D1570568

1

p0516022

DATE DUE

~~.5 / 8 / 97~~	
~~NOV 1 8 1997~~	

Philosophy and the Reconstruction of Culture

PHILOSOPHY AND THE
RECONSTRUCTION OF CULTURE

Pragmatic Essays after Dewey

EDITED BY John J. Stuhr

STATE UNIVERSITY OF NEW YORK PRESS

Published by
State University of New York Press, Albany

© 1993 State University of New York

For information, address State University of New York Press,
State University Plaza, Albany, N.Y., 12246

Production by Cathleen Collins
Marketing by Dana Yanulavich

Library of Congress Cataloging in Publication Data

Philosophy and the reconstruction of culture : pragmatic essays after
    Dewey / edited by John J. Stuhr.
        p.   cm.
    Includes bibliographical references and index.
    ISBN 0-7914-1529-5 (alk. paper). — ISBN 0-7914-1530-9 (pbk. :
alk. paper)
    1. Philosophy, American—20th century.   2. Pragmatism.
3. Culture.   4. Dewey, John, 1859–1952—Influence.
B936.P47   1993
144'.3—dc20   92-25799
                                                                    CIP

10 9 8 7 6 5 4 3 2 1

Contents

All peoples at all times have been narrowly realistic in practice and have then employed idealization to cover up in sentiment and theory their brutalities. But never, perhaps, has the tendency been so dangerous and so tempting as with ourselves. Faith in the power of intelligence to imagine a future which is the projection of the desirable in the present, and to invent the instrumentalities of its realization, is our salvation. And it is a faith which much be nurtured and made articulate: surely a sufficiently large task for our philosophy.
(MW 10:48)

In one of his best known essays, "The Need for a Recovery of Philosophy," American pragmatist John Dewey argued that philosophy recovers itself when it ceases to deal merely with the problems of philosophers, but instead becomes a method, cultivated by philosophers, for dealing with pressing practical problems of men and women. It is these problems that provide the initial subject matter for any genuine, living philosophy. Moreover, it is the progressive illumination and amelioration of these problems that supply the ultimate test of success for such a philosophy. As a result, in largest terms, the aim of Dewey's demand for a recovery of philosophy is not just to render philosophic theory more practical. Rather, it is to help make practice more intelligent. Simply put: *The recovery of philosophy is one with the intelligent reconstruction of culture.*

This need for a recovery of philosophy and an ongoing reconstruction of culture surely is no less urgent now than in the past. Dewey's commitment to infusing practices, associations, and institutions with intelligence and his insightful writings on a wide range of issues are an invaluable resource in this task. In fact, today this recovery of philosophy and reconstruction of culture must proceed in part *through* a critical recovery and renewal of the vision of Dewey's pragmatism.

Perhaps in fact the present time is especially ripe for this undertaking. There is now a remarkable renaissance of academic interest in both Dewey and pragmatism—in philosophy and in many other fields in the humanities, social sciences, and professions. Perhaps the time now has come for American philosophers to not only philosophize about pragmatism but to philosophize pragmatically. This book is a small step in that direction. Of course, this optimistic expectation can be countered with at least equal amounts of pessimism, skepticism, and cynicism. After all, some of this resurgent interest in Dewey and pragmatism, ironically, is little more than devotional, disciplined chewing and regurgitation of "historic cud long since reduced to woody fibre" (MW 10:47). Moreover, some of this interest, ironically in a different sense, flows from trendy neopragmatic and postmodernist misunderstandings and misappropriations of Dewey and pragmatism. These often are coupled with mistaken pronouncements about the nature and possibilities of philosophy in general, invalidly inferred from penetrating, accurate criticisms of a particular, limited sort of nonpragmatic philosophy. Perhaps more troubling still, intramural disputes and antiquarian studies aside, is the fact that this growing attention to Dewey and pragmatism is almost wholly academic. It exists almost entirely in little scholarly exchanges and publications (like this one) on the margins of a culture that, when it reads, prefers to consume sex fantasies, violent mysteries, instructions for thinning thighs and fattening savings accounts, and cartoon drawings of cats.

This book's project, however, is rooted neither in optimism nor pessimism about the present. Instead, it is rooted in pragmatic meliorism—in faith in the capacities of intelligent thought and action to bring to birth a world as yet unborn. In this pragmatic spirit, the essays in this volume seek to expand, deepen, and extend Dewey's concerns and conclusions. Collectively they constitute a project rooted in three straightforward convictions: that philosophy today in the United States of America is overly remote from the living pulse and problems of individual and social life; that, this situation notwithstanding, philosophy still has crucial reconstructive, ameliorative work to do in our culture; and, that this work can be undertaken fruitfully through a pragmatic cultivation of inquiry and communication.

The essays that follow seek to take up and advance this work in overlapping, interwoven, pluralistic ways. They do not aim to form a neat unity or tidy whole; they do not try to speak with a single voice, from a single standpoint, or on behalf of some supposed universal subject; and, they do not pretend to offer infallible analyses, surefire strategies, or the final word. Accordingly, from the Table of Contents onward, I have avoided editorial conventions that produce artificial neatness and contrived completeness. I have not arranged the essays to present the appearance of a single line of thought or single linear order. Following Charles S.

Peirce, I have attempted to fashion not a chain no stronger than its weakest link, but a cable made strong through the number and intimate connections of its slender fibers.

Similarly, I have not prepackaged the essays into distinct, antiseptic, familiar groupings—e.g., Pragmatism and Politics, Pragmatism and Postmodernism, Dewey and Feminism, Means and Ends in Dewey's Ethics and Aesthetics, Pragmatism and Epistemology, and so on. Instead, the essays individually and in relation to one another span these groupings in myriad, complex ways and, in so doing, subvert traditional under-standings of these categories as conceptual natural kinds or useful pedagogic simplifications.

Of course, devoted categorists should encounter no special difficulties in classifying (imperfectly) the book's contents according to their special interests and pigeonholes. Thus, for example, the book's essays span and may be arranged very roughly in terms of traditional branches of philosophy and the contemporary consequences of Dewey's pragmatism in those fields: philosophy of history (Lavine); metaphysics (Seigfried, Boisvert, Sleeper); metaphilosophy (Hickman); epistemology and logic (Manicas, Sidorov, Thayer); ethics (Gouinlock, Lachs); aesthetics (Alexander, McDermott); social and political philosophy (Campbell, Stuhr, Rosenthal); and philosophy of mind (Wilshire). Or, readers may group the essays in terms of their approaches to Dewey and pragmatism via other philosophical traditions and schools of thought: Modernity (Lavine); democratic theory, communitarianism, and liberalism (Campbell, Stuhr, Rosenthal); analytic philosophy (Gouinlock, Manicas, Thayer); critical theory (Lavine, Gouinlock); ancient philosophy (Lachs, Boisvert); naturalism (Lachs, Sidorov, Boisvert); feminism (Seigfried, Boisvert); modern philosophy (Boisvert, Sidorov); neopragmatism (Boisvert, Alexander, Hickman); Russian philosophy and East European thought (Sidorov, Sleeper); postmodernism (Alexander, Sleeper); phenomenology and existentialism (McDermott, Sleeper); and psychology (Wilshire). Finally, the essays may be sorted in terms of the contemporary issues they address: democracy, education, and community (Campbell, Stuhr, Rosenthal, Hickman); values, the good life, and the meaning of life (Gouinlock, Lachs, Alexander, McDermott); gender, body, and self (Seigfried, Boisvert, Wilshire); knowledge, reason, and science (Manicas, Thayer, Sidorov); and Modernity and Postmodernity (Lavine, Sleeper).

I also have resisted the common practice of summarizing or predigesting the book's essays by means of an introduction that sets forth superficially what is to come in much more depth. The essays are clear, compelling, and speak for themselves. The recovery of philosophy and the reconstruction of culture are not advanced or justified through easy introductory outlines. Instead, the book's central, basic convictions and the conclusions of the individual essays can be justified only through the *results* to which they gave rise—not before the fact, but only after the fact. This, of course, is the pragmatic test of pragmatism itself. This is not to say that a renewed pragmatic philosophy will single-handedly reconstruct culture or *solve* today's global cultural problems. As Dewey noted, "philosophy is vision, imagination, reflection—and these functions, apart from action, modify nothing and hence resolve nothing" (MW 10:46). Philosophy, however, must serve today as an impetus to action, and it can and must enrich and inform this action in service of desperately needed reconstructions of culture.

References and Abbreviations

All references to the writings of John Dewey are provided within the text of the chapters in this volume. These references are to the following:

John Dewey: The Early Works: 1882–1898, ed. Jo Ann Boydston, 5 vols. (Carbondale and Edwardsville, Ill.: Southern Illinois University Press, 1969–72).
John Dewey: The Middle Works: 1899–1924, ed. Jo Ann Boydston, 15 vols. (Carbondale and Edwardsville, Ill.: Southern Illinois University Press, 1976–83).
John Dewey: The Later Works, 1925–1953, ed. Jo Ann Boydston, 17 vols. (Carbondale and Edwardsville, Ill.: Southern Illinois University Press, 1981–90).

References to these volumes of Dewey's writings are abbreviated in the standard form: by initials for the series, followed by volume number and, following a colon, page number. Thus, for example, reference to *The Middle Works*, volume 10, page 137 would be abbreviated as (MW 10:137), and reference to *The Later Works*, volume 2, page 9 would be abbreviated as (LW 2:9).

All references to other authors and writings, except in special cases as noted in individual chapters, are provided in the Notes that immediately follow each chapter.

American Philosophy, Socialism, and the Contradictions of Modernity

THELMA Z. LAVINE

Introduction: Classical American Philosophy and the
End of Socialism

What bearing does classical American philosophy have upon recent momentous historical changes—for example, the collapse of socialism in Eastern Europe, in the Baltic States, and throughout the Soviet Republics? Here if ever there presents itself a concrete historical nexus of "problems of men" in urgent need of philosophical critique in the Deweyan sense: an identifiable subject, self, or community, surviving in its environment by means of available material and cognitive resources; the emergence of an immediate and/or long-range "problem" which is generative of stress, indecision, conflict; the genetic explanation of the problem—historical, causal, and circumstantial; the engendering of an interpretive structure which yields an understanding of the situation and projects a resolution-reconstruction, to be monitored in its outcomes in practice.

The same Deweyan critique must now be seen to apply reflexively to classical American philosophy itself, and the question must now be reversed: What is the bearing of the failure of socialism upon the social philosophy of classical American philosophy? The difficulties of Deweyan social philosophy that have been exposed by the collapse of socialist statist economics and politics present "problems of men" which are themselves in need of Deweyan philosophical critique.

Both questions, as to the bearing of American philosophy upon the collapse of socialism and the reverse question, as to the bearing of the collapse of socialism upon classical American philosophy point to a third question: What can be seen to be the role of classical American philosophy in the geopolitical world after the decline and death of socialism?

Smugness, Sour Grapes, and the End of the Cold War

It was only in the summer of 1989 that *The National Interest* gave us Francis Fukuyama's philosophical "The End of History?" announcing that Western liberal democracy has triumphed over socialist totalitarianism and is now universal as the final form of human ideology and government. The West has won, the long struggle for freedom is over, and history itself is coming to an end.

The West has won? Liberal democracy now becoming universal? The spectrum of response on the part of American journalistic opinion makers and academic intellectuals was predictable: smugness and triumphalism on the right, citing Reagan's Cold War policies for having hastened the erosion of the socialist economy and political order. Sour grapes and denial of defeat on the left, citing the economic and political costs of America's Cold War policies and the moral equivalence of the two imperialist powers. But American writers have been less concerned with the fallout in Eastern Europe and Russia from the defeat of socialism than with the consequences for America.

On the conservative niche in the spectrum, Charles Krauthammer looks back on the eighties as "the decade of the revival and triumph of the West."[1] And from the right, political theorist Jeane Kirkpatrick hails "the collapse of communism, the spread of democracy in Eastern Europe, the end of the Cold War and other good news. . . ." But this "good news" has been met, she says, with a barrage of repudiations "extraordinary for their passion, their confusion, and their pure malice" from commentators who have all along blamed the United States for the Cold War and are still embattled against U.S. policy in the Vietnam War.

Among the writers on the left who spurn the good news of the collapse of communism, the historian Christopher Lasch stands forth as the most intriguing. On June 10, 1990, the Institute for Policy Studies held a memorial colloquium for the historian William Appleman Williams, celebrated for his revisionist American history and his opposition to America's "containment" policy toward the Soviet Union. Lasch shocked and angered the audience by declaring: "We ought to admit the truth. . . that the West has won the Cold War—even if it goes against the grain, against our political inclinations. . . . We don't have to join the celebration of the free market to see that the masses in Eastern Europe and Russia no longer have much faith in socialism."[2] But by July 13, Lasch reversed himself on the op-ed page of *The New York Times*. The Soviet

Union has been defeated, he conceded, but the West has not won the Cold War, because the containment policy that destroyed the economy, domestic morale, and the world political leadership of the Soviets has had the same effect at home, driving America toward "secret policy organizations, the erosion of civil liberties, the stifling of political debate. . . ."[3] Masterfully, within a few paragraphs, Lasch has recanted his apostate insistence that the West has won, apologized to his revisionist colleagues and the memory of William Appleman Williams, and rallied the troops.

Although some commentators on the left hold America "responsible" for persisting in the Cold War which defeated Soviet socialism, and others, like Christopher Lasch, see America as a Cold War loser, Christopher Hitchens surpasses all others in the practice of denial by skeptically questioning whether communist totalitarianism (100,000,000 killed) ever really existed except in the rhetoric of American neoconservatives.[4] Such skeptical questioning is not without recent precedent: in the past decade questioning has begun as to whether the Holocause (6,000,000 killed) ever actually existed except in the rhetoric of Jews.

And in the academic world, some scholars are examining the significance for the intellectual culture of Fukuyama's end-of-history-West-has-won thesis. Writing in the *Chronicle of Higher Education*, Harvey Kaye, a professor of social change and development, argues that Fukuyama's claim of the universal victory of Western liberal democracy is a stratagem to create a neoconservative national consensus and a one-dimensional narrative of American history. "Thus, it appears all the more necessary," Professor Kay urges, "to recall the conception of historical practice that originally attracted so many of us to the discipline in the 60's and early 70's—a vision of critical scholarly studies and pedagogical activities linked to the experience and struggles of working people and the oppressed."[5]

Paradox: Socialism is dead in eastern Europe and Russia, the Communist bloc countries in which its ideas and economic and political practices held power. Why, then, is socialism vigorously alive in parts of capitalist America, as these rancorous debates about the Cold War make clear? Why, asks American sociologist Seymour Martin Lipset, have most left-wing political parties in the industrialized democracies been moving towards a free market economy and centrist politics—except for America, where socialist redistributionist and centralizing policies are still pursued by left-wing elements in the Democratic party and the universities?[6] How to explain paradoxical, exceptionalist America?

Lipset borrows an explanation from the sixties thinking of Richard Hofstadter and Lionel Trilling, that American socialist intellectuals' "attachment has been inspired and sustained more by a desire to be anti-establishment, to be adversarial toward bourgeois and national patriotic values than by a concern to implement specific political and social programs." Under these circumstances, Lipset concludes, "evidence that Marxism does not deliver is largely irrelevant." But Lipset leaves unexplained this adversarial, antibourgeois stance of left intellectuals. Nor does Lipset take note of conservatives' current complaint that leftist intellectuals dominate the media and give support to the implementation of favored programs, contrary to his view that American intellectuals are not politically involved.

The Contradictions of Modernity: American Romantic Transcendentalism and the Rise of Counter-Enlightenment Dissent

Only in the larger context of the contradictions of Modernity can sense be made of the Cold War debates, the paradox of the death of socialism and its survival in America, and the significance of these "problems of men" for American pragmatism. The contradictions of Modernity have formed the horizon of the West since the middle of the nineteenth century, when the concepts of the Enlightenment tradition, deriving from Locke and Newton, were already being fiercely opposed by a Counter-Enlightenment, Romantic tradition, deriving from Rousseau and the Romantic German, English, and American poets and philosophers. The Enlightenment thought-style: universal human rationality as the source of political and scientific truth; unalienable natural rights of the individual to life, liberty, property, and the pursuit of happiness; government by consent of the governed; the rule of law and equality under the law; liberation, by reason and science, from myth, religion, dogma, tradition, and prejudice; and the sustaining of a civil society of free and open social and economic relations. These are the Enlightenment ideas from which Fukuyama's victorious Western liberal democracy is a twentieth-century descendant.

Missing from Fukuyama's optimistic Enlightenment picture of Modernity are the ideas of the Romantic Counter-Enligthenment—ideas which have opposed, rejected, scorned, and feared the power of Enlightenment thought and practices to discredit and displace traditional economic, political, religious, and ethnic modes of cultural and personal life.

The Counter-Enlightenment thought-style: in opposition to abstract reason, the greater human significance of spirit, will, imagination; in opposition to objective science, the paths to truth are found in subjectivity, the arts, and culture; in opposition to the political autonomy of the individual, and natural rights democracy, politics has its source in the group and is sustained by a statism of left or right; in opposition to the self-interest of the rational individual, the primacy of the needs and aspirations of the community; in opposition to the achievement of a civil society and scientific and technological modernization, the concern of the Counter-Enlightenment is for the victims of Enlightenment civil society and modernization—the oppressed, the poor, the mentally or physically ill, minorities, rebels, revolutionaries, and martyrs.

Traditional nations of Europe began accommodating to the contradictions of Modernity during the nineteenth century, working out mixed modes of economics and politics within their respective historic situations, with traditional Britain evolving most clearly as a civil society in the Enlightenment style of modernity. Marx's mid-nineteenth-century philosophy was itself a mixed mode of Enlightenment science and human rights with Communist party statism. (It was twentieth-century Marxism-Leninism that became the totalitarian Other to Western liberalism.)

Unlike traditional nations, America was the first new nation, and its national and legal identity lay in Enlightenment philosophic truths of individual natural rights and constitutional democratic government, as these were Americanized in the unalienable natural rights of Jefferson's Declaration of Independence and Madison's Constitution with its separation of powers and machinery of representative democracy. It was the Enlightenment foundations of the new nation which significantly set its course and set the stage for ineluctable Counter-Enlightenment dissent—the American version of the contradictions of Modernity.

In 1830 Tocqueville saw in America "the image of democracy itself," a passionate consensus in the embrace of liberty, equality of social condition, an atomistic individualism; these were accompanied by the tyranny of the majority over intellect and wealth, by a "virtuous materialism" as the prevailing morality, and an aversion to the intellectual pursuit of philosophy.[7] Among the costs of the benefits of democracy was, he believed, that American democracy could not experience the elevation of mind, the scorn of material advantage, and the cultivation and love of the arts and philosophy which characterized the culture of the old French aristocracy. Tocqueville did not surmise that, at the very time of his pronouncement, there was arising in the vicinity of Concord, Massachusetts, the group of philosophers, poets, essayists, novelists, and political and cultural dissenters who became known as the Transcendentalists, affirming the very qualities which Tocqueville believed that Americans, in their egalitarianism and virtuous materialism, were destined to lack.

With the Transcendentalism of the 1830s–1850s the stream of European and British Romanticism entered the currents of American intellectual and political culture. Ralph Waldo Emerson, having been inspired by his encounters with the transforming powers of spirit conveyed by the Romantic, Counter-Enlightenment rhetoric of Wordsworth, Coleridge, and Carlyle, invented himself and a new conception of the individual human being, a new American self, and a new Emerson:

Man is not a farmer, or a professor or an engineer, but he is all. Man is priest, and scholar, and statesman, and producer, and soldier.[8]

It is intellectually astonishing to discover the echo of Emerson's "American Scholar" of 1837 and its new conception of the human being in Marx's *The German Ideology* of 1845–46.

[Under communism] society regulates the general production, and thus makes it possible for me to do one thing today and another tomorrow, to hunt in the morning, to fish in the afternoon, raise cattle in the evening, criticize after dinner, just as I have a mind, without becoming hunter, fisherman, shepherd or critic.

In the Emerson of 1837 and the Marx of 1845 there is expressed the same Romantic conception of the infinitude of potentiality within the human spirit, and the same Counter-Enlightenment indictment of existing repressive social conditions. Emerson concludes this passage with a criticism of American society:

The state of society is one in which the members have suffered amputation from the trunk, and strut about so many walking monsters,—a good finger, a neck, a stomach, an elbow, but never a man.[9]

"The American Scholar" has often been identified as a cultural declaration of American independence from Europe and Britain:

We shall walk on our own feet, work with our own hands, speak our own minds.[10]

It is also a declaration of independence of the American individual from the Enlightenment horizon of Jefferson's self-evident truths and Madison's external machinery of government. In the countervailing conception of "The American Scholar" Emerson invented (created) himself and a new American human being, and for both a new vocation, a secular calling to discern and teach "the other side," the truths of the inward path, of a spiritualized nature, a sanctified dailiness, and a unifying "Oversoul." And finally it may be seen that "The American Scholar" is a declaration of the entrance of American social thought and philosophy into the critique of the conflicting interpretive structures of Modernity, into what Dewey saw as the ongoing critical role of philosophy in civilization.

Progressivism, Pragmatism, and Counter-Enlightenment Politics

From the time of the Transcendentalists onward, their emerging Counter-Enlightenment thought became and was to remain a paradigmatic feature of American intellectual and popular culture. The Counter-Enlightenment dissent for which the Enlightenment foundation had set the stage had appeared in Transcendentalism and entered the enduring American expression of Modernity. Romantic Counter-Enlightenment modes of thought moved beyond the Transcendentalists' drift toward an antinomian mysticism and focused instead on a battery of social, economic, political, and cultural criticisms of the nation. Counter-Enlightenment criticism, varying with the historical situation, appears in the following characteristic modes: critique of abstract principles, by contrast with expressive incorporativeness; critique of absolute truths, values, norms, by contrast with Romantic process, change, growth; critique of the competitive capitalist economy, by contrast with the egalitarianism expressed by the democratic polity; critique of rights-based, atomistic individualism, by contrast with social unification or some type of communitarianism; the critique of American life and personality as diminished or impoverished by the complex of American institutions; criticisms of the absence in American culture of aspects of transcendence, or of a unifying civil religion, or moral uplift, or redemption.

In the Progressive Era, from the turn of the twentieth century through the pre–World War I decades, Counter-Enlightenment criticism became concretized and sharply politicized. A national crisis had mounted in the face of the acceleration of social and economic change: the post–Civil War rapid expansion of industrialization; the rise of a working-class population, augmented by huge waves of immigration; the growth of great corporate wealth, increasingly in collusion with federal and local government officials; urbanization and the concomitant disappearance of the old Protestant small-town culture and family-owned businesses; and the blockage to reform which decisions of the Supreme Court and the Constitution itself appeared to present. The dislocations produced by monopolistic capitalist forces of modernization brought into being not only the rebellion of the Progressive movement but a rethinking of the continued adequacy of the American Enlightenment tradition and a turning, again, to Counter-Enlightenment, European modes of thought (Hegelian, neo-Hegelian, Marxist, Schopenhauerian, Nietzschean, Bergsonian, Freudian) as an alternative way of understanding the problems of modernity. Classical American philosophy arose in the attempt to integrate the cultural styles of modernity, Enlightenment and Romantic Counter-Enlightenment, into a philosophy for America, whose national and legal identity was in Enlightenment truth.

Peirce, Royce, James, and Dewey attempted, each in his own way, to provide a fruitful reconciliation of the cognitive structures of Modernity which would offer a public philosophy for America. Yet only Dewey had a grasp of the formidable undertaking implicit in American pragmatism: to interpret the historical frameworks of Modernity in relation to their engendering problematic situations, to identify their consequences in historical practice, and to explore the prospects for their integration.

Dewey's writings constitute a remarkably successful exhibition of utilizing the major Counter-Enlightenment philosophical strategies to problematize the cognitive, moral, and political structures of traditional Enlightenment America. The Romantic category of unification dominates the developmental line of Dewey's thought from his early Hegelianism to his philosophic responses to the national crises of the 1890s and the 1930s. But the potent unification offered by Hegelian Spirit is displaced by an amplified Darwininan nature; and with the rise of the social sciences, nature is in turn displaced in Dewey's thought by "the social" as "the most inclusive category." In all versions, unification is linked to process: Hegelian, Darwinian, historicist; and process functions for Dewey as a universal solvent. There follows the celebrated Deweyan rejection of dichotomies (gaps, gulfs, dualisms, discontinuities) and absolutes ("fixities," finalities, "antecedent independent realities," the nonoperational, noninstrumental, nontestable). Dualisms and dichotomies (between organism and environment, subject and object, individual and society, is and ought) are overcome as separate structures by linking processes of interaction and transaction. Scientific, political, moral, and aesthetic experience are themselves differentiated only as distinctive contexts within "nature," "the social," or "culture." "Fixities" in all areas of thought and practice succumb to the solvent of process by being construed as functions of changing events, or as obsolete resolutions of past problematic situations, or as hypotheses to be tested.

Dewey may be seen to have swung away from the Emersonian Romanticism of the infinite potentialities of the self to the communal Romanticism of the collectivity.[11] Emerson's redemptive mystical unification of the spiritual self with nature and the Over-Soul was naturalized by Dewey into the unification of the socialized self with the community and the processes of nature. Yet the same redemptive symbolism of a sanctified unification is persistently evoked in Dewey's rhetoric of the uniting of the self with the life of the community and the ongoing affairs of nature. From its Transcendentalist inception the voice of American Counter-Enlightenment from Emerson to Dewey carries the themes of transcendence, communion, the sanctification of human life, covenant, mission, and redemption—themes lost in Enlightenment Modernity and generative of a powerful political critique against it.[12]

In *The Public and Its Problems, Individualism Old and New, Liberalism and Social Action*, Dewey's political philosophy reached its developmental peak. These volumes were written as journal articles or as public lectures during the boom years of the economy following World War I and the subsequent Great Depression, and within a political culture under the pervasive influence of socialist theory and the visible presence of Soviet socialist practice. Dewey rigorously formulates his political philosophy by attacking the inadequacies of traditional Enlightenment conceptions of the individual and government in the light of massive twentieth-century social and economic change.

"...Rugged individualism is praised as the glory of American life," Dewey reflects. "But such words have little relation to the moving facts of that life," since "the United States has steadily moved from an earlier pioneer individualism to a condition of corporate capitalism" (LW 5:58). Among the "eternal truths" of early liberalism was the conception of the individual as "ready made, already possessed, and needing only the removal of certain leqal restrictions to come into full play" (LW 11:30). But since early liberalism was pre–social scientific, it failed to see "the dependence in fact of individuals upon social conditions...."

> Such thinking treats individualism as if it were something static, having a uniform content. It ignores the fact that the mental and moral structure of individuals... change with every great change in social constitution. (LW 5:80)

Under the domination of "manufacturing, transportation, distribution and finance" in an interlocking corporate capitalism, Dewey asks, "Where is the wilderness which now beckons creative energy and affords untold opportunity to initiative and vigor?" (LW 5:80).

"The crisis in liberalism" stems from the need to develop a new form of "social organization" in the face of opposition from a regime which is "the agent of a dominant economic class" and from the continued moral influence of the old laissez-faire individualism. Dewey argues that "liberalism must now be prepared... to socialize the forces of production." A liberalism that is sincere in its creed of "free, self-initiated expression... must will the means of achieving its ends":

> Regimentation of material and mechanical forces is the only way by which the mass of individuals can be released from regimentation and consequent suppression of their cultural possibilities. (LW 11:63)

Dewey seeks to gain acceptance for socialism by identifying it as a type of corporatism such as already exists within capitalist enterprise and in the "organized intelligence" of the natural sciences. We are moving, he says, from an individualistic to a collectivist liberalism, from a capitalist to a socialist corporatism, from a socialism that is capitalist to a socialism that is public.

> We are in for some kind of socialism, call it by whatever name we please, and no matter what it will be called when it is realized. (LW 5:98)

It is of course to be hoped, he cautions, that the change will be undertaken by voluntary agreement rather than by governmental coercion or by violence. The outcome would surely signify the "doom" of capitalism, indeed "no phase of our culture would be unaffected." The function of "organized intelligence" would be carried out by a

> coordinating and directive council in which captains of industry and finance would meet with representatives of labor and public officials to plan the regulation of industrial activity [and] would signify that we had entered constructively and voluntarily upon the road which Soviet Russia is traveling with so much attendant destruction and coercion. (LW 5:98)

What then will be the new individualism, brought forth by the new political, economic, and cultural revolution, pursuing now the affairs of human life within a planned society? Dewey does not shirk the question:

> How shall the individual refind himself in an unprecendentedly new social situation, and what qualities will the new individualism exhibit? (LW 5:81)

Dewey's answer: "I am not anxious to depict the form which this emergent individualism will assume." A mentality which will be "congruous with the new social corporateness" cannot be predicted in advance of social change (LW 5:89).

Dewey ends *Individualism: Old and New* by invoking Emerson's Romantic natural supernaturalism, the discovery of transcendence in the everyday world, and the conception of the self-creating and world-creating possibilities of the human spirit.

> To gain an integrated individuality, each of us needs to cultivate his own garden. But . . . our garden is the world, in the angle at which it touches our own manner of being. By accepting the corporate and industrial world in which we live, and by thus fulfilling the precondition for interaction with it, we, who are also parts of the moving present, create ourselves as we create an unknown future. (LW 5:123)

In the fateful year of 1989 with the failure and collapse of socialism in the European countries in which it has prevailed, Dewey's social gospel and its scarcely concealed Marxist socialism appears to be the teaching of a false Messiah, except when placed in its historical situation. Enlightenment structures became for him, as for characteristic social critique in Modernity, the obstacles to social development. Dewey's Counter-Enlightenment negative criticisms attempt to delegitimate and desacralize the liberal tradition by examining the fixity of its "eternal truths" in the light of the limitations of its genesis and the distortions of its consequences. His sharpest criticisms are of the "old" individualism, laissez-faire economics, the incongruence between the professed ideals of traditional liberalism, visible in the judiciary and executive branches of government, and the existing corporate structures of industry, trade, finance, and politics. His call for a correcting socialism does not leave standing the right to private property, political and economic liberty, the Declaration of Independence, the Constitution, universal suffrage, the Supreme Court, the institutions of civil society, or the structures of the capitalist economy.

On the positive side of the Counter-Enlightenment mode of thought, Dewey presents the vast Romantic appeal of unification, the abandonment of self-interest, the redesigning of all aspects of culture to reflect the binding to the collective corporate organic totality, and the control of the nation through the central planning of "organized intelligence." But no provision is made for the continuation of civil society, those institutions (such as trade unions, political parties, social movements, free and autonomous churches and universities, independent industrial groups) which act as agents of the people and are not run by the state; nor for the independence of human rights from the purview and control of the state.[13] No constitution replaces the Constitution of the United States which Dewey reduced from its sanctified fixity to the status of an empirical hypothesis (thus endangering the bulwark of the civil rights movement), nor is there a replacement for universal suffrage which he views as flawed by its individualistic presuppositions. No answer is available to the crucial political query: *Quis custodiet ipsos custodes?* The Romantic sponteneity of self-creation is subordinated to the creation of the new society. But the Romantic aspiration to transcendence and redemption in the new society is left without content; only its polar opposite is clear, the proposed statist control by the planners of the polity, the economy, and the culture.

Despite the fervor of his Marxist rhetoric, Dewey retained the role of interpreter and integrator of the contradictions of Modernity by the number of significant elements he accepted from the Enlightenment side of Modernity. Science and democracy (both Romanticized) provide the pillars of his philosophy; scientific method is the sole adequate method of inquiry;

science and technology have the power to reconstruct the world; the forces of modernization, industrialization, bureaucratization, and urbanization are accepted by Dewey, along with the importance and dignity of work.[14] He had no Romantic/Marxist contempt for the bourgeoisie, nor did he seek to bring America down; he sought in these writings only a peaceful, voluntary revolution in America along the road which Soviet Russia was traveling with violence and coercion.

With the collapse of both communism and fascism, the two major embodiments of extremist Romantic politics, we seem to have learned that national statist installations of such Counter-Enlightenment ideas are human disasters. The failure of socialist economics and politics is now "writ large" for all the world to see, and exercises a potentially chastening influence on aspiring socialist-leaning political tendencies in America and abroad. As Barrington Moore, Perry Anderson, Jürgen Habermas, and most Western Marxists, have admitted to a new "chastened" Marxism in view of the failure of Marxism in its predictions and in the atrocities of its practices, so Dewey's quasi-Marxist socialism may be seen in retrospect as requiring an acknowledged chastening. And American left-liberalism which is committed to the pursuit of redistribution and centralized state controls, as Lipset points out, may be seen as still "unchastened" by the European experience with socialist redistributionism and statism.

Socialism as Counter-Enlightenment Symbolism

By the last decade of the twentieth century, Enlightenment America had developed a mixed, "welfare-capitalist" economy and a "civil rights" democracy. These changes came in response to a decade of intertwined social movements. Mounting social complexities fused with the powerful Counter-Enlightenment emotional appeal of community, contempt for monetary greed, shame in the presence of poverty, sickness, disabilities, illiteracy, and discrimination against minorities and women. But although most of the new social policies are adaptations of European socialism, they are not identified as such in America, but only within the context of the Enlightenment–Counter-Enlightenment contradictions of American liberal democracy. The right and the political center selectively accept these policies as rational, utilitarian reforms; the left sees them as redemptive of the sufferings caused by the American social system.

Thus the announcement of the death of socialism is premature. Defeated in the Cold War, and a self-confessed failure, socialism as a political and economic system can be pronounced dead. Socialism lives, however, as a symbol of the Counter-Enlightenment thought-style, a symbol of all perceived truths and moral values which the prevailing

Enlightenment-derived liberal democracy undermines or ignores. As a symbol of Romantic, Counter-Enlightenment Modernity, socialism draws out and identifies the negativities thrown up by liberal democracy: its intellectual limitations, its spiritual and religious emptiness, its moral impoverishment, its social and psychological fragmentation, its marginalization of unassimilable groups. Contradicting these negativities, socialism symbolizes the search for the self, for community, and for spiritual transcendence; the concern for minorities, the weak and oppressed; and a sensitivity to cruelties and to pain. "Socialism" is figurative language for the Counter-Enlightenment perspective upon the realities of Modernity. It is an umbrella term for 200 years of diverse Counter-Enlightenment protest in Western democracies. So long as Fukuyama's long peace of liberal democracy prevails, so long will the Counter-Enlightenment expressions of socialism also prevail and find their way into cultural and political life.

But there is no long peace. With the end of the Cold War another phase of the contradictions of Modernity has quickly arisen with the problems of the premodern Arab and Muslim world of the Middle East. The global oil dependency of the industrialized nations is confronted by Middle East nationalistic, religious, and tribal hostilities united only in the hatred and fear of modernization and the West.

Under the caption "How the 'West' Was Lost," essayist Meg Greenfield questions whether, after the West has won, the symbolic significance of America has not been lost. Truer to Hegel than is Fukuyama, Greenfield queries, ironically, that in winning the Cold War have we not lost the "Other" that we need for our self-definition, a sense of who we are? But the "Other," it appears, is not lost. At home in America the Other is present as the Counter-Enlightenment symbolism of socialism, tied as its shadow to the historic Enlightenment identity of America. Abroad, the Other hovers as the potentially global confrontation of the aspirations of Third World peoples with America as the national embodiment of liberal democracy. It is not Fukuyama's liberal democratic peace that is endless, but the horizon of the contradictions of Modernity in which we live.

Conclusion: American Philosophy and Modernity

Among the philosophies still flourishing in the Western world only American pragmatism, perhaps because of its Enlightenment founding, has a sharpened sense both of the Enlightenment thought-structures and of Counter-Enlightenment critique. It is the only philosophy which aspires (as does Habermas, alone among the Europeans) to bring the contradictions of Modernity "under one roof." This aspect of classical American philosophy sheds light upon the questions which introduced this essay. American philosophy, specifically the Deweyan paradigm of "inquiry" by way of the problematic situation, its complex genesis, the interpretive structure engendered, and the identifiable consequences present a model for the study of the collapse of socialism which draws upon explanation and understanding, hermeneutics and social science.

Secondly, Deweyan social philosophy may itself be critiqued by this paradigm, as the present chapter exemplifies. The reflexive use of Deweyan critique is itself a test of its instrumentality.

Most significant is the aspect of American philosophy in which it may be seen to be the philosophic interpreter of Modernity. American philosophy arose with the attempt to interpret and integrate the historical framework of Modernity in its Enlightenment universality of human rights, representative democracy, civil society, science and technology, and the Romantic expressiveness of personal and group life in subjectivity, community, transcendence, and redemption. Although bound to the Enlightenment in its origins as "the first new nation," America, because of that circumstance, is open to the Counter-Enlightenment mode of dissent. Despite the limitations of American "exceptionalism," American philosophy may now serve as a resource and model for Central and Eastern European intellectual culture as it reaches out from totalitarian socialism to Enlightenment liberal democracy—toward the reappropriation and unification of the long horizon of the contradictions of Modernity.

Notes
1. *Washington Post*, November 24, 1989.
2. *Washington Post*, June 12, 1990.
3. *New York Times*, July 13, 1990.
4. *Harper's Magazine*, July 1990.
5. *The Chronicle of Higher Education*, October 25, 1989.
6. *The National Interest*, Summer 1990.
7. Alexis de Tocqueville, *Democracy in America*, ed. R. Heffner (New York: New American Library, 1968), p. 32.
8. Ralph Waldo Emerson, "The American Scholar," in *Selected Writings of Emerson*, ed. D. McQuade (New York: The Modern Library, 1981), p. 46.
9. Ibid.
10. Ibid., p. 63.
11. See John J. McDermott, "Spires of Influence: The Importance of Emerson for Classical American Philosophy," in *Streams of Experience: Reflections on the History and Philosophy of American Culture* (Amherst: University of Massachusetts Press, 1986).

12. See, for example, the concluding passages of Dewey's *Reconstruction in Philosophy* (1920) and *Human Nature and Conduct* (1922). Also see Thelma Z. Lavine, "Pragmatism and the Constitution in the Culture of Modernity," *Transactions of the Charles S. Peirce Society* 20, 1 (Winter 1984), and "Individuation and Unification in Dewey and Sartre," in *Doctrine and Experience*, ed. Stephen G. Potter, S.J. (New York: Fordham University Press, 1988).

13. See Sir Ralf Dahrendorf, "Interview," *New Perspectives Quarterly* (Spring 1990).

14. See Thelma Z. Lavine, "John Dewey and the Founders: Human Nature and Politics," *Works and Days: Essays in the Socio-Historical Dimensions of Literature and the Arts* 3, 2 (Fall 1985), pp. 53–75.

2

Democracy as Cooperative Inquiry

JAMES CAMPBELL

Dewey's Social Philosophy: A Sketch

At the basis of all that John Dewey had to say about liberalism, freedom, community and social ethics was the conception of democracy as a cooperative inquiry. Both terms are equally important. He emphasizes that the process of living in democratic community requires a recognition that our political life "is essentially a cooperative undertaking, one which rests upon persuasion, upon ability to convince and be convinced by reason..." (MW 10:404). As he continues,

> the heart and final guarantee of democracy is in free gatherings
> of neighbors on the street corner to discuss back and forth what
> is read in uncensored news of the day, and in gatherings of friends
> in the living rooms of houses and apartments to converse freely
> with one another. (LW 14:227; cf. 13:153)

These interactions aim at being more than a diversion or pastime: their goal is to help advance the community. Dewey hopes to achieve, through "back-and-forth give-and-take discussion" (MW 8:443), a public opinion that can rise above tradition and appearance. Democracy requires, in addition to "sympathetic regard for the intelligence and personality of others," the additional step "of scientific inquiry into facts and testing of ideas" (LW 7:329).

The process of developing an informed public opinion used to be simpler, Dewey believes, because the social life with which it was concerned was simpler. Decisions were being made by people whose judgment "was exercised upon things within the range of their activities and their contacts" (LW 13:95). Although their overall range of information might have been limited, they knew more about what was related to their lives: "they were compelled to know, in the sense of *understanding,* the conditions that bore upon the conduct of their own affairs" (LW 13:94). The citizens of whom Dewey writes, on the other hand, found themselves awash in a sea of unorganized information.

To form public opinion that is more than " 'opinion' in its derogatory sense" (LW 2:346), it is necessary to uncover the meaning of this information, and to do this requires ongoing cooperative inquiry. Dewey believes that society had finally developed a method of social reconstruction that was appropriate to the modern, processive world, a method "of cooperative and experimental science which expresses the method of intelligence" (LW 11:58). It is important to recognize from the beginning that for him the notion of a method is better understood as a *mentality* for approaching and dealing with problems than a *protocol* for setting out in advance our responses to possible conditions. It offers no predetermined path of reform, no claim that individual reformers can be made irrelevant, and no guarantees of success. What sets this method off from other possible methods—like following custom or authority—is the nature of its justificatory process: its requirement of participation in and acceptance by a vibrant citizenry.

Dewey does not believe that the necessary reconstruction of social institutions is likely to result from foreseeable developments in the inherited two-party political system, whose adversarial operations he sees as ineffectual for addressing our social ills. On the contrary, he maintains that to accomplish the task of the reconstruction of the political framework of our society, it will be necessary to establish a broad spectrum of voluntary associations that would help inform and organize the members of the community and lead to the eventual establishment of a new kind of political organization based on more rational grounds.[1] In the short run, it would be the objective of these associations to "carry on the work of research and of education in order to build up that body of positive and constructive political policies which can alone give unity and endurance to a progressive party movement" (LW 5:348).

It would also be through these new associations that the abilities of experts for "discovering and making known the facts" (LW 2:365) could be successfully integrated, without granting them excessive power. The experts' ability to clarify and coordinate the formulation of problems serves us well. However, in the task of enacting solutions, of making the value choices from among the possibilities which we have before us, of deciding which possible solutions are most nearly adequate, there is no appropriate expertise. The individuals of the society may be at present part of a "submerged mass" and they "may not be very wise," Dewey notes facetiously. "But there is one thing they are wiser about than anybody else can be, and that is where the shoe pinches, the troubles they suffer from" (LW 11:219). The integration of scientific expertise within these voluntary associations would thus offer a legitimate grounding for public authorities. For Dewey, influence and persuasion are essential aspects of any democracy that recognizes that intelligence is social and that, when properly grounded, such means of influencing should be interpreted as mutual *guidance* rather than *manipulation*.

Dewey's understanding of democracy as cooperative inquiry cannot be considered apart from his understanding of the relationship of democracy and education. The intimate connection that he sees between the two can be recognized in such passages as: "Democracy has to be born anew every generation, and education is its midwife" (MW 10:139). To develop a society in which cooperative inquiry is actual, it would be necessary to "make our schools more completely the agents for preparation of free individuals for intelligent participation in a free society" (LW 13:297). Of course, Dewey recognizes, much more so than his critics tend to realize, the practical limits in the educational process. " 'Education' even in its widest sense cannot do everything," he writes (LW 9:110); and the school, although it is often treated as "the willing pack-horse of our social system" (MW 10:191), is only "one educational agency out of many" (LW 11:414). He continues, however, that "while the school is not a sufficient condition, it is a necessary condition of forming the understanding and the dispositions that are required to maintain a genuinely changed social order" (LW 11:414).

The role of education in social reconstruction has two distinguishable aspects. The first of these is to help the students develop as problem solvers, to help them to learn *how to think* rather than to fill them with *information*. Instead of turning out students "possessed *merely* of vast stores of information or high degrees of skill in specialized branches," Dewey writes, our goal as educators should be to produce students with "that attitude of mind which is conducive to good judgment in any department of affairs in which the pupils are placed..." (LW 8:211). This focus on *judgment* rather than on *knowledge* reminds us of his position that wisdom is "a moral term" (MW 11:44) related to evaluation and criticism of choices for a better future world. Because of our need for ongoing evaluation and criticism, he emphasizes the need to foster ongoing inquiry. "The most important attitude that can be formed," he writes, "is that of desire to go on learning" (LW 13:29; cf. 8:139). As a consequence, we need to cultivate in students not the love of random information nor the ability to display idle knowledge. "The criterion of the value of school education," Dewey writes, "is the extent in which it creates a desire for continued growth and supplies means for making the desire effective in fact" (MW 9:58; cf. LW 5:297).

The second aspect of education and schooling in social reconstruction is the importance of helping students become more social and cooperative. Educators have the job of socializing the student, of "saturating him with the spirit of service," Dewey write (MW 1:20). "Education should create," he continues, "an interest in all persons in furthering the general good, so that they will find their own happiness realized in what they can do to improve the conditions of others" (LW 7:243). He is not, of course, attempting to eliminate or prevent the development of individuality. His goal is, rather, to increase individuality by preparing the students to become "good citizens, in the broadest sense," citizens who are capable of "recognizing the ties that bind them to all the other members of the community, recognizing the responsibility they have to contribute to the upbuilding of the life of the community" (MW 15:158; cf. 11:57).

In addition, Dewey's emphasis upon the relationship between democracy and education is not just a point about schooling, but about the ongoing education of engaged citizens. "Full education," he writes, "comes only when there is a responsible share on the part of each person, in proportion to capacity, in shaping the aims and policies of the social groups to which he belongs" (MW 12:199). He continues that "freedom of thought in inquiry and in dissemination of the conclusions of inquiry is the vital nerve of democratic institutions" (LW 11:375). This emphasis upon the sharing of knowledge in a democracy requires once and for all the abandonment of the "purely individualistic notion of intelligence" and of "our ingrained habit of regarding intelligence as an individual possession. . ." (LW 11:38, 47). Such knowledge as our society possesses is gained through the cooperative efforts of human beings living together, and its proper role is social:

> There are few individuals who have the native capacity that was required to invent the stationary steam-engine, locomotive, dynamo or telephone. But there are none so mean that they cannot intelligently utilize these embodiments of intelligence once they are a part of the organized means of associated living. (LW 11:38)

For democracy to succeed, Dewey maintains, cooperative inquiry must become a deeply engrained process over the broad range of our social lives.[2]

Do We Measure Up to Dewey's Expectations?

Having sketched Dewey's understanding of democracy as cooperative inquiry, I would now like to explore briefly a series of three criticisms that challenge his position on the general question of its workability.[3] We can begin with what can best be called the apathy criticism. It proceeds as follows: Are people really that concerned about social problems or interested in this kind of cooperative democratic community? In a world of work and worry, of diversionary entertainment and compensatory recreation, are people that concerned about engaging in social action? Dewey offers us a method of social reconstruction that has a hope of working only if it can generate a high level of selfless involvement on the part of the citizenry. Yet, given what Dewey himself has written about the American situation, noninvolvement would not seem to be an irrational response. People have been systematically miseducated and propagandized, alienated in their working lives and exploited in their economic relations. They might well believe that a personally rational reaction to a nonresponsive, atrophied political system is apathy. It would be nice if the situation were otherwise, of course, if social action were a viable option; but, for now, no such expectations are realistic. And so on.

Thus runs the first criticism of Dewey's method of social reconstruction. Dewey of, course, does not deny the fact of apathy nor that such apathy demonstrates a kind of short-range rationality on the part of those who adopt it. He does, however, dispute the fatalistic assumptions about involvement of the citizenry that underlie it. From his point of view, what the failure of spontaneous involvement does point to is the end of political democracy as we have inherited it: the combat of two distant and self-serving national parties for positions from which to distribute the spoils of power. His intention, as we saw above, has been to sidestep the established party system and to use heightened involvement on the part of members of the community working in voluntary associations, to directly address social problems.

Two aspects of his view deserve to be mentioned here. The first is the theme noted above that education can help people find more value in involvement. The second theme is that serious efforts need to be undertaken to make cooperative inquiry more attractive to potential participants. Dewey disputes, for example, the assumption that the fruits of expert inquiry will necessarily remain "in secluded library alcoves... studied and understood only by a few intellectuals" (LW 2:349). He admits that "ideas are effective not as bare ideas but as they have imaginative content and emotional appeal" (LW 13:169), but this means that we need to develop a better manner of presentation of the materials of expert inquiry by enlisting the contributions of art. "The function of art," he writes, "has always been to break through the crust of conventionalized and routine consciousness" (LW 2:349). By offering our artists the task of publicizing this important social material and our need to address it, he believes we could create a flood of engaging and compelling exchanges that would carry public discourse forward. "The freeing of the artist in literary presentation," he writes, "is as much a precondition of the desirable creation of adequate opinion on public matters as is the freeing of social inquiry" (LW 2:349).[4] We thus come to recognize that, for Dewey, overcoming apathy is possible; but it will require efforts to make the material of expert inquiry and the activity of inquiry itself more attractive.

While I realize that the question of apathy is far from settled, I would like to turn to two additional criticisms of Dewey's view that are closely related to the apathy criticism. These two criticisms emphasize the intellectual and moral hurdles to be overcome in our attempts to carry on cooperative social inquiry, maintaining that even if apathy were overcome we are neither smart enough nor good enough to engage successfully in cooperative social inquiry. It will be beneficial to examine them separately as our second and third criticisms of Dewey's position.

If we attempt to formulate this second criticism—that people are, in some sense, too stupid for cooperative social inquiry—the result would be something like the following. Dewey offers, the critics say, a nice *theory*, but, realistically speaking, we need to consider whether the citizens with whom we are familiar are *smart* enough to play such an involved role in their shared lives. The human beings that we encounter simply do not demonstrate a level of intelligence sufficient enough to keep pace with the increasing complexity of our social existence. Consider the level of current political debate. There we find, for example, the citizenry requiring of candidates high levels of toughness, religious orthodoxy, and nationalism—and little else—before they can be considered seriously for political office. We find little or no interest in the vital issues of national, international, and global scope. Does not this sort of example suggest that our intelligence is just a thin veneer, insufficient for self-government, and that we cannot think our way through the complexities of our modern situation? One proposal to circumvent this lack of intelligence on the part of the voting public was put forward by Walter Lippmann (1889–1974) who suggests that the citizenry be relegated to a more spectatorial stance, concentrating on the choosing of leaders who would then make the informed choices. His essential point here is that, because the intellectual capabilities of our populace do not match up to the involved omnicompetence required of active citizens, we can attain *good* government only if we are willing to sacrifice *self*-government. Public opinion then becomes "a reserve of force brought into action during a crisis in public affairs," he writes. "To support the Ins when things are going well; to support the Outs when they seem to be going badly. . . is the essence of popular government."[5] Democracy as cooperative inquiry, however, will not work.

For Dewey, in response, there is first of all the serious question of how the uninformed citizenry is likely to choose the best leaders. More importantly for Dewey, there is always a distinction to be made between the conditions in our present transitional situation and what future situations might become. In particular, there is the need for faith in the intellectual possibilities that might be actualized through education. He readily admits that it is too much to expect of "the average citizen" that he or she be individually intelligent enough to be able to make sense of social events when "even superior minds are distracted and appalled by the intricacy and extent of the problems which confront society" (LW 6:185). But as we have seen, Dewey's claims about intelligence are not about the intellectual level of various individual members of the general population. His point is rather about the possible efficacy of cooperative inquiry using shared intelligence. If people begin to participate actively in the determining of their own lives, they will learn more; and the complaint that they are too stupid for the life of cooperative inquiry would have to be reevaluated.

If we turn to the third criticism—that people are, in some sense, too evil for cooperative social inquiry—we will find something like the following. Dewey offers, the critics say, a nice *theory*, but people simply are not *good* enough to play such a role in their shared lives. Their inherited selfishness is simply too strong. People are incapable of the level of *impartiality* that is necessary for the life of cooperative social inquiry that he proposes. Reinhold Niebuhr (1892–1971) is perhaps the most influential exponent of this view. "In the liberal world," he writes, "the evils in human nature and history [are] ascribed to social institutions or to ignorance or to some other manageable defect in human nature or environment."[6] In fact, however, the trouble with our social world is neither ignorance nor lag; the trouble is that the basic human material is not good enough to sustain cooperative attempts to reach a common good. Niebuhr continues that writers like Dewey mistakenly assume "that, with a little more time, a little more adequate moral or social pedagogy, and a generally higher development of human intelligence, our social problems will approach solution."[7] Niebuhr, however, has no such faith. "Not a suspicion dawns upon Professor Dewey," Niebuhr writes, "that no possible 'organized inquiry' can be as transcendent over the historical conflicts of interest as it ought to be to achieve the disinterested intelligence which he attributes to it."[8] People are simply too selfish to rise to the high level of impartiality that would be required to be truly disinterested and cooperative.

For Dewey, again, there is the need for faith in the possibilities of expanding our cooperative social horizon through education. Surely we must admit that much of our sense of public and private is learned in the process of our socialization. We *learn*, for example, that education through secondary school is a public matter, while health care is private. But neither of these evaluations is above challenge, let alone self-evident;

and, should we hope to expand the cooperative realm, education for service could help. Similarly, no one can claim to know in advance the limits of possible cooperation. We do not know how selfless we can become; but, Dewey's suspicion is strong that once we started, the complaint that people are too evil for the life of cooperative intelligence would have to be reevaluated.[9]

Does Dewey's Method Fit Our Social Practice?

We have considered a series of three related criticisms of Dewey's method of social reconstruction. They suggest, in order, that the people are not *interested* enough to make this method of social reconstruction work or the people are not *intelligent* enough to do it or the people are not *selfless* enough to do it. The Deweyan response in each case is to assert that, although at the present time such criticisms may be very persuasive, none of them should be seen as eliminating future possibilities. In our present "backward" state, he writes, "we are not even aware of what the *problems* are..." (LW 16:415); and, crippled in part by our assumption that our difficulties are based in our stupidity or our evil nature, we can rest in our apathy. With fewer diversions and increased participation, with more emphasis upon social morality rather than individual salvation, we just might be able to make the method of cooperative inquiry work.

I now want to turn to a different—and what I take to be a more fundamental—line of criticism, a line of criticism that is aimed not individually at the members of our society for failing to measure up to the challenges of *involvement* and *intelligence* and *morality* that are contained in Dewey's method of social reconstruction, but rather is aimed at the method itself. Dewey offers, this new criticism says, a nice *theory*, but when we stack the various *assumptions* that he is making about political life up against the political *reality* that we face, we recognize that his method of cooperative inquiry simply does not fit.

All that Dewey writes about the common good and collective social progress, about expanding cooperative participation within growing communities infused with trust, about experimenting toward the communal development of a program to advance the common good, about possibilities that will be developed through education, and so on, constitute in the words of C. Wright Mills (1916–62)—my focus here—"a set of images out of a fairy tale: they are not adequate even as an approximate model of how the American system of power works" (PE 300).[10] Dewey's method, therefore, simply does not fit the kind of political life that we experience. In most cases, Mills contends, individuals, voluntary associations, local groups, and the other key aspects of Dewey's view matter little; and, in the really significant political, economic, and military decisions of our society—decisions, Mills writes, that "carry more consequences for more people than has ever been the case in the world history of mankind"—they matter not at all. Such "key decisions," he continues, are made by "an elite of power" (PE 28).

Instead of seeing ourselves as living in a society in which publics interact to form opinions and collaborate to enact decisions, Mills believes that it is more accurate to describe our situation as one of "a society of masses" (PE 302). Such a society he analyzes as one in which the number of "givers of opinion" is much smaller than the number of opinion "receivers," in which these receivers have little possibility for "freely answering back," in which their opinion is ineffective "in the shaping of decisions of powerful consequence," and in which "institutional authority" chokes off autonomous discussion (PE 302-3). In fact, social action is, Mills maintains, neither *cooperative*—in the sense of shared efforts to advance the common good—nor *inquiry*—in the sense of a serious attempt to discover what ought to be done. Social action is rather politics; and, as politics, it "is a struggle for power," Mills writes (PE 171).

The challenge to Dewey's understanding of social action as cooperative *inquiry* is a rejection of his attempts to replace the squabbling and deal making of partisan politics with cooperative attempts at fostering scientific methods and attitudes. It will be recalled that it was this very aspect of Dewey's position that he offered as a possible defense against the criticism that people were too stupid for successful democracy. For Mills, however, Dewey fails to see that "the attempt to carry this laboratory technique over into social data precipitates methodological and political problems. . ." (PPP 466). Dewey's understanding of social problems, Mills writes, is grounded in what Dewey sees as "a social situation whose integration can occur by means of liberal individuals heavily endowed with substantive rationality." Such individuals, possessed of broad social perspectives and able to transcend their immediate situations, undertake careful and self-conscious actions to integrate past and future. "Adjustment is the term," Mills writes. Action "has to go slowly in order to squeeze the meaning and values from events it encounters. It is careful" (S&P 393). By maintaining that this kind of educative social inquiry is the rational method of social action, in conformity with his belief that aspects of society lag behind and require adjustment, Dewey has prejudged how politics is to be carried out. Mills maintains, however, that using the notion of lag veils choice: "To state problems in terms of cultural lag is to disguise evaluations. . ." (SI 89), to smuggle in the rationality of adjustment.

The problem, as Mills sees it, is that such an analysis of social action as inquiry has nothing at all to do with political action as it occurs in our current society. "His conception of action is *of an individual*," Mills writes, for example, the actions of "of a member of a free profession" (S&P 392–93) like an architect or a physician. Dewey's understanding of social action as cooperative inquiry finds itself well suited to a situation like a settlement house; but it is not "very well suited for action, *e.g.*, of a revolutionary scale, nor indeed for the large scale planning of society" (S&P 432). And it is this latter sort of action, in which conflicting powers attempt to get their way, that comprises the most important part of politics.

Rather than understanding social action as inquiry, Mills suggests that a more realistic analysis would be to see it as struggle. We thus return to his analysis of social action as power-oriented politics, and hence to a consideration of the role of political parties. "Parties," Mills writes, "live in a house of power. They are organizations for social fighting" (S&P 394). Their purpose is not inquiry but action, not the uncovering of truth but the enactment of policies; and their weapon is not the intellect, but the emotions. Dewey, of course, understood the importance of emotion to action. He writes, for example, that "no movement gets far on a purely intellectual basis. It has to be emotionalized; it must appeal to the social imagination" (LW 6:175). But, the aspect of social imagination to which Dewey wishes to appeal is the desire to participate in the intellectually driven advance of the society toward the common good. Political parties, on the other hand, attempt to excite group loyalties and mass followings, their focus upon victory and rewards, and this is what caused Dewey to want to do away with them. For Mills on the contrary, if what is wanted is "a chance at power," what is needed is a party (S&P 394).

The second aspect of Mills' challenge to Dewey's method of social reconstruction considers whether social action is to be considered as *cooperative* inquiry. It was this aspect of Dewey's position that he offered as a defense against the criticism that people were too selfish for successful democracy. Mills writes that Dewey's view of intelligent action assumes the existence of "a 'common ground,' a point of mediation" (S&P 395). This common ground is, for Dewey, the locus of our cooperation; for Mills, it is a mirage. Mills writes of the importance for Dewey of

> the assumption of a relatively homogeneous community which does not harbor any chasms of structure and power not thoroughly ameliorative by discussion. Always there must be the assumption that no "problems" will arise that will be so deep that a third idea-plan would not unite in some way the two conflicting plans (S&P 405).

But, as Mills continues, "this model of problem posing does not concern itself with two social interests in a death-clutch" (S&P 405). As an indication that Dewey has no clear recognition of such ultimate confrontations, Mills cites (S&P 438) Dewey's claim that "every serious political dispute turns upon the question whether a given political act is socially beneficial or harmful" (LW 2:245). In this case, Dewey uses, in the process of the resolution of the problem, the whole point of contention. For Mills, the question of whether a political act is simply "socially beneficial or harmful"—the question of whether a community exists—is still to be answered. Dewey, however, "never seriously questioned a fundamental and ultimately communal homogeneity of society" (S&P 412).

Emphasizing the complexity of our social interactions and the prevalence of the exploitation of some by others, Mills asks "what is *not* done in the name of the public interest?" (PPP 333). His aim here is to drive home the point that 'we' is "the most tricky word in the vocabulary of politics..." (M 19). For him, a more accurate analysis of our circumstances realizes that one person's or group's good is often another's evil: "What is a 'problem' to one 'group' is not at all problematic to another; it may well be a satisfactory 'solution' " (S&P 412). Different social groups have vastly different values; but, because of his "biological model of action and reflection," Mills continues, Dewey tends to minimize "the cleavage and power divisions *within society*," and ultimately to locate "all problems between *man and nature*, instead of between *men and men*" (S&P 382). Discussions of *the* problem, and correspondingly of *the* solution, thus imply the existence of a common good. In an actual community, where the advance of the common good was of central importance, cooperative revaluation would take place; but, for Mills, we have no such community.

For Mills, the political activity of our society is neither *cooperative* nor *inquiring*. It is a romantic, fairy-tale understanding of our democracy, he continues, to assume that the people discuss issues, formulate opinions, and decide social policy in a democratic fashion. The truth, he maintains in 1956, was that the United States had become "now in considerable part more a formal political democracy than a democratic social structure..." (PE 274). A powerful elite in our society—the central figures in our vital "political, economic, and military circles"—are the actual determiners of events. "In so far as national events are decided, the power elite are those who decide them" (PE 18). Consequently, the issues that "shape man's fate are neither raised nor decided by the public at large" (PE 300). Whether this elite decides issues in terms of its own private interests, or in terms of what it believes to be the common good, is irrelevant here. The point is that decision making about the pivotal issues of our society is out of the hands of the people.

In addition, underneath the level of the power elite, Mills believes that our centralized and myopic mass society is increasingly home to institutionalization and to the bureaucratic rationalization of procedures, both of which preclude any attempts on the part of the citizenry to reassume democratic control. The reason why the average individual does not gain the "capacity to act as a free man" is—and this is a point that Dewey emphasizes as well—that he or she does not participate in decision making. But, Mills continues, as outsiders, average citizens will never come to understand events. "Only from a few commanding positions or—as the case may be—merely vantage points, in the rationalized structure," Mills writes, "is it readily possible to understand the structural forces at work in the whole which thus affect each limited part of which ordinary men are aware" (SI 169). In general, however, Mills writes, "history is made behind men's backs" (WC 350).

Mills hopes that the impact of his more realistic analysis will cause people to question whether all of the participants in a social decision actually ought to try to understand their participation in the same way. Is social action a realm where we attempt to gain a careful understanding of social issues or to win, where we attempt to advance equality and justice or to force others to compromise by attaining a position of strength? Mills is concerned with keeping clear the difference between what he sees as political romanticism and political realism. For him, the heart of political democracy is power. For Dewey, on the other hand, "[t]he very heart of political democracy is adjudication of social differences by discussion and exchange of views" (LW 15:273). Mills' response would be to question whether this is an accurate description of our democracy or an embellished account modeled on Dewey's ideal. It may even be that the rhetoric of romantic democracy—of open participation in discussions on street corners and issues being fully and fairly presented in the media—is not only *false* but also *harmful*. That is, it may leave such open-minded and cooperative citizens unprotected and unprepared for the realistic democracy of power politics. To help make citizens open-minded and cooperative may be to undermine their already limited chances for self-defense.

In the place of Dewey's call for cooperative inquiry to make democracy work, Mills calls for a realistic assessment of "[t]he engineering of consent" (WC 110) and of attempts "to manage and to manipulate the consent of men" (SI 40) that are such an essential element of our current democratic practice. By "manipulation," Mills means "the 'secret' exercise of power, unknown to those who are influenced" (PE 316). Such manipulation, which Mills believes is "more insidious than coercion precisely because it is hidden. . ." (WC 110), cannot be totally eliminated from our social lives. This is so because, operating with a social theory of the self that he held in common with such figures as Dewey and George Herbert Mead (cf. PPP 426), Mills does not believe that we can stand free or independent of the contributions of our groups. "None of us stands alone directly confronting a world of solid fact," he writes. As social creatures, "men live in a second-hand world." People rely upon others. "The quality of their lives is determined by meanings they have received from others"

(PPP 375, 405). But, if the meanings we receive are tainted and we do not recognize it, then we will be manipulated.

Considering Mills' Critique

In this final section, I want to explore Mills' criticism of Dewey. The essence of this criticism, as we have just seen, is not that those who fail to adopt Dewey's method are not interested enough to care about, or too stupid to see, or too selfish to do, what ought to be done. Rather than putting forward these individual-oriented criticisms, Mills offers a social criticism: to see democratic practice as cooperative inquiry is simply to misunderstand how our political process works, and to adopt the stance of a cooperative inquirer in our society is to adopt a self-defeating stance. There are two themes that I want to develop in this exploration of Mills' criticism. The first is whether Mills offers us a full picture of Dewey's work; the second, whether this criticism is fully consistent with the rest of Mills' own work. The answer in each case is no.

To get a fuller sense of Dewey's radicalism, we can consider an aspect of his view that would allow for comparison with Mills' analysis of manipulation that we have just seen. What I have in mind here is the topic of propaganda. Although we find Dewey, in what might be called good liberal fashion, expressing great appreciation for the comment of O. W. Holmes, Jr., that "the best test of truth is the power of the thought to get itself accepted in the competition of the market" (LW 3:177), we do not find Dewey either praising the assaying powers of his own intellectual marketplace or claiming that all ideas that have won popular acceptance are therefore true. Dewey, as a witness to numerous governmental and business attempts at "manufacturing public opinion and sentiment" (LW 3:141), was cognizant of the power of propaganda. As he writes in 1918, the World War offered "a remarkable demonstration of the possibilities of guidance of the news upon which the formation of public opinion depends" (MW 11:118). This demonstration was not lost on those with an interest in control; and by 1932 he writes of "a multitude of agencies which skilfully manipulate and color the news and information, which circulate, and which artfully instill, under the guise of disinterested publicity, ideas favorable to hidden interests" (LW 7:360–61). Their success was due in part to the fact that, as we have explored above, people were being asked to decide about complex issues beyond their direct familiarity. Another part to this success was the fact that technological developments have "multiplied the means of modifying the dispositions of the mass of the population. . ." (LW 13:90) and thus afforded "an organ of unprecedented power for accomplishing a perversion of public opinion"

(LW 7:361). "Perversion" is, to Dewey's mind, the proper term to be used: "The very agencies that a century and a half ago were looked upon as those that were sure to advance the cause of democratic freedom," he writes, "are those which now make it possible to create pseudo-public opinion and to undermine democracy from within" (LW 13:168).

While in some technical sense popular consent must still be secured, Dewey reminds us that we should not necessarily assume any connection between the pliancy of the public and democracy. While in a democracy there is a focus on the development of the citizens and a requirement of participation in the definition of the common good, Dewey notes that we seldom have either. Instead of an attempt to foster the development of a vibrant popular opinion, "there is a premium put on the control of popular opinion and beliefs" (LW 3:141). Consequently, the fact that we ultimately have a democracy and the people could take over is not enough for the existence of a vibrant democracy. We must also live in active, inquiring communities. He did not believe such fundamental changes were likely under our present economic organization, in which "[t]he gathering and sale of subject-matter having a public import is part of the existing pecuniary system" (LW 2:349). Moreover, he did not anticipate that these necessary changes will be easy to bring about because "the system that nourishes these evils is such as to prevent adequate and widespread realization of the evils and their causes. . ." (LW 11:272). However, we still do ultimately have a democracy, he maintains, and we have the means of public inquiry. Thus, our efforts to advance inquiry further stand a chance of success. Here again, as we have seen so frequently, Dewey's emphasis returns to education as the most likely means of positive social reconstruction. He writes that the schools can help give students an "intelligent understanding of social forces" and that "unless the schools create a popular intelligence that is critically discriminating, there is no limit to the prejudices and inflamed emotion that will result" (LW 11:344). With the possibility of cooperative inquiry fostered in the schools, he looks forward to a time when the public has "located and identified itself" (LW 2:348) and is moving forward to advance the common good.

If we take this discussion of the possibilities of propaganda and manipulation seriously, we surely cannot consider Dewey to be—as Mills suggests he is—simply a naive proponent of a romantic sense of democracy. But it would also be a mistake to see Dewey as a hard-boiled realist of the sort that Mills at times claims to be. What shines through Dewey's critical stance toward his democracy is a sense of idealism. For example, although it is clearly too simple to suggest, as Mills does, that Dewey sees all problems as being "between *man and nature,* instead of between *men and men*" (S&P 382), there is a sense in which this claim is not completely false because in the final analysis Dewey does think there is a common good whose approximation will increasingly benefit the real interests of all. The fundamental point to emphasize behind his condemnations of social conflicts in which the participants seek "no common ground, no moral understanding, no agreed upon standard of appeal" and in which "each side treats its opponent as a wilful violator of moral principles, an expression of self-interest or superior might" (MW 14:59) is that such conflicts allow for no resolution other than through the continued use of force. Dewey continues to maintain, however, that to hope and act for a better future is worth a try even if it contains the danger of being duped on occasion. Thus, while it certainly is fairy-tale thinking to see our current situation as one of participatory democracy, it is not delusional thinking to hope to approximate participatory democracy by means of serious cooperative work in the future. And it is not fair to Dewey to fail to make this distinction.

It is also important to consider whether in this criticism of Dewey we have been seeing a full picture of Mills. On the contrary, it seems that in his later work, especially *The Sociological Imagination*, Mills begins to demonstrate a fuller sense of communal ideals and a greater concern with the *re*construction of society than previously. Understood in this way, Mills demonstrates several key similarities to Dewey himself, similarities that would seem to be worth exploring. One such similarity is in their conceptions of the ideal of democracy. Mills' sense of democracy, like Dewey's, refers to a social situation in which "those vitally affected by any decision men make have an effective voice in that decision" (SI 188). Democracy of this sort is constituted by "the power and the freedom of those controlled by law to change the law, according to agreed-upon rules—and even to change these rules...." Democracy thus means ultimately "some kind of collective self-control over the structural mechanics of history itself" (SI 116). In comparing Mills to Dewey here, it is important to emphasize that both stress the participatory and egalitarian aspects of democracy and play down the often overly stressed equation of democracy and freedom. For Dewey, effective freedom is a matter of the distribution of power in situations of social interaction. For Mills, similarly, freedom is "first of all, the chance to formulate the available choices, to argue over them—and then, the opportunity to choose" (SI 174). The goal of freedom within a democracy is therefore not "independence" but rather "control over that upon which the individual is dependent" (PPP 191).

A second similarity between Mills and Dewey can be seen in their generally negative evaluation of American democratic practice. Dewey spoke frequently of the need to recover our democracy. In 1959, Mills writes that the United States is "generally democratic mainly in form and in the rhetoric of expectation. In substance and in practice it is very often nondemocratic, and in many institutional areas it is quite clearly so" (SI 188). But similarly to Dewey, indicating this failing is not the end of the story for Mills. It is simply the first step in his attempt to increase the level of democratic involvement by making use of the "legal forms" that our society provides, and "formal expectations" that our democracy raises, "to make the society more democratic." Mills, sounding almost Deweyan, is here relying upon the potential effectiveness of "acting as if we were in a fully democratic society" for removing "the 'as if' " (SI 190-91, 189). He thus hopes, on the one hand, to engage more of those who presently are politically "inactionary" (SI 41), and, on the other, to contribute to the development of "parties and movements and publics" that will debate "ideas and alternatives of social life" and that will "have a chance really to influence decisions of structural consequence" (SI 190).

A third aspect of similarity between Dewey and Mills can be seen in their call for renewed efforts on the part of intellectuals to advance the common good. They both call for attempts to counterbalance manipulation and propaganda and to foster more adequate education and fuller democracy. Dewey maintains that the role of philosophical criticism in society is central: "the chief opportunity and chief responsibility of those who call themselves philosophers are to make clear the intrinsic kinship of democracy with the methods of directing change that have revolutionized science" (LW 15:274). Mills' view is parallel. "The intellectual ought to be the moral conscience of his society, at least with reference to the value of truth," he writes. They should be absorbed "in the attempt to know what is real and what is unreal" (PPP 611). Following the life of what he calls "the politics of truth" (SI 178) requires that, in addition to attempting to *know* the truth, intellectuals must also attempt to *tell* the truth: to present their fellow citizens "with genuine alternatives, the moral meanings of which are clearly opened to public debate" (PPP 338). And, whether this appeal to intellectuals is addressed primarily to philosophers (as in Dewey's case) or to social scientists (as in Mills') is surely irrelevant.

Mills, like Dewey before him, maintains that intellectuals should "conduct a continuing, uncompromising criticism of this established culture. . ." (PPP 233). The difficult task of the true educator thus begins with attempts "intellectually to transcend the milieux in which he happens to live. . ." (SI 184). There then begins the intellectual's dual "public role" (SI 186). One part of this dual role is to try to help individuals mired in aspects of social ills that they can see only as personal troubles to attain what he calls "adequate definitions of reality" (PPP 373). What the intellectual can do for individuals "is to turn personal troubles and concerns into social issues and problems open to reason—his aim is to help the individual become a self-educating man, who only then would be reasonable and free" (SI 186). The second part of the intellectual's public role is on a broader scale. It is to function as "a creative minority" that "might prevail against the ascendancy of the mass society, and all the men and apparatus that make for it" (PPP 372). Writing in a mood reminiscent of Dewey's call for "a minority having the requisite courage, conviction, and readiness for sacrificial work" (LW 6:189), Mills writes that it is part of the intellectual's public role "to combat all those forces which are destroying genuine publics and creating a mass society—or put as a positive goal, his aim is to help build and to strengthen self-cultivating publics. Only then might society be reasonable and free" (SI 186).

We have been considering a Deweyan response to the criticism, drawn from C. Wright Mills, that Dewey's understanding of democracy as cooperative inquiry is inappropriate to our social lives because it misunderstands the pervasive aspects of social power. This criticism is, I believe, an absolutely essential criticism of naive or romantic liberalism. However, I also believe, as I have suggested, that this criticism is in no way an adequate criticism of Dewey's position. Mills offers us, not a refutation of Dewey's method of social reconstruction, but a constant reminder to those who might want to adopt it of the importance of entering into cooperative inquiry with both eyes open. Dewey's method admittedly does not fit the normal sort of social situation with which we are currently familiar—his work does not comprise a handbook for contemporary political practice. Dewey's realistic point, however, is that if we ever hope to break out of our current political situation, we need to try to reconstruct our social situation to make something like the method he is proposing fit. To do so we must treat our current situation, as Mills himself does, as being potentially meliorable. Why challenge intellectuals and social scientists to play a role in overcoming the ills of mass society if the problems are completely intractable? Why write about participatory democracy and the evils of a society in the control of a power elite if not in the hope that such actions will contribute to a social situation in which cooperative inquiry will be the appropriate method?

Under the proper conditions—that is, as long as we recognize the limitations on cooperation and on inquiry in our current situations, and have some sense of our fellows' intentions, and see cooperative inquiry as a deliberate choice to be pursued beyond guarantees—it will not harm us greatly to have faith in the possibilities of Deweyan democracy. We may, in fact, have some success. And, although Mills himself is in no way overly confident of success,[11] he does suggest that the effort is worthwhile. If our focus is upon the long-range goals of society, we must try to rise above the limitations of our current situation. "No one knows the limits of possible human development," he writes. "What men might become, what kinds of societies men might build—the answers to such questions are neither closed nor inevitable" (CWW 94). And, while he realizes that such considerations introduce what "so-called practical men of affairs" see as "utopian ideals," Mills is proud to admit such ideals as his own (PPP 233). To say this, however, is simply to say that for Mills, as for Dewey, efforts to make our society the sort of place where social action could be carried on as a kind of cooperative inquiry are justifiable.

Notes

1.   Dewey was involved personally with all sorts of such voluntary organizations, the most significant of which were: the League for Industrial Democracy, the People's Lobby, and the League for Independent Political Action.

2.   For a further development of the themes discussed in this section, see James Campbell, *The Community Reconstructs: The Meaning of Pragmatic Social Thought* (Urbana, Ill: University of Illinois Press, 1992) pp. 38–58.

3. A second line of criticism—that I will not consider in this chapter—does not concern itself with whether a proposed system like Dewey's might work in our contemporary situation. Rather, this second criticism questions whether we should adopt Dewey's social approach as our fundamental stance. Instead of his social system of cooperative values, this criticism proposes an individualistic system that emphasizes the cluster of private goods and individual freedoms.

4.   While Dewey never explored fully this theme, certainly the *Thought News* project is relevant here. Some aspects of the Federal Writers' Project and the Federal Theater Project would seem to be a good starting point for an expanded consideration of this issue.

5.   Walter Lippmann, *The Phantom Public* (New York: Harcourt, Brace, 1925), pp. 69, 126; cf. pp. 40–44, 63–70, 124–30, 197–99. Compare Dewey (LW 2:213–20, 334).

6.   Reinhold Niebuhr, *The Irony of American History* (New York: Scribners, 1962), p. 4; cf. pp. 80–84.

7.   Reinhold Niebuhr, *Moral Man and Immoral Society* (New York: Scribners, [1932] 1960), p. xiii.

8.   Reinhold Niebuhr, *The Nature and Destiny of Man: A Christian Interpretation* – Vol.I, *Human Nature* (New York: Scribners, [1941] 1964), p. 111.

9.   For a further development of themes discussed in this section see James Campbell, *The Community Reconstructs*, pp. 91–109.

10.   The works of Mills to which I will refer are abbreviated in my chapter as follows: CWW—*The Causes of World War Three* (New York: Simon and Schuster, 1958); M—*The Marxists* (New York, Dell, 1962); PE—*The Power Elite* (New York: Oxford University Press, 1956); PPP—*Power, Politics*

and People: The Collected Essays of C. Wright Mills, ed. I. L. Horowitz (New York: Oxford University Press, 1967); SI—*The Sociological Imagination* (New York: Grove Press, 1961); S&P—*Sociology and Pragmatism: The Higher Learning in America,* ed. I. L. Horowitz (New York: Oxford University Press, 1966); and, WC—*White Collar: The American Middle Classes* (New York: Oxford University Press, 1951). It should perhaps be noted that although I see changes and growth in Mills' work, I do not see any reason for my purposes here to segregate his "pamphlets"—like CWW or M—from the rest of his work.

11.   In fact, at times Mills is explicitly pessimistic: SI 193; PPP 338.

3

Democracy as a Way of Life

JOHN J. STUHR

*The very idea of democracy, the meaning of democracy, must be
continually explored afresh; it has to be constantly discovered, and
rediscovered, remade and reorganized; while the political and
economic and social institutions in which it is embodied have to be
remade and reorganized to meet the changes that are going on in the
development of new needs on the part of human beings and new
resources for satisfying these needs. . . . Democracy as a form of life
cannot stand still. It, too, if it is to live, must go forward to meet the
changes that are here and that are coming. If it does not go forward,
if it tries to stand still, it is already starting on the backward road
that leads to extinction. (LW 11:182)*

Americans today face no shortage of complex social problems. Perhaps
earlier generations confronted equal difficulties, some similar and some
different, that are now more remote. In any case, there can be no question
that our current social ills range across all aspects of our lives, and appear
both already deeply entrenched and still multiplying and intensifying.
These deepening problems include: hunger and homelessness; debts and
deficits; illiteracy and illness; intolerance and illegality; physical and
psychic violence and scandal at both individual and institutional levels;
environmental degradation and international conflict; apathy, resignation,
contempt, and selfishness. Even politicians with infrared vision who sight
"a thousand points of light" or "new hope" and proclaim a "new world
order" or a "new covenant" must notice in moments of honesty the
surrounding vast cultural darkness and disarray.

From the perspective of the past, these current problems are horrible
reminders of the public and personal consequences of letting American

democracy "stand still." From the perspective of the future, these problems are also sobering reminders of the demands on our collective imagination, intelligence, and will. They are a challenge to extend, reconstruct, and renew our institutions, social practices, and individual life-styles. As such, these problems are a challenge to our commitment to democracy and to our very democracy itself.

Of course, some people may say that this is alarmist and exaggerated. They may deny that we face a problem that is this serious in character or wide in scope, particularly at present when it may seem that "the winds of democracy are blowing everywhere"—through Central and Eastern Europe, Africa, South and Central America, and elsewhere.[1] From this perspective, even if it does not soon become our largest export, democracy in America appears long ago established, at present firmly in place, and in the future secure from fundamental attack—no matter how serious the passing problems of the day at home or abroad. After all, on this view, Americans pledge steadfastly—if practice imperfectly—allegiance to majority rule and minority rights, the separation of powers, government by law, equality and opportunity, broad suffrage and fair elections, and civil liberties and justice for all. This, it may be held, was the enduring achievement of our nation's Founders. This is what they secured for us. This much, this view concludes, is safe, sure, and settled.

In part, this view of democracy may arise from and reflect a much deserved (when not uncritical) recognition and appreciation of democratic accomplishments and traditions in American culture. At the same time, this view of democracy in America, no matter how reassuring, is rooted in myopia about the past, unjustified reassurance about the future, and superficial patriotism in the present moment. Borrowing a term now familiar in ecology, I would like to contrast this superficial or shallow patriotism to a "deep patriotism." In developing this notion at a time when politicians and entrepreneurs rush to cloak themselves in the flag—in a time when democratic symbols have become substitutes for democratic reality (LW 13:301)—I am aware that many people may view social criticism as simply incompatible with patriotism. But patriotism must not be identified with complacency (LW 9:161). Genuine patriotism requires social criticism—and perhaps, in former President Nixon's campaign rhetoric, "now more than ever." In short, the view of democracy in America as settled and secure is mistaken in theory and dangerous in practice.

This view is mistaken in theory because it ignores both change and context. Change, not permanence, is a fundamental feature of individual and social life. The ongoing development of democracy in America is no exception and, in this regard, America is not exceptional. Moreover, this development is contextual. Change produces myriad particular demands and particular effects on institutions and ways of life in particular situations. To fail to recognize this fact of change-in-context is to render democracy a mere abstraction. It is to be blind to the sweeping actual differences of American democracy in the days of Jefferson from American democracy in the days of Dewey—as well as the differences of Dewey's America from today's America. It is to overlook within America today massive social differences of meaning and experience—differences of wealth, race, health, ethnic background, gender, age, religious belief, physical ability, sexual preference, power, and hope that constitute plural and different "democracies." And, it is to cover up the precariousness of the present and the openness of the future with illusions of permanence, fate, destiny, historical inevitability, and an end of ideology. We recognize such illusions when offered by others—illusions that range from imperialist manifest "destiny" to a war that will "permanently" end all wars; from an "inescapable" triumph of Nazism to an "invincible" superiority of the U.S. economy; and from the "chosen" character of racial apartheid to the "inevitable" global spread of communism. In recognizing these illusions, however, we must not manufacture, participate in, or sustain new fictions about the secure and complete character of democracy in America.

It is not only wrong in theory but dangerous in practice to treat democracy in America as a done deed, finished and final. This view is dangerous practically because it fosters both complacency and absolutism. It wrongly turns the urgent need for ongoing, never finished amelioration of pervasive social and personal problems into justification for passive optimism. Armed with the mistaken belief that democracy once and for all is an accomplished fact, we smugly may turn away from the uncertain practical tasks of continually reconstructing our global society in creative, new ways. As this happens, we become mere spectators, unwitting agents, or hapless victims to an increasing lack of fit between new problems and needs and earlier democratic institutions and practices. We fail to renew and revitalize our democratic inheritance, acting as though yesterday's hard-won investments and tomorrow's rosy projected earnings always will be adequate for needed social expenses today. We thus fail to bridge the growing gap, for example, between our new powers of inquiry and communication and their infrequent, haphazard actual employment for genuinely democratic purposes. Rather than exploring and realizing new possibilities for public inquiry, participation, and self-government, we instead achieve by default political, economic, educational, environmental, aesthetic, and religious exclusion of people from effective decision making about their own lives. At the same time, we fail to recognize that this increasing cultural disenfranchisement undermines and is incompatible with our democracy itself. Here complacency fosters absolutism. It converts social, economic, political, scientific, and moral arrangements that fostered democracy at earlier particular times and places into sacred, revered, timeless institutions, practices, and relations. It dogmatically turns once effective historical means into eternal ends—ends supposedly beyond the demands of progressive social reconstruction.

As a group, philosophers, of course, have been responsible for more than their share of this sort of ahistorical theory and complacent practice. There is, however, no reason to dwell on this fact here. To do so would only be to reduce philosophy to therapy for philosophers themselves, and to substitute the often barren problems of professional philosophers for critical, philosophical examination of the problems that arise in the actual experiences and lives of people. Still, in this light, there is ample reason to suspect that philosophers have little to contribute to genuine cultural concerns and problems. Having recognized rightly that they have no special access to Truth, Knowledge, Justice, Goodness, Beauty, or Reality, they wrongly have retreated to merely academic sanctuaries and logically possible worlds with special professional vocabularies, techniques, and issues. Even when they deal with public issues, they do it—ironically—largely only within this professional context or conversation.

In this situation, the philosophy of John Dewey stands as a striking exception. Throughout his long public career, popular writings, and many volumes of scholarly work, Dewey persistently sought to identify challenges to democracy and to articulate intelligent responses to these changing challenges. As he well knew, Dewey provided us no crystal ball, no ready-made solution, no blueprint, no formula, no formal decision procedures—not even a "Method," except the progressive development and application of intelligence in experience. As a result, it is not enough today to simply read and endorse, for example, *Democracy and Education* (MW 9), *Experience and Nature* (LW 1), *Liberalism and Social Action* (LW 11), or *Logic: The Theory of Inquiry* (LW 12). Instead, as Dewey—like other American thinkers such as Jefferson, Emerson, and William James all recognized—we must rewrite these books and reconstruct our institutions to accomplish democracy over again for our own time. In taking up this never finished task of "creative democracy," Dewey's writings on experience, inquiry, education, and democracy constitute an invaluable and rare resource for us today. It is time that we recognize, utilize, and extend this resource.

For philosophers, this can amount to a recovery of philosophy (MW 10:3ff) through a retrieval of Dewey's insight that philosophy is inherently criticism (LW 1:295ff.; 8:29ff.) and reconstruction (MW 12:80ff., 187ff., 256ff.). This point is badly missed even by many contemporary "neopragmatists" and some postmodernists who construe Dewey's pragmatism as an effective escape from their peculiar, self-induced "theory-guilt"—their apparent guilt for having no absolute, infallible, transcendentally justified philosophical theory.[2] This narcissistic concern, however, is irrelevant to the practical burden (or "guilt") that Dewey places on philosophers. The ultimate goal of philosophy, he made clear, is not practical theory but rather intelligent, meaningful practice.

In this light, what is democracy? What does democracy mean today in America? What can it mean? What should it mean? What is the value of democracy? What is its justification? How can we achieve it? What must we do and how can we at least begin to do it? It is not enough to fault philosophers for frequently failing to undertake the task of addressing these questions. We now must undertake this task ourselves. In 1936, Dewey called this study "the outstanding task of progressive education" (LW 11:190). It remains so today.

Two Meanings of Democracy

. . .democracy is much broader than a special political form, a method of conducting government, of making laws and carrying on governmental administration by means of popular suffrage and elected officers. It is that, of course. But it is something broader and deeper than that. . . .It is, as we often say, though perhaps without appreciating all that is involved in the saying, a way of life, social and individual. (LW 11:217)

"Democracy" is a vague term. It has many meanings and connotations, and it is used in a broad array of contexts for widely varying purposes. Nonetheless, it is now commonplace to understand democracy as a particular social organization or system for making decisions.[3] On this view, a decision is made democratically to the extent that it embodies the expressed preferences of the majority of the people, and results from a process in which the preferences of all people are included, informed, considered, contested, and counted equally. Democracy thus is both an adversary system designed to apply fair procedures to conflicting interests and opposing goods, and a system of public deliberation designed to create and promote common interests and shared goods. It is in this light, for example, that political theorist Robert Dahl formulates the criteria of an ideal democratic process as: virtually universal adult suffrage; equality in voting; equal and enlightened understanding of the issues; effective participation throughout the decision-making process; and final control over both the agenda of issues to be decided and the delegation of authority.[4] It is on this basis that democracy often is contrasted with other decision-making systems—such as monarchy, oligarchy, theocracy, anarchy, and totalitarianism. And, finally, it is on this same basis that familiar contrasts often are developed among different forms of democracy—such as direct democracy and representative democracy.

Of course, democracies (like all social forms of decision making) are not mere generalizations or abstractions. Actual democratic decision making (like actual nondemocratic decision making) always takes place within some particular context—at some time and place on some issues for some people. This context may be, for example, a family, a school, a research laboratory, an athletic team, a religious group, a neighborhood, a labor union, or a business. To the extent that any of these organizations, practices, or institutions embodies the characteristics of democratic decision making, then it is to that extent a democracy.

It is evident that today we think about democracy almost exclusively in the context of one social institution: government. From the standpoint of sheer authority and power alone, there may be good reason for this: government frequently is the final authority in society, and so often has, though it may not use, the power to determine partly the democratic or nondemocratic character of decision-making processes in other institutions and practices. Given this focus on government, historians have charted the emergence of democracy in small city-states, and its complex trans-formation and development in larger nation-states. This transformation often has been situated first in nineteenth-century America. Given this focus on government, sociologists and statisticians have determined the real number of democracies that exist today. Including recent changes in Central and Eastern Europe, that number has been estimated by many political scientists at about 35–40, or about 25–33 percent of the world total.[5] And, given this focus on government, social theorists, economists, and politicians have considered and argued problems concerning participation in, freedom from, and control of democratic decision-making processes. In short and in general, today democracy is understood as a form of government.

By contrast, John Dewey consistently understood democracy more broadly. For Dewey, democracy is primarily and most fully a form of *life* rather than a form of *government* alone. Democratic government, he argued, is a part—an important part but only a part—of a democratic society or democratic culture. It is a means for realizing democratic ends in individual lives and social relationships. Although it is the best and most expedient means yet invented to achieve these ends, it is only a means. Accordingly, Dewey radically cautioned that we must not treat means—that is, institutions and practices of democratic government such as universal suffrage, recurring elections, and majority rule—as ends, final or complete in themselves (LW 11:218). These structures of government are "external and very largely mechanical symbols and expressions" (LW 13:295) of a fully democratic life. They are not the core of democracy. They are only its political dimension or phase.

Because democratic structures of government have a value that is instrumental rather than final, they must be dynamic rather than static if they are to continue to promote a democratic way of life under changing conditions. This means that our democracy is not something fixed, "a kind of lump sum that we could live off and upon," something complete that can be simply "handed on from one person or generation to another" (LW 13:298–99), something so natural that it would simply maintain itself if once established. "I cannot rehearse," Dewey wrote, "the list of events that have given this naive faith a shock" (LW 15:259). Accordingly, we cannot afford to idolize passively practices and institutions that proved instrumental in the past; we continuously must appraise and be ready to revise them when necessary in terms of their present contributions to a democratic way of life.

Dewey began to articulate the nature of democracy as a way of life by exploring the basis of democracy as a way of government. He located the basis of democratic government in the conviction that no person or group of persons is sufficiently wise and good to govern others without their consent, "that is, without some expression on their part of their own needs, their own desires and their own conception of how social affairs should go on and social problems be handled" (LW 13:295). This conviction implies both equality—such that the "social will comes about as the cooperative expression of the ideas of many people"—and opportunity— such that all people have both a right and a duty to form and express convictions about their own places and welfare in the social order (LW 13:296; 11:219). This "expression of difference," inherent in a democratic way of life, is both a personal right and a means for public enrichment (LW 14:228). This means that all persons involved in and affected by social practices should participate in their formation and direction. Dewey called this the "democratic idea in its generic social sense" (LW 2:327) and termed it the "key-note of democracy as a way of life," "necessary from the standpoint of both the general social welfare and the full development of human beings as individuals" (LW 11:217–18).

Throughout his later work, Dewey returned to this theme, developing an extended account of democracy as a way of life. In his 1926 *The Public and Its Problems*, he offered a succinct measure of a fully democratic form of social life:

> From the standpoint of the individual, it [the idea of democracy] consists in having a responsible share according to capacity in forming and directing the activities of the groups to which one belongs and in participating according to need in the values which the groups sustain. From the standpoint of the groups, it demands liberation of the potentialities of members of a group in harmony

with the interests and goods which are common.... Regarded as an idea, democracy is not an alternative to other principles of associated life. It is the idea of community life itself....Wherever there is conjoint activity whose consequences are appreciated as good by all singular persons who take part in it, and where the realization of the good is such as to effect an energetic desire and effort to sustain it in being just because it is a good shared by all, there is in so far a community. The clear consciousness of a communal life, in all its implications, constitutes the idea of democracy. (LW 2:32–28)

This idea of democracy and the consequences of implementing it are revolutionary. Writing for *Common Sense* in 1937, Dewey argued forcefully and passionately that, understood as a way of life, "democracy is radical":

> *The fundamental principle of democracy is that the ends of freedom and individuality for all can be attained only by means that accord with those ends....The end of democracy is a radical end. For it is an end that has not been adequately realized in any country at any time.* It is radical because it requires great change in existing social institutions, economic, legal and cultural. A democratic liberalism that does not recognize these things in thought and action is not awake to its own meaning and to what that meaning demands. (LW 11:298–99)

Two years later, in *Freedom and Culture*, Dewey linked satisfaction of these demands of democratic life to the development of a distinctively democratic view of human nature:

> No matter how uniform and constant human nature is in the abstract, the conditions within which and upon which it operates have changed so greatly since political democracy was established among us, that democracy cannot now depend upon or be expressed in political institutions alone.... democracy is expressed in the attitudes of human beings and is measured by consequences produced in their lives. The impact of the humanist view of democracy upon all forms of culture, upon education, science and art, morals and religion, as well as upon industry and politics, saves it from the criticism passed upon moralistic exhortation. For it tells us that we need to examine every one of the phases of human activity to ascertain what effects it has in release, maturing and fruition of the potentialities of human nature. (LW 13:151–52)

The ongoing development of these potentialities requires appropriate social conditions in which all share and contribute. Belief in the power of human experience progressively to identify and attain these conditions coupled with unflagging action on this belief is what Dewey, at the age of eighty in 1939, called "Creative Democracy—The Task Before Us":

> We have had the habit of thinking of democracy as a kind of political mechanism that will work as long as citizens were reasonably faithful in performing political duties.... we can escape from this external way of thinking only as we realize in thought and act that democracy is a personal way of individual life; that it signifies the possession and continual use of certain attitudes, forming personal character and determining desire and purpose in all the relations of life. (LW 14:225–26)

To the extent, then, that a given person does not participate consistently and fully in the consideration, formation, and implementation of social values, decisions, and policies, democracy as an individual's self-determining and self-realizing way of life simply does not exist. And, to the extent that given social practices, groups, and institutions do not nourish shared interests, harmonious differences, and individual growth, democracy as a free community's way of life does not really exist.

This understanding of democracy as a way of life rather than a form of government radically expands the idea of democracy.[6] That this is a conceptual expansion is obvious. Given a Deweyan view, people's actual lives and social relations may fail to be actually and substantially democratic even when their government surely and formally is democratic. That this conceptual expansion is a theoretical improvement or, more importantly, that it might make any practical advance at all is at present less obvious. Moreover, while this expanded notion of democracy now should be clear in the abstract, the import and consequences for action of Dewey's account of democracy as a way of life still may seem difficult to imagine and understand, much less achieve. What, then, is the practical meaning of democracy understood broadly as a way of life? And, what is the pragmatic advantage of this view for us today?

Democracy as a Way of Life

The question of what is involved in self-governing methods is now much more complex. But for this very reason, the task of those who retain belief in democracy is to revive and maintain in full vigor the original conviction of the intrinsic moral nature of democracy, now stated in ways congruous with present conditions of culture. We have advanced far enough to say that democracy is a way of life. We have yet to realize that it is a way of personal life and one which provides a moral standard for personal conduct. (LW 13:155)

To view democracy as a way of life is not simply to substitute a broader account for a narrower one, a new definition for a familiar one, or a messy cultural notion for a neat political one. Instead, above all, it is to demand different personal conduct and far-reaching cultural reconstruction—deep changes in habits of thought and action, patterns of association and interaction, and personal and public values.

These changes may be facilitated, at least a little, by a grasp of the theoretical underpinnings (and their implications) of this broad view of democracy. For example, an understanding of democracy as a way of life overcomes: traditional dualisms about self and society, autonomy and association, experience and nature, thought and feeling, and fact and value; compartmentalized views of social life that keep antiseptically separate the political, economic, legal, scientific, aesthetic, religious, and moral dimensions of life; and, essentialist, ahistorical conceptions of culture and cultural change. In their place, an account of democracy as a way of life recognizes: the irreducibly social production and character of the self, its values, and its genuine individuality; the pervasive interconnections and mutual entanglements among all aspects of social life; and, the complex, varying historical efficacies of, and possibilities for, each of these dimensions of culture. These themes and concerns have been developed at length, thus establishing pragmatism as a middle ground between the extremes of irrelevant transcendentalism and desperate foundationalism on one side and quiescent neopragmatism and naive relativism on the other side. These themes have been repeated many times, and they bear this repetition, for sustained attention to them could serve as an effective antidote to much that ails contemporary professional philosophy. I will not rehearse once more these concerns here, however, for my immediate objective is less democracy's intellectual beginnings and more its personal and social ends.

Accordingly, I want to focus on the more immediately practical meaning and consequences of Dewey's broad view of democracy as a way of life. In doing so, I will stress three points. In the first place, to view democracy as a way of life is to highlight the fact that *democracy as a way of life is an ideal*. To deny this is to strip democratic life of its claims upon our future conduct, while mistakenly treating it as a reality ready-made and antecedent to that conduct. In this regard, democracy as a form of government differs from democracy as a way of life. While it may be impossible to identify an actual nation or state that fully embodies the criteria of a democratic government, there clearly are actual governments that fully meet most of these criteria and significantly meet all of them. From this descriptive or empirical standpoint, some existing governments are actual democracies. By contrast, there appear to be no existing large nations, states, or cultures that significantly, much less fully, meet the criteria of a democratic way of life. Surely the present United States of America is not an example. From this standpoint, existing ways of life are not actually democratic. This, of course, is what Dewey meant by terming democracy a radical idea and an undertaking still before us. Moreover, there is no guarantee that this undertaking will succeed: a democratic way of life is not now a reality and it may not become a reality.

Does this mean, then, that democratic life is a mere fiction, wishful thinking, or utopian fantasy? Does it mean that the democratic ideal is wholly separate from, and without support in, our actual existence? No. First, to claim that democracy as a way of life is an ideal is not to deny that some existing ways of life are more democratic than others. As Sidney Hook pointed out, the fact that no man is absolutely fat does not prohibit us from holding that one man is fatter than another.[7] Second, more importantly, as an ideal, democracy is not simply "unreal." As an ideal, it is a deep commitment, grasped by our imagination, that unifies our lives, makes meaningful our efforts, and directs our actions. As an ideal, it is generated through imagination, but it is not "made out of imaginary stuff." Instead, anything but "unreal" or "imaginary," it is "made out of the hard stuff of the world of physical and social experience"—the material and energies and capacities that are the conditions for its existence (LW 9:33–34; 13:174).

To describe democratic life as an ideal, however, is not so much to state a present fact as it is to recommend a future course of action—an admittedly radical course of action. To quietly favor, idly wish and hope for, or routinely assent to such a democratic course of action, however, is not thereby to make it an ideal. Today we still must make democracy an ideal; we have not done so yet. Thus, idealizing democracy is the first step in the task of realizing democracy. When, and if, our idealizing imagination does seize upon democracy as a way of life, personal life will express this ideal in action. In Dewey's terms, communication, freedom, and cooperation will become loyalties or values in action, instead of mere values in name only (LW 14:275). As an ideal, democracy requires this committed expression and action from each of us.

This makes clear, in the second place, that *democracy as a way of life is a moral notion*. Indeed, it is "moral through and through: in its foundations, its methods, its ends" (LW 13:173): "We have to see that democracy means the belief that humanistic culture *should* prevail; we should be frank and open in our recognition that the proposition is a moral one—like any idea that concerns what *should* be" (LW 13:151). In stressing the moral dimension of democracy, Dewey, like Thomas Jefferson, argues that the demands of democracy coincide with those of liberty, equality, and justice. Democracy as a form of government may be the best means to the fullest possible realization of human nature (LW 13:155), but democracy as a way of life is that realization itself in process.

This means that democratic processes are not value neutral, consistent with all preferences, or tolerant of all loyalties—even when these loyalties are rooted in old habits or reflect the present desires of a majority. Instead, this explicitly moral formulation of democracy furnishes a basis in experience for criticism and reconstruction of experience itself. In fact, this is a defining trait of democracy: democracy "is the sole way of living which believes wholeheartedly in the process of experience as end and as means; as that which is capable of generating the science which is the sole dependable authority for the direction of further experience and which releases emotions, needs and desires so as to call into being the things that have not existed in the past" (LW 14:228). Recognition of the moral character of democracy directs us to assess and revise institutions, practices, and social relations in terms of the extent to which they yield and embody democratic concern for the free, intelligent, and harmonious development of individuals. It leads us to question repeatedly to what extent our social arrangements promote "living together in ways in which the life of each of us is at once profitable in the deepest sense of the word," profitable to the individual and to the individuality of others (LW 13:303).

If this questioning is successful in theory, it undercuts worries about emotivism, subjectivism, and irrationalism, as well as demands for foundations, a priori justifications, and final proof. If it is successful in practice, it enlarges and secures the democratic character of our lives. But it is not an easy task. For the most part, it has not been achieved, and it will not be achieved by armchair philosophizing or speculative theorizing. Dewey put this nicely: "Not all who say Ideals, Ideals, shall enter the kingdom of the ideal, but those who know and who respect the roads that conduct to the kingdom" (LW 3:151). The roads to the kingdom of democratic life are inquiry and communication; they are prerequisites of democracy as a way of life, prerequisites of what Dewey called the formation of the Public and the transition from a Great Society to a Great Community (LW 2:324, 345, 350). It is hard to satisfy these prerequisites. The roadblocks to inquiry and communication are many: exclusion from participation and denial of access; control of publicity and the dissemination of knowledge; manipulation of opinion and thought; interference with experimentation and dishonest research; ignorance and inarticulateness; distance, time, and cultural difference; conservative habits of belief and emotion; fear, greed, and selfishness; specialization and mediation; and, illusions of intellectual freedom in the absence of known external oppression. These are immense obstacles to a democratic way of life, and the weight of history is on the side of those who are cynical about the prospects of overcoming them.

This situation is a measure of the enormous cultural distance—evident in the life of each person—between what morally should be and what actually is. It highlights, in the third place, another key characteristic of *democracy as a way of life*: *the central role of democratic faith*. This faith carries no overarching or advance guarantees. It provides no specific assurances about the future existence or expansion of democratic life. Indeed, it provides no general warrant for any complacent expectation of progress. It finds nothing in human history, human nature, or the world situation today to support a rosy or comfortable vision of the future. Such mistaken visions merely treat present hopes as future realities. As Dewey often noted, it simply is no longer possible to hold the happy Enlightenment faith in the assured advance of science and its production of free institutions and fulfilling lives. This democratic faith, then, supports neither utopian thinking nor even optimism in the abstract.

At the same time, it stands in opposition to all pessimism, cynicism, and fatalism. It opposes every uncomfortable, but still in consequence complacent, dystopian future vision. Such mistaken visions merely treat present contingencies—for instance, social relations of power and personal traits of stupidity, selfishness, impatience, and laziness—as future, eternal necessities. There is every reason to recognize soberly the serious problems that these realities pose for democracy, but there is no reason to treat them as fixed and impossible to change.

Instead, democratic faith is melioristic faith in possibility: It is the conviction that associated human imagination, intelligence, and will, if exercised, can fashion progressively a more fully democratic existence. It is the belief that these things, if given a show, "will grow and be able to generate progressively the knowledge and wisdom needed to guide collective action" (LW 11:219).

This faith, Dewey said, is the basis or foundation of democracy. Democracy is a way of life controlled by and infused with this faith. Is this faith warranted? The pragmatic answer is neither a final "yes" nor a final "no." Instead, it is "experience so far indicates that it is, but let's find out more fully." That is, despite the best efforts of clever political theorists and traditional epistemologists, there is no advance theoretical foundation or justification for democracy. There is no transcendental basis, no non-question-begging deduction, no final, binding empirical proof. (Similarly, there is no advance theoretical foundation or justification against democracy.) This sort of "epistemological" justification in advance of trial is impossible, and search for it is misguided. The matter can be decided only by experiment, not by argument.

Democracy requires faith in order to sustain the action necessary for its fuller realization. Accordingly, this faith may be warranted only through experimental trial, only after the fact or eventually, only by means of its consequences, only in relation to its results (rather than its origins). At present, as Dewey noted, this trial still stands before us because faith in democracy has emerged only recently and has been adopted only partially, haphazardly, and infrequently (LW 11:219). Even under democratic governments today, thoughts and feelings are saturated with earlier preferences for authority rather than community, experimentation, and publicity. In fact, we still lack a common vocabulary to articulate the values involved in the realization of democracy (LW 13:178). Still, results of adopting this democratic faith have broken the "hypnotic spell" (LW 14:250) of earlier, failed alternatives (LW 11:144; 14:250), and now warrant the extension of democracy. Those who "do their best to make the extension actual" expect no speedy victory: "They are however, buoyed by the assurance that no matter how slight the immediate effect of their efforts, . . . they are projecting into events a large and comprehensive idea by experimental methods that correct and mature the method and the idea in the very process of trial" (LW 11:145). And, if experience and history teach anything at all, Dewey added, it is that this is the surest possible promise of practical advance (LW 6:68).

Democratic Challenges and Democratic Methods

Democracy is the faith that the process of experience is more
important than any special result attained, so that special results
achieved are of ultimate value only as they are used to enrich and
order the ongoing process. Since the process of experience is capable of
being educative, faith in democracy is all one with faith in experience
and education. (LW 14:229)

Can we produce a democratic culture? Can we execute our democratic ideals directly in our own lives (LW 6:48)? Is democracy as a way of life possible? These are open questions. Their answers depend on and await our action. Still, these questions point directly to the central pragmatic issue facing democracy today: *How* can we produce a genuinely democratic way of life? To sidestep this question is to demonstrate greater concern for the problems of philosophers than for the problems of men and women.

A *first* important, straightforward way to answer this question is to attempt to identify particular roadblocks to a democratic way of life, formulate specific strategies to remove these roadblocks, and then implement these strategies (making revisions in light of successful and unsuccessful results, new problems, and the need for new approaches). All of this, it should be remembered, requires pragmatic inquiry (and not just neopragmatic "conversation"). Dewey frequently pursued democracy in just this critical way. He tirelessly advocated far-reaching changes in, for example: American politics, political parties, and political action; international relations and foreign policy; labor, business, and the production and distribution of economic opportunities and material wealth and profit; divisions and relations of race and class; social welfare programs; entertainment, propaganda, and the direction of what passes for public opinion; and, of course, schooling and educational administration. "The struggle for democracy has to be maintained on as many fronts as culture has aspects" (LW 13:186), he summarized simply.

This same struggle confronts us today. In some respects, of course recent events, fresh concerns, and new knowledges have refocused this struggle—on, for example: feminism and gender, internationalism and multiple cultures, information and new technologies, and environmentalism and nature. The struggle for democracy has to be carried to these new battlegrounds.

Sadly, in many other instances and details, the struggle for democracy remains much the same for us as it was for Dewey. Worse yet, some of the conditions that Dewey recognized and analyzed as most threatening to democracy now appear even more pervasive and pernicious. Two problems stand out here. The first is economic, and concerns what Dewey called "the scandal of private appropriation of socially produced values" (LW 5:95), the emergence of the "business mind" (LW 5:69) and spread of a "corporate mentality," and the narrow use of intelligence for selfish ends and class interests (LW 9:111). Today outdated ideas of economic "liberty" and "free" markets—the same ideas that Dewey debunked repeatedly in *Individualism: Old and New, Liberalism and Social Action,* and *Freedom and Culture*—still grip our minds and conduct. But these ideas now have little basis in social life. Instead, the gaps between wealthy and poor, idle and meaningfully active, and powerful and powerless have never been greater, in this country and abroad. The poverty and insecurity of much of the economic underclass has never seemed more permanent or hopeless. Our institutionalized disregard, intolerance, and waste of the welfare of the sick, the weak, the hungry, and the homeless have never been more far-reaching. And, the cynical equation of maximum material consumption, private prosperity, and pecuniary profit with the good life has never been more commonplace. Unlike Dewey, we almost must "admit that our outer civilization is attaining an inner culture which corresponds to it, however much we might disesteem the quality of that culture" (LW 5:69). Still, this situation is pathetic and outrageous, and it must be intolerable to anyone really committed to democracy. In short, we must invent ways to make our economy democratic. There is a second problem that seems to threaten and undermine democratic life much more now than when Dewey confronted it. It cuts across our culture and concerns what Dewey called propaganda, cheap amusement, and the control of opinion (MW 11:118; LW 2:321, 348; 3:141; 7:361; 13:168). Today naive beliefs about "freedom" of thought and "free" expression, "public" opinion, and "self-determination"—the same beliefs that Dewey thoroughly criticized in *The Public and Its Problems* and many subsequent essays—still shape our images of ourselves and our society. But these beliefs now have little correspondence to reality. Instead, we are the unwitting, usually unconscious, targets of powerful public relations techniques and subtle marketing campaigns that promote everything from automobiles to philosophies, luxury cruises to news magazines, and domestic wines to foreign wars. We are inundated by influential sound bytes and carefully controlled images that wash over us but do not wash us clean. We have become habituated to institutionalized restrictions and private economic influences on the gathering and dissemination of information. And, we are happy consumers of entertainment, constantly craving and everywhere institutionalizing it (rather than criticism)—even in our schools. Unlike Dewey, we almost have given up concern for the eclipse of a community or public and effective publicity. Still, we must realize that this state of affairs is incompatible with a democratic way of life: in short, we must find ways to transform mass communications and mass media into public communications and public media—communications and media of, by, and for a public.[8]

There is a *second* related important way to answer the question about how to create a thoroughly democratic way of life. This second approach does not concentrate primarily on specific existing obstacles to democracy. Instead, it articulates the general preconditions or requirements of democratic life, and then inquires as to how to satisfy these conditions. Not surprisingly, Dewey frequently proceeded in this way too, explaining how inquiry and communication are intrinsically and reciprocally related to democracy:

> The prime condition of a democratically organized public is a kind of knowledge and insight which does not yet exist. In its absence, it would be the height of absurdity to try to tell what it would be like if it existed. But some of the conditions which must be fulfilled if it is to exist can be indicated.... An obvious requirement is freedom of social inquiry and of distribution of its conclusions....The highest and most difficult kind of inquiry and a subtle, delicate, vivid and responsive art of communication must take possession of the physical machinery of transmission and circulation and breathe life into it. When the machine age has thus perfected its machinery it will be a means of life and not its

despotic master. Democracy will come into its own, for democracy is a name for a life of free and enriching communion. It had its seer in Walt Whitman. It will have its consummation when free social inquiry is indissolubly wedded to the art of full and moving communication. (LW 2:339, 350)

It is important to emphasize that this relation between democracy and both inquiry and communication is in practice a reciprocal, circular relation. Democracy as a way of life both requires and is required by inquiry and communication. This, of course, creates no logically vicious circle; it does not force us to decide whether chicken or egg came first. Instead, it indicates that a democratic way of life is not a separate entity or by-product of inquiry and communication. Instead, the progressive development of culture by, in, and through inquiry and communication constitutes fully democratic social life.

This progressive development is an educational matter, in the broadest sense of that term, and it is for this reason that Dewey characterized democracy as a challenge to education. This suggests an important *third* dimension or way to address the question concerning how to create democracy as a way of life. On this view, education must be the practical or strategic focus. In its broadest sense, education is the creation of habits of mind and character (LW 11:44), and in this context all social institutions and arrangements—not just the schools—"are educational in the sense that they operate to form attitudes, dispositions, abilities and disabilities that constitute a concrete personality" (LW 11:221). In this light, democracy simply stands for a particular sort of education; it is a particular educational principle, measure, and policy (LW 13:294, 304). What principle? Democracy as an educational principle is this: The social aim of education is the production of democratic attitudes, dispositions, and abilities—the free interaction and participation of individuals and their mutual inter-penetration of interests in and through shared community life (MW 9:92: LW 2:327). This democratic educational principle receives little more than lip service from the most powerful educational institutions in America today—the economic system, the government, the military, the media, the family and neighborhood, and the school.[9] To this extent, remarkably, America today is committed neither to democratic education nor to democracy.

Any democratic reconstruction of American society is one with the democratic reconstruction of these institutions. And this, in turn, involves nothing less than the thoroughgoing change and adoption on all cultural fronts of democratic educational principles and their democratic social aims.

This demand for democratic educational principles is doubly radical: it is the pursuit of radically democratic *ends*, undertaken through radically democratic *means*. As a way of life, democracy cannot be achieved, sustained, or expanded in any other way. To employ on behalf of democracy means of social change other than those of intelligent inquiry and communication is, to the very degree in which those other means are used, to postpone and undermine democracy as a way of life. Experience supplies ample evidence of this, for in the past we regularly have depended on non-democratic means (LW 11:170, 299)—whether explicitly violent, authoritarian or totalitarian, or implicitly coercive, elitist, or merely bureaucratic. We may do so again in the future, as Tatyana Vorozheikina, writing about recent democratic changes in Russia points out: "And if winter does come, the pressure for an alternative [to democracy] will become increasingly urgent because, unlike nature, society cannot expect the automatic arrival of spring. Whenever people who call themselves democrats embrace the 'objective necessity' of an authoritarian regime, democracy is dead."[10] Our first defense from this, Dewey wrote, "is to realize that democracy can be served only by the slow day by day adoption and contagious diffusion in every phase of our common life of methods that are identical with the ends to be reached" (LW 13:187)

There is nothing flashy or catchy about any of this (and, for this reason, it is easy to miss the thoroughly radical character of democracy as a way of life). At best, democratic means of social change will extend democratic life only slowly and bit by bit. As a result, democracy is an unsure and difficult path to follow. On the other hand, it is a path open to us all. As a way of life, democracy has personal (as well as institutional) meaning and message. The message is straightforward: Democracy exists only on paper and in statute unless individuals enact it in their own transactions day by day and face-to-face in local communities. That is, a society of individuals can become a democracy only as those individuals act democratically. This is the *personal* (but not private) challenge of democracy to each of us—as parent and child, teacher and student, friend and lover, neighbor and citizen, in recreation and work, and in relation to the rest of nature. In our various personal relations and associations, throughout our lives, even recognizing social limits and constraints, we each must seek to expand democracy, to invent new ways to extend free inquiry and full communication on behalf of shared values. We must realize in thought and action that democracy is a personal way of individual life (LW 14:226), and we must rededicate our lives to its realization—now.

Notes

1.   Oldemiro Baloi, Mozambique's vice minister of cooperation, as quoted by Rick Lyman, Knight-Ridder News Service, December 2, 1990.

Days later, in a speech in Argentina, President Bush echoed his own 1988 Inaugural Address, proclaiming that "the day of the dictator is over," *Los Angeles Times*, December 5, 1990. More soberly, conservative Irving Kristol argues that modern democracies have gotten what they wanted, producing a new malaise in America: "The new, distinctive feature of our modern democracies is the contempt of this citizenry for their governments and politicians. They demand more and more of their governments, since they have been taught that this is their democratic duty, but at the same time they expect less and less." "America's Mysterious Malaise," *The Times Literary Supplement*, May 22, 1992, p. 5. For an analysis that is less conservative and more grim still, see Noam Chomsky, *Deterring Democracy* (New York: Verso, 1991).

2. This term, "theory-guilt," coined by Thomas C. Grey in his "Hear the Other Side: Wallace Stevens and Pragmatist Legal Theory," is utilized and expanded by Richard Rorty in his "The Banality of Pragmatism and the Poetry of Justice." Both these essays are part of the important "Symposium on the Renaissance of Pragmatism in American Legal Thought," *Southern California Law Review* 63, 6 (September 1990). My criticism is directed not at Grey but at Rorty and his neopragmatism, particularly as it is developed in his *Consequences of Pragmatism* (Minneapolis: University of Minnesota Press, 1982) and *Contingency, Irony and Solidarity* (Cambridge: Cambridge University Press, 1989). I discuss this at greater length elsewhere: "Revisioning Philosophy," *Philosophy Today* 33, 3 (Fall 1989); review of Rorty's *Contingency, Irony and Solidarity, The Personalist Forum* 5, 2 (Fall, 1989); and, "Dewey's Reconstruction of Metaphysics," *Transactions of the Charles S. Peirce Society* 28, 2 (Spring 1992).

3. See, for example: David Truman, *The Governmental Process* (New York: Alfred A. Knopf, 1951); Alan Altshuler, *Community Control* (New York: Pegasus, 1970); William Alton Kelso, *American Democratic Theory: Pluralism and Its Critics* (Westport, Conn.: Greenwood Press, 1978); J. Roland Pennock, *Democratic Political Theory* (Princeton, N.J.: Princeton University Press, 1979); Robert A. Dahl, *Democracy and Its Critics* (New Haven: Yale University Press, 1989); Jane Mansbridge, *Beyond Adversary Democracy* (New York: Basic Books, 1980) and *Beyond Self-Interest* (Chicago: University of Chicago Press, 1991); Sara M. Evans and Harry C. Boyte, *Free Spaces: The Sources of Democratic Change in America* (New York: Harper and Row, 1986).

4. Robert A. Dahl, *Dilemmas of Pluralist Democracy: Autonomy vs. Control* (New Haven: Yale University Press, 1982), p. 6.

5. See, for example, Frank Bealey, *Democracy in the Contemporary State* (Oxford: Clarendon Press, 1988), p. 2.

6. Here once more it is interesting to note similarities between Dewey's philosophy and the work of political theorist Robert Dahl.

Although Dahl defines democracy as a kind of government rather than a way of life, he is quick to caution that democracy in this restricted sense may be necessary but not sufficient for sound policy. At the same time, like Dewey, he also is quick to point out the need to reconstruct our political order, values, and beliefs: "For the most powerful ideologies of our age all suffer from having acquired their shape and substance in the eighteenth and nineteenth centuries, or very much earlier, before the world in which we now live had come fully into view. They are like medieval maps of the world, charming but dangerous for navigating unfamiliar seas.... Liberalism, conservativism, capitalism, socialism, Marxism, corporatism, anarchism, even democratic ideas, all face a world that in its form and thrust confounds the crucial assumptions, requirements, descriptions, predictions, hopes, or prescriptions they express." *Dilemmas of Pluralist Democracy: Autonomy vs. Control*, p. 3. Although they seem wholly unaware of Dewey's work and its parallels with their own, see also: Carol Pateman's discussion of a "participatory society" in *Participation and Democratic Theory* (New York: Cambridge University Press, 1970); Anne Phillips' analysis of the implications and uses of feminism for democratic theory in *Engendering Democracy* (University Park: Pennsylvania State University Press, 1991); and Chantal Mouffe's views on citizenship and community in *Dimensions of Radical Democracy* (New York: Verso, 1992).

7. Sidney Hook, "The Democratic Way of Life" in his 1940 *Reason, Social Myths, and Democracy* (Buffalo, N.Y.: Prometheus Books, 1991), p. 285. It is very unfortunate that this book (that I encountered only after finishing this essay) now is generally neglected and not well-known.

8. In this vein, Hook writes: "A political democracy cannot function properly where differences in economic power are so great that one group can determine the weal or woe of another by non-political means. Genuine political democracy, therefore, entails the right of the governed, through their representatives, to control economic policy. He continues succinctly: "A further consequence of 'freely given consent' is the absence of a monopoly on education where education includes all agencies of cultural transmission, especially the press.... Not many years ago this would have been a commonplace. Today apologists have so muddied the waters of truth that its reaffirmation must be stressed." Hook, *Reason, Social Myths, and Democracy*, pp. 286, 287.

9. In this reconstruction, the schools, and intellectuals within them, have a special role to play in fostering critical inquiry and cooperative communication. At the same time, however, this role and its effectiveness are limited by external (LW 3:273; 9:110; 9:207; 11:222; 11:414; 13:296) and internal (LW 5:103) forces. See also Boyd H. Bode, " 'The Great American Dream,' " in *American Philosophy Today and Tomorrow*, ed. H. Kallen and S. Hook (Freeport, N.Y.: Books for Libraries Press, 1968), pp. 65–79.

10.   Tatyana Vorozheikina, "Why Not Try Democracy?," in *The Nation*, May 4, 1992, pp. 594–96.

4

The Individual, the Community, and the Reconstruction of Values

SANDRA B. ROSENTHAL

Community and pluralism are often held to be at odds with each other, with a choice to be made between group conformity and individualism, and this dilemma has dominated much of contemporary discussions of social and moral philosophy. Following the general thrust of Dewey's pragmatic position, the ensuing discussion will develop the view that the creativity of the individual and the constraints of group conformity are not two conflicting alternatives, but rather two mutually dependent, interrelated poles in a dynamic temporal process which manifests itself as two poles within the self, two poles within the community, and two poles in the experience of value. This view in turn incorporates an open perspectivalism and temporalism which at once points to the importance of the past and denies the stultifying self-enclosement of a relativism of arbitrary selection or a historicism of present happenstance. These various features involve, as well, the pragmatic understanding of the temporal spread of human existence as embodying the dynamics of scientific method, the understanding of the stretch of experience as inherently experimental.[1]

The above general context as providing the framework for under-standing the reconstruction of values can best be approached by focusing first on the perspectival and experimental nature of experience. These features go hand in hand with the radical rejection of spectator philosophy. All knowledge and experience are infused with interpretive aspects, funded with past experience, and stem from a perspective or a point of view. In being inherently perspectival, experience and knowledge are at once experimental. The very nature of human experience involves selective, purposive activity guided by intentional creativity and trans-formative of its environment in ways which turn problematic or potentially problematic situations[2] into meaningfully experienced unities, and the adequacy of such intentionally directed transformations are judged by their workability in the ongoing course of experience.[3] All experience is experimental, then, not in the sense that it is guided by sophisticated levels of thought, but that the very structure of human behavior, both as a way of experiencing and as a way of being, embodies the above features of scientific or experimental method.[4]

The creative, perspectival nature of experience yields a worldly environment which incorporates a perspectival pluralism, for diverse groups or diverse individuals bring diverse perspectives in the organization of experience. Not only are these perspectives real within our environment, but without them there is no environment. The universe exists indepen-dent of our intentional activity, but our worldly environment is inseparable from our meaning or intending it in certain ways, and these ways are inherently pluralistic. However, such pluralism, when properly under-stood, should not lead to the view that varying groups are enclosed within self-contained, myopic, limiting frameworks or points of view, cutting off the possibility of rational dialogue, for two reasons. First, perspectives by their very nature are not self-enclosed but open onto a community perspective. Second, perspectival pluralism provides the very matrix for rational dialogue and ongoing temporal development. These points will first be briefly discussed in relation to the self, for it will be seen that in a certain sense, the dynamics of community are the dynamics of the self "writ large."

As Dewey stresses, mind, thinking, and selfhood are not aspects of some mental substance. Neither, however, are they reducible to the material functioning of the brain and the nervous system. Mind, thinking, and selfhood are emergent levels of activity of organisms within nature. Meaning emerges in the interactions among conscious organisms, in the adjustments and coordinations needed for cooperative action in the social context. Mental processes are part of a process that is going on between organism and environment, and language itself is possible because of the communicative interactions on which the existence of meaning is based. In communicative interaction, individuals take the perspective of the other in the development of their conduct, and in this way there develops the common content which provides community of meaning. This in turn requires the ability to go beyond the limitation to the present, to be aware of the future possible phases of social activity. And, this awareness relates, strictly speaking, not to the actual reaction of the other, but rather to the *relation between* one's own actions and the anticipated possible responses of others to them. In this way there emerges not just consciousness but self-consciousness. To have a self is to have a particular type of ability, the ability to be aware of one's behavior as part of the social process of adjustment, to be aware of oneself as a social object, as an acting agent within the context of other acting agents. Not only can selves exist only in relationship to other selves, but no absolute line can be drawn between our own selves and the selves of others, since our own selves are there for and in our experience only in so far as others exist and enter into our experience. The origins and foundation of the self, like those of mind, are social or intersubjective. As Dewey notes in *Art as Experience*, it is through social interaction that "the self is both formed and brought to consciousness" (LW 10:286).

In incorporating the perspective of the other, the developing self comes to take the perspective of others as the group as a whole. In this way the self comes to incorporate the standards and authority of the group; there is a passive dimension to the self. Yet, in responding to the perspective of the other, it is this individual as a unique center of activity that responds; there is a creative dimension to the self. Any self thus incorporates, by its very nature, both the conformity of the group perspective and the creativity of its unique individual perspective.[5] Accordingly, in "Authority and Social Change" Dewey holds that the tension between conservative and liberating factors lies in the very constitution of individual selves. Freedom does not lie in opposition to the restrictions of norms and authority, but in a self-direction which requires the proper dynamic interaction of these two poles within the self. Thus Dewey notes that "the principle of authority" must not be understood as "purely restrictive power" but as providing direction (LW 11:133). Because of this dynamic interaction constitutive of the very nature of selfhood, the perspective of the novel, "liberating" pole of the self always opens onto a common, "conserving" perspective. From the backdrop of the above brief overview of the self, the ensuing discussion will turn to the nature of community.

It has been seen that the unique individual both reflects and reacts to the common perspective in its own peculiar manner. And, when the individual selects a novel perspective, this novelty in turn enters into the common perspective which is now "there" as incorporating this novelty. This novel perspective is an emergent because of its relation to institutions, traditions, and patterns of life which conditioned its novel emergence, and it gains its significance in light of the new common perspectives to which it gives rise. In this continual interplay of adjustment of attitudes, aspirations, and factual perceptions between the common perspective as the condition for the novel emergent perspective and the novel emergent as it conditions the common perspective the dynamic of community is to be found. Thus the creativity of the individual can be contrasted with the conformity represented by the common perspective, but not with community. True community requires myself as both partially constituted by and partially constitutive of the common perspective. Further it requires this in the dynamic and changing manner of ongoing adjustment embodying authentic communication. The act of adjustment between the novel perspective and the common perspective is the essential communicative dynamic of community.

This adjustment is neither assimilation of perspectives, one to the other, nor the fusion of perspectives into an indistinguishable oneness, but can best be understood as an "accommodation" in which each creatively affects, and is affected by, the other through accepted means of mediation of some sort. Thus a community is constituted by, and develops in terms of, the ongoing communicative adjustment between the activity constitutive of the novel individual perspective and the common or group perspective, and each of these two interacting poles constitutive of community gains its meaning, significance, and enrichment through this process of accommodation or adjustment. A free society, like a free individual, requires both the influencing power of authority as embodied in institutions and traditions and the innovative power of creativity as contextually set or directed novelty. Thus, in Dewey's terms, "No amount of aggregated collective action of itself constitutes a community. . . . To learn to be human is to develop through the give-and-take of communication an effective sense of being an individually distinctive member of a community; one who understands and appreciates its beliefs, desires, and methods, and who contributes to a further conversion of organic powers into human resources and values. But this transition is never finished" (LW 2:330, 332).

The individual is neither an isolatable discrete element in, nor an atomic building block of, a community. Rather, the individual represents the instigation of creative adjustments within a community, adjustments which creatively change both poles which operate within the adjustment process. The very intelligence which transforms societies and institutions is itself influenced by these institutions. The operation of individual intelligence, the particular habits of intelligent activity which individuals utilize, are products of the cultural, educational, and other institutional practices into which they are thrown. In this sense even individual intelligence is social intelligence. And, social intelligence, as the historically grounded intelligence operative within a community and embodied in its institutions, though not merely an aggregate of individual intelligence but rather a qualitatively unique and unified whole, is nonetheless not something separable from individual intelligence. There is an intimate functional reciprocity between individual and social intelligence, a reciprocity based on the continual process of adjustment. Novelty within society is initiated by individuals, but such initiation can occur only because individuals are continuous with others and with social institutions of which they are a part. As Dewey emphasizes, "Wants, choices and purposes have their locus in single beings," but the content is not "something purely personal." The "along with" is part of the very life process (LW 2:249).

It can be seen that the common perspective changes as it incorporates or adjusts to its own creativity emerging as novel individual perspectives. That which both founds and is founded upon this activity of ongoing adjustment is a community, and in its historical rootedness it develops its own particular organs for the control of the process. The ability to provide the means of mediating within the ongoing dynamics of adjustment constitutes a community of any type as a community.[6] The very nature of community requires the openness of perspectives. And, no community is constricted by closed community perspectives either in terms of possibilities of penetrating to more fundamental levels of community or to wider breadth of community. Indeed such an either-or is itself a false dichotomy, for expansion in breadth is at once expansion in depth, for the adjustment of incompatible perspectives at any level requires not an imposition from "on high" of abstract principles but a deepening to a more fundamental level of community. As two communities recognize their openness of horizons in coming to understand the perspective of the other, there can be adjustment founded on a deeper or broader community.

The demands of the human condition, in its deepest sense, can be understood as the community of communities, not in the sense that it contains many self-enclosed communities, but in the sense that it is that grounding community upon which all other communities must be founded and upon which they all open. As Dewey states, the demands of adjusting the old and the new, the stability of conformity and the novelty of creativity, "is inherent in, or a part of, the very texture of life" (LW 11:133). Thus, Dewey stresses the ideal of a world community, and holds that what would make the great community precisely a community as opposed to a mere society is "intercommunication," expressed above as the organs of accommodation which allow for the ongoing interplay of novelty and conformity (LW 2:367).[7] The understanding of a radically diverse way of life, or way of making sense of things, is not to be found from above by imposing one's own reflective perspective upon such diversity, but rather from beneath, by penetrating through such differences to the sense of the various ways of making sense of the world as they emerge from the essential characteristics of beings fundamentally alike confronting a common reality in an ongoing process of change. Such a deepening may change conflict into community diversity, or it may lead to an emerging consensus of the wrongness of one of the conflicting positions. Such a deepening of course does not negate the use of intelligent inquiry, but rather opens it up, frees it from the products of its past in terms of rigidities and abstractions, and focuses it on the dynamics of concrete human existence. In this way, over the course of time, incompatible perspectives, though not proved right or wrong, are resolved by the weight of argument as reasons and practices are worked out in the ongoing course of inquiry. If such adjustments do not emerge, then community has broken down.

To understand one's own stance on any issue is to understand its inherently perspectival approach and the illuminating light which other perspectives can rightfully cast upon it. In coming to understand the perspectival pluralism and the dynamic of adjustment or accommodation which constitute community, one can at the same time come to recognize the enrichment to be gained by understanding the perspective of the other and, as importantly, to recognize the enrichment to be gained by understanding what is implicitly operative in one's own perspectival approach. The development of the ability both to create and to respond constructively to the creation of novel perspectives, as well as to incorporate the perspective of the other, not as something totally alien, but as something sympathetically understood, is at once growth of the self. Growth of self incorporates an ever more encompassing sympathetic understanding of varied and diverse interests, thus leading to tolerance not as a sacrifice but as an enlargement of self. It involves as well the concomitant reconstruction of the institutions and practices which become incorporated within the self's "conserving" dimension, and at times demands also a reconstruction of the very organs of adjudication for controlling the process of the community adjustments which ground such reconstructive dynamics. Thus to deepen and expand the horizons of community is at once to deepen and expand the horizons of the selves involved in the ongoing dynamics of adjustment.

The sense of history is very much tied to the pragmatic understanding of the reconstruction taking place in the present. Perspectival pluralism, though incorporating at its deepest level the endless activity of adjustment rather than convergence toward final completed truth, does not involve the stultifying self-enclosement of a relativism in terms of arbitrary conceptual schemes or a historicism in terms of present happenstance. Rather, it involves an ontologically grounded temporalism in which perspectives emerge within the context of a past which presents itself in the richness of the present and which is oriented toward an indefinite future. Knowledge as cumulative and knowledge as changing do not lie in opposition, but rather knowledge as changing is also knowledge as cumulative, for any novel perspective emerges from a cumulative process or history of adjustment which yields enrichment of intelligibility both of the old and of the new. It has been seen that in any community, the eliciting of new community organs for adjustment in cases of incompatibility cannot be imposed from on high by eliciting the standards of a past which does not contain the organs of resolution, but must be created by calling on a sense of a more fundamental and creative level of activity. Yet, this activity must itself be based on the problem situation and the history within which it has emerged. By looking backward we can view the historical development within the social process, the direction of the movement. However, this looking backward is not some passive recovery of what once was but rather is a construction taking place in the present, and the past, as interpreted in the present, sets goals for the future. Indeed, the conformity of the group which delineates and typifies not only facts but attitudes and institutional practices is in a sense a past which enters into the future-oriented choices of the individual as it creatively structures its emerging present. Thus Dewey stresses that historical materials, in their most important sense, do not signify "the past and gone and the remote," but rather heightened perception of "elements active in present experience, elements that are seeking expansion and outlet and that demand clarification and which some phase of social life. . .brings to the focus of a selective, coherently arranged and growing experience" (LW 11:209–10).

The dynamics of experimental method, which embody "the fundamental principles of the relationship of life to its surroundings" (LW 2:106–7), is the vehicle by which the past becomes effective in the reconstruction of the present, leading to integration and fulfillment through organized movement. In this way, science is "operative art" (LW 1:269). The proper functioning of experimental method is precisely the artful functioning of experience. Indeed, in the "immediate" sense[8] of the qualitative character of *an* experience as a unified whole, or, in other terms, experience in its aesthetic dimension, the experimental method is embodied in its most intensified concrete unification or fusion. The sense of the qualitative character of an experience as a unified, integrated whole involves a sense of its temporal flow, of its own "little history," of the dynamics of experimentalism as providing the creatively organizing and ordering movement which brings to fruition the internal integration and fulfillment of the experience. As Dewey stresses, the dynamics of experience as experimental have "consequences *in* the individualized experiences, one that is immediate," and without these dynamics "immediate esthetic perception would have neither rich nor clear meaning immanent within it." (LW 4:190).[9] The concern with growing integration and fulfillment brings us to the pervasive value dimension of experience.

Communicative adjustments can work only when there are values held in common. As Dewey stresses, to have "anything that can be called a community in its pregnant sense there must be values prized in common"

(LW 13:71). Any community, qua community, is a moral community. From the backdrop of the above understanding of selfhood and community, the ensuing discussion will turn to the value dimension of experience as it reflects the bipolar dynamics of adjustment.

Value, as Dewey holds, is not something subjective, housed either as a content of mind or in any other sense within the organism, but neither is it something "there" in an independently ordered universe. Objects and situations, as they emerge in human experience, possess qualities that are as ontologically real in their emergence as the processes within which they emerge. These objects and situations possess qualities not just of colors, sounds, resistance, etc., but qualities of being alluring or repugnant, fulfilling or stultifying, appealing or unappealing, and so forth. These latter types of qualities, like all qualities, are real additive and irreducible features within nature. Value and valuings or valuing experiences are traits of nature, novel emergents in the context of organism-environment inter-action. Like all traits of nature, they have an aspect of the relatively stable or continuous, and an aspect of the precarious or novel. Further, the experience of value emerges as both shared and unique, as all experience is both shared and unique. The adjustment between these two aspects, the shared and the unique, gives rise to the novel and creative aspects within moral community. Finally, value situations, like all situations, are open to inquiry and require the general method of scientific experimen-talism by which progressive movement from a problematic situation to a meaningfully resolved or secure situation takes place. As seen above, this method involves creatively organizing experience through meanings, directing one's activity in light of that creative organization, and testing for truth in terms of consequences: does the organization work in bringing about the intended result? In the case of value, intelligent inquiry, as the embodiment of experimental method, moves from a situation filled with problematic valuings to a resolved or meaningfully organized experience of the valuable.

The difference between valuings and the experience of the valu*able*, between valuings and evaluations, is the difference in stages in inquiry. The distinction between valuings and the valuable is the distinction between experiencings which make no future claim and those judgments which make future claims by linking present experience to other experiences in terms of interacting potentialities or causal connections. In brief, valuings are turned into the experience of the valuable by the organizing activity of mind in the ongoing course of experience as experimental. Claims concerning the valuable emerge from the context of conflicting valuings and are dependent for their validity upon their ability to produce harmonious valuing experiences. In Dewey's words:

To say that something satisfies is to report something as an isolated finality. To assert that it is satisfactory is to define it in its connections and interactions. The fact that it pleases or is immediately congenial poses a problem to judgment. How shall the satisfaction be rated? Is it a value or is it not? Is it something to be prized and cherished, to be enjoyed? The latter "involves a prediction; it contemplates a future in which the thing will continue to serve; it *will* do. (LW 4:208)

Dewey distinguishes between ends as termini, casual valuings which are not the result of experimental inquiiry (LW 1:86), and ends which are "fulfillments, conclusions, completions, or perfections" (LW 4:212), ends which are the result of intelligent inquiry and hence are "intrinsic qualities of events in their consummatory reference" (LW 1:9). However, for Dewey, there are no absolute endings, but rather, any ending is at once a new beginning, and the valuings which set a problematic context may themselves be either casual valuings or previous consummatory valuings. Valuings of any kind, as they conflict and hence initiate inquiry, are problematic valuings which must be evaluated. The resolution of any problematic context, however, can be understood only in terms of consummatory valuings as fulfillments of reflectively organized anticipations, fulfillments that result from the intervention of "operative art," from the organizing activity of experimental method. Such artful functioning of experience allows for the emergence of the valuable as the potentiality for objectivities of some sort to yield other valuing experiences.

Here it becomes important not to fall, within the understanding of value, into what would parallel the remnants of a spectator theory of knowledge. Even at the most rudimentary level of human experience, the purposive, anticipatory character of human activity which constitutes its very structure demands fulfillment of expectation. The temporal stretch of human behavior carries the felt continuity of creative anticipation and fulfillment into the very texture of valuing experience even at its most rudimentary level. Thus the structure of human behavior, in being anticipatory, is at once inherently consummatory. Further, even the most rudimentary valuings result from anticipatory activity directed in light of past consummatory experiences, and thus this activity incorporates incipient evaluations at least implicitly operative in even the most primitive "choices." Finally, even at this level valuings have been partially molded by the organism's interaction with other organisms. The valuings of an isolated individual are artificial abstractions. The presence of the other active organism, like the environment in general, shapes the direction of anticipatory activity toward the consummations which yield valuing experiencings. Even at the most rudimentary level, the temporal stretch of anticipatory fulfillment is intertwined with the anticipatory consummations of the other with resulting adjustments of each. Thus all valuings, including both the most rudimentary and the most casual, have a dimension of consummatory valuing, are tinged with the effects of objects taken as valuable, and incorporate a social aspect.

As potentialities for the production of valuings become incorporated into the structure of developed objective value meanings, and as valuings are experienced within the context of these meanings, and promoted because of these meanings, there develops the "full-blown" experience of the valuable. These moral meanings and accompanying beliefs become embodied in the institutions and practices of a community and thus the, valuings which reflect these meanings and beliefs reflect as well the norms and standards of the community. In brief, the value quality of immediate experience is structured in large part by the context of moral beliefs within which it emerges. As Dewey notes, "Even in the midst of direct enjoyment, there is a sense of validity, of authorization, which intensifies the enjoyment" (LW 4:213). The extent of one's awareness of this functional relation between valuings and evaluations or, in other terms, the extent of one's awareness of the moral meanings that enrich experience, determines the extent of the consummatory versus casual valuings within experience. The difference between a more casual valuing and a consummatory valuing lies in the difference in the utilization of objective value meanings within which value experiences emerge, in the difference in the richness of, and the conscious awareness of, the meanings within which they function. Thus, moral awareness enhances value experience, for the level or intensity of the richness of consummatory valuing is a function of the meanings which infuse it. New ideals, new assertions of the valuable, are new moral meanings which emerge in the organization of conflicting valuings. Moral action is planned rational action rooted in the awareness of meanings.

Part of the development of the harmonious life is to make valuings as reflective of valuations as possible. Such cultivation can proceed only when one is aware of the relation between the valuing experiences and the network of processes which can culminate in their occurrence. Thus taste, as Dewey notes, far from being that about which one cannot argue, is one of the most imoortant things to argue about (LW 4:213). The cultivation of taste is the cultivation of the correct infusion of valuings with evaluations, with a sense of the valuable. Only when immediate valuings are valuings which reason sees are or can be organized into the objectivity valuable can there be a life of harmony and a truly integrated self. If one can get valuing experiences only from what reflective inquiry shows not to be valuable, then one is living a life of internal conflict in which the experience of value and the claims of reason are at odds with each other.

Reason thus performs its proper moral function by enriching the immediacy of value experience in a way which reflects awareness of moral meaning and validity of application in concrete situations.

When habitual modes of organizing behavior do not work in resolving problematic situations involving conflicting valuings, new moral objectivities emerge which in turn give a different funded quality to the immediacy of valuings. The functional relation between valuing experiences and objective value claims must work as an organic unity in the ongoing course of experience in increasing the value ladenness of experience. Such a workable relationship, to remain workable, requires not stagnation but constant openness to change through intelligent reconstruction incorporating the dynamics of experimental inquiry. The source of the vitality for such ongoing evaluation and reconstruction is to be found in the creative drive of the individual in its entirety, which can perhaps best be captured by employing and further developing Dewey's concept of "impulsion." While an impulse is specialized and particular, impulsion "designates a movement outward and forward of the whole organism to which special impulses are auxiliary" (LW 10:64). In its concreteness impulsion is inexhaustible by any number of actualization of tendencies which, beginning as the diversity of impulses, settle into habits of response as some emerging tendencies fit adequately with the possibilities presented by the surrounding environment, while others do not. Impulsion is that wellspring of human creative activity which prevents the repetition of habitual modes of behavior and the formalized institutions they involve from settling into sterile rigidity. It keeps the moral situation, when rationally directed, flexible, vital and changing, for its creativity and ongoing development cannot be understood as a collection of impulses and habits but as the inexhaustible concrete foundation for their emergence. Indeed, similar habits stem from unique impulsions, and thus are embedded in a unique concrete center of creativity which enters into the course of novel direction takings. Impulsion provides both uniqueness and unity to one's way of approaching experience; it makes this particular organic center of creativity unique and uniquely unified, and overflows any attempt to render it precise through reflection or to exhaust it through specific activity.

One's sense of impulsion is a sense of the ontological density and vitality of self-creativity which, as seen above, incorporates an essential social dimension; a sense of the body-self, the decentered subject, in its vital concrete functioning. This elusive awareness provides a vague "moral sense" of fittingness which, far from being the result of learned principles, of socially accepted norms, is the source of, or foundation for, their acceptance or eventual overthrow. Because emerging, changing energies of impulsion immersed in emerging, changing situations cannot be captured in the confines of institutionalized or habitual ways of acting, the moral order must be in a continual process of development, and thus, in Dewey's words, "Man is under just as much obligation to develop his most advanced standards and ideals as to use conscientiously those which he already possesses" (MW 12:180). And, as new standards and ideals emerge through the play of imagination,[10] the rational order which underlies a moral community and which provides the process of adjustment is recreated as well. Though the slow evolution of such a recreation may at times be difficult to discern, it may at times seem to manifest itself with startling energy and immediacy.

In the workable moral situation, habitual tendencies prevail, and the sense of impulsion may slip into the background. The moral situation becomes unreflective, stagnant, and unperceptive. In this situation, rules and practices which stifle the growth of the human may develop yet be ignored. However, the demands of impulsion will eventually assert themselves and moral crises will arise. In the breakdown of the workable value situation, in the reconstruction and reintegration of values, the sense of impulsion comes to the fore. Thus there is the opportunity for a new integration which more adequately fulfills its demands, for though habitual behaviors and beliefs are thrown into question, indeed, precisely *because* they are thrown into question, the sense of impulsion is heightened. The acceptance of learned habits and the formalized rigidities to which they lead, the focus on unchanging moral objectivities, prevents the reconstruction and reintegration of values, and at the same time prevents the heightened experience of impulsion as that which demands fulfillment and which provides the elusive sense of moral "fittingness" to the particularities of the habits to which it gives rise.

It can be seen, then, that though the social context itself affects the vital drives, the energies operative within a situation, and though neither the emergence of moral norms and practices nor the emergence of the most "casual" valuings occur apart from the social interaction of concrete organisms, yet the creative impulsion of the individual in its uniqueness brings unique tendencies and potentialities into the shaping processes of social change, brings creative perspectives to the resolution of the conflicting and changing value claims, and restructures the very moral behavior or moral practices and the institutionalized ways of behaving that helped shape its own developing potentialities. Thus Dewey claims that though moral deliberation involves "social intelligence," the reaction of the individual against an existing scheme becomes the means of the transformation and restructuring of habits and institutional practices (MW 5:173).

The ongoing reconstructive process, properly directed, should lead to a moral situation not of mere change, but rather of real growth. Because of the concrete richness of impulsion, integration and harmonizing cannot be achieved by the stifling of emerging energies which overflow the rigidity of habits and institutions, but rather by their incorporation into new workable patterns of behavior. As Dewey so eloquently proclaims, more "passions, not fewer, is the answer.... Rationality, once more, is not a force to evoke against impulse and habit. It is the attainment of a working harmony among diverse desires" (MW 14:136). Moral crisis provides the opportunity for a surge of revitalized growth; the creative, self-directed organism must take advantage of such an opportunity through sensitivity in the awareness of the demands of impulsion and intelligent reorganization of moral objectivities. As Dewey emphasizes,

> Life itself consists of phases in which the organism falls out of step with the march of surrounding things and then recovers unison with it.... And, in a growing life, the recovery is never mere return to a prior state, for it is enriched by the state of disparity and resistance through which it has successfully passed... Life grows when a temporary falling out is a transition to a more extensive balance of the energies of the organism with those of the conditions under which it lives (LW 10:19–20).

Dewey, then, can hold that growth involves the rational resolution of conflict, conflict between duty and desire, between what is already accomplished and what is possible (MW 5:327); that growth itself is the only moral "end"; and that the moral meaning of democracy lies in its contribution to the growth of every member of society (MW 12:181, 186); indeed, that this moral import of democracy is the ideal of community life itself.[11] Rationally directed change leads to growth both for the individual and the community, and authentic growth of self as well as of the institutions and practices of the community is inherently moral.

Though Dewey refers to growth as an "end," he does not intend this in a technical sense of "end," and indeed, growth can best be understood not as an end to be attained but as a dynamic embedded in the ongoing process of life, just as experimental method is not an end to be achieved but a dynamic embedded in the very structure of human activity. Experimental method, as applied in the moral context, is in fact the attempt to increase the value ladenness of a situation through a creative growth of perspective which can incorporate and harmonize conflicting or potentially conflicting values. It should be stressed here that the expansion of a moral perspective, though not independent of intelligent inquiry, is not merely a change in an intellectual perspective but rather is a change which affects and is affected by the impulsion of the organism in its total concreteness. It is this pathway which is ultimately at stake in the choice of values. The full significance of the consequences of choice among values can be found in Dewey's claim that:

> The resulting choice also shapes the self, making it, in some degree, a new self. . . . In committing oneself to a particular course, a person gives a lasting set to his own being. Consequently, it is proper to say that in choosing this object rather than that, one is in reality choosing what kind of person or self one is going to be. Superficially, the deliberation which terminates in choice is concerned with weighing the values of particular ends. Below the surface, it is a process of discovering what sort of being a person most wants to become. (LW 7:287)

Or, as he summarizes,

> In short, the thing actually at stake in any serious deliberation is not a difference of quantity, but what kind of person one is to become, what sort of self is in the making, what kind of a world is making. (MW 14:150)

Growth of moral perspective is growth of the self as an organic whole, and such growth is rooted in the sense of impulsion at the core of human existence, guided by the use of reflective intelligence in organizing its demands through imaginatively projected unifying and universalizing ideals. The deepening involved in the expansion of horizons incorporates the deepening of imagination as well. The universalizing and unifying ideals which hold sway over us involve the play of imagination, but imagination, as well as the ideals it presents, emerges from the ground up. It was seen that the demand of adjusting the old and the new is inherent in the very texture of life. This adjustment as conscious involves, or, as Dewey states, this adjustment as conscious *is*, imagination (LW 10:276).[12] The deepening of imagination involved in the expansion of ideals can be seen in Dewey's understanding of the encompassing imaginative ideal incorporated within religious experience. Such an imaginative ideal, which allows one to "rise above" the divisiveness of a relativism founded in supposed perspectival closure, as well as the conformism of an absolutism founded in supposed perspectival absence,[13] comes in fact by a "delving beneath" to the imaginative sense of the possibilities of a deep-seated harmonizing of the self not just with humanity as a whole but with the totality of the universe within which the human condition emerges (LW 9:14). Such an ideal, it would seem, is the limiting ideal of fully attained growth. It can be seen then that the vital, growing sense of moral rightness, which comes not from the indoctrination of abstract principles but from attunement to the way in which moral beliefs and practices must be rooted naturally in the very conditions of human existence, ultimately requires a deepening attunement of individuals in their entirety.

A true community, as by its very nature incorporating an ontologically grounded temporalism and perspectival pluralism requiring ongoing growth or horizonal expansion, is far from immune to the hazardous pitfalls and wrenching clashes that provide the material out of which ever deepening and expanding horizons are constituted. When there is lacking the reorganizing and ordering capabilities of intelligence, the imaginative grasp of authentic possibilities, the vitality of motivation, or sensitivity to the "felt" dimensions of existence, all of which are needed for ongoing reconstructive horizonal expansion, then irreconcilable factionalism results. A community, then, to maintain itself *as* a community, requires the education of the whole person. This in turn indicates, in Deweyean fashion, that education is not fundamentally the transmission of information but rather the development of creative, attuned intelligence.

The development of creative intelligence requires nourishment of the skills of experimental inquiry, needed not just for the adequate exploration of specific subject matter but for the possibility of the interrelated ongoing reconstruction and expansion of the self, values, and the institutions and practices of the community, including the very organs of adjudication for the communicative adjustments which make possible such ongoing reconstructions and expansions. The proper method of education is in fact, for Dewey, the road to freedom, for we are free when our activity is guided by the outcome of intelligent reflection, when we do not let ourselves be passively pushed this way and that by external factors bombarding us, but can take what comes to us, reconstruct it through intelligent inquiry, and direct our activity in terms of the unique synthesis of the data brought about by our unique creativity. To the extent that we do not passively respond but intelligently participate, independently think, we are free, for we, not external factors, determine the nature of our responses. As morally responsible beings we are free, but moral responsibility does not involve the learning of rules and regulations, the following of rigid principles handed down. Rather, it involves the ability to recognize moral problems and to reconstruct the moral situation according to experimental method in order to bring about a reintegration of value experiences. Thus, in learning to think, we are learning at the same time to be free moral beings. To be free moral beings in an authentic sense, however, we must also cultivate a deepening attunement to the "felt" dimensions of experience: to the consummating phases of integral experiences; to diverse ways of making sense of the world and the diverse valuings this involves; and to the general pulse of human existence in which the diversity of valuings is ultimately rooted, and toward the expansion and development of which valuings and claims of the valuable should be shaped. And, none of this is possible without a historical awareness which itself is not a passive recovery but a creative reconstruction manifested in a present oriented toward a future. The function of the play of imagination is "the extension and thickening of experience" (LW 11:210), but this play can extend and reintegrate experience in productive ways only if it is not capricious but rather seizes upon real possibilities which a dynamic past has embedded in the changing present.

The above understanding of the role of education in the reconstruction of values necessary for the ongoing development of a true community has several suggestive concrete implications for the problems facing American education today. America seems to be moving from the ideal of the grand melting pot to the ideal of the grand accumulator of aggregates. Within the multiculturalism of today, many want not to assimilate but to isolate in terms of their heritage and customs. Yet, the debates and arguments over these two alternatives are wrongheaded in both directions, for both extremes are destructive of the dynamics of true community The multiculturalism of today offers the opportunity for the enrichment of all, but only if the collection of aggregates is woven into the dynamic interplay of a pluralistic community. The uniqueness of diverse cultures, as representative of the individual perspective, must maintain its uniqueness not through separation from, but through a dynamic interplay with, the common perspective, bringing about a resultant enrichment of each through the dynamics of accommodation constitutive of community. For this to occur, however, students from diverse cultures cannot sit in different classrooms, nor is a solution to be found by merely locating them within the same classroom, or by lectures to all on the importance of tolerance. The answer to the divisive selfishness and factionalism of American life today is not sacrificial external tolerance. Rather, the educational process must provide the vehicle by which the sympathetic understanding of diverse cultures through the incorporation of diverse perspectives leads to the internalized tolerance of enlarged selves.

An important vehicle for achieving the above-mentioned goals is the focus on the educational process as nourishing the skills of creative intelligence or experimental inquiry, attunement to the sense of values, and the expansion of the imagination. These cannot be adequately developed through different courses focusing on each, for one does not educate the whole person through an accumulation of aggregates. Rather all have to be brought to bear on, and in turn nourished by, diverse subject matter. Educating the entire person through the development of these skills in one sense fosters the dimension of commonalty, for regardless of the particular types of content that particular cultures may prefer to focus upon, the development of the skills of experimental inquiry transcends any particular content. Yet, in another sense it fosters the expression of, and sympathetic understanding of, diverse cultures. For, the play of imagination and sense of valuing operative in the diverse demarcations of the significance of the problems and issues of the content to be dealt with, as well as in the evaluation of the consequences of the proposed solutions, can lead to a sympathetic understanding of diverse perspectives and sensitivities within the common endeavor of problem solving.

This is perhaps most clearly brought to light in a discipline that is too often reduced to a series of facts—history. Diverse perspectives within the present are situated within the pasts from which they have emerged, and the common endeavor of identifying problems, issues, and possible alternative solutions within historical situations can bring forth culturally diverse, historically rooted sensitivities to these problems and issues and possible solutions. This can bring about at once the enrichment and enlargement of the selves involved in this common endeavor and a heightened attunement to the human condition and the felt value dimensions of existence.

When the educational process allows individuals to remain oblivious to the value dimension pervasive of concrete human existence, then artificial values will be substituted. The consumerism of today is partially the product of a desperate substitute for the experience of felt value. When the educational process fragments the individual, then the holistic skills needed for the reconstruction and expansion of values necessary for community growth cannot occur, and the result is the factionalism, intolerance, or at best external toleration which abounds today. If the educational process fails to utilize the enriching potentialities of multi-culturalism, then the destructive alternatives of assimilation or isolation will reign supreme.

The education of the whole person provides education for life in a true community, for it provides the tools for ongoing adjustment or accommodation between the new and the old, the precarious and the stable, the novel and the continuous, creativity and conformity, self and other. Further, it nourishes the common "end" which must characterize a community, even a highly pluralistic one, for it helps bring to fruition the universalizing ideal of ongoing self-directed growth. Such growth, as has been seen from the entire discussion, is made possible by the dynamic ongoing interaction of the interdependent features of novelty and conformity, features which manifest themselves as two poles within the self, two poles within the community, and two poles within the experience of value. The proper functioning of these two inseparable, dynamically interrelated poles results in the authentic reconstruction of values by free individuals within a free community. Such reconstruction involves the dynamics of experimental method embedded in the very life process, and the proper functioning of experimental method requires the proper nourishment of the whole person, for the proper functioning of experimental method is precisely the artful functioning of human experience in its entirety.

Notes

1. This switch from the term 'existence' to the term 'experience' is not an inadvertent slip but rather a deliberate attempt to emphasize the denial of any ontological gap between existence and experience.

2. Since all situations have an element of indeterminateness, all situations are potentially problematic until organized by experimental activity.

3. I develop this brief statement of the features of scientific method as well as the following claim of its pervasiveness within experience in *Speculative Pragmatism* (Amherst: The University of Massachusetts Press, 1986; Peru, Ill.: Open Court, 1990).

4. Dewey holds, for example in *The Quest for Certainty*, not only that experimental method is embodied in even the simplest perception of a common sense object (LW. 4:189–90), but also holds, for example in "Does Reality Possess Practical Character?" that even the most rudimentary awareness invoves such dynamics (MW 4:137–38).

5. This view is found in its most developed form in pragmatic literature in the writings of George Herbert Mead, and involves his well-known concept of "the generalized other."

6. A person may be a member of more than one community, for there are diverse levels and types of communities. Any community consists of many subgroups. Individuals may feel alienated from a particular group, but can't really be alienated from society in general because this very alienation will only throw them into some other society. Dewey makes this point in *The Public and Its Problems* (LW 2:353–54).

7. This transformation involves not only "intercommunication" but also shared values, as discussed later.

8. Immediate experience is not, of course, the experience of pure immediacy—which in fact does not exist in experience.

9. Thus Dewey notes that "scientific and artistic systems embody the same fundamental principles of the relationship of life to its surroundings," and indeed the differences between the work of the scientist and the work of the artist are "technical and specialized, rather than deep-seated" (LW 2:106–7).

10. Within pragmatic philosophy, there is no longer a Kantian type distinction between productive imagination and understanding as the

faculty of judgment. Rather, both understanding and imagination are unified and transformed into the creative functioning of habit. Thus Dewey makes a distinction between two kinds of habit—the creatively intelligent and the merely routine (MW 14:51).

11.   Dewey makes a distinction between democracy as a social idea and democracy as a system of government, but notes that the two of course are connected (LW 2:325).

12.   See note 10 for the interrelation of imagination, habit, and creative intelligence.

13.   In so doing, one avoids the respective extremes of irresponsible tolerance and dogmatic imposition.

5

Dewey and Contemporary Moral Philosophy

JAMES GOUINLOCK

In the last two decades—dating from Rawls' *A Theory of Justice*[1] and, later, from Gewirth's *Reason and Morality*[2]—philosophers have delivered themselves of some impressive looking normative moral theories. They ascended all the way from the deserts of relativism and metaethics to the empyrean of rationally conclusive systems. A number of major thinkers have contributed to this movement, among them Dworkin, Ackerman, Hare, MacIntyre, Nozick, Nielsen, and Gauthier.[3] Many other philosophers, as we know, have not been persuaded by any of them; and, believing that the alternative to such high ambitions is resignation to historicism or some other form of relativism, they have given up on the entire enterprise of normative ethics. Hence the current scene is roughly divided between those who would dwell in the heavens and those who still see no escape from the ever-shifting sands.

The dispassionate observer could not fail to note in all this that the skeptic seems to have a point: the substance of the "rational" systems varies quite dramatically from one author to the next. Hardly a comforting observation for one who hopes for some sort of rationally determined intersubjective agreement! While viewing this scene, one cannot help wondering whether there really are any characteristics of the subject matter that would constrain our ethical convictions in a manner to bring them into some common accord.

This is no small matter, and the doubter might be right in the end. Nevertheless, I am convinced, if any headway is to be made on the question, it will require the adoption of a mode of philosophizing very much after the manner of Dewey. There are two crucial questions in this context that must be faced squarely: What *is* the fundamental subject matter, and what is the philosopher's relationship to it? For Dewey, the subject matter of moral philosophy is the moral life itself—real moral experience—with its characteristic vicissitudes, perplexities, instrumentalities, and promises of fulfillment. His aim was to understand and clarify these conditions in such a manner that ordinary persons could appropriate them effectively. Being real, not fictional, people, already caught up in the moral life, they are not going to create or accept a morality out of whole cloth. They are deeply vested with specific loyalties, convictions, and purposes. The aim of Dewey's philosophy is not to obviate vital concerns with abstract theory, but to provide the means to contend effectively with just those characteristic human perplexities and aspirations—to develop powers of criticism and conduct appropriate to their real condition.

In the final analysis, our constraints and inspirations must come from moral experience itself. Our lessons are *there*—hidden, confused, unsytematic, conflicting, as they may be. Honest and intelligent reflection on this experience might make the lessons clearer, more orderly, and compelling; and realistic possibilities for human welfare might be discerned. It is our apprehension of these lessons that will prompt us, if anything can, in the direction of moral consensus. The phenomena of the primary subject matter itself are moving, as they portend good or ill. Argument, inquiry, reasoning, and discourse have efficacy in drawing our attention to such lessons. This is not a weakness of human nature, to be remedied by education; it is a simple fact about human motivation. *Whatever constraints and inspirations there are for thought and action, they lie ultimately in this primary subject matter in its own right.* If a more agreeable order can be introduced into human affairs, it can come, finally, only from the lessons of *experience*. The philosopher might be especially gifted at discerning and refining those lessons, and he might have proposals for reordering the structures of experience that would draw our attention to possibilities that move us to novel efforts. "One ought to keep his promises" might not be a cognitive truth, much less a moral absolute, but the conditions and efficacies of associated life themselves are such to assure that promises will be made and kept. Likewise, the prohibition of murder is sure to be very strongly supported, the cultivation of virtue widely taught and esteemed. Such are among the simplest lessons of life itself. Dewey believed that there are powerful constraints and inspirations in the moral life, sufficient to move us into some good measure of concord.

Philosophers become haughtily aloof from these essential concerns. The problem with most current thinkers, as with many in the past, is that they have become almost wholly alienated from any useful subject matter. The typical contemporary moral philosopher, whether from the heavens or deserts, is preoccupied with issues that are of little relevance to the acute human concerns that bring forth earnest moral reflection and give it point.[4] His or her inquiries are not of a nature to espy whatever life conditions there might be that could prompt responsive and perhaps unifying movement in the moral life itself. Recent moral philosophers have been obsessed with such approaches as the analysis of ordinary language, the systematic ordering of moral "intuitions," the definition of the precise nature of rational agency, or the determination of ideal conditions of choice. These are the sorts of things a philosopher thinks about these days—and also, of course, about the swarm of writings on the same topics produced by his or her peers. Hence they do a lot of talking to each other, even if no one else cares to listen in.

I will elaborate some of these differences and suggest what difference they make. Although the topic requires fuller treatment than I can give it on this occasion, I must be content with leaving a number of analyses rather undeveloped, but the momentous differences between Dewey's enterprise and those in favor today will be evident.

The Subject Matter of Moral Theory

"There is a special service which the study of philosophy may render, Dewey writes in *Experience and Nature*. "Empirically pursued it will not be a study of philosophy but a study, by means of philosophy, of life experience" (LW 1:40). (Don't pass over this oft-quoted remark lightly. *Experience* is the subject matter.) The book was written with explicitly moral intent. In its culminating chapter he wrote,

> The more sure one is that the world which encompasses human life is of such and such a character, . . . the more one is committed to try to direct the conduct of life, that of others as well as himself, *upon the basis of the character assigned to the world*. And if he finds that he cannot succeed, that the attempt lands him in confusion, inconsistency and darkness, plunging others into discord and shutting them out from participation, rudimentary precepts instruct him to surrender his assurance as a delusion; and to revise his notions of the nature of nature till he makes them more adequate to the concrete facts in which nature is embodied. (LW 1:309, emphasis added)

Given the typical paradigms of moral reasoning, these lines are certain to be misunderstood. *Dewey has no intention of deducing normative propositions from descriptive.*[5] His intention is disarmingly simple: to characterize our existential condition in a manner that will display those characteristics that are salient for life activity. Every chapter of *Experience and Nature* that introduces one of these characteristics begins with references to conspicuous and undeniable features of common life. Whatever else it is, Dewey's "metaphysics" is not a foray into the recondite, wholly abstract speculations of the tradition. Notoriously, traditional metaphysics (such as absolute idealism or reductive materialism) had obscured the pressing realities of our situation—the realities we must contend with and take account of in thought and action. It is crucial for us to know, for example, that nature has orders of various kinds, orders subject to some modification by human intervention. Under certain conditions, nature also produces qualitative immediacies. It is manifestly precarious as well: we are interminably beset with all manner of contingencies in life experience. These problematic events are not sequestered within putatively subjective mind. Earthquakes, floods, epidemics, wars, spoiled milk, and losing the house keys really happen. They are eventuations of natural processes, and as such they are subject to being known and perhaps controlled. Nature has histories, too: processes of qualitative change hurrying to fateful but uncertain outcomes. Enmeshed in histories, for the very life of us we need methods of inquiry and conduct that might permit us to predict and control these outcomes. Novel relations and ends might be instituted. Goods might be *constructed*.

Dewey's metaphysics is the attempt to discern and characterize these generic conditions.[6] He stressed that they do not constitute a monistic order: alternative histories will be incompatible with one another and their ends will clash. Our power to construct goods does not exclude uncertainty, error, conflict, tragedy, and defeat. Vested with intelligence, however, it can yield unifications and satisfactions otherwise unattainable. The "chief import" of his metaphysics, Dewey says, "is to afford understanding of the necessity and nature of the office of intelligence" (LW 1:315). And this is of the utmost consequence. Success in life— including the moral life—depends upon our well-considered appropriation of the realities and potentialities of actual existences, including human relationships. Early on in his career, Dewey wrote, "Moral value [is] not equivalent to preaching or *moralizing*. Truth has its own moral value, all the greater because not deflected to serve some immediate end of exhortation." He adds that "salvation" is "the freeing of life reached through knowledge of its real nature and relations" (EW 4:226).

In *Experience and Nature* he sometimes calls intelligence *criticism*. Any reader familiar with Dewey's writings hears much about the functions of intelligence, or criticism. Generically, they include the determination of the various powers and constraints of our condition that we may be effective in converting the blind forces of physical events into human consummations; and it functions best, Dewey believed, as a deliberately cooperative process. The pragmatists were the first philosophers to develop this notion of intelligence—an epochal achievement. It must be sharply contrasted, Dewey urged, with the classical conception of intelligence ("reason"), in accordance with which one identifies a present event as conforming to the fixities of antecedent form or law. This is a classificatory and deductive procedure, not creative and experimental; and it is inept in contending with the world as it really is.

Dewey's own "criticism" drew him into many fields: a theory of value and art, theory of inquiry, philosophical anthropology, sociology, and the discernment of the principal moral relations and goods available to us. In specific reference to ethical problems, he begins his "Theory of the Moral Life" in Part II of *Ethics* by saying, "Realization that the need for reflective morality and for moral theories grows out of conflict between ends, responsibilities, rights and duties defines the service which moral theory may render, and also protects the student from false conceptions of its nature" (LW 7:165). Note that Dewey explicitly binds moral theory organically to actual practice; and he does not attempt to reduce ethical concerns to the teleological (nor to any single and changeless criterion). There is a plurality of moral relations: for example, "ends, responsibilities, rights, and duties," all of which are conspicuous in the moral life. The point of philosophizing is not to banish such concerns into nonbeing, but to investigate how they can be intelligently criticized and utilized.

For many, it has been easy to conclude that there are insufficient constraints of any kind to bring us to confidently shared conclusions about moral conduct. Others, in contrast, have been certain that they possess rationally incontestable principles. Dewey's studies of the primary subject matter led him to the position that neither stance is warranted. If seriously embraced, relativisms preclude social life itself; and no tolerably sane person finds that acceptable. Associated life must be *somehow* sustained. This is a prime example of finding constraints and opportunities in experience itself. Professors and students can engage at will in theoretical discourse defending relativism, but life itself prevents them from *living* it. The typical philosophic prescription for sustaining social order, however, is to deliver up putatively unassailable principles. For many reasons, Dewey rejected that possibility too. There are and can be no such principles; and the demand for their observance in real life is a form of tyranny. And, in the name of absolutes, tyrannies there have been.

Dewey's analysis of the moral condition yields another option: the most serviceable moral method would be social intelligence, as he called it, or democracy as a way of life. It is a deliberately consultative and experimental procedure, and it requires the cultivation of pertinent virtues, for which Dewey looked to education. These include open-mindedness; sensitivity; cooperativeness; even-handedness; willingness to inquire, learn, adapt, and grow; and readiness to submit to well-authenticated evidence about the realities at issue. Even with some measure of these traits, social intelligence will lead neither to perfect unanimity nor to infallible principles; but, Dewey believed, it has better prospects for creating concert in human affairs than any other method hitherto conceived, and it is more apt to satisfy and enrich the plurality of values in the moral life.

His allegiance to social intelligence was predicated on a number of assumptions. We live in a world of change, and there are always possibilities for contriving ways of bettering the human lot. No institutions or policies should be regarded as beyond modification. Every situation presents more or less novel contingencies and opportunities; and we should be prepared to address them creatively. We also have an irreducible plurality of values: goods, obligations, entitlements; and they cannot be reduced to an all-sufficing or uncontroversial norm, nor to a single form in each category. We must, accordingly, be willing to be accommodating in some measure. There is, moreover, no reason to suppose that any one individual by himself can decide questions for other mature individuals or can reach verdicts for interpersonal enterprises by consulting himself alone. Consultation, communication, is essential. Just as the isolated individual is impotent in scientific inquiry, he is likewise impotent in moral affairs. One would be moved to adopt social intelligence not by virtue of an anteceent definition of moral rationality, but in response to the conditions and possibilities disclosed in honest and penetrating study of moral realities.

Although this is a most novel approach in ethical theory, it is entirely familiar in everyday life. No association of free persons can function without these accustomed procedures. Even the closest of friends have significant and enduring disagreements, and the persistence of their friendship requires them to be tolerant and flexible; and so must it be for any community. But such is not good enough for the typical philosopher, who turns his back on the facts of life in order to produce an omnicompetent principle, or to wash his hands entirely of ethical theory. See how long your community will endure when each of its members holds intransigently to his or her preferred absolutes!

Dewey believed the possession of the habits appropriate to social intelligence is within the reach of any normal person; and he believed their exercise would bring a greater good to human beings than any other mode of social life. Accordingly, democracy as a way of life is both practicable and inherently precious. It is eminently suitable to the moral condition. In this he is perhaps unwarrantedly optimistic. It may be that we aren't supremely well suited to any form of moral life. This is not a fault of philosophy, but a condition that philosophers must wrestle with. All the same, in many contexts its efficacies are well displayed; the promise of social intelligence might have more realistic claim on our allegiance than any other of which we know. In any case, what we can do and cannot do are limiting conditions for any philosophy, and no moral philosophy can be other than an idle posture if it does not engage in the sorts of inquiry that Dewey pursued to such effect.

Today we contend with innumerable moral controversies. Putative rights and duties of every description vie with one another for recognition. Treating them as absolutes is hopeless; and letting them contend just as they sprout is ineffectual. Consider the intensely important concerns regarding current changes in family structure: the contested rights and obligations of mothers and fathers, of children, and of the state. To address these issues in a Deweyan manner there is much that we must try to find out: the determination of workable and even happy relationships for the several members of a family; the good offices of perhaps novel roles, as well as the emotional (and other) costs to men, to women, and to children in assuming them; the conditions under which children are apt to learn and flourish; the institutions that might or might not be competent to perform such functions. The possession of trustworthy answers to these questions will certainly be of crucial importance to those who are striving to contend with the realities themselves; they have no wish to engage in ill-fated behavior. They must communicate with each other to contrive plans of action that are truly responsive to the peculiarities of their shared circumstance and to formulate advocacies for public policy.

These are topics about which there are many more opinions than responsibly ascertained conclusions, and the opinions take the guise of heatedly proclaimed rights and duties. Inquiries of a Deweyan sort do not guarantee peace, love, and harmony; but they will surely go further to answer to the perplexities of the moral life than do the mere artifices of current philosophy.

The Poverty of Contemporary Theory

Dewey's thinking contrasts with the sterility of characteristic current endeavors, which adopt and confine themselves to artificial subject matter. Hence they can be neither convincing nor efficacious. I will review some representative specimens. In this survey, Rawls and Habermas will receive more extended (but still all-too-brief) attention. Rawls' work is regarded in many quarters as masterful, and Habermas at least appears to bear close resemblance to Dewey.

The project of determining the nature of a truly rational moral agent has been thought promising. What would be his generic aims and principles? With the suitable definition of rationality, that question is answered, and we possess the holy grail: clearly established norms for everyone! The project is plagued first of all by the fact that its various champions have displayed a remarkable propensity to define rationality in a manner to endorse their antecedently held convictions. Gauthier's rational agent prescribes a form of libertarianism: while Nielsen's (who employs the Rawlsian strategy of wide relflective equilibrium) becomes a socialist. Gewirth also pursues a strategy of "ideal" rationality and comes out with routine welfare state liberalism. One becomes suspicious that "moral rationality" is an inherently controversial notion and not the sort of pristine idea that bears us inexorably to definite conclusions.

But secondly, and of even more importance, such paradigms of rationality exist only in heaven. Actual persons are not rational beings in that way. We are creatures of nature and history, and our intelligence functions in a context that already nourishes and protects particular and variable moral loyalties. We run the gamut from extreme individualism to communism, or perhaps to tribalism. From person to person, as the case may be, we are devoted to such a medley of causes as reproductive rights, right to life, property rights, complete egalitarianism, animal rights, childrens' rights, environmental rights, affirmative action, pacifism, militarism, and so on almost interminably. And we know that such devotions are not easily revised, much less abandoned. The imposition of an abstract theory of moral rationality on such variety would be the acme of impertinence, and it would create endless social convulsion. It could be accomplished only by oppressive methods (some forms of which have come to be known as reeducation camps). Rest assured that devotees of alternative schools would fight to establish camps of their own. Absolutism, however "rational," is a sure invitation to strife and oppression.

R. M. Hare's moral thinking issues in a different kind of theory. It does not prescribe specific institutions and practices, but it requires them all, whatever they may be, to conform to the dictates of general utility. Utilitarianism is an initially attractive theory, for it aims to maximize pleasure, and we are all interested in that. But it makes utility the *only* criterion, while we find again and again in moral experience the persistence of moral values that are not reducible to utility. Many of us have obligations, for example, that we would not compromise for the sake of an increase in marginal utility. A sacred promise would not be foresworn for the sake of providing incremental pleasure to anonymous persons to whom we have no established obligtions, or no relationship whatever. Or one's duties to his family could take precedence over the opportunity to give added pleasure to persons who weren't even needy.

But Hare's reduction is even more radical than this. He founds utilitarianism on the way we use "ought." Truth to tell, he declares, our use of "ought" commits us to being perfectly impartial regarding anyone's preferences, when they are both prudent and weighted according to their intensity. Now, can anyone really believe we make such a commitment when we say "ought?" Perhaps some people do (but I doubt it). But even if this is what "ought" happens to mean today in the English language, why should that fact be morally compelling? Why is the local idiom the ultimate court of moral appeal? Some linguistic usages embody noble and generous sentiments; others embody greed, bigotry, and hatred. Many regimes attempt to install one form or another of newspeak, and such forms might become part of ordinary language. Just consider it! The trials, hopes, loves, and aspirations of the moral life resolved by consulting the dictionary! Rarely has the moral condition been left so high and dry. But we may be assured that with such an impoverished subject matter, this approach to moral reflection will not be found widely compelling by the real partcipants in the moral life.

Nozick's *Anarchy, State and Utopia* employs what he calls "state of nature theory." He postulates certain absolute rights in this mythical state, deriving from them exact limits to the province of government. The problem here is not just with the a priori postulate, as such. The deeper problem is that he proceeds explicitly on the premise that his derivation requires no attention to the actual beliefs, hopes, fears, and loyalties that have moved real people to reflect on their condition and to strive to better it through political action. The urgent, diverse, and changing historical contingencies that have called forth various demands for state action merit no attention; nor does the historical record itself, wherein we witness the real effects of different kinds of institutions for the weal and woe of actual populations. No, "A theory of a state of nature that begins with fundamental general descriptions of morally permissible and impermissible actions, . . . and goes on to describe how a state would arise from that state of nature will serve our explanatory purposes, *even if no actual state ever arose that way.*"[9]

Many of a libertarian persuasion, however, have seemed to find Nozick's arguments persuasive. But, in fact, it is doubtful in the extreme that Nozick's analyses are what made them into true believers. The sympathetic reader outwits himself in judging such reasonings to be compelling. He is *already* of that persuasion. Why? It is most improbable to attribute such allegiance to a priori argument. Rather, the devotee's experiences, beliefs, and hopes have been such that the idea of very limited state authority is highly agreeable to him, and likewise with the idea of possessing unbreachable rights. He might well be convinced that the state is and has been an agent of exploitation and suffering. He might believe that human beings exercising such rights will bring forth enterprise, prosperity, peace, contentment, and creativity on a broader and richer scale than could any other arrangement. (He might just be confident that *he* would attain such things.) *These* are the sorts of conditions that inspire allegiance and effort; *these* are what we become devoted to; and these are features of the primary subject matter. Yet we are too easily lulled into thinking that some abstract demonstration provides the real justification for our position. So one nods agreeably, and mindlessly, in reading arguments like Nozick's.

Those who are not libertarians will, of course, find abstract arguments of another persuasion, we may be sure. Or, perhaps, they will study the concrete subject matter of political, social, and economic life in its own right. There and there alone do we locate the experience that really matters.

Rawls' theory of justice almost touches ground at two points. Otherwise, it is simply an excogitated theory, oblivious to experience. At its outset, however, it appears to be a herculean attempt to take into account the widest possible panoply of human values—moral intuitions, or considered judgments, as he alternately calls them. His procedure is to survey them all in order to establish his proximate aim: definition of the original position. With this in hand, we have determined ideal conditions of choice, such that perfectly definite principles of justice are derivative of them. Utilizing the full assortment of considered judgments, we make a provisional definition of the original position, and then we see what follows from it. The result might be incompatible with some of our judgments, however; and we do not want to give them up that easily. Perhaps the hypothesized choice conditions yield a form of utilitarianism, for example, but this clashes with our judgment that no innocent individual should be sacrificed to the general welfare. So we think of a way to revise our definition. At the same time we don't rule out revision of considered judgments either. Thus the dialectic continues—shaping our definition and pruning our judgments until they make a coherent whole. The coherent whole is that which we seek. This settled, the rest is geometry. At least it *aims* at geometry.

One of the most powerful considered judgments that survives the entire dialectic is the requirement for absolute impartiality: no one may be in a position to "tailor" the constraints of the original position in a way that would particularly benefit himself or his favorites. Hence the veil of ignorance. No one has *any* identity; so he can't possibly select principles that are to his peculiar advantage. The main preoccupation of the faceless legislators is to avoid calamity. Rather than bet that they will be personally well-favored on the other side of the veil, they want assurance that no matter how much of a bungler, idiot, or incompetent they might really be, such a person will still be in a good position. This gives us the difference principle, which states that inequalities in the real world will be justified if and only if they have the effect of improving the condition of the least advantaged. Any and all inequalities will be decided upon by determining what the effect on the least advantaged will be, exclusive of all other considerations. Thus everyone is as safe as can be, allegedly.

A further consequence of the requirement for perfect impartiality is that the principles settled upon in the original position *are not subject to experimental revision*. If it turns out in the nonideal world that a given person or group decides they don't like this justice, it is too late to change. The animus for change has arisen in conditions where we *do* have a particular identity. Hence partiality inevitably arises.

There is only one condition in which change might be legitimate. Though having no personal identity, the legislators of justice are endowed with truly enviable knowledge: "...[T] hey know the general facts about human society. They understand political affairs and the principles of economic theory; they know the basis of social organization and the laws of human psychology."[10] The point of possessing this information is to determine whether the *implementation* of any given set of principles is *feasible*. They need only be *feasible* in the nonideal world—the world that we actually inhabit for better or worse. That is, the principles need not be found *morally* acceptable to real populations. They needn't even be preferable to any other principles, or even to be especially welcome. They need only be tolerable. For his part, Rawls believes we have adequate knowledge right now to be sure of the feasibility test.

> It is hard to imagine realistically any new knowledge that should convince us that these ideals are not feasible, given what we know about the general nature of the world.... Thus such advances in our knowledge of human nature and society as may take place do not affect our moral conception, but rather may be used to implement the application of its first principles of justice and suggest to us institutions and policies better designed to realize them in practice.[11]

Many critics will be skeptical that we have anything resembling such a science. Moreover, Rawls is confident that individuals in the temporal realm will in fact embrace his fundamental tenets. We might not *now* accept them, but assuredly we would if we thought about them long enough. "...[W]e can say that when persons act on these principles they are acting in accordance with principles that they would choose as rational and independent persons in an original position of equality."[12] These principles, in fact, "manifest" one's "nature as a free and equal rational being."[13]

Throughout *A Theory of Justice* we read of "our" considered judgments, "our" moral sense, "our" sense of justice, "our" intuitions; and one has to wonder to whom "our" refers—especially in those cases when one's own "considered judgments" are not recognized. The preceding paragraph suggests that "our" is *anyone*. So *anyone* would find these principles fully congenial to his "true" moral personality. Given the manifest diversity in basic moral orientations, this seems the utmost in preposterous claims. But it turned out in his subsequent amplifications that Rawls was not quite so imperialistic; so his claim was slightly less preposterous. There *is* a certain ideal of the person implied, but it is the *political* and *normative* ideal implicit in Western liberal democracies.[14] He said he was referring to the ideal latent in constitutional democracies; so his principles are definitive of that population only.

Remarkably, Rawls made *no* effort to substantiate this claim. There is no reference to history, popular culture, sociological research, political behavior, constitutional debates, or judicial interpretations. Neither was there reference to the two greatest philosophers of liberalism of the past hundred years, Mill and Dewey. Of course, he couldn't substantiate his claim. Our heritage was, and is, far more pluralistic than that. The claim that his principles articulate a single and shared ideal is both undefended and false. Accordingly, to lay these principles upon us with the bland assumption that we "really" have subscribed to them all along is, at best, sophistry. At its worst it is tyranny.

Consider, for example, another of "our" considered judgments. We "look for a conception of justice that *nullifies* the accidents of natural endowment and the contingencies of social circumstance as counters in quest for political and economic advantage..."[15] How many people subscribe to this thesis, which contributes to the eradication of the condition of being deserving, the denial of fundamental property rights and freedom of contract, experimentalism, and, in due course, to the adoption of the difference principle? Certainly all of these matters are controversial, and readers of this chapter will take sharply divergent positions on them. Such differences will be attributable to *many* factors: conceptions of human nature, interpretation of the historical record, study of comparative politics and economics, understanding of the nature of the moral life and our resources for contending with it, alternative moral conceptions and ideals—all, perhaps, in a deliberately provisional amalgam. My point is not to settle such disputes, but to point out that none of them can be conveniently swept under the rug with a priori theories. Rawls claims that his theory shows the utmost in respect for persons. But is does not. It respects only his own philosophic confection of the moral person. The real creatures of nature and history are left out of account.[16]

I mentioned above that this theory appears to engage experience at two points. The first is in his reliance on empirical social theory to determine the feasibility of implementing principles of justice. The second is in his claim to embody the actual political ideals embedded in our traditions. In neither case is he convincing. All the same, with these gestures at engaging reality, he proceeds to put our moral intuitions into a coherent whole. And what matters here is that they *be* a coherent whole. Coherence is the test. He does not examine a given moral conviction by asking what its consequences for experience would be—how it would serve or sacrifice the actual and possible values of the moral life. He doesn't ask what sorts of experience and concern have led to the adoption of intuitions. He doesn't undertake the more complex inquiry into where varying constellations of convictions might lead us. No, he just takes the "intuition" as an irreducible datum. The only matter of importance is their coherence in and of themselves; and once the system is established, its principles are unconditional. Fancy that![17]

Rawls has sytematically neglected the moral life. The seeming herculean effort to do justice to it is an imposture. If moral philosophy is judged by the adequacy with which it answers to the very exigencies that bring it into existence, then it must address them directly, honestly, and thoroughly, and for their own sake.

Jürgen Habermas might seem to be an exception to the dreary failures of contemporary moral theory. His explicitly communicative ethics, after all, seems to resemble Dewey's philosophy of social intelligence. In truth, however, Habermas has a greater resemblance to Rawls than to Dewey. Rawls' original position is a stacked deck (and a very slender one at that). Habermas' model of ethical discourse is likewise designed sytematically to exclude certain vital positions from having any voice whatever in moral discourse. Moreover, he justifies this model by recourse to considerations that do not touch upon the existential realities of the moral life.

Valid ethical communication, says Habermas, requires the satisfaction of at least three inseparable conditions. First, there must be generalizable (i.e., potentially common) interests among the participants. Hence, second, inequalities of power are morally intolerable, for they negate the very possibility of generalizable interest. Third, the participants must be adequately enlightened. (They are not afflicted with false consciousness.) Otherwise, their judgments have no weight. Inequalities in power represent inequalities in the respective relations to the means of production. Only a form of egalitarian socialism, then, provides one of the indispensable conditions for communicative competence. Moreover, those who have "already successfully completed processes of enlighten-ment" recognize the "incapacity for dialogue on the part of the strategic opponent," making free and equal discourse "impossible under the given circumstances."[18]

This is convenient, to say the least. The complex, urgent, and conscientiously contested controversies about the merits of forms of capitalism relative to forms of socialism are ruled out of order. That matter is already settled, and the champions of capitalism in one incarnation or another are declared incompetent. Thus, as in Rawls, a conjectured ideal and exclusive speech situation is presupposed as the only source of legitimate discussion.

The procedure is flagrantly question-begging—a form of special pleading; and it attempts to evade, rather than confront, the urgencies and difficulties of our moral situation. Those who earnestly inquire about the relative merits of competing political economies want to know what conceptions of human nature and institutions are at work in them and what verification in history these conceptions will endure. They want to know about such mundane matters as productivity, social mobility, the condition of the poor, oppressions, social services, tendencies to corruption, and the like. What are the conditions for the flourishing of the arts and sciences? For personal opportunity and adventure? What sorts of individualities flourish and what sorts are stymied? What are the explicit and symptomatic expressions of satisfaction or discontent? We might well wonder, too, whether the assumption of generalizable interests is not utopian.

Every sort of regime promises definite results of various kinds in regard to such matters, and our allegiances are largely determined by the credibility of competing promises. Although these are often extremely difficult questions, perhaps Habermas has already satisfied himself that he knows the answers to them. If so, let him produce empirical verifications for his theories, and then he would address the moral life pertinently. The results would not lead us to unambiguous allegiances. The moral condition has its inevitable uncertainties and ambivalences, but this is hardly to say that conscientious inquiry must leave us indiscriminate and impotent. Our convictions about alternative social schemes do, in fact, attain more confident direction as a consequence of just such experience.

Habermas' philosophy is evasive in an additional way. In his way of thinking, the norms of ethical discourse are not determined by making judgments about their possible efficacies in addressing the needs and imperatives generated in the moral life. They are, he says, transcendental. They are always already presupposed in any speech situation. The presupposition is not a product of human need or deliberation. It is necessarily resident in any speech situation, just because it is a speech situation.

The problematic that arises with the introduction of a moral principle is disposed of as soon as one sees that the expectation of discursive redemption of normative-validity claims is already contained in the structure of intersubjectivity and makes specially introduced maxims of universalization superfluous. . . . A cognitivist-linguistic ethics (*Sprachethik*) has no need of principles.

It is based only on fundamental norms of rational speech that we must always presuppose if we discourse at all.[19]

This transcendentalism is dubious in the extreme. Although everything is said to depend upon it, my point here is not to challenge it in itself. Just suppose, rather, that the antecedently given nature of speech as such implies (for one thing) that a speaker intends to tell the truth. Now, for obvious reasons we regard telling the truth as one of the consummately important functions in human conduct. Such precious things as reliability, trust, affection, and concerted social action are impossible without it. Without it we suffer such ills as paranoia, loneliness, and chaos. But according to Habermas this is not why telling the truth is a principle. It is so because it is a transcendental condition of engaging in speech at all. The question of the *functions* of honest speech is *not* pertinent.

Not only does this argument deliberately disregard the existential demands and benefits organic to forthright communication, it also assumes that a transcendental condition, just because it exists, is *therefore* good. There might be many sorts of unavoidable presupposition in mortal life, but that fact doesn't make them *desirable*. Let them be as transcendental as you like, they might be of a nature to make us miserable. Maybe the devil himself is a transcendental. We would have to *analyze* such conditions of existence to see what they are worth. We would judge them in respect to how they serve us for good or ill. If truth telling were somehow transcendental, we would be apt to be grateful—not because it is transcendental *simpliciter*, however, but only if that condition were somehow conducive to a more welcome social order.

Habermas' transcendentalism would seem to commit him to the view that the necessities of existence, just as they are, whatever they are, are necessarily good. But of course he doesn't really hold such a view. Rather, he has, in effect, attempted to circumvent the very rigors of moral experience that prompt us to propound and defend moral principles. But the result is that he has presented these deservedly cherished norms on the slimmest and most impertinent of reeds. The hard realities upon which our fortunes depend are left out of the reckoning.

The Renewal of Moral Philosophy

Too often, the subject matter adopted in moral philosophy is pretty thin soup. There seem to be many reasons for the starvation diet. The thinker's love of system and finality for their own sake cannot be discounted. But they are loved for other reasons as well. Such attachment can be born of a neediness to sustain one's antecedent convictions in the face of ambiguities and uncertainties; or, on the other hand, it can be inspired by simple intolerance and an inordinate desire to be authoritative. As Dewey repeatedly complained, one of the most conspicuous causes of philosophic malnutrition is this: The typical academic takes as *his* problematic situation the current state of *philosophic* reflection. He is hypnotically absorbed in what philosophers think. He does not attend to the trials and yearnings that haunt the moral life itself; and he is satisfied with his efforts insofar as they contend effectively with the arguments and counterarguments of his professional colleagues—however the moral predicament of human beings may waggle. How easy it is—how satisfying, indeed—to be a prisoner within the dialectic of ideas! Of course, once the hermetic system is completed, its author has no hesitation to visit it upon the problems of the workaday world.

Be that as it may, the search for the philosopher's stone is in any case futile. The endeavor to incorporate certainty and exactitude into moral thought will end in embarrassment, for such systematic results can be purchased only by introducing arbitrarily simplifying, and inherently controversial, assumptions. Hence we witness the proliferation of philosophic cults. *Of course* we must try to bring reflection and order to the plurality of contingencies, loyalties, and aspirations of moral existence; and we have had some success in doing so. Moral communities do, after all, exist and even flourish in the midst of plural and sometimes inconsistent concerns. But the would-be heaven dweller pursues the aim of simplification to a fault. In effect, he sweeps aside the pervasive traits of nature articulated in Dewey's metaphysics. According legitimacy to neither irreducible variety, persistent heartfelt disagreement, change, nor tragedy, he would make light of our lives by forcing them into the straitjacket of an abstract theoretical order.

A Deweyan, by contrast, will confront moral experience and its conditions in all their vicissitudes, to learn of their restraints, powers, and promises, to be both chastened and inspired. Of course, knowledge of such experience and sensitivity to it do not lead inescapably to an ultimate set of moral principles. Our situation is too complex, varying, and tragic for that. Yet it is not without resource and direction, and it will deeply repay conscientious study. Reflection upon the moral life, including human capabilities, has yielded valuable lessons, and it will yield more. Witness—again—Dewey's philosophy of social intelligence, which is founded on neither artifice nor intuition, but upon a searching examination of the entire human condition.

A Deweyan must endure a measure of uncertainty and second thoughts. Yet despair is not his only alternative. Studying the moral life in its fullness, he can identify invaluable lessons for the conduct of life; and in consequence of the honesty and discernment with which the search is pursued, the lessons will have real credibility. He cannot lead the way to paradise, but he might help to make expanses of desert bloom.

Notes

1. John Rawls, *A Theory of Justice* (Cambridge, Mass.: Harvard University Press, 1971).
2. Alan Gewirth, *Reason and Morality* (Chicago: University of Chicago Press, 1978).
3. Bruce A. Ackerman, *Social Justice in the Liberal State* (New Haven: Yale University Press, 1980); Ronald Dworkin, *Taking Rights Seriously* (Cambridge, Mass.: Harvard University Press, 1978); David Gauthier, *Morals by Agreement* (Oxford: Clarendon Press, 1986); R. M. Hare, *Moral Thinking* (Oxford: Clarendon Press, 1981); Alasdair MacIntyre, *After Virtue* 2d ed. (Notre Dame, Ind.: University of Notre Dame Press, 1984) and *Whose Justice? Which Rationality?* (Notre Dame, Ind.: University of Notre Dame Press, 1988); Kai Nielsen, *Equality and Liberty: A Defense of Radical Egalitarianism* (Totowa, N.J.: Rowman and Allanheld, 1985); and Robert Nozick, *Anarchy, State, and Utopia* (New York: Basic Books, 1974).
4. MacIntyre's work is to some extent an exception. It is still subject to severe criticism from a Deweyan point of view, however. It is intolerant of pluarlism, for example, and has no room for social intelligence. Limitations of space forbid a discussion of MacIntyre in this text.
5. See my "Dewey's Theory of Moral Deliberation," *Ethics* 88, 3 (April 1978), pp. 218–28.
6. One of the keys to understanding Dewey's metaphysics is to recognize that he is not atempting to describe the generic traits of the *universe*. He is characterizing *nature*, as he says, "when its properties are most fully displayed (LW 1:201). The greatest exhibition of nature's potentialities open to our observation is in evidence in the organic transactional field constituted by the interaction of humans and the environment. Neither human beings nor the environment can be reduced to substances, to self-complete entities. Processes constitutive and inclusive of both bring new traits into existence, and these traits are as real as any other sort of natural outcome. They are the subject matter of Dewey's metaphysics.
7. *Ethics* was written with James H. Tufts. The passage quoted was written by Dewey.
8. I have elaborated Dewey's philosophy of social intelligence in *Excellence in Public Discourse: John Stuart Mill, John Dewey, and Social Intelligence* (New York: Teachers College Press, 1986), esp. chap. 5. See also

my essay "Dewey" in *Ethics in the History of Western Philosophy*, ed. R. Cavalier, J. Gouinlock, and J. Sterba (New York: St. Martin's Press, 1989).

9. Nozick, *Anarchy, State, and Utopia*, p. 7.

10. Rawls, *A Theory of Justice*, p. 137.

11. John Rawls, "Kantian Constructivism in Moral Theory," *The Journal of Philosophy* 87 (September 9, 1980), p. 566.

12. Rawls, *A Theory of Justice*, p. 252.

13. Ibid., p. 255.

14. John Rawls, "Justice as Fairness: Political Not Metaphysical," *Philosophy and Public Affairs* 14, 4 (Summer 1985), pp. 223–51.

15. Rawls, *A Theory of Justice*, p. 15. Emphasis added.

16. Instances abound in *A Theory of Justice* of the outright unconditional rejection of any values incompatible with the theory. For example: "As we have seen, a certain ideal is embedded in the principles of justice, and the fulfillment of desires incompatible with these principles has no value at all" (pp. 326–27). Or: ". . . [T]he contract view requires that we move towards just institutions as speedily as the cirucumstances permit irrespective of existing sentiments" (p. 451).

17. It is difficult if not impossible to attain coherence in one's own convictions. *But for an entire culture?* Moreover, it is by no means clear even for an individual that coherence is the ultimate *desideratum*.

18. Jürgen Habermas, *Theory and Practice* (Boston: Beacon Press, 1973), p. 39.

19. Jürgen Habermas, *Legitimation Crisis* (Boston: Beacon Press, 1975), p. 110.

6

Aristotle and Dewey on the Rat Race

JOHN LACHS

Aristotle put his stamp on the history of Western thought by inventing the concepts of activity and process. This is not the only way in which he exercised a formative influence over much subsequent philosophy nor are these the only novel concepts that flowed from his fertile mind. But these ideas became cornerstones of a distinguished series of metaphysical systems. They also came to articulate a vision of the good life or the life proper for humans.

The simple observation that underlies the distinction between activity and process is that some actions appear to be complete while others seem to point beyond themselves for their completion. In digging and pouring foundations, for example, we find that the acts make sense only by reference to further things to be accomplished in the process of building. Foundation work is, in this way, intrinsically incomplete: it requires a significant sequence of additional performances to render it meaningful or whole. A moment or two of pleasure, by contrast, demands nothing further: it is experienced as complete and satisfying simply by itself. Extension of the feeling is, of course, welcome but it is not necessary to render the initial pleasure a complete and self-contained moment of joy.

On careful inspection, this incompleteness is revealed as not a random or accidental feature of some acts. Complex physical performances, in particular, appear to be rent by a sort of fragmentation that renders them imperfect and unsatisfactory. The reason is their integrated complexity itself. Within such processes, each part is tied to the rest and none makes sense alone. Pouring the foundations is incomplete without building the basement, nothing can be a basement without a first floor, and for the structure to become a house requires that we build each of its parts in its proper place and in the right sequence. This seems neither surprising nor altogether bad and we may well decide that such processes achieve completeness only when finished: they are whole in the totality or whole of their existence, but always fragmented in the parts. This whole, however, never actually exists because the parts that constitute it are successive. Past and future infect the entire process: all the parts necessary to make it whole never coexist and, paradoxically, at the moment when it reaches completion with its last constituent act, all of it has sadly ceased to be.

Sequential actualization is, in this way, essentially imperfect since it is structured by time: it must always rely on the dead or the yet to be for its completion, which means that it can never be complete. Its fate, both as human action and as metaphysical event, is expectation and grief. It is a yearning after what is to come and the sadness over what is irretrievably gone. Aristotle and others have, therefore, concluded that it can serve neither as a foundation for our understanding of what *is* nor as a design for how to lead a satisfactory life.

In sharp contrast with this, activities are complete at each moment of their occurrence. Their simplicity assures that they can be actualized at once. In this way, they liberate themselves from the tyranny of time; even when they exist for a while, as when happiness endures for a precious hour, they are complete and self-contained at each portion of that stretch, gladly accepting continuance, but losing nothing if it fails to be granted. Activities constitute, therefore, human acts that are gems: they are meaningful, self-contained achievements free of the corrosive influence of time, of all expectation and sadness. They are eternal not in the sense of lasting forever, but in that they transcend or defang the temporal to reach perfection in a moment.

This notion of timeless actuality became the foundation of our understanding of the divine. Aristotle himself thought of his odd god as consisting of just such an eternal act in which the timeless timelessly contemplated itself. Thinking of God as being constituted of activity assures divine completeness and perfection. One of the ideas of substance, that of an existent in need of nothing beyond itself in order to be or to be complete, captures this notion of a being shielded from time, growth, decay, need, desire, and imperfection. This manner of conceiving the ideal being permeated not only theology; it became the grounding notion of many of the great metaphysical systems. It has a remarkable history through the Middle Ages and was memorably introduced to the modern world in Spinoza's *Ethics*. It haunted German metaphysics after Kant, as a long series of system builders struggled to work through their love-dread relation to Spinoza. In one form and context or another, it has survived to ground much of the metaphysics of the twentieth century.

In spite of this distinguished past, the idea of activity would not command the interest it does if its use had been purely theoretical. Conceptions of God, however, typically also serve to articulate ideals for human life. Activity was viewed precisely in this light from the first. Aristotle thought of it not only as a way of understanding God, but also as an ideal to which we needed to aspire in order to actualize the best in us. He knew that, as temporally embodied, we could never escape the world of labored processes. But contemplation of the changeless beckoned to him as at least a momentary completion of imperfect lives and, therefore, as a manner in which we could be godlike. The same ideal, in typically exaggerated form, was present in Spinoza, who saw absorption into eternal, pure act as the only life worth living.

A fundamental disagreement separates Aristotle and Spinoza. The resolutely sensible Greek could think of no way of breaking down the distinction between process and activity and of thereby escaping temporality and death. As natural creatures with mind, we always remain both temporally fragmented and, potentially at least, eternally complete. The Stoics showed Spinoza a way to avoid this undesirable ambiguity in human life. Their belief in the power of the mind convinced them that the distinction between process and activity was not absolute: by taking the correct attitude to what we do, they maintained, we can convert any process into an activity. If what renders an action a fragmented process is that it is performed to obtain an ulterior end, we can change it into an activity simply by doing it, and each part of it, as an end in itself. This breaks the process into a sequence of activities, each of which is meaningful and complete without reference to anything beyond. The Stoic insight suggested to Spinoza that a life in the eternal was really possible. His account of how passive emotions can be converted into active ones was his version of the transmutation of process into activity and his explanation of how, though finite, we can completely fade, or rather brighten, into the eternal.

The ideal of self-contained activity, of life in the eternal, has remained powerful to this day. Some people advocate attitudinal adjustments to unpleasant tasks, others continue to draw a sharp line between the realm of means and actions that are of intrinsic value. Many condemn commercial and industrial life because of its endless cycle of fragmented acts and trivial demands. All of these critics tacitly assume the process/activity distinction and embrace pure act in some form as our only hope of satisfaction.

A fine, though perhaps surprising, twentieth-century philosophical articulation of the same ideas can be found in the work of George Santayana. Although he studied with William James and found himself in sympathy with some of the central ideas of pragmatism, when it came to thinking through the nature of the good life, Santayana reverted to Aristotle's time-honored distinction. He viewed the physical world as an endless sequence of events and animal life within it as a cycle of needs and fleeting satisfactions. Nothing caught in this web of the tenuous, not even the temporarily successful life of reason, could escape the ultimate inadequacy of all processes.

Santayana was more explicit than Aristotle in identifying process with the material world and activity with a phase of consciousness or mind. Accordingly, he maintained that nothing is of ultimate value except conscious feeling. But even the realm of mind is permeated by the anxiety and incompleteness characteristic of temporal process: since, referring to what is beyond, neither belief nor emotion shows itself satisfied with the immediately present content of consciousness, they cannot constitute self-complete moments of activity. We reach fulfillment only in the spiritual phase of awareness, which is free of all restless striving and of all reference to the absent or the beyond. Santayana deliberately identified this "spiritual life" with activity in Aristotle's sense.[1] It consists of a string of pure intuitions (contemplative acts of consciousness), each complete in itself and presenting some form for cognitive grasp or direct enjoyment. Placid aesthetic immediacy is thus the only thing perfect in the world, the only act whose performance does not in the end dissatisfy.

The broader context of Santayana's theory of the spiritual life was naturalistic. He thought that absorption in the given constituted a perfection open to certain animals, and that it required the continued support of a living body. Nevertheless, the view amounted to a reaffirmation of the supremacy of mind and, in the form of aesthetic immediacy, of a sort of cognition. It also identified time and its attendant imperfections as the enemy. We could not hope to defeat this antagonist but, by momentary escape, we could cheat it of victory.

This depiction of Santayana's view of the perfection open to us reveals its remarkable similarity to Schopenhauer's theory of art. Schopenhauer thought of the aesthetic intuition of universals as one of only two ways of escaping the ravages of an ever hungry and never satisfied will. The ultimate form of escape was denial of the will to live; if resolutely executed, this terminated life. Contemplation of the beautiful offered a less radical, and therefore less permanent, solution to the problem of endless frustrated striving. It enabled one to eliminate desire for a moment by providing absorption in a pure, uselessly beautiful object.

The resemblance is important to note because it shows the close connection between application of the process/activity distinction to the question of how to live well and the deepest, most devastating pessimism. So long as we think that time is the enemy and set ourselves an ideal of godlike, eternal act, we cannot avoid seeing much of life as worthless, if not positively evil. In such a sea of imperfection, with nothing but momentary glimpses of beauty to redeem us, we can readily decide that life is without hope and significance.

If we think of divine perfection in terms of activity, we can hope to achieve a state similar to God's blessedness by engaging in activity ourselves. Our inevitable failure to sustain such pure actuality need, then, not plunge us into ultimate despair; with God, we can have the promise of another life in which eternal activity will go on unabated. The pessimism of Schopenhauer and Santayana becomes unavoidable if we retain the process/activity framework but eliminate the theocentric metaphysics that has been its historical partner. Contrary to what some philosophers think, Schopenhauer and Santayana were not pessimists simply because they failed to believe in the existence of God. The sense of hopelessness they felt was due to the fact that they rejected God's existence and the promise of a future state while, for purposes of elucidating the ideal human life, they retained the very concepts that, employed in metaphysics, lead at once to God. The lesson may well be that we end up paying a high price if we refuse to employ a set of concepts in one area while we retain their related use in another.

The process/activity distinction rests on the claim that there is an essential incompatibility between ends-in-themselves and means, between ultimate value and utility. Philosophers since Aristotle have, accordingly, maintained that whatever aims at some goal beyond itself cannot also carry intrinsic worth. Astoundingly, no one challenged this idea until the twentieth century. Much in Hegel hinted at its wrongheadedness. But Dewey was the first to bring it into question and to develop an alternative conception.

In *Experience and Nature*, Dewey acknowledges that much of what we do "in home, factory, laboratory and study" (LW 1:271) is devoid of intrinsic value. The ends we prize, by contrast, are "spasms of excited escape from the thraldom of enforced work" (LW 1:271). Labor is merely useful while enjoyment is good in and of itself. Its value resides in our being satisfied with it independently of where it may lead or precisely because it leads nowhere beyond itself. It appears, therefore, that work is intrinsically incomplete process and enjoyment is luminous and perfect activity.

Dewey, however, is quick to dispel this appearance. In reality, work can be seen as useful only if "we arbitrarily cut short our consideration of consequences" (LW 1:272) by focusing on the commodities it produces to the neglect of its cost in the quality of human life. Enjoyments, in turn, approximate ultimate ends only if we detach them from the full context of their conditions and consequences and thereby convert them into passivities devoid of meaning. The process/activity distinction applies, therefore, only to life fragmented by improper institutional arrangements and to events we abstract from their place in experience. The extent to which it applies is a measure of how far "experience fails to be art" (LW 1:271).

To speak of experience as art is to say that in it means and end, the useful and the valuable, fully coincide. This sounds at first as a restatement of the idea of activity: since such divine acts are performed for their own sake, they display no distinction between means and end. The reason, however, why we can see no such distinction is that activities contain no means at all. Means are realities not in themselves desirable that tend to bring about what we seek. We turn to them for their causal features or for their mediating role in leading us where we want to be. There is simply no such mediation in activity; we perform what is wanted directly, for its own sake. In activity, we transcend time and achieve perfection by refusing all contact with the merely useful.

Dewey speaks of the genuine unity of means and end, not of the absence of means. This demands rethinking the traditional notion of means, which is the "coerced antecedent of the occurrence of another thing which is wanted" (LW 1:275). Such causal conditions, serving as external necessities, appear to have nothing in common with the ends they help bring about. Dewey rejects this as the only, or the proper, idea of means and introduces in its place a notion according to which the means is an intrinsic element of the end. In addition to being a causal condition of the end to which it leads, a means must meet two criteria: (a) to be freely chosen and used to bring about a consequence, and (b) to be an integrated portion of that consequence (LW 1:275).

It is generally agreed that if they are not chosen and used, causal antecedents simply result in effects without being means to them. Dewey goes a step beyond this and notes that, under normal circumstances, the love for the end extends to whatever helps us attain it. Achieving results by control over the generative conditions of things and events is a characteristically human endeavor. Such deliberately and intelligently caused consequences are, in Dewey's language, "meanings." The need for meanings runs deep in our lives; their attainment constitutes art (LW 1:370). The first criterion connects means, therefore, with the prized and enjoyed ability of humans to take control of their lives, or at least of important portions of them.

The second criterion amounts to a rejection of the separateness of causes and effects. Affecting the tone of an exasperated instructor, G. E. Moore thought he wreaked havoc with Mill's wayward attempt to show that music, virtue, and money could have both instrumental and final value.[2] Dewey picks up Mill's mantle and maintains that nothing can be a means *unless* it is both useful and a part of the desired end. He presents telling examples of means that are, at once, elements of the whole to whose creation they contribute. Flour and yeast, he argues, are both means to bread and ingredients of it. And a "good political constitution, honest police system and competent judiciary, are means to the prosperous life of the community because they are integrated portions of that life" (LW 1:275).

Dewey's alternative to the notion of activity, of what can be done as an end directly, is the idea of action that is both means and end. Events in experience present this double face: they play a role in the sequential (causal) order and also display qualities we can immediately enjoy. Dewey does not think that these divergent features of actions are matters of perspective. Everything actually has both relational and intrinsic, both instrumental and consummatory, properties. We need neither adjustment of attitude nor act of will to gain access to them; a growth in sensitivity is enough. Such growth, if Dewey is right, enables us to realize that instrumental and final values are not incompatible. Accordingly, intelligent human beings will seek satisfaction by participating fully in both the labor and the delights of life.

This notion of means-end integrated actions is a far more worldly ideal than Aristotle's. It abolishes the supremacy of the cognitive and the contemplative, and opens the entire range of human activities to the legitimate search for satisfaction. It eliminates the prerogatives of the eternal and turns attention away from the age-old fixation on transcending time to the use of the time available. It restores the dignity of everyday activities and establishes them as proper elements in meaningful human lives. It refuses to view the totality of our condition as flawed (along the lines of the idea, for example, that we are rational beings tied to an absurd body in an irrational world) and looks, instead, for concrete ways to enhance enjoyment in the present and to increase it in the future.

Dewey's claim that we can perform actions both for their own sake and for the sake of what they bring is heartening. If true, it would make life richer and satisfaction in it easier to attain. By redirecting our efforts in accordance with it, we could engage in actions that are both fulfilling and useful; we would not have to sacrifice pleasure to service. But is Dewey's claim true and his ideal workable?

Utopian thinkers have an easy way of sidestepping these questions. Dewey himself readily admits that many of our current practices fall short of being both means and ends; these include "much of our labors in home, factory, laboratory and study" (LW 1:271). A single easy step from here could take him to the declaration that means-end integrated actions constitute an ideal in the sense of that which defines how things would be if humans were rational, the world sufficiently pliable, and social arrangements optimal. Such standards beckon from afar: nothing need live up to them now or at any time until the millennium or some astounding change in human nature. This insulates the ideal from criticism as impractical; its function, it might be urged, is precisely to articulate a standard that is difficult, if not impossible, to meet.

Such an approach has satisfied framers of abstract ideals throughout the history of thought. To his great credit, Dewey sees no appeal in it. His denotative method requires him to anchor all his views, including his ideas of the good, in actual experience. We must, therefore, be able to find cases of action that are valuable both as means and as end, and that we undertake to do in order to secure both sorts of good. Such actions, Dewey asserts, must be both instrumental and consummatory simultaneously "rather than in alternation and displacement" (LW 1:271). Moreover, much of the rest of what we do should be reorientable so that it approximates this ideal of the coincidence of utility and intrinsic value.

At least two sorts of ordinary practice qualify by Dewey's criteria: love and play. Kissing, done in the right context, clearly displays both instrumental and final values. It is unquestionably pleasant and tends to lead to additional fine activities. As enjoyed for its intrinsic qualities, it is an end; as freely chosen to bring about a larger, more orgiastic, consequence of which it is an integrated portion, it is a means. Those engaged in it may, moreover, be reasonably viewed as initiating and continuing it for the double reason of how nice it is and what exciting things grow from it. It is, therefore, both instrument and consummation, as is every other element of the act of love.

The same holds for games and for play. Dribbling the ball downcourt is not a coerced antecedent of going for the lay-up. It is an activity enjoyable for its own sake, but also for the sake of the basket that may come from it. As freely chosen instrument of scoring and as an integrated element of the larger scoring drive, it is a means; as fun experience and display of ball-handling skill, it is an end. Those who like playing the game, moreover, dribble for both reasons: they enjoy fast movement with control of the ball and they look forward to the opportunities for scoring it creates.

Unfortunately, not many other examples of human conduct appear to qualify as optimal by Dewey's high ideal. Some ends we seek, such as entertainment and beer-soaked highs, lack useful outcomes. The majority of actions we perform as means can be enjoyed only by idiots or by those sufficiently unconscious not to note or object to repetition. Means and ends are, in this way, fragmented and sequential, and we pay a high price for fleeting satisfaction. At first sight, therefore, Aristotle's view of the human lot as pervaded by incomplete and ultimately unsatisfying processes appears more accurate about the bulk of life than Dewey's more optimistic assessment.

Two well-known psychological phenomena operate to reduce the onerousness of means. The pleasure of attaining the objective tends to spread to the instruments that helped us in the quest. Shaving, an otherwise unpleasant or indifferent act, can in this way become suffused with excitement if it is a condition of morning love. Brokers on the floor of the stock exchange report that long train rides to work cease to be objectionable when their trading goes well. Such anticipatory pleasures do much to make life bearable, even if the delight they offer is bittersweet or ambiguous.

The second psychological mechanism of relief is the remarkable human capacity for acceptance. Unavoidable, debilitating routines can become bearable with the years. Their assurance and predictability offer comfort and the force of habit makes them expected, even essential, parts of life. Boring and menial work may seem a depressing way to earn one's living. But vacations reveal how much even such miserable routines can come to function as important elements of at least acceptable days. Given a choice, perhaps only a few would opt for such lives, but swallowed up in them we do all we can to make the pain subside.

Although these mechanisms render existence centered around unpleasant instrumentalities a little better, they fail to achieve satisfaction beyond the compensatory. They fall far short of endowing instruments with intrinsic value or of making dehumanizing tasks a pleasure to perform. So long as there are disagreeable but necessary actions, they are, therefore, inadequate to attain Dewey's ideal of means that are at once consummations.

Is it, however, the case that we must always face disagreeable necessities? We face them now and, if they are to disappear, it will be either because we refuse to view them as unpleasant or because they will no longer be needed. The former leads us back to the attitudinal adjustments of the Stoic and is unlikely to gain Dewey's support. The latter points to increased control over the conditions of our existence and thus to applied intelligence and technology.

We find that many onerous tasks have been eliminated in the last few hundred years. We no longer have to gather wood for heat, haul our own water or take an oxcart when we visit friends. In many respects, we live in what James called a "wishing-cap world," in which:

> We want water and we turn a faucet. We want a kodak-picture and we press a button. We want information and we telephone. We want to travel and we buy a ticket. In these and similar cases, we hardly need to do more than the wishing—the world is rationally organized to do the rest.[3]

In such a world, we have to do much less, or at least much less that is objectionable, to attain our ends. One part of the reason is that we have reduced the amount of human labor necessary to meet our desires; the introduction of machines, for example, makes our efforts more efficient. Another is that much necessary work has been shifted to others who, since they are specialized and have access to the right equipment, can do it more easily or better. Very few people raise their own food, for example, and few could even think of making their own car.

These vast and, on the whole, beneficial changes appear to favor the view that industrial life moves us in the direction of Dewey's means-end integrated actions. The appearance, however, is deceptive. Industrial society makes life more comfortable at the cost of a momentous separation between means and ends at the workplace. The tasks we perform in huge organizations are routine and restricted. As the sheet metal worker in the airplane factory, we make small and anonymous contributions to large social products. Our actions constitute the means, or fragments of the means, to ends we have not intended and may not understand. These means may well be "integrated portions" of the ends, but they are not freely and intelligently chosen by the individuals involved. Even if instruments and products stand in a consummately rational relation in the institution, those who work there find it difficult to connect their efforts with the objectives they subserve.

The gulf between means and ends is widened by the fact that necessary specialization makes tasks narrow and repetitive. Competition with others generates internal pressure to work relentlessly and the demand for productivity causes haste. Under these circumstances, it is difficult to view fragmentary tasks as intrinsically enjoyable ends. Perhaps the work of those who shape metal sheets does have an intrinsic quality that, if only they could focus on it, would give them satisfaction. Their situation at work, however, is not well adapted to promote such focusing. And even if they succeed for a day or two, their need for work will outlive their ability to see it as meaningful or fun.

All of this may, of course, be true only because we are at an intermediate stage of industrialization. In another hundred years, all jobs unworthy of humans, all routine, repetitive, and boring tasks, will possibly have been eliminated. This could leave for us only acts, such as love and play, in which everything is both means and end. All the rest of the work of the world may well end up being done by intelligent machines.

If we do not destroy the human race and the planet in the process, this is a plausible scenario. Suppose that it comes about. Would human life then consist only or largely of means-end integrated actions? The likely answer is no. For the mechanization of productive tasks does not substitute pleasurable means for unpleasant ones; instead, it trivializes means or eliminates them altogether. The development from raising, killing, and plucking a chicken and then cooking it on a wood-burning stove to warming prepackaged microwave fowl makes the point obvious. In reading, we have to move the eyes and turn the page; television requires little more than a grateful stare. We do not have to go to science fiction accounts of electrically stimulated brains in pleasure vats to know that people gladly choose and often dream of passive sensuous delights. The mechanization of the world is propelled by this desire and serves it. The promise and ultimate reward of such a society is to convert much of life into enjoyed ends. This is closer to Aristotle than to Dewey, with the difference that such ends are passivities, not activities. A large additional increase in technology offers, therefore, little of benefit to Dewey's ideal.

It may be better to look for the growth or distribution of means-end integrated actions by starting from the example of professionals and their work. Physicians, presumably, do not have to engage in disagreeable routines. The actions they undertake are freely chosen and the treatments they administer (especially in preventive medicine) are integral parts of the sustained health of their patients. It appears, therefore, that doctors have the privilege of performing only or mainly those actions which feature both instrumental and consummatory value. Perhaps we could all be like doctors and other professionals and thereby enhance our enjoyment of what we do.

This picture of physicians is, unfortunately, selective and therefore inaccurate. It romanticizes their work by overlooking the everyday context in which they operate. In reality, doctors can enjoy what they do only because they hand over much of what is unpleasant or routine to nurses, orderlies, assistants, bookkeepers, and secretaries. And even with these tasks delegated, it takes a wild stretch of the imagination to see their daily work as similar to making love. Particularly is this true after the fifteenth Pap smear or when examining, late in the afternoon, the fiftieth baby with colic. Even love, I suppose, loses its allure when there are too many customers.

The key, then, we might suppose, is to do what one wants for as long as one wants to do it. This is not a bad, brief account of freedom. Most people know the connection between freedom and pleasure because they find that they tend to enjoy what they choose without constraint. If we keep this in mind, we might conclude that the first criterion a means must meet according to Dewey, namely that it be freely chosen and used, may be adequate by itself to assure a significant improvement of the human condition. If only all of us could do what we wished, embracing ends and choosing means without external interference and without the demands of necessity, we would be able to experience each means as at once a consummation.

What is there to stop us from growing in this direction? Dewey himself stresses the importance of freedom and sees it as indispensable for a satisfactory moral and political life. What we need here, however, is radical freedom for the individual. Each person must be in a position to decide what he or she wants to do, even if the decision disregards legitimate social needs. Can a society operate with this much liberty? Only if it finds a way to make people want what is needed. But this is excessively difficult to accomplish. We can force individuals to do the socially necessary; to pay taxes, for example. We can train people to do what is useful (to take care of their parents, for instance) by creating in them a sense of obligation. Human beings get used to having to do such things and accept them as unavoidable parts of life. But they do not come to like or to enjoy them and they certainly do not seek them out. Socialization has its limits. Although some psychologists claim that they can make anyone like anything, it is clear that no one can make enough people like enough unpleasant things to enable a society to run on the basis of free choice alone.

Friends of Dewey must by now be anxious to set me right. Since the search for large-scale or utopian improvements in human life did not appeal to Dewey, it is unfair, they might assert, to saddle him with a view that requires us to turn most of the actions of the largest number of people into meaningful, means-end integrated acts. This is a good reminder, even though it misses the point of what I have said. Of course, Dewey is a meliorist looking for incremental change. Of course, such change is possible: we can reduce the unpleasantness of means a little here and there by making life more like love, by selective advances in technology, by modeling more jobs on the professions, by expanding the sphere of freedom. Those, however, were not the questions we set out to examine.

Dewey presents his idea of means-end integrated actions as an alternative to Aristotle's notion of activity. As such, the conception articulates an ideal of human conduct in the most general terms: although it does not tell us in detail what to do, it gives precise instructions on how to do it. I have been examining the warrant for this ideal and its scope. I had little trouble identifying its source and instances in experience. Its range, however, gets Dewey in trouble. For he advances it as a condition at which human action in general should aim, bemoans the fact that such action falls short of it, and attributes this failure to current institutional arrangements (LW 1:272, 276). This suggests that there are some strategies we can pursue to bring our conduct closer to the ideal. I have explored what these strategies might be, but found none that offers significant relief.

Aristotle was satisfied to note that some things we did were by nature processes, others activities. The Stoics developed this distinction into a technique useful for dealing with the rat race. In order to maximize satisfaction in life, they admonished, we need simply to convert processes into activities by doing each element of them for its own sake, as an end. This requires only a change in aim or attitude and that, they believed, is always within our power. If we followed the Stoic, we would perform whatever actions were needed without concern for their ultimate success. Such focus on the present would, presumably, make our personal lives and social actions meaningful at least for the moment.

Dewey's ideal, more robust and less resigned about the future, provides a better expression of the modern temper. But how can we turn it into a useful strategy for dealing with the pressures and the meaningless necessities of existence? Can we hope to spend our days as though we were making love to life? Having Marx before him as a failed example, Dewey shied away from recommending revolutionary social changes to institutionalize means-end integrated actions. Unfortunately, even if he had wanted to advance such recommendations, my discussion shows that it is not at all clear what they might have been.

There is one sure way in which we can all enjoy the intrinsic qualities of otherwise objectionable means. We can simply perform the acts of which they consist as ends in themselves, for their own sake alone. All this takes is a change of attitude or a firm resolve to focus on the immediate. The only trouble is that it is the Stoic gambit and it converts means-end integrated actions into activities.

Notes

1.   George Santayana, *Scepticism and Animal Faith* (New York: Dover, 1955), p. 217.

2.   G. E. Moore, *Principia Ethica* (Cambridge: Cambridge University Press, 1951), Chapter 3.

3.   William James, *Pragmatism* (Cambridge, Mass.: Harvard University Press, 1975), p. 139.

7

Validating Women's Experiences Pragmatically

CHARLENE HADDOCK SEIGFRIED

Carolyn Whitbeck says that she regards "feminist philosophy as primarily concerned with the construction and development of concepts and models adequate for the articulation of women's experience and women's practices."[1] Denise Riley, on the other hand, questions the possibility of an experience that is specifically women's when she deconstructs the category of 'woman' in *"Am I that Name?"*.[2] She examines the ambivalent attitudes towards the designation of 'woman' that feminists have exhibited over the centuries. The recurring difficulty is that the more women are differentiated as women, the less they embody the characteristics of humanity.[3] The instability of the designation, woman, is particularly problematic for political organization and emancipatory campaigns, since "to be named as a woman can be the precondition for some kinds of solidarity."[4] The indeterminacy of 'women' means that "while it's impossible to thoroughly be a woman, it's also impossible never to be one."[5] The undecidability of the issue is magnified in debates over women's experience.

Riley does not simplistically solve the problems she raises, since she expects that feminism will continue to oscillate between asserting and refusing the category of 'women.' She takes her stand "on a territory of pragmatism," and argues that "it is compatible to suggest that 'women' don' t exist—while maintaining a politics of 'as if they existed'—since the world behaves as if they unambiguously did."[6] She is using "pragmatism" in its conventional sense and not referring to the philosophical tradition of pragmatism, but her further explanation is remarkably consistent with pragmatist philosophy: "And the less that 'women workers' can be believed to have a fixed nature, as distinct from neglected needs because of their domestic responsibilities, the more it will be arguable that only for some purposes can they be distinguished from all workers. Feminism can then join battle over which these purposes are to be."[7]

John Dewey, like Whitbeck, defends the primacy and ultimacy of concrete experience, understood as the process "of continuous and cumulative interaction of an organic self with the world" (LW 10:224). He also, like Riley, rejects fixed natures, and replaces them with explanations of relative stabilities within the flux of experience which have developed over time. What has traditionally been called a nature is a way of effectively organizing experience to answer our needs, intentions, and purposes. Therefore, the traits of experience, whether of women's or of some other designated group, cannot just be read off from nature but must be reconstructed within a historical process with which we are continuous. We are not contemplatively detached from experience, but are ourselves formed within it as "desiring, striving, thinking, feeling creature(s)" (LW 1:67).

In this chapter I explore those aspects of Dewey's analysis of experience which seem particularly apt for enriching feminist explorations of women's experiences. These are (a) the identification and rejection of philosophical dualisms which have systematically distorted our understanding of everyday experience, (b) the thesis that ignoring the perspectival nature of experience is a source of oppression, (c) the development of standards of judgment and values out of concrete experience, and (d) the role of feeling in experience. Dewey's explanation of experience is interrogated throughout from the perspective of feminist analyses of women's oppression. In the final section I suggest that the systematic identification and rejection of Dewey's gender bias will begin to yield an analysis of actual existences and events capable of guiding those decisions that both feminists and pragmatists seek about ends to strive for, goods to be obtained, and evils to be averted.

Lifting the Burden of Tradition: Attack on Dualism

In *The Quest for Certainty* Dewey seeks the origins of present-day beliefs, assumptions, and values by turning to history and anthropology. He strips away the veneer of pure rationality that is attributed to widely held attitudes by showing that they arose within definite human communities in answer to felt needs. He specifically wants to account for the hierarchical dualisms that have systematically distorted experience. The four, in particular, which must be rejected in order to clear the way for pragmatist philosophy, turn out to be the same ones that feminists have also identified as oppressive: (a) the depreciation of doing and making and the over-evaluation of pure thinking and reflection, (b) the contempt for bodies and matter and praise of spirit and immateriality, (c) the sharp division of practice and theory, and (d) the inferiority of changing things and events and the superiority of a fixed reality. The criticism of dualism is also central to most varieties of feminist analysis.[8] Susan Sherwin, for instance, points out that most traditional philosophical methodologies accept dichotomous thinking that "forces ideas, persons, roles, and disciplines into rigid polarities. It reduces richness and complexity in the interest of logical neatness, and, in doing so, it distorts truth."[9] Dichotomies undergird patriarchy, which is sustained by power relations that both assume and construct unbridgeable differences between the sexes.

Dewey also argues that philosophers who denigrate doing and making and praise theory above practice are self-serving (LW 4:4). They perpetuate these dualisms by first rationally formulating and then justifying them, but philosophers did not originate the position. The subordination of practice to theory originates far back in history, when physical work was onerous and done under the compulsion of necessity, and intellectual work was associated with leisure. The least pleasant and more burdensome practical activity was forced on slaves, serfs, and women. The social dishonor attributed by those in power to the slave class and to women was extended to their work. Dewey asks why such attitudes to social castes and emotional revulsions should be raised to dogma. A class-based genealogy alone, however, cannot explain why the body should be held in contempt in relation to spirit.

This is not just a historical question, because the negative effects of these dualisms are still with us. Morals, for instance, have been understood as the province of an inner, personal attitude and not as "overt activity having consequences" in those areas in which action is manifested, such as industry, politics, and the fine arts (LW 4:5). Theories of knowledge and of mind also suffer from the separation of intellect from action. Dewey argues that the historical grounds for elevating knowledge above making and doing is the quest for certainty to overcome the perils which daily beset us in a hazardous world. We can change the world directly through "the complicated arts of associated living," such as building shelters and weaving garments (LW 4:3). Alternatively, we can try to coerce unpredictable forces by ritual, sacrifice, and supplication. In earlier times the security that could be obtained by an individual or a community through overtly changing environing conditions was inadequate to overcome the dangers encountered. Recourse to religious or rational absolutes was therefore more comforting.

Certain traits of practical activity account for this preference. A brief comparison with the absolute standards of rational thinking can bring them out. Practical activity involves individualized and unique situations, which undergo change, while rational categories are universals, and rationality privileges invariant neccessity. In contrast to Platonic Forms, Aristotelian essences, and Cartesian clear and distinct ideas, overt action involves risk because eventual success is never entirely in our control. Since unforeseeable conditions can always thwart us, our intent alone cannot bring about a successful outcome, but we can unerringly assert the Kantian categorical imperative. If the perilousness of existence has tended to evoke a corresponding search for security, including intellectual stability, then one can understand why the absolute predictability of abstract principles comes to be more highly valued than the relative predictability of even the best understood practice. But this separation of theory from practice, of truth from the messy details of experience, of absolute good from particular, limited goods has had dire consequences.

A radical change is needed in our understanding of knowledge and value. When once values are connected with the problem of intelligent action, then we can investigate what must be done in order to make objects of value more secure in existence. Traditionally, philosophers obtained cognitive certification, whether through intuition or a process of reasoning, by seeking to identify an antecedently existing, immutable truth and goodness (LW 4:35). This understanding of knowledge as disclosure of a reality independent of the knowing process perpetuates the vain search for values subsistent in the properties of Being apart from human action.

All the ways that human individuals experience things, whether through love, desire, fear, or need, are real modes of experience, not reducible to cognitive judgments. But these emotional and practical realities remain fragmentary and inconsistent and subject to forces beyond our control until they are intellectually grasped. A new way of dealing with these experiences is needed, one which does not simply reduce them to cognitive objects. Dewey proposes examining the relations and interactions with one another of the widest range of experienced objects. This will yield a new kind of experienced object, no more or less real than unintellec-tualized experiences of objects, "but more significant, and less over-whelming and oppressive" (LW 4:175). The monopoly of more specialized forms of knowing can be broken by turning to the ways that welfare mothers, artists, students, daughters, and untold persons in everyday life manage to solve problems and thereby extract knowledge from their daily concerns.

Dewey advocates that philosophers cease trying to formulate general theories that seek to settle for all time the nature of truth, knowledge, and value.[10] Instead, we should find out "how authentic beliefs about exis-tence as they currently exist can operate fruitfully and efficaciously in con-nection with the practical problems that are urgent in actual life" (LW 4:36).

Experience Is *Reality*

Taking over James' characterization of experience as a double-barreled word, Dewey says that "like its congeners, life and history, [experience] includes *what* men do and suffer, *what* they strive for, love, believe and endure, and also *how* men act and are acted upon, the ways in which they do and suffer, desire and enjoy, see, believe, imagine—in short, processes of *experiencing*" (LW 1:18). Dewey spoke more accurately than he knew when he defined experiencing as what men do, feel, value, and imagine. Historically, men have had disproportionate power to inscribe their point of view on the world.

Given the exaggeration of gender differences in most organizations of society, it would be expected that women's experiences will differ in various ways from men's, and certainly women's access to dominant structures of power has been severely restricted in most societies at most periods of history. Dewey most likely did not realize that he was privileging a masculine perspective, since he did not do so in his political activities, but his gendered discourse nonetheless testifies to a male bias. However, since he was also alert to hidden forms of oppression, this bias does not vitiate what he says, but disappears once it is exposed. If anything, it provides unintended—and therefore even more forceful—evidence for his claim that our experiences influence our perspectives and value judgments.

What he said can easily be appropriated by feminists to good effect. By taking the integrated unity of what is experienced and the concretely embodied way of experiencing as the starting point of philosophic thought Dewey not only avoided the extremes of materialism and idealism, but he provided a means of legitimating women's special angles of vision and tendency to theorize on the basis of our experiences. The concrete specificity of Dewey's explanation of experience stands in stark contrast to the practice of philosophy as sterile argumentation and symbol manipulation. He says, for instance, that " 'experience' denotes the planted field, the sowed seeds, the reaped harvests, the changes of night and day, spring and autumn, wet and dry, heat and cold, that are observed, feared, longed for; it also denotes the one who plants and reaps, who works and rejoices, hopes, fears, plans, invokes magic or chemistry to aid him, who is downcast or triumphant" (LW 1:18). The "him" can be replaced by "her" without distortion, which is not true of most male-biased theoretical discourse.

Long before the current wave of poststructuralism, Dewey argued that "our analysis shows that the *ways* in which we believe and expect have a tremendous effect upon *what* we believe and expect" (LW 1:23). Following Hegel, and anticipating Foucault, he showed how our inherited beliefs and institutions continue to influence our perceptions, that is, how historicity is constitutive of our peculiarly human interactions with nature. "We learn, in short, that qualities which we attribute to objects ought to be imputed to our own ways of experiencing them, and that these in turn are due to the force of intercourse and custom." Moreover, he argues that "this discovery marks an emancipation; it purifies and remakes the objects of our direct or primary experience."

As far back in history as we have records of women's denunciation of their situation, we have evidence that women have recognized the emancipatory potential of the discovery of the effect of preconception on reality. When once it is realized that what we take to be straightforwardly matters of fact are actually active transformations of experience which include socially transmitted preconceptions, then we can dispute historically widespread claims that women's perceived inferiority is due to a fact of nature and is therefore inalterable. Even facts can be questioned.

Not only presuppositions, but social, political, economic, and psychological practices contribute to the facticity of facts. There is no way to strip away all subjective factors and just reductively identify the facts that remain. So-called subjective factors are constitutive of the objectivity of the facts. Therefore, it is not irrelevant to respond to a cited statistic about the different mathematical ability of boys and girls by asking for the underlying cultural expectations and political agenda which helped constitute the experimental procedure. Expectations, values, and beliefs are already part of any experimental situation. By drawing our attention to them feminists and pragmatists are not politicizing an otherwise neutral, objective field, but they are seeking to disclose the full complexity of the actual situation. It is pernicious to deny minority groups and women the means to develop the intellectual skills needed to function successfully in a highly technological society just because such denial does not leave the victims intact; the assumption of lesser ability contributes to bringing about as an actual result what was initially merely a preconception.[11]

But some feminist theorists presuppose that it is possible to expose the misogynist biases of explanations which perpetuate distorted views of reality and replace these with objective claims which transparently capture reality as it really is, apart from any presuppositions or value orientation. They think that anyone could just look and see that the feminist explanation is the one true one. According to William James as well as Dewey, this belief in a univocally true transcription of reality, which is the possession of any one group or theoretical stance, is itself one of the bases for many oppressive practices over the centuries.

That one has good intentions in pointing out what reality really is does not lessen the oppressive results of the belief. It is the belief itself that one has a privileged access to reality that does the harm. If I am simply right about reality, for instance, in some absolute way, and you oppose my claim with a different one, then it follows that you are necessarily wrong. This accounts for the confrontational basis of so many academic and wider social disputes. The stronger the belief in one's own integrity, the greater the confrontation.

That reality is always as much a function of one's angle of vision and lived experience as it is of what is available to be experienced has been dramatically enacted over the years in challenges to feminist theory from within. African American feminists charge white feminists with racism, lesbian feminists charge heterosexual feminists with homophobia, and third world feminists charge first world feminists with colonialism.[12] The early feminist agenda of speaking out on behalf of women has been challenged as distortive by those who want to speak in their own voice about their own experiences. This phenomenon could simply be interpreted as being that of an initially false theoretical position being challenged by the true one. The earlier theories were homophobic, sexist, and racist and the new ones replacing them are not. But this does not adequately describe the complexity of the dynamics. Earlier feminists conscientiously argued against oppression as they saw it. But their angle of vision was necessarily partial. They recognized some aspects of the situation, but not all. This does not show that their original position was false, but that it was finite, incomplete, and in principle revisable when new experiences and reflective interpretations became available. These were quickly supplied by women who felt that their experiences were not being accurately described.

In the sixties, through consciousness-raising sessions and critical reflections on personal experience, it became possible to recognize, name, and criticize the web of social, cultural, and political structures within which experiences took on the particular oppressive dimensions they did. The very homogeneity of the white, middle-class experiences being expressed generated a sense of sisterhood and conviction that their political analyses truly named and provided a remedy for the felt oppression. It soon became evident, however, that not everyone had the same experiences or shared the same values. It took different perspectives to recognize the hidden biases that had not been recognized. But these challenges were often put forth as themselves complete and the final word. Some lesbians, for instance, accused heterosexual feminists as not only perpetuating homophobia, but as also being fundamentally flawed in their way of life. They said that these misguided sisters could not be totally emancipated until they gave up their sexual orientation and became completely woman-identified.

The finite partiality of lesbian experiences allowed lesbians to recognize the one-sided nature of heterosexual experiences, but not of their own, just as the one-sided nature of the heterosexual experiences had blinded heterosexuals to their homophobia. If one looks at the complex dynamics of the sometimes confrontational dialogues over the years, it is obvious that the wrong position was not simply replaced by the right one, but that gradually each modified their initial stance as they assimilated different ways of naming the contested experiences. The quality of the experiences themselves changed as beliefs changed and beliefs changed in response to new experiences.

How, then, can we appeal to experience as a bulwark against the ideological distortions which we have absorbed merely by growing up as a member of a particular community? Dewey's philosophy is a major achievement precisely because it combines explanations of the perspectival character of our grasp of reality, which is active and transformative, with analyses of the ways in which we can legitimately distinguish merely subjective from warrantably objective claims about reality. Dewey denies that the unavoidably subjective element in our active dealings with the world makes it impossible to objectively determine genuine aspects of any given situation. He also denies that there is an infinite regress or infinite plurality of interpretations of experience, just as he denies that there is one, hegemonically definitive transcription of reality.

Dewey's accomplishment cannot be grasped unless it is realized that he rejects the privatization of experience that has come to be taken for granted. The recognition of the contributing influence of personal attitudes and their consequences, which was liberating in actual life, had pernicious results in philosophy (LW 1:24ff.). When philosophy took the subject matter of psychology to be the interior or subjective response to objective reality, then experience was reduced to the act of experiencing, and experience to the single aspect of perceiving (LW 1:11). Dewey asserted instead "the primacy and ultimacy" of the material of ordinary experience (LW 1:24). Experience is primary in uncontrolled form and ultimate as regulated, given significance through "the methods and results of reflective experience." In rejecting the subjectification of primary experience, Dewey provides arguments for acknowledging the reality of the material conditions, the objectivity, of women's experience.

Life Experiences

Pragmatist philosophy begins with life experiences, which consist of both doings and undergoings (LW 10:9, 50–53). Experience is not just naively undergone, it is overlaid and saturated not only with previous philosophical interpretations, but also with past beliefs, values, and classifications. Since the origins and validity of these earlier interpretations are for the most part lost, they differ little from prejudices. But whether they are taken as the incorporated results of past reflection or as prejudices, they are welded onto genuinely firsthand experiences and can be a source of enlightenment when reflected upon. They distort present experience just to the extent that they are not detected. "Clarification and emancipation follow when they are detected and cast out; and one great object of philosophy is to accomplish this task" (LW 1:40).

Dewey moves back and forth between labeling earlier interpretations of experience, which continue to influence our understanding of present events, as sources of enrichment or causes of obfuscation. Consequently, it sometimes seems that the reflective effort to identify them should properly issue in deliberate recovery, and then again, in rejection and emancipation. This ambiguity is deliberate because we ought to continually and critically reflect on these inheritances. Some will be found to be enhancements of present experience and others to be distortive and counterproductive. Which is which cannot simply be decided hegemonically by a privileged elite or tradition, nor can it be determined beforehand by purely rational analysis. Instead, we should find out "what wearing them does to us" (LW 1:40).

Dewey calls the discriminative judgment by which we decide to continue or reject aspects of our culture the cultivation of a naïveté of eye, ear, and thought. But this is not a return to an original innocence, rather it is a genuine grasp of experience acquired through a discipline of severe thought. In fact, traditional philosophy has failed the ordinary person by denigrating just such a concern with everyday experiences. The authoritarian arrogance of much philosophizing has given the impression that only those few who have access to the classical thinkers of the past are qualified to judge what is important and what not. The denigration of ordinary experience and praise of pure thought or rational analysis for its own sake is one of the greatest failings of traditional philosophy precisely because it denies to the nonspecialist the authority of their own experience. By almost exclusively focusing on classical texts or papers given at professional meetings or articles published in professional journals, philosophers "have denied that common experience is capable of developing from within itself methods which will secure direction for itself and will create inherent standards of judgment and value" (LW 1:41). An avowed pragmatist goal, therefore, is to create and promote respect for concrete human experience and its potentialities.[13]

But "Whose experience?" feminists want to know. Not only have classical texts and elite professional discourse characterized traditional philosophizing, but also male reflections and experiences have been exclusively privileged. Dewey does explicitly raise the issue of "Whose experience?" as a criticism, but only in order to deny its relevance (LW 1:178ff.). His intention in doing so is a good one, namely to undercut the subjectivity traditionally ascribed to experience as a basis for excluding it from the abstractly rational deliberations of philosophers. However, good intentions do not override the harm done by not taking the objection more seriously. Unlike Dewey, I cannot ignore the source of experienced claims because, from my point of view as a member of a marginalized group, the male-centered angle of vision of supposedly generalized experiential claims is both obvious and oppressive. I grant the validity of Dewey's rejection of the subjectification of experience, since women's experiential perspectives have consistently been dismissed by philosophers as being merely subjective. But defenses of the objective character of experience can be made without denying that gender, as well as race, class, sexual orientation, and many other distinctions contribute to its objectivity, and therefore it is not only appropriate but imperative to question whose experience is being used as a paradigm for explication.

My objection, therefore, is not meant to undercut Dewey's explanation that experience is dependent on the objectively physical and social structures of natural events. "It has its own objective and definitive traits," which are describable without reference to a self, if by self is meant the isolated individual in the privacy of consciousness (LW 1:179). Moreover, selves are specifiable, definable events within experience and not occurrences outside, underneath, or beside experience, as they are traditionally held to be in the pernicious dualisms of spirit and matter, mind and body.

Dewey also argues that for some purposes and consequences, it is imperative to recognize and acknowledge personal ownership. The self can be objectified, just as other objects like trees and planets are discriminated as aspects of experience. "To say in a significant way, 'I think, believe, desire,'. . . is to accept and affirm a responsibility and to put forth a claim" (LW 1:179–80). It signifies the self as an organizing center, who accepts future benefits and liabilities as the consequences of one's deliberate actions, rather than crediting them to nature, family, church, or state.

"Existentially speaking, a human individual is distinctive opacity of bias and preference conjoined with plasticity and permeability of needs and likings. One trait tends to isolation, discreetness; the other trait to connection, continuity. This ambivalent character is rooted in nature" (LW 1:186). For certain purposes we can distinguish what pertains more to the subject and what more to the object. Dualisms are objectionable when they convert dynamic principles of formulation and interpretation into antithetical absolutes. "Sociability, communication are just as immediate traits of the concrete individual as is the privacy of the closet of consciousness" (LW 1:187).

In chapter 3 of *Experience and Nature* Dewey explains that one of the most striking features of human experience is direct enjoyment, as found in feasting, ornamentation, dance, and festivities of all kinds. Luxuries and embellishments transform the everyday even at the subsistence level, so that those living in hovels, for instance, nonetheless erect and decorate temples of worship and adorn their bodies, even if clothing is scarce. Useful labors are transformed by ritual and ceremony. Dewey gives the following example: "Men make a game of their fishing and hunting, and turn to the periodic and disciplinary labor of agriculture only when inferiors, women and slaves, cannot be had to do the work" (LW 1:69). This example passes without comment or criticism. Dewey is too intent on demonstrating the connection of the consummatory phase of the direct appreciative enjoyment of things with instrumental, laborious productivity.

Not until the end of the chapter does he remind us that "to point out something as a fact is not the same thing as to commend or eulogize the fact" (LW 1:97). He criticizes the class structure which permitted a privileged elite to engage in pure intellectual activity without the need of making a living. The ultimate contradiction for the philosophical tradition is that it praised thought as universal and necessary and the culminating good of nature, but did not bother to condemn the restriction of its exercise to a small and exclusive class, and therefore did nothing to extend it to those not privileged by birth, economic, or civil status.

Obviously, why women were taken to be inferiors is not an issue which interests Dewey to the extent that class does, nor does he seem aware of the male-centered view uncritically expressed. He does continually criticize and seek to overturn the class-based nature of traditional philosophizing, pointing out its dependency on slave labor, but he does not similarly reject its gender bias. His arguments for the objectivity of experience can be supported without agreeing that the question of whose experience it is should not be raised. We can only realize the full emancipatory potential of the analysis of experience by bringing in those whose experience has been excluded in the past.

Feeling as a Quality of Life Forms

Pragmatist explanations of the relation between self and world, experience and knowledge, theory and praxis deny the strict separation of emotions and intellect that feminists frequently criticize as a masculinist distortion pervasive in the Western tradition of philosophy.[14] In Dewey's transactive model of experience feelings and intellect are continuous, although distinguishable for certain purposes. Needs, efforts to satisfy needs, and satisfactions distinguish living from nonliving things (LW 1:194). When the activity of need-demand satisfaction acquires certain additional abilities to secure the interactive support of needs from the environment, the subsequent organization is psychophysical. The perpetuation of patterned activities as an aspect of organizing capacities serves as the basis of sensitivity. Selective bias in interactions with environing conditions serves to perpetuate both the organism and the whole of which it is a part. Sensitivity is thus always discriminative. On a more complex level of organization, biases become interests and satisfaction of needs are reflectively determined to be values, rather than simply mere satiation.

Dewey's use of the term 'organism,' instead of person or body, is deliberate. He speaks of the "organism in its entirety" (LW 10:64) and "the whole of the live creature" (LW 10:87). This usage emphasizes the post-Darwinian awareness of the human continuity with other animals and recognizes that we are not embodied minds but interactive organisms with many ways of taking in the world and responding to it.[15] The mind/body split is an inherited dualistic classification, which either distinguishes the body and mind so rigidly that it becomes impossible to figure out how they are related, or pits each against the other in an adversarial relationship. Both feminists and pragmatists have pointed out at great length the oppressive consequences of this split. It is difficult to retain one side of the dualism, the body, without its ghostly double distorting what is meant by body, embodiedness, or lived body. By contrast, we experience organic transactions within situations and are aware that this process does not leave either pole of the transaction unchanged.

Sensitivity and interests are realized as feelings, which can be sharp and intense or vague and diffuse, such as in massive uneasiness or comfortableness. "Activities are differentiated into the preparatory, or anticipatory, and the fulfilling or consummatory" (LW 1:197). Anticipation of food or sex or danger is suffused with the tone of the consummated activity. This capacity to sensitively anticipate an outcome is actualized in feeling. Feelings, therefore, are not simply private, internal events, but a valuable "susceptibility to the useful and harmful in surroundings," a premonition of eventual lived consequences.

When the consummated satisfactions or disappointments accrue, they reinforce the anticipatory activities, including feelings. The experience is no longer haphazard, but becomes an integrated accumulation. "Comfort or discomfort, fatigue or exhilaration, implicitly sum up a history, and thereby unwittingly provide a means whereby (when other conditions become present) the past can be unravelled and made explicit" (LW 1:197). Although feelings themselves are relatively undifferentiated, they have the capacity to take on innumerable distinctions. As they are refined they can vary more and more in quality, intensity, and duration.

Feelings are thus distinctively related to environing conditions and interactive outcomes. They *have* these connections, but not necessarily mentally, as an explicit grasp of meaning. When feelings are meaningful as well as experienced, then mind has emerged. In an intricate but succinct summing up, Dewey adroitly manages to avoid dualistic explanations while retaining the complexity of human organisms. "As life is a character of events in a peculiar condition of organization, and 'feeling' is a quality of life-forms marked by complexly mobile and discriminating responses, so 'mind' is an added property assumed by a feeling creature, when it reaches that organized interaction with other living creatures which is language, communication" (LW 1:198). Feelings become suffused with meaning as they serve to objectively discriminate external things and relate past and future episodes. They recall and foretell. As language develops, pains, pleasures, colors, and odors acquire the capacity to objectify the immediate traits of things. Qualities do not essentially reside in organisms or in things but emerge in interactions with each other. But for purposes of control they may be treated as if located in one or the other. Psychologists, for instance, have traditionally treated women hysterics for their symptoms, thus substantializing the subjective pole and privatizing it, rather than taking the hysteric behavior as a quality of their interactions with their human and material surroundings. The latter would make it possible to objectively identify the hysteria as a process whose roots, and therefore cure, is deeply entangled in an objectively identifiable situation.

Sensory qualities do not identify themselves. They exist as the indispensable means of any noetic function, but must be transformed through a system of signs. When a particular feeling of listlessness is identified as a response to repeated beatings, then attention is directed to a particular, objective interaction and it becomes possible to change the conditions which are bringing it about. Qualities just merge into the general situation until, through communication, as shared meanings to social consequences, they acquire objective distinctiveness (LW 1:199). When the same listlessness is interpreted by society as inappropriate behavior for a wife, and the woman internalizes this explanation, then she is likely to cooperate in therapies designed to change her behavior rather than her surroundings, including the actions of the aggressor.

Feelings inhere neither in matter nor mind, but are qualitative aspects of a particular field of interacting events. A battered woman feeling badly enough to seek help can be aided or obstructed in the identification of the objective interactions defining her situation, depending on the meanings projected onto the events by others. It cannot be assumed that the woman already has an explicit understanding of the full reality of her situation, which is why she can be caught in a series of inappropriate responses. Neither can it be assumed that neutral observers, such as social work professionals or law enforcement officials, have a privileged access to the truth of her situation. Interactive communication is required for a progressively better understanding of the situation. But the battered woman has one advantage no one else has. She knows how she feels and what she observes, and these can be articulated ever more accurately as meaningful connections begin to be appropriately named.

The View from the Fringe

For all his sensitivity to different angles of vision, Dewey does not finally recognize how much his philosophic perspective derives its strength from the fact that it is a view from a privileged center. He comes so close to the realization, and even provides the philosophic resources for doing so, that the fact that he does not gives added weight to his own claim that there is something authoritative about experience that cannot be had any other way. He deliberately and consciously subverts the hegemony of privileged centers, and the means by which he does so can still be appropriated to good effect. Nonetheless, he, himself, is not a member of any group whose experience has been systematically distorted and therefore has not developed a sensitivity to some specific limitations of his own experiential understanding. Pragmatist feminists can profitably criticize, incorporate, and develop Deweyan pragmatism further, just as socialist feminists have moved on from Marxism, but first it is important to see just what is missing.

In *Experience and Nature* Dewey says that "it is natural to men to take that which is of chief value to them at the time as *the* real" (LW 1:31). Dewey takes "men" as a generic term for "human." The intention in doing so is benign, but the consequences are not. Compare Dewey's statement with a superficially similar one from Simone de Beauvoir, where by "men," she means males as distinguished from females: "Representation of the world, like the world itself, is the work of men; they describe it from their own point of view, which they confuse with absolute truth."[16] Oddly enough, Beauvoir and Dewey are making substantially the same point, namely, that what we take to be objectively given reality is actually filtered through our presuppositions and values. Given a different perspective we would literally be experiencing a different reality. They are also making the point that we are usually blind to this intersubjective character of the constitution of reality and that its realization is the first step to liberating ourselves from the pernicious effects that follow from not doing so.

The consequences of not recognizing his own gender bias is apparent in Dewey's subsequent remark that "in ordinary experience this fact does no particular harm." According to the context of his discussion, equating reality with what we value does no harm in everyday experience because it is easily compensated for by simply turning to other practical experiences exhibiting other interests. The harm comes from reflective disciplines like philosophy, which are deliberately removed from everyday experience and, therefore, encounter no corrective influence from counterindicating events. This indictment of modern philosophy for substituting categorial analysis for reflections on concrete experience is well taken, but not the claim about the self-corrective nature of ordinary experience. At the very least, some qualifications about how it is corrective have to be introduced.

Elizabeth Cady Stanton, in a speech before the New York legislature in 1860, pointed out precisely what harm is caused in everyday life by men's conflating what they value with what is real. She said that "man, the sculptor, has carved out his ideal. . . . He has made a woman that from his low stand-point looks fair and beautiful, a being without rights, or hopes, or fears but in him—neither noble, virtuous, nor independent. . . . We have bowed down and worshiped in woman, beauty, grace, the exquisite proportions, . . . her delicacy, refinement, and silent helplessness—all well when she is viewed simply as an object of sight"[17] She contrasts this type of womanhood carved by man, with "our type of womanhood," namely, "the women who are called masculine, who are brave, courageous, self-reliant and independent, . . . they who have taken their gauge of womanhood from their own native strength and dignity— they who have learned for themselves the will of God concerning them." Stanton is not just pointing out women's disadvantages relative to men in nineteenth-century America. She also identifies its source in the masculinist angle of vision and suggests how this perspective can be contested when she refers to those "who have learned for themselves." The reasons she gives for this disparity can still be usefully applied in our own century.

Stanton points to the *deliberate* maiming of women to make them appear lesser—to themselves as well as to men. Such distortion of women's own experience is motivated by the drive to gain, consolidate, or extend power. This strategy works best when some noble motivation is explicitly claimed. For one thing, this renders plausible the accusation that those pointing out the implicit motivation hidden under the explicit one are inventing ill will where none exists. There are many ways to explain situations, depending on the aim in doing so. The same situation can be described neutrally, that is, as a slice of life, as if causes were too diffuse to identify. The causes can also be described in moral or psychoanalytic terms, so that the larger structural or institutional web in which they are embedded is ignored. For instance, it is reported that a husband shoots his wife because he has been drinking or is jealous, as though this were an isolated incident, totally explainable in terms of the man's moral shortcomings or pathology.

The behavior can instead be related to many others very similar to it in order to bring out the full dimensions of the societal structures which contribute to such behavior patterns. The fact that assaults against women by men is much greater than women against men and that less violence against women is perpetrated by strangers than by intimates, is often not mentioned as relevant to the incident. Many newspapers and magazines follow this policy of isolationist, know-nothing reportage. This false neutrality is defended as keeping editorializing off the news pages. But it obscures relevant causal factors, ignores aspects of the situation which have to be understood in order to bring about effective changes, and neutralizes critics by making their obviously politicized rhetoric appear by contrast to seem shrill, self-serving and ideological.

Those on the sidelines, who do not have an immediate stake in the particular incident being reported, are often attracted to calm recitals of facts rather than to seemingly shrill rebuttals by feminists who point out connections that are being ignored or distorted. This preference reinforces our sense of ourselves as rational beings, calmly considering the facts of the case. Since every single significant improvement in women's situation—from property rights, access to education, divorce, and birth control, to enfranchisement—has been controversial, bitterly contested, and won only after many years of struggle, we can begin to perceive one source of the otherwise puzzling phenomenon of women actively opposing their own betterment. Isolated incidents of men pathologically or evilly assaulting individual women, for instance, do not sum themselves up into an indictment of marriage as an institution or of patterns of behavior and expectations in a particular society. When more immediate and acceptable explanations are available, more far-ranging and radical ones appear less plausible.

Geneva Overholser's adoption of a feminist perspective in *The Des Moines Register*, of which she is editor, illustrates how the rejection of a falsely neutral perspective can provide not only a fuller understanding of events, rather than a lesser or distortive account, but also one which is perceived as both plausible and fair. Her newspaper won a Pulitzer Prize in 1991 for a graphic story on rape. In reporting the story *Newsweek* credited Overholser with fashioning "what may be the most feminist daily in America," by which it meant one which proves "that so-called women's issues can be important to every reader."[18] Acknowledging that the *Register* formerly reflected the interests of its mostly male editors, *Newsweek* said that "Overholser has not so much altered the paper as added to it. Topics such as day care, sexual harassment and the safety of contraceptives receive prominent, thoughtful coverage. Reporters and editors have come to view routine stories through new prisms: last week a homicide account noted that five other Des Moines women had died in recent domestic assaults."

Philosophical analyses of the objectivity of experience that ignore the central role of power among the complex motivations which structure our perceptions of the world are themselves part of the problem of discrimination against women which feminists address. In other words, self-proclaimed neutral analyses, whether put forward by philosophical realists or by feminists, are actually biased in a way that is eventually harmful to women and other oppressed groups. The radical political agendas of feminists are better served by radical analyses of the relation of self and world.

Conclusion

Dewey stands out, even within the pragmatist tradition, for attacking the supposed neutrality of our perceptions of reality. He analyzes the complex ways our perceptions are enmeshed in past beliefs, current anticipations, and values. I have interrogated his analyses of how our experiences interactively construct reality from the point of view of a feminist critique of the structures of women's oppression. This interrogation is consistent with Dewey's contention that we are interested in purposely managing the traits of experience so that we can avoid being victimized by inherited structures and develop ones more conducive to growth. Reflection is not a luxury reserved to a leisure class, but "exists to guide choice and effort" (LW 1:67). Only through thoughtful observation and experiment can the frail and transient goods we experience be substantiated, secured, and extended. But since observations are always from a particular perspective and the good outcomes desired are relative to concretely experienced needs, it follows that feminist angles of vision will extend Dewey's insights in new and unexpected ways.[19]

Dewey empowers individuals to trust their own experiences as a litmus test of theoretical explanations. Philosophical theories have long served to repress and distort women's experiences because, like Plato's Forms, they have provided Procrustean beds on which women had to fit at the pain of seeming irrational. Dewey's emancipatory move reverses this priority by making theory answer to practice. This does not mean just repeating what we know or do already, but can include strikingly different interpretations and actions and even the unmasking of our own misconceptions. The relevant criterion is that they clarify rather than distort our lived-through experiences: "A first-rate test of the value of any philosophy which is offered us: Does it end in conclusions which, when they are referred back to ordinary life-experiences and their predicaments, render them more significant, more luminous to us, and make our dealings with them more fruitful? Or does it terminate in rendering the things of ordinary experience more opaque than they were before, and in depriving them of having in 'reality' even the significance they had previously seemed to have?" (LW 1:18).

Notes

1.   Caroline Whitbeck, "A Different Reality: Feminist Ontology," in *Women, Knowledge and Reality: Explorations in Feminist Philosophy,* ed. A. Garry and M. Pearsall (Boston: Unwin Hyman, 1989), p. 69, n.1

2.   Denise Riley, *"Am I that Name?" Feminism and the Category of 'Women' in History* (Minneapolis: University of Minnesota Press, 1988).

3.   Ibid., p. 13. A recent example can be found in Sheila Ruth, *Issues in Feminism: An Introduction of Women's Studies,* 2d ed. (Mountain View, Calif.: Mayfield Publishing Co., 1990): "How, generations of women have asked, can one integrate claims to full equality with a sense of women's special identity?" (p. 413).

4.   Ibid., p. 99.

5.   Ibid., p. 114.

6.   Ibid., p. 112.

7.   Ibid., p. 113.

8.   A brief literature survey of feninist critiques of dualism is included in Caroline Whitbeck's "A Different Reality: Feminist Ontology" p. 69, n.1.

9.   Susan Sherwin, "Philosophical Methodology and Feminist Methodology: Are They Compatible?," in *Women, Knowledge, and Reality,* p. 32.

10.   See my "Like Bridges without Piers: Beyond the Foundationalist Metaphor," in *Antifoundationalism, Old and New,* ed. T. Rockmore and B. J. Singer (Philadelphia: Temple University Press, 1992), pp. 143–64.

11.   For the pernicious effects of the construction of racial and gender differentiation and a call for a reconstruction of difference, see Paula Rothenberg, "The Construction, Deconstruction, and Reconstruction of Difference," *Hypatia* 5, 1 (Spring 1990), pp. 42–57.

12.   See Bell Hooks, *Ain't I a Woman: Black Women and Feminism* (Boston: South End Press, 1981) and Patricia Hill Collins, *Black Feminist Thought* (Hammersmith, London: Harper Collins Academic Press, 1990); Jill Johnston, *Lesbian Nation: The Feminist Solution* (New York: Simon and Schuster, 1974) and Nancy Myron and Charlotte Bunch, eds., *Lesbianism and the Women's Movement* (Baltimore, Md.: Diana Press, 1975); Maria Lugones and Elizabeth V. Spelman, "Have We Got a Theory For You! Feminist Theory, Cultural Imperialism, and the Demand for 'The Woman's Voice,'" in *Women and Values: Readings in Recent Feminist Philosophy,* ed. Marilyn Pearsall (Belmont, Calif.: Wadsworth, 1986), pp. 19–32.

13. For an analysis of pragmatist appeals to concrete experience, see my *William James's Radical Reconstruction of Philosophy* (Albany: State University of New York Press, 1990), pp. 75–116, 183–90, 263–68, 299–306, 317–24, and 356–60.

14. See Genevieve Lloyd, *The Man of Reason: 'Male' and 'Female' in Western Philosophy* (Minneapolis: University of Minnesota Press, 1984); Susan Bordo, *The Flight to Objectivity* (Albany: State University of New York Press, 1987); Robin Schott, *Cognition and Eros: A Critique of the Kantian Paradigm* (Boston: Beacon Press, 1988); and Karen J. Warren, "Male-Gender Bias and Western Conceptions of Reasons and Rationality," *APA Newsletters* 88, 2 (March 1989) pp. 48–58.

15. Linda Holler also argues for an embodied rationality in "Thinking with the Weight of the Earth: Feminist Contributions to an Epistemology of Concreteness," *Hypatia* 5, 1 (Spring 1990), pp. 1–23.

16. Simone de Beauvoir, *The Second Sex* (New York: Vintage Books, 1974), p. 161.

17. Ruth, *Issues in Feminism: An Introduction to Women's Studies*, pp. 469–70. For contemporary accounts of how women are still being molded to men's ideals see Rita Freedman, *Beauty Bound* (Lexington, Mass.: D.C. Heath and Co., 1986) and Jenijoy LaBelle, *Herself Beheld: The Literature of the Looking Glass* (Ithaca, N.Y.: Cornell University Press, 1989).

18. *Newsweek*, April 22, 1991, p. 69.

19. See Lisa Heldke, "John Dewey and Evelyn Fox Keller: A Shared Epistemological Tradition," *Hypatia* 2, 3 (Fall 1987), pp. 129–40; Lisa Heldke, "Recipes for Theory Making," *Hypatia* 3, 2 (Summer 1988), pp. 15–29; my "Where Are All the Pragmatist Feminists?," *Hypatia* 6, 2 (July 1991), pp. 1–20; my "The Missing Perspective: Feminist Pragmatism," pp. 405–16; and Eugenie Gatens-Robinson, "Dewey and the Feminist Successor Science Project," *Transactions of the Charles S. Peirce Society* 27, 4 (Fall 1991), pp. 417–33.

8

Heteronomous Freedom

RAYMOND D. BOISVERT

*The inward space where the self is sheltered against the world must
not be mistaken for the heart and mind, both of which exist and
function only in interrelationship with the world.*
—*Hannah Arendt*

Introduction

A recent history of the United States features a picture of freed blacks after
the Civil War together with the following caption from a Confederate
general: "[They] had nothing but freedom."[1] His meaning, juxtaposed with
the picture and narrative, is obvious. The legal category of "slave" had
been removed. But the only immediate benefit was an abstract sense of
no longer having that legal status. With regard to everyday life, opportunity
for growth, education, and augmentation of wealth, the prospects were
not at all hopeful.

In Deweyan terminology, the ex-slaves possessed "merely legal" as
opposed to "actual" liberty; or, putting the matter in a slightly different
way, "purely formal" rather than "effective" liberty (LW 11:27, 34). The
contrast between "merely legal" and "effective" freedom identifies the plot
of the story I wish to narrate in this chapter. Democratic cultures prize
freedom as, if not the main, then certainly one in the small cluster of most
highly valued goods. In examining contemporary culture from the
perspective of pragmatist reconstruction, freedom remains as central a
topic as it was in the nineteenth century.

What an examination of the histories of philosophy and of cultures
makes clear, however, is that the meaning of important leading ideas is
not given once and for all. Their meaning changes with time and shifts

with the cultural contexts within which they are framed. The sense of freedom expressed in Thucydides' "Funeral Oration" is not the same as that articulated by Epictetus. Augustine and Aquinas, Hegel and Mill have all made important yet diverse, if not incompatible, contributions to our understanding of this important ideal. The lesson of historical change is a challenge for each new generation of philosophers. An ideal is a living thing which must not only be cared for, but pruned and transplanted.

Dewey's distinction between "real" and "purely formal" liberty can best be interpreted by tracing the philosophical story of several interconnected notions: personhood, freedom, and autonomy. My aim is to indicate that one important reconstruction involves articulating a view of freedom that is allied with heteronomy, not with autonomy. In order to streamline the narrative which culminates in the harmonizing of freedom and heteronomy I will begin by providing a somewhat simplified division of philosophers into two families. Following Aristotle's example in criticizing the "friends of Forms," I call them "the friends of *Mathema*" and the "friends of *Bios.*"

The friends of *Mathema* tend to privilege mathematics as somehow getting at the kernel of reality. They are attracted by fixed forms, computational certainties, and the unambiguous clarities associated with numbers. One branch of this family, while preserving the assumption that rationality must approximate the mathematical paradigm, does not believe that it is possible to attain this degree of precision. This branch then turns to raw feeling, subjectivity, intuition, and other forms of nonrationality. The safest generalization about all branches of this family is that they are "discrete." They prize discrete, individualized, clearly separated elements. Purity is an important family ideal. Messy entanglements are its greatest scandal. The friends of *Mathema* are influential, prominent, and diverse. My own listing of members would include such otherwise disparate thinkers as Pythagoras, Descartes, Parmenides, Augustine, Kant, Rousseau, Kierkegaard, Sartre, and Quine.

The friends of *Bios* tend instead to root themselves in the biological realm and utilize organic metaphors.[2] They see change and interdependence as basic to any ontology of existence. These family members may be described as "close-knit." They prize relationships, connections, and continuities. Abstract simplifications or decontextualizations are unpardonable offenses. The whole period of modernity, dominated as it was by the friends of *Mathema*, provided unsuitable breeding conditions for the friends of *Bios*. Perhaps the most prominent member of this group, Aristotle, was premodern. Most of its other members came to the fore as modernity began to wane: Bergson, Ortega y Gasset, Whitehead, Dewey, and more recently, Marjorie Grene and Mary Midgley.

The two lineages are well represented in the ongoing conversation regarding cultural criticism. For those who prize *Mathema*, the notions of person and freedom crystallize around the concept of autonomy. "Autonomy" in this tradition, is a cluster word, combining the self-regulating will of Kant with that ability for self-formation and self-description that characterize what it means to be a person. One of the most prominent and sensitive defenders of autonomy, Gerald Dworkin, recognizes that the term is used in an "exceedingly broad fashion." Some of its senses include "self-rule or sovereignty," "freedom of the will," "dignity, integrity, individuality, independence, responsibility, and self-knowledge." One commonality to which this diverse list points is that of an individual who is not a puppet pulled to and fro by external strings. Rather, the individual is an agent capable of making choices affecting his or her life. This capacity for self-generated choice is linked to dignity, and brings responsibility in its wake.

The different renderings of autonomy do not prevent it, according to Dworkin, from remaining an important ideal: "About the only features held constant from one author to another are that autonomy is a feature of persons and that it is a desirable quality to have."[3] Bruce Ackerman goes even further, asserting of autonomy: "It is, in short, not necessary for autonomy to be the only good thing; it suffices for it to be the best thing there is."[4]

It may seem strange to suggest that an important element in the reconstruction of culture for the twenty-first century is the marginalization of such a seemingly beneficent characteristic as autonomy. Yet that is precisely what I wish to do. Within the postmodern world, more and more populated by the friends of *Bios*, the notions of integrity, responsibility, individuality, dignity, and freedom are altered in a way that rehabilitates heteronomy. Autonomy, on this view, should go the way of epistemology, a growth once so robust that it was almost equated with the whole garden of philosophy itself, but now a more humble plant among many others.

What I am suggesting is not new. Encomiums to autonomy such as those uttered by Dworkin and Ackerman have been challenged by those whose sympathies are more with *Bios*. Seyla Benhabib is a good example. The examination of women's oppression, she claims, must uncover "those symbols, myths and fantasies" that keep both sexes in the grip of unquestioned gender roles: "Perhaps one of the most fundamental of these myths and symbols has been the ideal of autonomy conceived in the image of a disembedded and disembodied male ego."[5] Echoing a similar sentiment, Annette Baier has attacked autonomy while articulating a sympathetic appraisal of Hume. He lived, she says, at a time when Rousseau was making autonomy an obsession with moral and social philosophers. Nonetheless, his own opposition to "contractarian doctrines of social obligation," his recognition of "interconnection" and "mutual vulnerability and enrichment, . . . make autonomy not even an ideal, for Hume."⁶

Significantly, as we think in terms of the twenty-first century, these critics of autonomy are female. One great failing of both lineages I am examining has been their treatment of women. Both clans have been nearly uniform in depicting women as deficient, as not manifesting the fullness (determined by degree of maleness), of humanity. Nonetheless, I wish to indicate the manner in which the friends of *Bios* offer intellectual affiliations which provide a more welcoming environment in which the new flora planted by women philosophers can best thrive.

Charlene Seigfried has already argued that the pragmatist cousins in this family, although still widely neglected by feminist philosophers, have "much to offer feminist theory".⁷ Pragmatism's emphasis on the biological, the concrete, the contextual, its tolerance of ambiguities, its embrace of pluralism, mean that "on a scale of traits, assumptions and positions that range from the stereotypically masculine to feminine, pragmatism appears far more feminine than masculine."⁸ Dewey himself, true to his anti-totalizing attitude, predicted in 1918 that women's experience would contribute a new dimension to philosophy, one which, understandably, would be different "in viewpoint or tenor as that composed from the standpoint of the different masculine experience of things" (MW 11:45).

What I am suggesting, following Seigfried's lead, is that certain dimensions of Deweyan pragmatism (or "empirical naturalism")⁹ make of its adherents a sympathetic *salon* in which the until-now marginalized voice will receive a sympathetic hearing. In its general outline, empirical naturalism begins and ends with the context of human action. That action, in turn, is understood as continuous with the natural environment. Experience, especially ordinary, everyday human experience, is regarded as the source for and the final arbiter of philosophical positions. One typical strategy of those who celebrate *Mathema*, that of seeking out a "really real" behind the world of lived experience, is rejected by Dewey. Such a strategy leads inexorably to a problematizing of the affections, accomplishments, and activities of ordinary human life.

The best short slogan for characterizing the method of empirical naturalism would be "start with the here and now." Negatively, empirical naturalism suggests the injunction: avoid fictive constructions. The need to stand outside ordinary experience and project ideal conditions or theoretical entities may be crucial to success in geometry and science. Philosophy, though, is neither geometry nor science, and following their procedure would be a mistake. The aim of philosophy is a wisdom by which to guide human lives. Because of this, it must be concrete. It cannot eliminate what might be inconvenient for mathematical exactitude. The concretely experienced world with all its complexity and messiness is its province. It must, as James recognized, be radically empiricist, that is to say, accept experience in its comprehensiveness.

Modern philosophy, with one eye on the mathematically formulated sciences, set about projecting what we should now recognize as fictions of various sorts. These became foundations for erecting philosophical systems: universal doubt, original situations, mind/body dualism, windowless monads. Empirical naturalism strenuously makes the attempt to avoid make-believes of all kinds.

The Masturbatory Self

Benhabib has identified the two make-believes that inform the support for autonomy: the assumptions of (a) a disembedded and (b) a disembodied self.[10] It is, of course, possible to consider an individual separately from the community to which he or she belongs. It is possible, imaginatively, to separate someone from the affiliations that come with birth to particular people in a particular place and time, from the specific language and from the particular tradition of that community. It is also possible to consider humans as essentially minds whose association with their bodies is accidental. Imaginative dislocations, however, must not be confused with concrete, recurring associations.

To highlight the manner in which the fabrications of a disembedded and disembodied self affect the interrelated subjects of personhood, freedom, and autonomy, I will discuss two influential friends of *Mathema*. The first is Rousseau, the second is Kant. Rousseau gave the West an important version of that modern myth, "the state of nature," which helped sustain the ideal of autonomous selves. Kant provided the first philosophical corpus in which "autonomy" had an explicitly central place. These men did not view individual/community disembeddedness and mind/matter disembodiedness as projective fictions. Instead, they assumed them as foundational for their analyses. The here and now of concrete, lived experience receded as the appropriate place from which to initiate philosophical reflection. They preferred a clearer, simpler, (seemingly) more solid basis on which to erect their philosophies. Autonomy as an ideal grew easily and well in this land of make-believe. Instead of a flesh-and-blood human being (child, spouse, friend, parent), philosophers could now speak of the autonomous agent. This agent, in turn, would seek emancipation from bodily and societal constraints, replacing these with self-sufficiency, self-legislation, and self-description.

ROUSSEAU

The Discourse on Inequality reveals a Rousseau who is willing to follow through in a thorough manner the implications of disembeddedness. The fictive projection associated with Rousseau was the existence of a completed self, somehow endowed with freedom, reason, and individuality outside of social connections. Rousseau's state of nature story imagines an early time in man's development (masculine used advisedly) when he was happier because less dependent. In this posited world humans existed as fully self-enclosed monads. Even nature herself did little to incline men toward social bonds.

> But whatever these origins [of language] may be, we see at least from the small pains which nature has taken to unite man through mutual needs or to facilitate the use of speech how little she has prepared their sociability and how little she has contributed to what they have done to establish bonds among themselves.[11]

Rousseau here reads back as original givens what are more likely subsequent products of a particular sort of human development: strong ego boundaries, asocial selves. Once these are accepted as givens, a particular understanding of freedom readily follows. Rousseau first asserts that freedom is one of the "gifts of nature, and then characterizes it as a form of "indifference towards every other object" such that even the *ataraxia* of the Stoics pales by comparison.[12]

Rousseau's model self is autonomous in the sense of being a detached entity impervious to the connections, solicitations, and constraints of the world around him. Freedom then becomes what might be called "cointoss indifference." Choices need not be linked to deliberation/reflection which takes into account contextual conditions. These might include needs, circumstances, concern for others, appraisal of consequences. We are free, rather, to the degree that we can exercise our free choice independently of constraint by external factors.

"Choice" is a perfectly good word whose etymology links it with perception, testing, trying, discerning. It has come, however, to signify something almost wholly internal. Rousseau's version of the Augustinian *liberum arbitrium* as an autonomous, inner source of decision, provides the context within which the term "choice" is now understood. An alternative connotation associating "choice" with selection for good reasons, or selection as dependent on contextual conditions, is all but forgotten. In its place, Rousseau stresses indifference to surroundings. Connection to others, cultural traditions, family relations, even commitment to a life partner cannot on this view but be seen as impediments to the indifference that defines freedom. As he admits explicitly, Rousseau is content to out-Stoic even the Stoics.

Those too weak to rise above dependence are compared by Rousseau to once robust, wild animals who have degenerated as a result of domestication:

> The same is true even of man himself; in becoming sociable and a slave, he grows feeble, timid, servile; and his soft and effeminate way of life completes the enervation both of his strength and his courage.[13]

Not surprisingly, one strategy for avoiding this domestication is to avoid entanglements with women. "Intercourse with women," declared Rousseau, "distinctly aggravated my ill health."[14] Joel Schwartz describes what, as an instance of the exceptional few, Rousseau sought: "Rousseau himself, by contrast [to men who cannot be independent of women] would like to be an asexual anarchist. He would like to be truly independent, to avoid ruling and being ruled."[15]

Even he, however, had trouble embracing this ideal of freedom based on the fabricated assumption of original isolation. At one point he vowed continence and substituted masturbation for sexual relations with his long-time companion, Therese.[16] This strategy of Rousseau's repeats the practice of Diogenes the Cynic who had also, 2,000 years earlier, celebrated isolation, indifference, and antidependence. Astonishing people in the agora by publicly masturbating, he dismissed the fuss by saying simply that he wished "it were as easy to banish hunger by rubbing the belly."[17] This response typifies the attitude of antidependence that reached a later apex in the eighteenth century. Rousseau, although he did not practice his habit publicly, spoke openly of it in the *Confessions*. The masturbatory self symbolizes the enclosed, antiembedded, antidependent, indifferent-to-others ideal that Rousseau envisioned as the highest level of human freedom.

KANT

Rousseau's *Emile* was apparently the only distraction that could keep Kant from his daily turn on the philosopher's walk in Königsberg. Kant moved beyond Rousseau by giving the term "autonomy" its present role in philosophy. He pronounced solemnly that "the *autonomy* of the will is the sole principle of all moral laws."[18] This autonomy was linked to freedom as independence "of determination by causes in the sensible world."[19] Kant's anthropology so identifies humans with disembodied selves that he speaks, not of human beings, but of "rational beings" or "rational essences" (*vernüftigen Wesen*). Starting philosophical reflection from the point of view of particular, embodied, encultured humans is rejected out of hand:

> ... We should not dream for a moment of trying to derive the reality of this principle from *the special characteristics of human nature*. For duty ... must therefore hold for all rational beings (to whom alone an imperative can apply at all), and *only because of this* can it also be a law for all human wills.[20]

In this simple, deft stroke, Kant manages to transform human beings into rational essences, dismiss as insignificant particular wants and needs, and eliminate from purview historical, cultural, and personal considerations.

This eliminative anthropology also tends to separate masculine from feminine. Once the transformation from human beings to rational essences is made, an important shift in outlook follows. A sentiment begins to grow that what the rational agent ought most to guard against are the entanglements, constraints, and dependencies associated with the material world. As the example of Lewis White Beck shows, interpreting the Kantian position invites a particular use of feminine imagery:

> Against the eighteenth-century position that man is a part of nature and ought to be subservient to her laws, Kant reacted by inverting the order and making nature what she is because of how she appears to us. Then he transcended even this Copernican venture by daring to weigh nature in the scales of reason and to declare that she is wanting and does not contain the destiny of man..... Nature produced man but brought him to the stage where he can finally assert his independence of her.[21]

"Escaping *her* clutches" may well be one way to identify a dominant motivating force in modern philosophy.[22] Beck's metaphors allow us to recognize that philosophies which start with assumptions that we might identify as fictions, translate nonetheless into very real practical orientations. One of these is the domination of nature. Kantian philosophy continues the Baconian attitude that nature is mere formless stuff to be controlled, shaped, and made subservient to man.[23]

The other consequence of the make-believe assumptions that guided Kant is the marginalization, if not the outright disappearance, of women.[24] Humans became "rational essences", for example, masculine philosophers enthralled with abstract, mathematical thought. Within the network of such assumptions, human differences disappear and a criterion for full humanity is readily available. Since masculine = rational essence = full humanity, difference can only be read as divergence, as somehow falling short of full humanity. In the middle decades of this century, Kohlberg followed out in experimental psychology exactly this scenario. The result was a scale on which could be ranked a person's moral maturity. Not surprisingly, this scale rated increase in maturity as inversely proportional to considerations of body, emotions, and concrete situations. The critique which Carol Gilligan has articulated against Kohlberg (for example that universal claims about human beings should not be made by using only male subjects in the studies, and that including female subjects would provide an alternative "care" perspective) represents the voicing of a position that is rooted in a different anthropology. It also represents the voice which is not only different, but which had been made inaudible under the guise of objective, universal, apodictic claims.[25]

The Waning of the Masturbatory Self

As we look back genealogically on how the celebration of autonomy emerged, we come to recognize that it is linked to a particular anthropology centered on assumptions of detachable rationality and presocial selves. This anthropology, in turn, is woven into an ontological fabric. The primary descriptive characteristic of the world in this ontology is that it is composed of ultimate simples. Discrete substances are said to mark the fundamental fact of existence.[26]

Such an ontology was understandable in an age dominated by classical physics. Today, it is neither so readily acceptable nor so easily justifiable. As Werner Heisenberg has pointed out, interaction between humans and nature has replaced the older view of distinct units, "observer" and "observed." "Science no longer is in the position of observer of nature, but rather recognizes itself as part of the interplay between man and nature."[27] Biology, with its emphasis on systematic interconnections has, since the time of Darwin, begun to gain more prominence and to rival physics as the science from which philosophy draws inspiration. In ecology, as Barry Commoner has made clear, the first law is "everything is connected to everything else."[28] What results from these changes is an ontological climate in which it is difficult to defend the priority of ultimate simples. Revisions in physics and the emphasis on biology both point to an ontology in which interrelationships, interactions, fields, and ecological interconnections take on a fundamental prominence.

Accompanying the metaphysics of ultimate simples was an anthropology that culminated in the Rousseau-type claim that humans are completed selves prior to and outside of relationships with others. The realm thus envisioned now strikes us, in Benhabib's words, as a "strange world":

It is one in which individuals are grown up before they have been born; in which boys are men before they have been children; a world where neither mother, nor sister, nor wife exist.[29]

Strange though it may have been, this vision held European philosophy in its grip for at least the last three centuries. In some ways, it was liberating and helpful, but its limitations became more and more pronounced as we entered the twentieth century.[30]

In an important sense, Deweyans cannot argue against this view on its own grounds. They do not accept its foundations concerning either transhistorical, nonexperiential starting points or fictional states of nature. Pragmatists cannot provide contradictory deductions from alternative apodictic first principles. All apodictic first principles are viewed as fictions. What can be done, what I have tried to do, is to provide a genealogy which indicates the manner (a) in which such positions do not represent embodiments of eternally valid essences, but are instead products of particular strains of thought developing at specific times, and (b) indicate the ways in which that network of connected ideas is no longer philosophically suitable.

In a Deweyan context, this latter task always sends philosophers back to ordinary experience. The anthropology or perhaps better the "andrology" (since it is concerned mostly with masculine experience) of the masturbatory self withers in the soil of lived human experience. To test whether a philosophy would wither or thrive, Dewey claims, we should ask whether it terminates in conclusions which,

> when they are referred back to ordinary life-experiences and their predicaments, render them more significant, more luminous to us, and make our dealings with them more fruitful? Or does it terminate in rendering the things of ordinary experience more opaque than they were before, and in depriving them of having in "reality" even the significance they had previously seemed to have? (LW 1:18)

What to do with "ordinary life-experiences" is a special problem for the friends of *Mathema*. By stripping humans of their particularities and transforming them into either the rational essences of Kant, or the anonymous sexual partners of Rousseau's state of nature, this lineage does not meet the Deweyan criterion for a philosophical orientation. Several important "things of ordinary experience," friendship, parent-child affection, husband-wife love, concern for others, are indeed deprived of "the significance they had previously seemed to have." Rather than celebrate the opportunities presented by the natural world, by their own bodies, by social connections, these thinkers transformed their antidependence crusade into a narrowly focused understanding of freedom as the act of a will indifferent to and indeed withdrawn from the real conditions of human existence.

Some more recent inheritors of this tradition wonder aloud whether it might indeed be too one-sided. Thus, Robert Paul Wolff begins by admitting that in the tradition to which he adheres "the accidents of birth and death, the phenomena of growth and parenthood, the facts of the social origin of personality itself... are treated as mere intrusions or embarassments or marginal imperfections."[31] Having made this admission, he falls back on ordinary experience and asserts that we have to come to grips with the fact that "each of us is an historically, culturally, socially located individual." "What," he is forced to ask, "is the relationship between each person's human personality and his pure rational agency?"[32] The question as phrased cannot be answered. It only makes sense within the anthropology that views humans as discrete simples defined as rational essences. The appropriate reply is to examine the genealogy of the question and eliminate the make-believe assumptions which give it any coherence at all.

Dewey's Pragmatist Anthropology

As we saw earlier in this chapter, two interconnected assumptions which provide the context for Wolff's dilemma, monadic individualism and metaphysical atomism, are rejected outright by Dewey. Drawing on Darwinian biology, Dewey resituates human beings within the web of relationships that make up the natural world. Instead of distinct units, defined as rational agents, Deweyan anthropology understands humans as individuals in a context, primarily concerned with developing the sort of praxis that will optimize well-being. Within this new framework "freedom" comes to signify something different from the autonomy favored by those whose ontologies encouraged an antidependence attitude. "A *distinctive* way of behaving in conjunction and *connection* with other distinctive ways of acting, not a self-enclosed way of acting, independent of everything else, is that toward which we are pointed." (LW 2:352–53).

Unlike the philosophers who began their work by placing themselves in a make-believe situation, Dewey starts with the fullness of lived experience. "Now empirical method is the only method which can do justice to this inclusive integrity of 'experience.' It alone takes this integrated unity as the starting point for philosophic thought" (LW 1:19). "Inclusive integrity" is the expression to keep in mind when trying to understand the manner in which Dewey differs from the friends of *Mathema*. Instead of ignoring difference, isolating individuals, looking for a "really real" either in some internal self or in some hypothesized aboriginal epoch, Dewey's orientation begins by taking ordinary experience seriously. Rather than pursue a reductive, essentialist kernel that ignores real differences, he attempts to articulate an emergent, burgeoning philosophy that welcomes experiential differences. As we have already seen, on the now significant question of women and philosophy, Dewey predicted a novel contribution based on the distinct experience of women.

What is interesting from the perspective of the reconstruction of culture is that Dewey does not recoil from such a modification of philosophy. Nor does he dismiss it as violating the purity of *the* proper philosophical stance. Indeed, he welcomes the opportunity for enhancement presented by contact with the new formulation of human experience. This opportunity for enhancement provides us with an important clue for understanding the Deweyan position on freedom. The contrast with Robert Paul Wolff is instructive here.

For Wolff the "rational agent" judges the daily experiences of life to be "intrusions," "embarassments," or "marginal imperfections." Dewey, by contrast, rejects the anthropology that would lead a philosopher to problematize ordinary life experiences. Two pivots are central to his pragmatist anthropology. (a) Interdependence is a fundamental, inherent fact of life.[33] Such a realization is consistent with changes in twentieth-century science. This position has an immediate negative implication for the subject of freedom. "No man and no mind was ever emancipated by being left alone" (LW 2:340). (b) The second assumption, which grows out of the biological model, is that humans are not "completed selves." Change, growth, and the possibility for enhanced experiences are always part of the human condition. Emergent properties and capacities are here the focus:

> The idea of a natural individual in his isolation possessed of full-fledged wants, of energies to be expended according to his own volition, and of a ready-made faculty of foresight and prudent calculation is as much a fiction in psychology as the doctrine of the individual in possession of antecedent political rights is one in politics. (LW 2:299)

As this quotation makes clear, Dewey's anthropology requires that the state of nature story be once and for all recognized as a fiction. Within the new anthropology, that of emerging selves in a context, autonomy as tied to self-sufficiency and antidependence can play no central role.

Autonomy does play a central role where freedom, reason, and individuality are treated as original givens. On such an understanding, surrounding conditions, including even other people, are seen as obstacles to the full manifestation of these original possessions. Dewey's biological pragmatism treats freedom, mind, and individuality as products or results. They do not preexist in full-blown form, requiring only the elimination of constraints for their manifestation. They mature as a result of certain sorts of interaction. Freedom becomes the actual capacity to carry out courses of action.

> Liberty is that secure release and fulfillment of personal poten-
> tialities which take place only in rich and manifold association
> with others: the power to be an individualized self making a
> distinctive contribution and enjoying in its own way the fruits of
> association. (LW 2:329).

Freedom is not an all or nothing property. It involves the enhancement of powers such that continuity of growth and degrees of achievement are important considerations. "Personal potentialities" can be actualized, but the actualization occurs in increments and involves the participation of others. We might say that in the world of empirical naturalism, others are welcomed, indeed recruited, to help *increase* freedom.

The model on which Dewey's view of freedom is built is that of an artist. In order to develop the talent, say, of piano playing, it is not enough to find oneself in conditions that do not forbid practicing. Restriction of limitations provides the beginning of freedom, not the completed state of freedom. For the embryonic talent to grow, certain kinds of dependencies are sought: on people who will allow place, time, and access to a piano, on a teacher, on music publishers, on exemplary pianists.

As students, thus interrelated to others, grow in proficiency, they are more and more able to claim that they are free to play the instrument. The claim, in this instance, means having the actual ability to perform a piece of music. As their talent develops, so does their freedom to undertake more difficult pieces. In ordinary discourse, people often make the claim "I am free to play the piano" and mean simply "no one would forbid me, were I to want to learn." When asked to sit down and play a piece of music, they cannot. Using language in this way confuses "formal" freedom, the conditions of freedom, with the "actual," "effective," incremental flowering of freedom. "I am free to play the piano" in the fullest, concrete sense, means "I am actually able to play music on this instrument."

In a philosophical landscape reconstructed along Deweyan lines, the terms made pejorative by the friends of *Mathema*, "dependence" and "heteronomy" would be revalued. These are terms indicative of human situations that can be positive and fruitful. Dependence does not represent a shameful weakness; heteronomy does not inherently connote being shackled to deterministic, mechanistic processes. Both present opportunities and, as such, can be properly used or perverted.

My suggestion that one important direction for pragmatist reconstruction involves the rehabilitation of heteronomy and dependence will no doubt strike many Deweyans as controversial, if not entirely misguided. One prominent champion of pragmatism has indeed articulated a position quite different from my own. In a recent book, Richard Rorty repeats the refrain "thus I willed it."[34] He also celebrates the fact that it became possible toward the end of the nineteenth century "to take the activity of redescription more lightly than it had ever been taken before."[35] Rorty's ideal is what Harold Bloom has called a "strong poet," someone whose great horror is being influenced by others, finding himself to be only a "copy or a replica."[36] "Thus I willed it" thereby translates into a new version of the antidependence movement, one which can look without irony to the self-sufficient process of "giving birth to oneself."[37] The strong poet celebrated by Rorty manifests in the twentieth century what Susan Bordo, in her analysis of the seventeenth century, has called "The Father of Oneself Fantasy."[38]

In my taxonomy, Rorty would belong more to the friends of *Mathema* than to the friends of *Bios*. He is, despite protestations to the contrary, still drawing upon the capital deposited by modernity: disembodiedness and disembeddedness. The radical redescriptions envisioned and celebrated by Rorty would work only for disembodied intellects envisioning playfully one self-description after another. They do not work so well for concrete human beings who have bodies, are parts of families, make up the fabric of a particular culture, and in general are imbedded in a network of caring relations. It is one thing to say as an abstract, general pronouncement that "most of reality is indifferent to our descriptions of it."[39] It is another to be a concrete, embodied individual living in a particular social and natural environment. In the latter case, continuous redescriptions are neither so possible, nor such ideals.

As a father, I suppose I could, following Rousseau and Gauguin, refashion myself, use a new vocabulary and redescribe myself apart from continuing and sustaining connections to my children. Of course, such behavior is possible. It may even be an open question whether it should be deemed praiseworthy or blameworthy. But as a reasonable human being this sort of decision should not be undertaken as a simple voluntaristic directive: "thus I willed it." Selection and intellection should work together. It should not (unless we assume the existence of the disembodied and disembedded self) issue solely from an inner free will. The decision should issue from reasonable, intelligent deliberation. Such deliberation means that choice involves a selection among alternatives. To decide intelligently among these alternatives means paying attention to a variety of factors.

This kind of choice is heteronomous, and rightly so. We are embedded and embodied as well as intelligent.

The followers of *Mathema* have tended to parcel out the philosophical landscape into cold, disembodied rationality on the one hand, and a self-directing *liberum arbitrium* on the other. "Rationality" leaves little room for reasonableness, or embodied (heteronomous, dependent on surrounding conditions) intelligence. "Thus I willed it" might be a meaningful incantation if we were disembodied intelligences capable of unrestricted redescriptions. Embodied individuals, by contrast, can more easily accept the fact that they are continuous with a particular people and tradition. The great horror of the strong poet, being influenced by others, is a horror occasioned by an anthropology which, whether it recognizes it or not, contains lingering elements of disembodiedness.

Surely, Rorty's emphasis on "thus I willed it" is an exercise in hyperbole. Continual modifications, ameliorations, changing, and tinkering with ourselves in light of newly articulated aspirations are no doubt worthy. They are necessary if humans are to avoid stagnation. Rorty has properly rejected the Enlightenment ideal that sought the "view from nowhere" which would once and for all make investigation, experimentation, and critique of existing social practices no longer necessary. But why is he so afraid of our biology? The world of Rortyan radical redescriptions, of strong poets who abhor being influenced by others, who seek to give themselves birth, is surely the sort of false, make-believe world which Bordo has appropriately labeled "The Dream of Everywhere." The "Dream of Everywhere" seeks to attain a "critical standpoint free of the locatedness and limitation of bodily existence." This latest erasure of the body is not accomplished in Cartesian fashion by a trip to nowhere, "but in a resistance to the recognition that one is always *somewhere* and limited."[40] As someone who refers to Dewey as a hero, Rorty should be more sensitive to this concrete sense of personal and cultural embodiment. Indeed, it is perhaps some lingering Deweyan sense of contextuality that gives Rorty's positions some of their charm. In the end, though, Rorty remains too much a friend of *Mathema*.

A friend of *Bios*, such as Dewey, will tend to emphasize deliberation, "social intelligence," and even choice, if this good word could be rescued from the connotations of an autonomous will. Deweyan "social intelligence" takes into account the associations of which we form a part (some given, some chosen), response to our needs and those of others, our own past, consequences of actions on others as well as ourselves, and general views about what is important. Most fundamentally, it recognizes that we are inherently social creatures, not disembedded monads.[41]

Within the andrology whose story I have been tracing, choice is too narrowly allied to a voluntaristic act issuing from an inner, independent self. Primacy is given to the *liberum arbitrium*, not to social intelligence focusing on communication and shared deliberation. Such an ideal of severed connections did not result from an ineluctable deduction starting from apodictic first principles. Its prominence became most pronounced as the friends of *Mathema* achieved philosophical hegemony during the seventeenth and eighteenth centuries. The resultant andrology focused so intently on self-sufficiency, self-definition, and the radical freedom of an indifferent will that it relegated to oblivion much that humans hold dear. This modern sense of freedom, as Midgley observes, "has spread itself to cover the isolation of the individual from all connection with others." What results, predictably, is detachment from "most of what gives life meaning: tradition, influence, affection, personal and local ties, natural roots and sympathies."[42]

The emergence of concrete liberty, of effective powers of action and growth, depends to a great degree on intelligent choice. Intelligent choice cannot be summarized by the slogan "thus I willed it." In fact, this is a distortion of *intelligent* choice which selects for appropriate reasons, reasons which include factors that form part of the context to which we belong. For Dewey, intelligent choice begins by communicating with others. It develops by applying what he so misleadingly called the "scientific method," that is gathering information in a systematic fashion and judging the information experimentally, by paying attention to consequences.

In place of autonomy, self-definition, and antidependence, empirical naturalism admits that we live in a world where heteronomy and dependence ought to be viewed as opportunities for growth and liberation of capacities. Human beings are both embodied and embedded. We do not carry bodies around with us as deadweights, nor are our cultures simply prisons. As we enter the twenty-first century, philosophy should articulate an understanding that is ample and generous enough to accommodate more than the experience of mathematically intoxicated European males. Deweyan pragmatism has done much to set out the rudiments of such an orientation.[43]

Notes

1. George B. Tindall and David E. Shi, *America: A Narrative History* (New York: W. W. Norton and Co., 1989), p. 446.

2. Mary Midgley has articulated succinctly the central orientation of the leading figure in this group, Aristotle. "On the positive side, however, he stands as *the* biologist among philosophers—indeed as the inventor of the biological attitude, which takes the world as a continuous organic whole to be accepted on its own terms, not as a tiresome mass

of matter tolerable only because it instantiates mathematical laws. This is beyond praise." *Beast and Man* (New York: New American Library, 1978), p. 260.

3. Gerald Dworkin, *The Theory and Practice of Autonomy* (Cambridge: Cambridge University Press, 1988), p. 6.

4. Bruce Ackerman, *Social Justice in the Liberal State* (New Haven: Yale University Press, 1980), p. 368.

5. Seyla Benhabib, "The Generalized and the Concrete Other," in *Women and Moral Theory*, eds. E. Kittay and D. Meyers (Totowa, N.J.: Roman and Littlefield, 1987), p. 171.

6. Annette Baier, "Hume, the Women's Moral Theorist?," in *Women and Moral Theory*, p. 46.

7. Charlene Haddock Seigfried, "Where Are All the Pragmatic Feminists?" read at the annual meeting of the Society for the Advancement of American Philosophy, Buffalo, N.Y., March 2, 1990, p. 1.

8. Ibid., pp. 11, 7.

9. Both "pragmatism" and "instrumentalism," two labels traditionally associated with Dewey's position, carry with them the unfortunate and un-Deweyan connotations of narrow expedience and antirealism. "Emprical naturalism" is an expression used by Dewey at the very beginning of *Experience and Nature*: "The title of this volume, Experience and Nature, is intended to signify that the philosophy here presented may be termed either empirical naturalism, or naturalistic empiricism, or, taking 'experience' in its usual signification, naturalistic humanism"(LW 1:10).

10. Seyla Benhabib, "The Generalized and the Concrete Other," in *Women and Moral Theory*, p. 5. "I want to argue that the *definition* of the moral domain as well as the ideal of *moral autonomy*, not only in Kohlberg's theory but in universalistic, contractarian theories from Hobbes to Rawls, lead to a privatization of women's experience and to the exclusion of its consideration from a moral point of view. In this tradition, the moral self is viewed as a *disembedded* and *disembodied* being."

11. Jean-Jacques Rousseau, *A Discourse on Inequality*, ed. M. Cranston (London: Penguin Books, [1755] 1984), p. 97.

12. Ibid., pp. 128, 136. Rousseau here runs together the "apathy" of the Stoics and the Epicurean ideal of "ataraxy."

13. Ibid., p. 86.

14. Cited in Jacques Derrida, *Of Grammatology* (Baltimore: The Johns Hopkins University Press, 1976), p. 156. What Diogenes Laertius reports was Pythagoras's answer to the question "when should one consort with a woman?": "When you want to lose what strength you have." Diogenes Laertius, *Lives of Eminent Philosophers* (London: Loeb Classical Library, 1931), vol. 2, p. 329.

15. Joel Schwartz, *The Sexual Politics of Jean-Jacques Rousseau* (Chicago: University of Chicago Press, 1984), p. 99.

16. See Joel Schwartz, *The Sexual Politics of Jean-Jacques Rousseau*, p. 99; and, Jacques Derrida, *Of Grammatology*, pp. 152–57.

17. Diogenes Laertius, *Lives of Eminent Philosphers*, vol. 2, p. 71.

18. Immanuel Kant, *Critique of Practical Reason* (Indianapolis: Bobbs Merrill Co., [1788] 1956), p. 33.

19. Immanuel Kant, *Groundwork of the Metaphysics of Morals* (New York: Harper and Row, [1785] 1964) p. 120.

20. Ibid., pp. 92-93.

21. Lewis White Beck, *A Commentary on Kant's Critique of Practical Reason* (Chicago: University of Chicago Press, 1960), p. 125.

22. Such an escape in the case of Descartes has been traced by Susan Bordo, *The Flight to Objectivity: Essays on Cartesianism and Culture* (Albany, N.Y.: State University of New York Press, 1987).

23. This modem dream of dominating nature, of treating it as if it were made *for us*, is, as Mary Midgley has put it, a "childish and megalomaniac notion." "We are at home in this world *because we were made for it.*" *Beast and Man*, p. 195.

24. The place of women in Kant's precritical writings has been examined by Mary Bittner Wiseman, "Beautiful Women, Dutiful Men," *American Philosophical Association Newsletter on Feminism* 89 (1990), pp. 71-75.

25. See Carol Gilligan, *In a Different Voice: Psychological Theory and Women's Development* (Cambridge, Mass.: Harvard University Press, 1982).

26. Cf. "Hume, as so often, is bogged down by his mysterious ontology by which 'all beings in the universe, considered in themselves, appear entirely loose and independent of each other.' Not in this universe they don't." Mary Midgley, *Beast and Man*, pp. 275-76.

27. Werner Heisenberg, "The Representation of Nature in Contemporary Physics," in *Symbolism in Religion and Literature* (New York: George Braziller, 1960), p. 231.

28. Barry Commoner, *The Closing Circle* (New York: Alfred A. Knopf, 1971). p. 33.

29. Seyla Benhabib, *Women and Moral Theory*, p. 162.

30. Cf. "Western thought has long occupied itself with prying individuals loose from their surroundings in this way, with making them autonomous. Initially the process is enormously liberating. But, carried through systematically, it comes to a point where it means severing all personal bonds." Mary Midgley, *Beast and Man*, p. 356.

31. Robert Paul Wolff, *The Autonomy of Reason: A Commentary on Kant's Groundwork of the Metaphysics of Morals* (New York: Harper and Row, 1973), pp. 226-27.

32. Ibid., pp. 227, 228.

33. "Conjoint, combined, associated action is a universal trait of the behavior of things" (LW 2:257). For a detailed treament of Dewey's metaphysics and its emphasis on relations, see my *Dewey's Metaphysics* (New York: Fordham University Press, 1988).

34. Richard Rorty, *Contingency, Irony and Solidarity* (Cambridge: Cambridge University Press, 1989), pp. 29, 37, 40.

35. Ibid., p. 39.

36. Ibid., p. 24.

37. Ibid., p. 29.

38. "More subtly, the Cartesian project of starting anew through the revocation of one's actual childhood (during which one was 'immersed' in body and nature) and the (re)creation of a world in which absolute separateness (both epistemological and ontological) from body and nature are keys to control rather than sources of anxiety can now be seen as a 'father of oneself' fantasy on a highly symbolic, but profound, plane." Susan Bordo, *The Flight to Objectivity*, p. 108.

39. Rorty, *Contingency, Irony and Solidarity*, p. 7.

40. Susan Bordo, "The View from Nowhere and the Dream of Everywhere: Heterogeneity, Adequation and Feminist Theory," *American Philosophical Association Newsletter of Feminism*, 88 (1989), pp. 20, 21.

41. For a good introduction to Dewey's "social intelligence," see James Gouinlock, *Excellence in Public Discourse* (New York: Teachers College Press, 1986), chap. 5.

42. Mary Midgley, *Beast and Man*, p. 288.

43. I wish to thank my colleagues, Richard Gaffney, David Rice, Paul Santilli, and Jennifer McErlean who read earlier drafts of this essay and made many helpful comments.

9

Naturalizing Epistemology: Reconstructing Philosophy

PETER T. MANICAS

Introduction

It is surely plausible to think of the histories of humankind as a series of discontinuous and sometimes continuous intersecting movements marked by accidents, some benign, some fortuitous, and some disasterous. In this regard, if nothing else, history is radically contingent—even if looking back, we can often provide altogether satisfactory explanations of what happened and why.[1] One such legacy is the intertwined conceptual and institutional legacies of science and academic philosophy.

Yet not all is well as regards these. Dewey could lament that we had failed to replace old habits of thought with more scientific ways. This was one aspect of the reconstruction in philosophy for which he called. We wonder, not unreasonably, whether the authority of science was but Western provincialism, the rationale for the imperialist obliteration of non-Western cultures. On the other side, while Dewey was aware that science had been misappropriated and misapplied, he remained optimistic that this could be changed, that democratic processes could be brought to bear on expert claims to authority. This, too, was an aspect of his call for reconstruction. Yet, as above, Dewey's hopes strike us as naive. Wholly disjoined from experts, we stand in terror of their so carefully considered decisions. What, heaven help us, will be the unintended consequences of genetic engineering or a confrontation in Saudi Arabia? If the nineteenth century had Frankenstein, we have energy-obsessed Dr. Strangeloves.

This chapter pursues the idea of reconstructing philosophy; thus, if very indirectly, of reconstructing culture. With Dewey as both guide and foil, the focus is on the implications of the current debate over the effort to naturalize epistemology, that is, to study knowledge scientifically. Dewey was surely correct that we need an alternative to dogmatism and to skepticism; but as perhaps Dewey did not clearly see, we cannot take science for granted. A second goal of this chapter, then, is to raise some questions both about current scientific practices and our understanding of these.

The Epistemological Problem

We can begin with Barry Stroud's critique of Quine's influential essay, "Epistemology Naturalized."[2] Quine argues that naturalized epistemology is "the empirical study of a species of primates, or, in the particular case, of an individual human subject in interaction with his environment."[3] Thus, now quoting Quine:

> This human subject is accorded a certain experimentally controlled imput—certain patterns of irradiation in certain frequencies, for instance—and in the fullness of time the subject delivers as output a description of the three-dimensional external world and its history.[4]

The story continues: we observe the subject as she interacts with her environment. Given then that we know her environment and have an adequate psychology, we then explain her "output," seeing that, in the fullness of time, what she says is true.

But, of course, the situation just described is not the situation of our naturalizing epistemologist, since, of course, like our knower, he is (as everyone!) utterly denied that independent, theory-neutral access to the world which could be the only basis for determining whether inputs from it ever result in outputs which are *true*. Stroud concludes that Quine simply fails to address what he takes to be the traditional question of epistemology: How do we know that the external world is what *anybody* says it is?

This problem is not the problem of *whether* there is an external world or, for that matter, whether it has *some* structure. As Peirce and Dewey insisted, we can call into question any particular version of *how* the world is, but Cartesian skepticism cannot be reasonably motivated.[5] But as the foregoing seems at least to show, one can assume an external and structured world, the method of science, and *still* ask if what is presumed to be known is known.

Dewey might add there that this presumes an absolute conception of reality.[6] On this (commonsensical) view, reality means reality as it is independently of you and me, independently of what it is known as. *My* skeptic demands that we show that knowledge of this reality is possible. If the only knowledge we can have is from *some* viewpoint, how can we know whether it—our or some other—is valid? That is, given an absolute conception of reality, it would seem that we are forced to accept a relative conception of knowledge. It may be, of course, that we can justify some viewpoint. Perhaps (as I argue below) there are modes of fixing belief which should be preferred. Such a relationalism could then be contrasted to relativism: understood as the thesis that no viewpoint, no mode, can claim privilege over any other.

It may be doubted that we *need* an absolute conception of reality. But we surely do—if we want to avoid relativism and to anchor our fallibilism.[7] Even if we can privilege some mode of fixing belief, we will need to aspire to the ideal of grasping the world as it is, independently of what you and I might believe. The problem of historical knowledge is, perhaps, the clearest case. We must acknowledge that we shall never have more than a fragment of the possible evidence and that alternative histories are always possible. But surely what transpired transpired independently of these. It is just this which grounds the limits of all perspectives and thus our fallibilism.

More, we need an absolute conception of reality if criticism and persuasion is not to collapse into sophistry, to be *merely* a struggle to win opinion. As rhetoricians know, truth-talk plays a vital role in argument, persuasion, and criticism. Indeed, if we could dispense with the conception of an absolute conception of reality, truth-talk might be dispensable, replaced by pragmatic "works/does not work" or "predicts/does not predict." Language (and theories about the world) are surely (our) tools for coping with our world; but for *social animals*, they could not serve if they did not have a rhetorical function.[8]

There is another form of answer to Stroud. We don't need independent access to the world if we can assume there is a *necessary* connection between some method, say, the method of science and truth. Thus, with persistent application of our method, our (un-Peircean) individual, given a (Peircean) fullness of time, *will* arrive at truth. But even this act of faith does not help us. Since we will *always* lack independent access, we can never know whether we have arrived!

Here we can pause to consider, even if too briefly, an argument put forward by Michael Friedman. He points out (rightly) that there is no necessary connection between confirmation and truth and that what traditional philosophy of science has to offer on the relation cannot be sustained.[9] In particular, he argues that if scientific method (or any other) is to show that it achieves (or even approximates) truth, the Tarskian theory of truth (shared by all traditional candidates) must be supplemented to include a causal theory of reference. Since our methods cannot guarantee success, "we have to know facts about the actual world if we are to know which method is best; and we have to know facts about the actual world to know even that any given method has any chance at all of leading to truth."[10] To do this in a nonviciously circular way "we need general laws connecting physics and psychology [*sic*] with the theory of truth; and it is precisely this kind of generality that a theory of reference tries to provide."[11]

There are two fairly obvious objections. First, even given these laws, it is by no means clear what scientific method *is* and thus what and how it is to be tested (of which more below). But, second, as Friedman says, we lack utterly such general laws. Worse, I believe that there is little reason to suppose that such are possible. To anticipate, Friedman's program seems, at least, to follow Quine's in being committed to an epistemological individualism.[12]

Epistemological Individualism

There are, I believe, about nine (or forty?) ways into this. One way is to observe, with Dewey, that:

> . . .the whole history of science, art and morals prove that the mind that appears *in* individuals is not as such individual mind. The former is in itself a system of belief, recognitions, and ignorances, of acceptances and rejections, of expectancies and appraisals of meanings which have been instituted under the influence of custom and tradition (LW 1:170).[13]

The epistemological problem that is at issue here was surely propelled by modern science, but contrary to what Quine (and Dewey) imply, acknowledging this is no advantage for the naturalizing epistemologist. It is, indeed, *because* of modern science that, as William James rightly saw (versus Spencer), the epistemological problem is so intractable. Naive realism could (and does!) sustain epistemological individualism: if you don't believe there are red apples in the world, then just look and see! But if you take modern physical science *and* Dewey's remark seriously (as I think we must), then it is a rather gigantic system of belief, recognition, and the rest, which has been instituted under the influence of custom and tradition. Given this, how can we be so confident that our beliefs correspond to a world that exists independent of either you or me?[14]

This does not mean that I am deluded in saying "there is a red apple" when I *see* a red apple. That is not the issue. Plainly, science did not undermine our ordinary ways of thinking and speaking. When a G. E.

Moore says, "I know that there are red apples," and a neuroscientist says "The experience of red apples is the product of physical and biochemical transactions between something and us" and the skeptic says, "Nobody could know that there are red apples," the same words are being used differently.[15] What Moore and the rest of us say, even if true, is not decisive as regards either the epistemological *or* the scientific investigation of knowledge.

We began with Quine's psychological program; this is the appropriate point to refer to recent sociology of knowledge, to the so-called "strong programme."[16] Its key insight is what Barry Barnes calls "the naturalistic equivalence of the knowledge of different cultures."

> "Naturalism... implies the most intensely serious concern with what is real.... Everything of naturalistic significance would indicate that there is indeed one world, one reality, "out there", the source of our perceptions if not their total determinant [that is, *though* not their total determinant], the cause of our perceptions being fulfilled or disappointed, of our endeavors succeeding or being frustrated. But this reality should not be identified with any linguistic account of it, or needless to say, with any way of perceiving it, or pictorial representation of it. Reality is the source of our primitive causes, which, having been presupposed by our perceptual apparatus, produces changes in our knowledge and the verbal representations of it which we possess. All cultures relate symmetrically to this reality. Men [*sic*] in all cultures are capable of making reasonable responses to the causal imputs they receive from reality—that is, are capable of learning. That the structure of our verbal knowledge does not thereby necessarily converge upon a single form, isomorphous with what is real, should not surprise us. Why should we ever expect this to be a property of our linguistic and cognitive capacities?[17]

Because, like Quine, Barnes and Bloor take science seriously, they believe (a) there is an independently existing world, but (b) they also believe with Dewey that human cognition is *always* socially mediated.

An example may here be useful. According to Bulmer, the terminal taxa of Karam correspond very well in approximately 70 percent of the cases with species identified by a scientific zoologist.[18] The cassowary is an interesting instance of noncorrespondence. Karam have the taxon "yakt" for birds and bats, but the cassowary is not placed in this taxon. Instead, it appears in a special taxon, "kobity," making it a nonbird/nonbat. For Bulmer, of course, this is an error, an error explained in terms of a Karam willingness (unlike us!) to allow culture to supercede "objective biological facts." The problem is not whether there is an external world nor whether

Karam fail to see *something* which we call a "cassowary." Rather, the problem is: How can we say that reality is not parsed the way the Karam say it is?[19]

The idea that knowledges of different cultures is naturalistically equivalent is both a premise and a conclusion of strong program science.[20] Strong programmers are interested in understanding belief, and therefore, *for scientific purposes*, beliefs which we think of as rational—including accordingly, those which are fixed scientifically—must be treated as on the same footing as all others. The belief "I see a Panda now" involves *language*. Hence social considerations are relevant. Just because our only access to a world is causal, and epistemological individualism cannot be sustained, a naturalistic epistemology interested in explaining knowledge must appeal to social facts. Not only do these enter into concept formation (enormously complicating empirical psychology), but we need to acknowledge that the problem of reproducing the cognitive order could not possibly be explained without a sociological understanding of the relevant social mechanisms, for example, how belief is authorized and stabilized.

On the other hand, because our best science implies that all we can have is a representation of reality, and because there is no way to measure any representation against reality-in-itself, we cannot escape a relationalism. But it does not follow from this that all truth claims are equally *good*. At this point, we can turn to Dewey.

Dewey's Program

It is not *perfectly* clear what Dewey would say to a Karam defender of *his* system of classification. Who here has the truth? He might say that the question is badly posed. He might say that since "true" presupposes an absolutist conception that is neither necessary nor possible, both are *right*. Although the world is structured, *it* does not allow us to discriminate between contrary taxonomies. It does constrain these: A culture could not, for example, treat what we have identified as poisonous as foods, for their biology will not allow them to survive. But there is nonetheless plenty of room for alternative and contrary schemes depending on a host of alternative contingent factors regarding beliefs about the gods, the good, etc. On this view of the matter, there are *too many* truths and it is idle to suppose that any can be privileged.

There is an attractive aspect to this move. Given that peoples have different interests and different ideas about the gods and the good, we need to acknowledge that they may very well be able to justify their beliefs about the way the world is—however strange these may seem to us. There is, unfortunately, an unattractive aspect to this posture. Not only does it disavow an attempt to give any special credence to the claims of science (perhaps not such a bad thing?), but it disavows any effort to provide guidance about how we *ought* to go about finding out what to believe, including here, lest we forget, beliefs about what is good and right. I think that we can do better. So, too, did Dewey.

Dewey's Naturalizing of Epistemology

Dewey wrote that "the methods of knowing practiced in daily life and science are excluded from consideration in the philosophical theory of knowing" (MW 10:37). Presumably, "the actual process of knowing," involves "operations of controlled observation, inference, reasoning, and testing." While this seems true enough, it does not help us in the present instance. Surely, Karam do all these things even as they are arriving at a different taxonomy than ours. Are the Karam going about the business of inquiry wrongly? Perhaps what is needed is a more systematic attempt at discriminating the special features of successful knowing. Dewey set this as the goal of inquiry into inquiry. Thus, he writes:

> The position here taken holds that since every special case of knowledge is constituted as the outcome of some special inquiry, the conception of knowledge as such can only be a generalization of the properties discovered to belong to conclusions which are outcomes of inquiry. Knowledge, as an abstract term, is a name for the product of competent inquiries. (LW 12:16)

That is, by examining the outcomes of inquiries, we can discover why these are knowledge and, conjunctively, by examining inquiries we can discover what makes for competence.[21]

It is important to see what this program is and is not. Not only was Dewey not altogether clear regarding what is involved, but more troublesome, the program does not neatly join with work being carried on today in academic disciplines as they are generally practiced. Perhaps Dewey was off the mark, or perhaps the fault is with much current social science.

Inquiry into Inquiry: I

It may be best to proceed indirectly and to begin by noting that Dewey's program is *not* akin to the psychologically oriented programs of Quine or, for example, William Lycan.[22] Quine has not said very much about the sort of psychology he assumes will explain how we know, but we may guess that it is some sophisticated version of behaviorism. By contrast, Lycan is very clear in his commitments to a Fodor/Dennett-inspired homuncularism, a currently fashionable version of cognitive psychology.[23]

But in either case, Quine, Lycan, and the psychologies they presume are epistemologically individualistic and Dewey's psychology was not. Moreover, these writers and the psychologies they want to include are committed to a *logical* theory which Dewey found to be misdirected.

Throughout his career, from his brilliant essay on the reflex arc, through the 1903 studies in experimental logic, to *How We Think* (1910), to his ill-understood *Logic,* Dewey developed a naturalistic theory of inquiry that totally went against the dominating and now taken-for-granted Frege-Russell conception of logic.[24] In this view, logical relations hold between abstract predicates and inference (deductive and inductive) depends on there being some sort of objective relation between propositions.[25] Because this assumption was a feature of what Dewey called "intellectualism," he looked at the matter entirely differently. As Thomas Burke says, Dewey's conception of inquiry "has to be understood not so much as cognitive problem solving but more generally in terms of an adaptive stabilization propensity of organism/environment relations."[26] This basic naturalistic starting point led Dewey to totally refashion "inference," "propositional content," "kinds," and other critical terms in standard logical theory. Thus, as I understand Dewey, "inference" is fundamentally a way of handling information which does not require human language. The logician's concept of inference is not, of course, to be abandoned; it is rather to be seen as a highly useful abstraction, regimented for particular purposes.[27]

This is hardly the place to develop the radical implications of Dewey's revision. Continuing along lines just suggested, one example will have to suffice. Enormous effort in psychology has been directed at solving Meno's paradox: "If imputs require concepts to be meaningful, then concepts must precede 'imputs' as in nativism; but if concepts (to be at all useful in the real world) require 'imput' for their content, then 'imputs' must precede concepts as in empiricism (either of the ontogenetic or phylogenetic variety)."[28] For example, behaviorist learning theory needs to assume that the organism has made the relevant abstraction if it is to be reinforced. But this assumes exactly what needs to be explained. On the other hand, recent cognitive psychology, by conceiving of mind as an information processing system, assumes that information comes sententially prepackaged, ready-made for use by the linguistically apt learner.

If I am correct we can now identify three obstacles to an adequate understanding of knowing: a pervasive intellectualism, an epistemological individualism, and third, a pervasive assumption, shared by the main contending views, that, as Kelly and Kreuger put it "the only relations between contents of cognitive states which makes a process involving those states a cognitive process are the sorts of logical functions used in classical experiments." [29] But, of course, on the standard view of logic, logical functions can hold *only* between abstract predicates. Meno's dilemma is then inescapable! Indeed, until psychology breaks from those philosophical dogmas which have formed it, we shall not have an adequate psychology of learning, and we shall not naturalistically understand knowing. Dewey's path, if I am right, was the right one.

But even if we accept completely Dewey's picture of inquiry (including a host of details yet to be filled in), this would not, of itself, respond to the problem of judging between the belief systems of the Karam and the Western zoologist. Presumably, Dewey's account applies to both. If only the zoologist gets it right, then something more is being assumed, likely that something called the method of science privileges the findings of the zoologist. But we have yet to see the argument for this.

Inquiry into Inquiry: II

There is an entirely different program which is rightly construed as inquiry into inquiry. Dewey offered (as we noted) that "through examination of the *relations* which exist between means (methods) employed and conclusions attained as their consequence, reasons are discovered why some methods succeed and other methods fail." This might be understood as meaning that the task is not *only* to frame theory which describes and explains the general feature of inquiry, but consistent with this, to consider *empirical science empirically*. It might then be possible to generate warranted methodological rules, thus satisfying the demand that we be able to judge between contrary beliefs and belief systems. This version of a naturalistic program has had some recent advocates, among them, most outstandingly, Nicholas Rescher and Larry Laudan. There are, I think, three main features which distinguish this approach.

First, the Deweyan inspiration is in the effort to avoid a vicious circularity in which one either justifies outcomes by assuming that means are competent, or warrants the means by assuming the truth of the outcomes. If as Rescher puts it, "justification is here an essentially two-way process—its results legitimate the method as proper and appropriate, and the method justifies its results as 'correct' " then one needs either to break the circle or to show that it is nonvicious.[30]

Briefly, Rescher argues that "any *experiential* justification of a truth-criterion must pull itself up by its own bootstraps—it needs factual imputs, but yet factual imputs cannot at this stage already qualify as truths." "To meet this need," accordingly, Rescher appeals to "truth candidates," "data which are no more truths than candidate-presidents are presidents. . . ."[31] Rescher then envisages "a feed-back loop" in which "the *reasonableness* of the over-all process. . . rests not only on the (external) element of success inherent in the factor of pragmatic efficiency, but also on the (internal) factor of intrinsic coherence and the mutual support of self-substantiation that the various stages of the whole are able to lend to one another."[32]

Laudan offers what he calls a "reticulated model of scientific rationality" which explicitly introduces values:

> The reticulational approach shows that we can use our knowledge of the available methods of inquiry as a tool for assessing the viability of proposed cognitive claims. . . . Equally, the reticulated picture insists that our judgments about which theories are sound can be played off against our explicit axiologies in order to reveal tensions between our implicit and explicit value structures.[33]

For Laudan, fully in the spirit of Dewey, "axiology, methodology, and factual claims are inevitably intertwined in relations of mutual dependency."[34]

Second, both writers (Rescher explicitly, Laudan implicitly) reject a thesis (or propositional) pragmatism in which the problem is to vindicate particular truth claims. Instead, they opt for a methodological pragmatism in which the problem is to justify *methods*. Thus, "pragmatic considerations are never brought to bear on theses directly. The relationship becomes indirect and mediated; a specific knowledge claim is supported by reference to a method, which in turn is supported on pragmatist lines."[35] Beliefs arrived at with warranted methods may very well be false. The aim, however, is to find methods which are reliable in the sense that they answer to human purposes, critically assessed."

Thesis pragmatism is highly vulnerable to a wholly idiosyncratic mode determining what counts as warranted assertibility. This is, of course, a long-standing objection to pragmatism. Methodological pragmatism offers hope since beliefs are warranted only insofar as they are the outcome of an explicit method which has been warranted independently of this or that particular belief. As Rescher points out:

> Considerations of the *suitability* and *effectiveness* of methods introduce an inherently rational orientation which serves to assure the logical properties. Moreover, methods are intrinsically public, interpersonal, and communal. A method is not a successful *method* unless its employment is generally effective—otherwise we are talking about a knack or skill rather than a method. A skill can

> only be *shown*, it cannot be *explained*.... This line of thought indicates the fundamentally social dimension of methods....They can be examined and evaluated *in abstracto*, without any dependency on particular practitioners.[36]

These are certainly desirable features of this program, even if as I shall shall suggest, instead of methods, we are better advised to try to warrant practices. But we should first notice that *if* the program carries, we will have escaped subjectivism, we will have warranted our method and thus beliefs which are determined by means of these methods, but we will *not* have secured truth. But, of course, Dewey's shift to warranted assertibility was a rejection of the search for truth (understood, as always, in the absolutist sense).[37]

Excursus: Truth about the World and Moral Truth

It will be important to notice the bearing of the foregoing on the question of moral relativism. In my view, this is surely the most important of the troublesome questions raised by relativism. Plainly, I cannot pursue this here. Yet, it seems to me that it is just here that the foregoing is most helpful. The reason is clear enough. The skeptical objection forecloses the possibility of securing a perspectively neutral truth about a world which exists independently of you and me. But since *on naturalistic grounds, our* ideas about what is good and right are *our* ideas, the skeptical objection has no force. All that we need as regards questions of the good and the right is warranted assertibility. Moreover, in this context, the public, interpersonal, and communal aspects are fundamental. While the effort to secure ever inclusive representations of the external world cannot secure truth about it, the effort to secure ever inclusive *goods* is exactly what is called for as regards moral matters.

Methodological Pragmatism

There is a third aspect to methodological pragmatism. It presumes that an empirical study of science will yield clarity about aims and methods, and that there is a way to reflexively test methods against aims, once identified. As far as I know, Laudan (and his associates), have been in the forefront of actually engaging in such research.[38] But I think that on this count, there are some very difficult problems.

First, there is the abstraction science. It is easy to suppose that although there are manifest differences in the sciences, the term, "science" is meaningful because the sciences share in goals, for example, prediction and control, and/or because there is something called "scientific method," again, usually defined in terms of a series of abstractions about the formation, deductive elaboration, and testing of hypotheses. Dewey was, I believe, utterly uncritical in this.[39] Laudan acknowledges that goals do differ and that, pertinent to this and to subject matter, methods (not merely techniques) may vary. Still it would seem that an adequate empirical picture would show some *fundamental* differences, not only in the sites and goals of the practices of the sciences, but in their methods and standards as well.[40]

Consider first the idea of the goals of these practices. Even a cursory examination would show, I believe, that there are at least four fundamentally different goals currently operative in the sciences.

1. Description: for example, ethnographic work in anthropology; quantitative research in economics or demography; much geography; and taxonomic work in botany and zoology (motivated, I believe, by very different goals than the pre-scientific taxonomy of the Karam!).

2. Prediction and control: behavioral social science, most psychology, meteorology, the engineering sciences, and applied sciences.

3. Understanding: basic science, including work in space/time theory, quantum mechanics, evolutionary theory, some (but surely the smallest part) of theoretical work in psychology and the social sciences.

4. The explanation of concrete events: history and the historical sciences (including here, some social science, some geology, some evolutionary biology, some psychology).

It has been easy to collapse these cognitive goals. For example, by means of the idea that the discovery of laws is *the* goal of science, it has been easy to believe that explanation, understanding, and prediction are of a piece. But while the point cannot be pursued here, it is easy to show that these are conceptually, and in practice, distinct aims. Empirical examination of practice would show, I believe, that those practices which aim at prediction and control (implicitly or explicitly) offer *nothing* in the way of understanding or in the explanation of concrete events. For example, behaviorist psychology gives no understanding of learning; and it cannot explain the most elementary concrete act, for example, my response, "fantastic," to seeing Guernica for the first time. But—and this is not to be minimized—behaviorist psychology has been an effective tool for manipulation and control.

But the point of this sketch is not to settle issues, but to raise questions for the empirical program that I have called "Inquiry into Inquiry: II." Speaking now within its frame of reference, if the goals are different, then we can expect the methods to be different. For any particular goal, there still will be methods that are most effective and suitable. And we can still endorse the basic Deweyan effort to self-referentially bootstrap. But not all these goals will be pertinent to the problem with which we began. The skeptical objection is plainly irrelevant if the aim is prediction and control. Moreover, it is very easy to justify science as the preferred mode if prediction and control is *the* goal. Indeed, this is a major motive for continuously attractive instrumentalist theories of science. If, however, one is interested in understanding or in explaining what happens, then inquiry into the practices of sciences with those aims will be pertinent. Laudan and his colleagues look at the "basic" natural sciences (depite their antirealism). If they had looked at most mainstream psychology, indeed at most mainstream social science, things would look very different.

But let us assume that the intention is to get an "empirically well-grounded picture" of those practices which in fact (and not merely in intention) aim at giving an account of how the world is. Of course, it will not do, as Laudan has himself so strenuously insisted, to accept those descriptions of science that are written with manifest assumptions imported from the two dominating traditions of twentieth-century philosophy of science. These studies cannot count as tests because they are self-authenticating. Nor can we, uncritically, accept what practitioners *say* are their methods (or for that matter, their standards and goals). As Einstein remarked, "If you want to find out anything from the theoretical physicists about the methods they use, I advise you to stick closely to one principle: Don't listen to their words, fix your attention on their deeds."[41] We have the best chance of getting some understanding about what they do if we can study activities directly. For standard historiographical reasons, things get much more difficult when we consider past practices. Indeed, in the face of these problems, there may be a temptation to *assume* methods and then to *assume* that they determine outcomes. We then enter history less problematically, with an eye merely to these.

Laudan's program risks this. Thus, he seems (at least) to begin with hypotheses regarding methodological rules which derive from philosophies of science. The idea then is to enter into history and seek either confirmation or disconfirmation of these. But there are now two additional problems. First, if as Laudan asserts, science changes, it is not clear how much generalizing will be possible,[42] and thus, to what degree we can regard conclusions drawn from such inquiry as tests. For example, consider but the institutional differences between Newton's scientific research and the big science of today. Assuming (what is likely contrary to fact) that the goals are comparable, can we be confident that abstracted methodological rules effective then would now be effective?

Second, as recent studies surely show, agents making decisions in science are complexly affected. Not only are they capable of self-delusion (like everyone else), but rules, even if they are crisply formulated and form a consistent set, need to be applied concretely. This is hardly to say that methods are irrelevant. Rather it is to assent to Kuhn's view, rejected by Laudan, that methodological criteria rarely if ever determine choices between rival theories. As Kuhn (and strong program writers) have insisted, this is not to deny rationality; it is to affirm that rationality is both changing (as Laudan admits) and *concrete*, exactly in a more Deweyan sense that we cannot explain choices by subsuming them under rules.

One thrust of my argument has been against philosophers (and those influenced by these) who, despite the best intentions, have been unable to free themselves from the shackles of traditional epistemology. Another thrust has been to sympathize warmly with pragmatic approaches, but to suggest that among the most outstanding of these, there are serious problems to be faced. Before concluding, I summarize:

First, if we are to understand knowing naturalistically, we need to rethink, in Deweyan terms, the psychology *and* logic of knowing. This will require, if I am correct, some important changes in the mainstream practices of empirical psychology.

Second, since knowledge is inescapeably a social product, we need to welcome the efforts of recent sociology of scientific knowledge. Our "naturalism" cannot be "half-hearted."

Third, having achieved a better understanding of the production of knowledge, if we are to seek warrant for beliefs (or to prescribe norms for belief), we will need to embrace a Deweyan approach to the fact/value dichotomy. We need to acknowledge, straight out, as Sleeper puts it, that since "*all* judgment is practical . . . there is no gulf between intellectual and practical judgment."

Fourth and finally, instead of trying to warrant methods, we will be better advised to try to warrant practices. I conclude with a sketch of what I mean by this.

The Warranting of Practices

Practices are, roughly, ways of doing. Practices include the beliefs of practitioners, the tools they use, their explicit goals, and much else besides. Practices are institutionalized (structured) activities, activities which presuppose habits in Dewey's sense, dispositions which carry the legacy of training and custom. The shift from methods to practices has consequences:

First, we will not be stymied if, as seems to be the case, much of what is known by practitioners is not formulable in terms of rules, but is tacit, craftlike, and learned at the side of experienced mentors. One learns how to use the tools, not merely the instrumentation, but the special languages, for example, the mathematics, and the standards for employing them. One learns what counts, what are the pitfalls, what are the ongoing standards of adequacy. Indeed, understanding these is precisely what would count as understanding a practice.[43]

Second, the shift to practice allows us to acknowledge that structured activities have unintended consequences. This includes not merely the uses to which basic work can be put, but the potential that outcomes may be surprising and hence not subject to control, and that intentions may be frustrated and transformed. Third, as part of the picture, we can include the real possibility that actors engaged in a practice can have false consciousness: they may have beliefs which are essential to the practice in the sense that if they have believed otherwise, they would not do what they do, but these beliefs might be false in the sense that actors may not fully understand just what they are doing. For example, they may believe that they are Popperians or instrumentalists when in fact they are not; they may believe that they are explaining when they are merely controlling; they may believe that their research is uncontaminated by interests foreign to their aims, etc.

A fourth advantage of this shift is that it allows us to incorporate as critical the fact that scientific practices are enmeshed in, effecting and effected by, a host of other practices: economic, educational, and political. Thus, the political economy of "big science" is critically relevant to understanding how its problems get defined and how it approaches and resolves them.[44] The issue is not merely that the goals and methods of the practice of big science are not autonomous, but that nonscientific factors are playing critical roles in constituting these practices.

Finally, we can be sensitive to the fact that scientific practices are very differently constituted, not merely between and among disciplines, but across time. Given this, a global defense of science may not be possible. On the other hand, we do not need a global defense. We need only to learn by inquiry what it is that makes a practice warrantable.

Harré's Justification of Theoretical/Experimental Physics

With these considerations in mind, there is at least one recent work to which we can point. Rom Harré is a trained physicist/philosopher who takes fully to heart the idea that (a) we had best look at scientific practices, (b) that a defense of practice in theoretical/experimental physics is not, *tout court*, a defense of science or of scientific method and (c) that such a defense must recognize the skeptical challenge with which we began. Plainly, this is not the place to detail Harré's important work, but I believe that (with some minor amendations), it is entirely congenial to the views of this chapter.

Begin with (c). Harré rejects what he calls "truth realism," roughly that a belief is true if and only if it corresponds to reality. Sensitive to arguments from Hume to Laudan, he defends "referential realism," roughly, the idea that "some of the substantive terms in a discourse denote or purport to denote beings of various metaphysical categories such as substance, quality or relation, that exist independently of that discourse."[45] In terms of our earlier discussion, not only is there an external world, but given what we know, the most plausible causal theory of perception is Gibsonian. That is, "while one must concede that there could not be psychological laws which explain how someone came to see a pencil, it does not follow that there could not be psychological laws which explain how someone came to see long, thin things, causal sequences, and other generic perceptibles."[46] On this view, these are natural "affordances," possibilities of action ecologically offered to naturally evolved species and found in the exploration of the ambient array. But plainly, this story will not suffice to explain our relevant taxonomies since, as above, Karam see (mediately) kobity and we see birds (or if we are birdwatchers, we see cassowary).

We need to make room for the social component of knowledge. Harré exploits Dretske's explication of "seeing that..." Thus,

1. S sees b.
2. The conditions under which S sees b are such that it would not look the way it does look, say L, unless it were P.
3. S, believing 2, takes b to be P.

Here, b is a Gibsonian invariant; condition 2 introduces S's corpus of prior belief. That "b is P" is knowledge, but, plainly, it is relative to the corpus of beliefs held by S, and there is no way to find some original, terminal, or foundational belief! We have found a toehold on the world, but we have not secured an absolutist conception of knowledge. Nor have we secured science.

We can imagine a discourse, Harré calls it Realm I discourse, which made reference only to the states and relations of beings known in actual experience (the heaven of empirical realisms!). Could such a discourse sustain a science? No doubt, human communities have put considerable attention on classifying beings in Realm I discourse, but as is now sufficiently clear, the boundaries "which serve to maintain discrete groupings in any human classificatory practice cannot be justified without reference to unobservable properties and structures of the beings in question."[47]

Harré's problem is now clear. Can he justify theoretical/experimental physics as a preferred mode of fixing belief about the external world? Grasping fully the idea that "the science we consume, so to speak, is the final product of the complex interplay of social forces and cognitive and material practices" (and *not* the product of a "logic engine"), he argues that one must acknowledge that scientific communities control their products "by the informal yet rigorous maintenance of a moral order."[48] Indeed, on Harré's view, a great deal of the best work by philosophers of science is most usefully understood as sketching an ideal *moral* order, not an ideal (or still less, real) epistemic order. On this reading, the (epistemic realist) manifesto, "Scientific statements should be taken as true or false by virtue of the way the world is" as a moral principle becomes: "As scientists, that is, members of a certain community, we should apportion our willingness or reluctance to accept a claim as worthy. . . only to the extent that we sincerely believe that it somehow reflects the way the world is." Similarly, the idea that we should seek falsification cannot be sustained as an epistemic principle. But it has manifest merits as encapsulating moral injunctions: for example, "However much personal investment one has in a theory, one should not ignore contrary evidence."[49]

For Harré, then, "facts" *are* socially constructed, but not only are they not constructed from whole cloth (the burden of referential realism), but *to the extent that the ideal moral order is functioning, then the results are to be preferred.*[50]

Why We Are Epistemically in Trouble

Harré appeals to empirical studies of scientific practices to identify what, pertinent to the problem of knowledge, is distinctive of these and, then, why, ideally speaking, they should be preferred. Speaking as a naturalizing epistemologist, this is all that we can demand. He does not, to be sure, say very much about the *social conditions* that would seem to be requisite to sustaining the ideal moral order. In general terms, these are the ideas that we familiarly associate with Peirce and Dewey, critically, the ideas of publicity and access.[51] But it is also clear that under conditions of industrialized science, it is just these conditions that are now under threat.

"Shoddy science" becomes possible when published papers are not being read and thus not subjected to critical scrutiny.[52] But since they easily become part of the construction of facts, how can we know what to trust?

"Entrepreneurial science" allows contractors to establish huge mission-oriented, capital-intensive enterprises in which researchers lose all independence and everyone else is denied access. Since these products are not assessed by consensus, why should they be trusted? "Runaway technology" can produce "reckless science." Here ready to access to millions of dollars aimed at some specific technical power, for example, the manipulation of genetic materials, can produce shoddy science now accompanied by the risk of catastrophic consequences. Finally, there is "dirty science" in which opportunities to fund research projects aimed at realizing understanding are converted into technologies for state purposes of destruction, or control, or manipulation.

We thus come full circle. We *are* stuck with our history. With the invention of modern philosophy as a discipline pretending not only autonomy but a privileged role in the intellectual division of labor, philosophers unwittingly conspired in mystifying a world in which science has played a profoundly important role. Seventy years after Dewey's called for reconstruction, the need is, if anything, even more urgent.

Notes

1. I have made two efforts at this, in *A History and Philosophy of the Social Sciences* (New York and Oxford: Basil Blackwell, 1987) and *War and Democracy* (New York and Oxford: Basil Blackwell, 1989).

2. Quine's 1969 essay and Stroud's 1981 "The Significance of Naturalized Epistemology" are reprinted in Hilary Kornblith's influential anthology, *Naturalizing Epistemology* (Cambridge, Mass.: MIT Press, 1985), cited in what follows.

3. Ibid., p. 77.

4. Ibid., quoted from "Epistemology." Quine's picture, presumably, is that, in Carnapian fashion, our knower can continually revise C-functions or in Popperian fashion, she can continue indefinitely to conceive hypothesis which she tries to falsify. These two programs in philosophy of science have been the most influential epistemologies in our century, but, as Laudan observes, they "have run into technical difficulties which seem beyond their resources to surmount" ("Progress or Rationality: The Prospects for Normative Naturalims," *American Philosophical Quarterly* 14, 1 (January 1987), p. 19.

5. See John Dewey, "The Existence of the World as Logical Problem" (MW 8:94–95). Of course, there are other forms of skepticism. See, e.g., Thomas Nagel, *The View From Nowhere* (New York: Oxford University Press, 1986), p. 71. J.E. Tiles, in *Dewey* (London: Routledge and Kegan Paul, 1988), quotes Russell's complaint that 'Professor Dewey ignores all fundamental

skepticism. To those who are troubled by the question: 'Is knowledge possible at all?' he has nothing to say" (p. 14). Tiles retorts that this is not fair: "what Dewey had to say was that the question lacked foundation" (p. 14). But 'the question' is ambiguous. Whether there is an external world which is at least partly structured *cannot* be motivated. But whether knowledge is possible, given *our* history, does have a point. See below.

6. See Tiles, *Dewey*, pp. 70–76. 116–23, 127–29. My account departs, however, from Tiles (and from Dewey?). Holding to an absolute conception of reality does not commit one to an absolute conception of knowledge. It is not my contention that we could describe the world "from no point of view." Knowing is *necessarily* a relation between a situated knower and "the world." But unless being depends upon knowing, this does not make whatever is at the object end either featureless or unknowable. On the other hand, Dewey was correct to insist that objects of knowledge (the character of things *as* known) were *produced* by inquiry. But because they are not produced from whole cloth (either by individuals or groups!), the skeptical problem arises.

7. Fallibilism, according to Nagel in *The View from Nowhere*, holds that our beliefs "go beyond their grounds in ways that make it impossible to defend them against doubt" (p. 68). Nagel here is defining *skepticism*, not fallibilism! It is hard to say how much disagreement in epistemology turns on different usages.

Peirce's limit conception of truth provides an anchor, but at a cost. See below. Dewey seemed at least to subscribe to Peirce's conception. See John Dewey, *Logic: The Theory of Inquiry* (LW 2:345).

8. See David Bloor, *Knowledge and Social Imagery* (London: Routledge and Kegan Paul, 1974), p. 32ff. In his *Dewey*, Tiles holds that Dewey's fallibilism was secured by the idea that inquiries comprise a continuum and suggests that Dewey was correct to de-emphasize Peirce's limit theory (pp. 106–8). I doubt this. Where there is no doubt, there is no inquiry. But the limit notion of truth does, at least, give the dissenter a rhetorical tack which is otherwise lacking.

9. Michael Friedman, "Truth and Confirmation," in *Naturalizing Epistemology*. Friedman offers what seem to me to be fatal objections to positivist views and to those views, like Peirce's, which seek to ensure a connection between confirmation and truth by giving a special meaning to truth. This would include Popper and at least some contemporary versions of instrumentalism—perhaps Larry Laudan. As regards the theory of reference, see my sketch of Harré's approach, below.

10. Ibid., pp. 155–56.

11. Ibid., p. 161. Notice that sociology is omitted. Presumably, what it has to offer is irrelevant to epistemology?

12.   Quine waffles on just what he is claiming. Susan Haack holds that Quine is "ambivalent" between a reformist "Modest Naturalism" in which epistemology is an integral part of empirical belief and a revolutionary "Scientistic Naturalism" "according to which epistemology is be conducted wholly within the natural sciences." See her "The Two Faces of Quine's Naturalism," *ms*, nd. On his more notorious ambiguities regarding the "validation" of claims to knowledge, see Ken Geme, "Epistemological Vs. Causal Explanation in Quine, or Quine: *Sic et Non*," *ms*, nd.

13.   Another is to observe (versus Quine) there is no way (as far as we can know) to go from "molecules upon our sensory surfaces" to the rat perception of, e.g., an edible object, to the (linguistically modeled) belief that there are red apples in the world. We return to this.

14.   See my "Modest Realism, Experience and Evolution," in *Harré' and His Critics* ed. Roy Bhaskar (Oxford: Basil Blackwell, 1990).

15.   Barry Stroud, "The Significance of Naturalized Epistemology," *Naturalizing Epistemology*, p. 76.

16.   See P. T. Manicas and Alan Rosenberg, "Naturalism, Epistemological Individualism and 'The Strong Programme' in the Sociology of Knowledge," *Journal for the Theory of Social Behavior* 15 (1985), pp. 76–101; and "The Sociology of Scientific Knowledge: Can We Ever Get It Straight?" *Journal for the Theory of Social Behavior* 18 (1988), pp. 51–76. As we indicated in the latter essay, there are important differences between researchers as regards questions in philosophy, between (say) Barnes, Harry Collins, and Steve Woolgar. Confusion over the claims of Barnes and Bloor is now joined by confusion over these differences.

17.   Barry Barnes, *Interests and the Growth of Knowledge* (London: Routledge and Kegan Paul, 1977), p. 25.

18.   I take this example from Barry Barnes, "On the Conventional Character of Knowledge and Cognition," *Philosophy of the Social Sciences* 11 (1981), pp. 303–33. Barnes puts it to the same purpose. See R. Bulmer, "Why is the Cassowary not a Bird?" *Man* 21 (1967), pp. 4–25.

19.   See Derek Bickerton, *The Origin of Language* (Chicago: University of Chicago Press, 1991).

20.   Thus drawing the rage of philosophers. It is presumably one thing to explain irrationally fixed belief by appeal to sociological facts; it is quite another thing to suppose that rational belief needs these. Presumably, one must contrast my belief that some figure presently in my vision is the Virgin Mary with my belief that some figure presently in my vision is a panda. Anthony Flew, now speaking for countless epistemological individualists, thinks that the former belief admits of a sociological explanation, but that if it is being argued (and it is!) that "intrusive, non-social, physiological, and biological facts" are not sufficient to explain this latter belief, then

the view is "manifestly preposterous and in its implications, catastroph-ically obscurantist." "A Strong Programme for the Sociology of Belief," *Inquiry* 25 (1982), pp. 366–67.

21. Dewey continues: "Through examination of the *relations* which exist between means (methods) employed and conclusions attained as their consequence, reasons are discovered why some methods succeed and other methods fail" (LW 12:17).

22. See his *Judgment and Justification* (Cambridge: Cambridge University Press, 1988).

23. According to Lycan, "occurent beliefs are sentencelike represen-tations stored and played back in our brains" (*ibid.*, p. 6). A belief, then, "is epistemically justified if and only if it is rated highly overall by the set of all-purpose, *topic neutral* canons of theory-preference that would have been selected by Mother Nature for creatures of our general sort. . ." (p. 160).

24. See Ralph W. Sleeper's important *The Necessity of Pragmatism* (New Haven, Yale University Press, 1986); and Thomas Burke, "Dewey on Defeasibility," in *Situation Theory and Its Applications*, eds. R. Cooper, K. Mukai, and J. Perry, (Stanford: CSLI Publications, 1990), pp. 233–68.

25. Confirmation theory is the skeleton in the closet of empiricist epistemologies of this century. For some of the key papers, see P. T. Manicas, ed., *Logic as Philosophy* (New York: D. Van Nostrand, 1972).

26. As Burke writes:

> The basic scenario is that a given organism/environmental system is constantly performing certain *operations* as a matter of course—employing sensory mechanisms, scanning, varying, probing, and otherwise moving about and altering things. Inquiry is initiated by some unsettling perturbation. . . . None of this needs be "deliberate." Dewey's picture of inquiry is supposed to describe general architectural and dynamic features of virtually any constituent subsystem of living animals, characterizing the simplest cellular life-functions as well as the most complex motor activities." ("Dewey on Defeasibility," p. 236.)

Classical epistemology is intellectualist in that it miscontrues "experience" and then conflates "having of an experience" with knowledge. Experience is "an affair of the intercourse of a living being with its physical and social environment"; it is *not* primarily "psychical," nor "a knowledge-affair"; and it is "pregnant with connexions" and "full of inference" (MW 10:6).

27. Compare Barnes and Bloor, " "Rationalism and the Sociology of Knowledge," in *Rationality and Relativism* eds. Hollis and Lukes, (Cambridge, Mass.: MIT Press, 1982), p. 44. For a provocative treatment in the context

172   PETER T. MANICAS

of recent philosophy of mathematics, see Mary Tiles, *Mathematics and The Image of Reason* (Cambridge: Cambridge University Press, 1991).

28. M. T. Turvey, R. E. Shaw, E. S. Reed, and W. M. Mace, "Ecological Laws of Perceiving and Acting: In Reply to Fodor and Pylyshyn (1981);; *Cognition* 9 (1981), p. 285. See also W. B. Weimer, "The Psychology of Inference and Expectations: Some Preliminary Remarks," in *Minnesota Studies in the Philosophy of Science*, Eds. G. R. Maxwell and A. R. Anderson vol. 6 (Minneapolis: University of Minnesota Press, 1975).

29. David Kelly and Janet Kreuger, "The Psychology of Abstraction," *Journal for the Theory of Social Behavior* 14 (March 1984), p. 64.

30. Nicholas Rescher, *Methodological Pragmatism* (Oxford: Basil Blackwell, 1975), p. 27.

31. Ibid., p. 28. See Guy Axtell, "Logicism, Pragmatism and Meta-Science," in *Philosophy of Science*, forthcoming.

32. Ibid., p. 36.

33. Larry Laudan, *Science and Values* (Berkeley: University of California Press, 1984), p. 62.

34. Ibid., p. 63.

35. Rescher, *Methodological Pragmatism*, p. 73.

36. Ibid.

37. Of course, the pragmatist, rejecting the problem of knowledge *überhaupt* and alive to differences in aims, cognitive and otherwise, is open to the possibility that different communities with different aims, cognitive and otherwise, might well be justified in their beliefs about the world. Thus, it is not clear that Karam methods, perhaps informed by and tested against goals which, for example, emphasize harmony with the natural world, are not justified.

38. Expanding on work in his *Progress and Its Problems*, Laudan has provided a "test" of "realist axiology and methodology" in his *Science and Values*, chapter 5. He construes realism as a truth-realism and then argues that a great deal of what physicists have believed to be true has been given up. Accordingly, realist methodological advice cannot be historically vindicated. However, as Harré says, this conclusion is vulnerable to a "modest" objection: "While physicists perhaps have not been able to keep their stock of deep fundamental theories unscathed by later developments, there has been a continual refinement and growing repetoire of very plausible items of information about many kinds of being whose existence can no longer be seriously called into doubt." (*Varieties of Realism* [Oxford and New York: Basil Blackwell, 1987], p. 41). Indeed, once realism is construed as by Harré, not only can Laudan's bullet be dodged but an excellent case for what Harré calls policy realism can be made: "If a substantive term seems to denote a being of certain natural kind (and some special conditions are satisfied by the theory in which that term functions)

it is worth setting up a search for that being" (p. 59). That is, by including in their working vocabulary a robust referring expression, there are "features of theories which historical experience shows are good bets for having anticipated experience..." (p. 60).

For other suggestions for rules worth testing, see Rachel Laudan, Larry Laudan, and Arthur Donovan, *Scrutinizing Science* (Holland: Kluwer Academic Publishers, 1988).

39.   I have suggested that Dewey held to an instrumentalist theory of science in which prediction and control exhaustively defined the goals of the sciences. See my "Pragmatic Philosophy of Science and the Charge of Scientism," *Transactions of the C.S. Peirce Society* 24, 2 (Spring 1988), pp. 179–219. In his antirealism as regards theoretical terms, he shares much with my colleague, Larry Laudan.

40.   Think of astrophysics at Princeton's Advanced Institute and at Rome ARDC, research in solid state physics at Stony Brook or at Roswell, N.M., DNA/RNA research at Cold Spring Harbor and at Texas Medical Center; biochemists working at Max Factor, or on bonding metals ions to antibodies at Scripps Clinic, or neurotransmitters at the University of Hawaii; economists at the Bureau of Labor, the American Enterprise Institute, or Cambridge University, England; psychologists at Merrill Lynch, in the social welfare services of the City of New York, at the New School for Social Research, at MIT; unfunded anthropologists in Thailand and anthropologists working for AID in Thailand. One could easily go on.

41.   Quoted by G. Holton, "Mach, Einstein, and the Search for Reality." in *Ernst Mach, Physicist and Philosopher*, eds. R. S. Cohen and R. J. Seeger (Dordrecht: Reidel, 1970). The text is from Einstein's 1933 Herbert Spencer Lecture.

42.   Feyerabend surely goes too far here. Harré points out that Feyerabend aims his guns at "the logicisms of the alleged inductive method and the fallibilism of Popper," but this target is too restricted. More importantly as regards the present context, "there may be more than one but not indefinitely many contexts of enquiry, in each of which different methodological and metaphysical principles, each cluster of which could be taken as defining a scientific inquiry, could be rationally defended" (*Varieties of Realism*, pp. 24–25). This would, I think, still undermine Laudan's program.

43.   Compare, of course: Michael Polanyi, *Personal Knowledge* (London: Routledge and Kegan Paul, 1958); Jerome Ravetz, *Scientific Knowledge and Its Social Problems* (New York: Oxford University Press, 1971).

44.   Merely by way of illustration, what are we to make of the fact that sixty billion dollars will be spent in the 1990s on a half-dozen projects—a space station, a human genome project, a supercollider. And what are we to make of the criticism that "big science has gone berserk,"

that "good minds and a lot of money are going into areas that are not relevant to American competitiveness, American technological health, or even the balanced development of American science" (*New York Times,* Sunday, May 27, 1990, p. 1).

45.   Harré, *Varieties of Realism,* p. 67.

46.   Ibid., p. 154.

47.   Ibid., p. 179. They will, for example, require dispositional attributions. The clearest examples are in everyday discriminations, for example, salt and sugar. But consider also classifications of modern zoology, sustained (or not) by appeal to beliefs deriving from neo-Darwinian theory (just as the Karam classifications are sustained [or not] by appeal to beliefs which run past Realm I discourse).

48.   Ibid., p. 12.

49.   Ibid., p. 90.

50.   I have, of course, omitted all of his argument in favor of policy realism. This takes us onto more familiar ground in the philosophy of science.

51.   See Dewey's remarkable *The Public and Its Problems* (LW 2). Dewey pointed out that the conditions for assessing claims were, in general, being eroded. Thirty years later, C. W. Mills picked up this theme: As "experts" constrained dialogue, "publics" were being converted to "masses."

52.   The term "shoddy science," the analysis, and the other categories that follow are thanks to Jerome Ravetz, *Scientific Knowledge and Its Social Problems,* chap. 10.

10

Rationality and a Sense of Pragmatism: Preconditions for a New Method of Thinking

IGOR N. SIDOROV

Philosophy is—or can be—an expression of fundamental spiritual life and culture. As such, it is of great importance for understanding and developing a socially progressive world order and outlook. The pressing cultural (as opposed to academic) question for philosophy thus is this: Is it possible to transform the existing basic functions of philosophical knowledge, the methods of its attainment, and the goals of its application? The present day surfeit of ways of philosophizing makes this question a genuine problem. What are the preconditions for a substantial dialogue among various world cultures in the context of values shared by all people? How, if at all, may these preconditions be realized?

It must be recognized, of course, that the narrow, one-sidedness of our present technocratic culture and stage of human development points to the urgent need for active and sustained search for alternatives. In this experimental search and social reconstruction, new possibilities for philosophy and new formulations of philosophical problems, in keeping with philosophical traditions, may be of great value.

Attention to American pragmatic philosophy of our age uncovers one such possibility. Following the precepts of its own "golden age," contemporary American philosophy displays a striving to bring new elements to the classical scheme of analysis of cognitive relationships. These new elements are formulated from a point of view which recognizes and emphasizes the leading role of the *practical* activities of human beings. This stress on practice is not only theoretical, but also practical: any new development of philosophical problems must be set forth and decided on practical terms. Journal articles and book essays will not suffice.

This point of view, embodied and articulated in pragmatism, has deep roots in American culture and American philosophy. It is oriented toward substantial—that is to say active—humanism. As John E. Smith writes: "There are three dominant or focal beliefs through which our philosophic spirit can be articulated. First the belief that thinking is primarily an *activity* in response to a concrete situation and that this activity is aimed at solving problems. Second, the belief that ideas and theories must have a cutting edge or must *make a difference* in the conduct of people who hold them and in the situations in which they live. Third, the belief that *the earth can be civilized* and obstacles to progress overcome by the application of knowledge. Taken together, these beliefs define a basically humanistic outlook...."[1] This orientation of American thought, in the context of Western humanistic ideals, toward the practical resolution of practical problems broadly manifests itself. It is explicitly evident, for example, in social and political thought, in legal theory, and in moral and aesthetic conceptions.

This orientation, that even now so strongly irritates self-absorbed proponents of traditional and more speculative approaches, connects philosophy with the day-to-day activities and fundamental interests of the people. To realize its present possibilities, it is not necessary that philosophy attain speculative truth. Rather, it is more that philosophy must develop and exhibit the ability to recapture the living meaning of—and thus to reconstruct in light of new attention to justice, gender, and the environment—the thesis of Protogoras that man is the measure of all things.

"This sort of study," comments Marcus Singer, "may not be philosophy as philosophy has been understood in Anglo-American analytic circles for some forty or fifty years, and it may not be philosophy as it is understood in the haunts and graveyards of existentialism, but it is philosophy nonetheless. The standards for evaluating instances of it as good or bad may not be the same as those for evaluating other instances of philosophy. There are such standards nonetheless, which derive from the activity itself, not from something other than it."[2] In such a manner there has formed, and survived, in American philosophy a nontraditional principle in accordance with which the wellspring of the philosophical method of thinking can be and must be related to practical activities.

This principle was for the most part fully embodied in the methodology of pragmatism. Peirce placed at the center of his philosophy the problem of the epistemological status of action and the meaning of faith. Before Peirce, this had occupied often only peripheral spheres of philosophical interest. Even Immanuel Kant, who understood the philosophical significance of action and pragmatic faith, did not tie together with this understanding a deep, radical perspective of a philosophical method of practice. He supposed, in part, that faith only fills in for the lack of knowledge when necessities arise and require a decision to be reached without delay. In this compensatory role, faith has turned out to be fortuitous—for in the this role it could not operate where resolution of a situation on the basis of knowledge is possible. The relative application of faith as a condition for adopting the correct decision, that is for the attainment of success, is in Kant's view a reflection of the fluctuation of diverse interests that are motivated by the origins of the given faith. In other words, in the doctrine of the author of "Criticisms of a Pure Mind," faith, although it is recognized as a basis of successful action, is, however, in essence inferior in this role to knowledge.

The view of the founders of pragmatism toward the mutual relationships of knowledge, faith, and action was from the beginning principally different. They believed that the demand for knowledge prior to and independent of action and the quest for a purely theoretical resolution of problems brought on by life cannot be reached and cannot be realistic under actual life conditions. Men and women are constantly engaged in active efforts to make effective decisions and in attempts to formulate effective principles and methods for decision making. These principles and methods must reflect the results of these active efforts— the results of action. For this reason, a faith in action provides an authentic basis for genuinely human knowledge.

Guided by these convictions, the founders of pragmatism changed in a material way the substance of philosophical problems. Despite the continued misunderstanding of critics, this allowed them to reach nontrivial solutions and dis-solutions of philosophical issues. It allowed them, in short, to recover philosophy.

This recovery of philosophy amounts to a naturalistic reconstruction of the entire spectrum of philosophy by means of an account of a naturalistic, *natural* way of thinking. As already formulated by Peirce in his pragmatic maxim, the principle of thinking as a natural human activity stands in opposition to all accounts of persons as inorganic investigatory programs. Instead, it supports a view of thought as an instrumental activity of a fully natural being striving for self-realization. As if following Kant in his representation of human life as an end, and not as a mere means for the realization of external goals, pragmatism's empirical method and naturalistic account of thinking are interwoven intrinsically with a humanistic idea—an ethical ideal—*of human self-realization*.

From a methodological perspective, this idea is mainly directed against logical or scientistic reductionism. It infuses any reductionist scheme with all the richness of cognitive, aesthetic, temporal, social relationships that traditionally are not expressed in the language of formal logic. Pragmatism exposed the conservatism of traditional/formal accounts of rationality and opened the way for radical change. A radically empirical account of experience and nature, thought and action, logic and inquiry, quality and mediation, and meaning and reference is made possible in direct relation to links to the process and results of practical interaction between the subject and object of cognitive (and other) transactions.

This undertaking by American pragmatism and its new methodology oriented toward practice is both promising and principally correct. Many of these ideas also were developed successfully and independently in several Russian investigations during approximately the same time. The most significant and fundamental in this regard is development of a pragmatic, practical psychological theory of activity, dating from the work of the Russian psychologist L. S. Vygotski (1896–1934). This theory of human activity develops an understanding of the subject-object relation-ship as a nondualistic structure. That is, there is a third element, to which special attention is paid: subject-activity-object. This third element is activity as a means of real communication and transformative constitution between subject and object. In the context of philosophy, this theory aims to terminate the dependence of epistemology on the so-called "axioms of spontaneity." These axioms, according to Vygotski, have postulated the subject-object connection as outside and independent of action or practice—as a kind of spontaneous imitation. But, the form of such a connection, its number or varieties, and its logical expression cannot possibly be spontaneous and independent of activity: ". . . the role of activity in the formulation of a psychological model of consciousness is that it transfers the property of the cognitive/reflected subject from its substantive form in activity, into the form of operations, of a scheme of action with this subject, but this active form of existence of the subject, *which is permitted to be made the object of his cognition*, has a middle ground, in which is created the ideal form of the subject, i.e. his psychological model in view of knowledge."[3]

This point of view of practical activity also provides an answer to the highly material question of why cognition is directed at some, rather than other, aspects of its subject matter, its object. The answer is fully determined: selectivity is necessary to cognize those aspects and characteristics of a situation and its subject matter that are in fact included in activity, actual or proposed. Contemporary empirical investigations have shown that ". . . external subjects so reflect themselves in the psyche of man that they enter into his activity, i.e. they represent those aspects of the object, which they open up to man and in the process of influencing man they are determined not indirectly as subjects, but instead they mediate between that activity which is directed at this subject and the structure in which it is included as an object."[4] In such manner the active, practical approach to thinking is conducive to the elimination from philosophy of both the traditional ideal of objectivism—where knowledge is proclaimed as an imitation of all attributes of an independent object—and also the commonplace methodology of logical reductionism—where metaphysics is derived from logic, and knowledge is presented as a modification of the so-called "logical substance."

Furthermore, the fuller development of the active, practical, naturalistic approach to thinking has led, in Russian philosophy, for example, to the notions of: a) the singularity or intrinsic connectedness in cognition of logic and intuition, and b) the mutual coordination and supplementation in philosophical theory and method of formal and substantial aspects. Neither the supposed "laws of logic" nor the supposed formal requirements of theory are adequate to understand the actual execution of cognition. An understanding of thinking cannot be reached simply by putting into action all the clever engines of logical-formal apriorism.

The mutual connection of logic and intuition, of the formal and the substantial, of theory and practice is evident in and determined through human activity. These intrinsic connections are aspects of all knowing transactions, and these transactions are inconclusive, anything but final, and elements in the unbroken, continuous processes of practical transformations. If one looks at any element in such a process from the point of view of the entire process—that is, from the point of view of activity as a practical whole—that element reflects the general/universal content of practical activity. As demonstrated by contemporary research: "for active interaction in the world it is necessary to present all of these [objective] correlations in view of the regulated and logical aspect of the system;" as the result of such regulation "is created a synonymous context."[5]

However, merely having knowledge—existing knowledge—can prove to be useless or ineffective in the active effort to attain new goals. For this reason, the need to develop new knowledge—knowledge not contained in or simply logically deduced from existing knowledge—arises. The effort to solve this sort of problem characterizes the intuitive, practical phase of the creative process, where an unexpected decision, often called insightful, "arises owing to that which proves to be a *satisfied requirement* which had by this time reached a high tension."[6] The subsequent verbalization and formalization of an intuitive decision cloaks it in a logical form. In other words, belief becomes knowledge through practice; that is, practical knowledge—art—becomes fact—science—when it leads from the polysemantic practical context of thought to a synonymity of logic. Such synonymity opens up the possibility of effective action in the future. In the case of the confirmation of this effectiveness, knowledge must be admitted as scientific in character.

This synonymity of scientific knowledge means that science, as science, is indifferent to the source of an idea or plan of action. It also means that science is indifferent to its form. The objective content of knowledge—that is, that which makes up its meaning—does not depend merely on its modality—that is, on that method by which perceptible information comes into consciousness. In other words, scientific knowledge is not defined simply by the channel of transmission of information used—that is, visual, audio, or tactile. Instead, it is characterized by the practical goals of its application—application that determines its meaning. This meaning is objective from the standpoint of practice, and in this sense may be understood as independent of the language in which it is expressed. In the semantic relationship it is regarded as isomorphous, admitted/allowed/spoken, gesticulative (*symbolic*) expression. Here also everything is determined mostly by context and the goals of the practical activity—in whatever formulation in language that may be natural or artificial, scientific or artistic, indicative or symbolic.

The advancement of this theory of activity, briefly rehearsed above, allows one to evaluate freshly pragmatism's perspective on the nature of rationality and the relation of thought to action in rationality. In any event, pragmatism provides an opportunity—one that philosophy often has squandered—to understand more deeply the substance of the problem of rationality itself.

Before addressing this issue directly, it may be useful to recall briefly its historical and philosophical context. Under the strong influence of Descartes, Spinoda, Leibniz, and others in the rationalist tradition, the model of rationality was supplied by mathematics and geometry, the criterion of knowledge was logical certainty, and the definition of truth was correspondence. Hegel, however, realized and argued that this is internally inconsistent and dubious. Remarking on the wide range of opinion concerning the view that in geometry the synthetic method of final cognition reaches full perfection, Hegel thereupon exposed a deep contradiction in the traditional interpretation of this perfection as the form of rationality itself. In the "Encyclopedia of Philosophical Science," he writes, "It is remarkable, however, that moving on its own path, geometry also is pushed in the end to incommensurable and irrational magnitudes, where it, if it wants to go further along the path of specification, is obliged to go beyond the boundaries of the principle of reason. And here, as in other spheres, the terminology turns out to be false: that, which we call rational, in reality belongs to the sphere of reason; to that which we call irrational there is a quicker commencement and trail of rationality."[7] The principle of reason is, in such fashion, in a conditionally strict definition. The transition to a still stricter definition to the extent that it becomes necessary, requires a paradoxical repudiation of this principle and of the point of view of reason as such.

The paradox is that it is impossible to call this point of view of reason a wholly bankrupt one in theory, for it and the definitions that stem from it conform to the prior level of knowledge. But in practice, this rational knowledge is without force. As Hegel puts it, "it pays no heed to the fact that it has come up against its own boundary, it does not know that it is in a sphere, in which the definitions of reason already are without strength, and it continues to coarsely employ them there, where they are already inapplicable."[8] Even in this past account of rationality, rationality did not ensure the adequacy of cognition to its task. Thus it points to a new, alternative account of rationality, an account that recognizes the basis, goals, and test of cognition in activity.

In this way, Hegel showed that in the dialectical tradition, rationality and irrationality constitute reciprocal, flexible characteristics of knowledge—characteristics that depend on the practical goals of cognition.

Pragmatism represents an especially deep and sizeable further development of this theme of the practical, active, expedient character of rationality. Moreover, this pragmatic development has fundamentally influenced subsequent philosophy. Dewey, for example, made clear that the traditional, logical, formal, theoretical account of rationality is rooted in the development of science, from the geometric beginnings of Euclid to the mathematic beginnings of the natural philosophy of Newton. Such an absolutist view of reason always finds powerful support from dogmatic adherents of speculative philosophies. In this manner, formal logic, beginning with Aristotle, was deliberately abstracted from substantial definitions and actual contexts of thought and reason. More recently, this dogmatism has embraced a "strict" definition of ideal and pure forms, images and essences, in a mystical dependence on imaginary attributes in which are supplied the entire wealth of real phenomenon and concrete experience. In any event, this dogmatic conformity of logical forms or speculative categories with pre-Western abstractions or with forms of high sophistication is said to meet the supposed criteria of knowledge.

Recognizing, with Hegel, that genuine knowledge cannot have the status of the finished form or absolute, Dewey uncovered the fundamental conditions for the formation of actual human knowledge. For the substantiation of an adequate methodology, it is important, in his opinion, to take into consideration that the real basis of cognition lies in the concrete activites of man. These activities are directed toward the ongoing transformation of the natural or objective world, including one's self. These activities and their expediency and effectiveness must be safeguarded, but not by the rules of supposed pure reflection or pure reason. Dewey wrote that logic is a systematized and clarified formulation of the procedures of thinking that enables the desired reconstruction to go on economically and efficiently: "If thought or intelligence is the means of intentional reconstruction of experience, then logic, as an account of the procedures of thought, is not purely formal.... If ideas, meanings, conceptions, notions, theories, systems are instrumental to an active reorganization of the given environment, to a removal of some specific trouble and perplexity, then the test of their validity and value lies in accomplishing this work" (MW 12:157, 169). This means that it is impossible to look at thought as some autonomous wellspring of pure logical forms. Such forms come last, not first; they derive from practical goals in particular situations.

This view has widespread explanatory force for philosophical thought. Compare the contemporary Russian scientific interpretation of philosophy as a metaphysical study on the fundamental, organic traits of being: For philosophy, ". . . not in the least do we mean its value-semantic component, the knowledge from which derived has obtained the status of conviction and has entered into a relationship with the intimate-personality plan of human life. [Philosophical truths] are convictions and therefore in their final expression are personal truths. The scientific interpretation of philosophy, which places it under the prevailing standards of natural knowledge, severs from it exactly that by which is fed its specific outward-looking influence."[9] This recognition that philosophical truth is irreducibly truth conviction overcomes scientism and the negative influence in philosophy of a supposed scientific ideal of reason.

This recognition is possible, in other words, only through a revival of the naturalistic method and naturalistic view of thought and reason set forth by pragmatism. In this context, it may be necessary to add, at least with respect to Russian philosophy, that there is no reason to reduce or lower this naturalism to a kind of economism, an exclusive focus on the level of everyday "economic" elements. Here it is interesting to note that the Russian philosopher Vladimir Solovyov correctly predicted that "it is insufficient for a natural being to have economic relationships, but instead it is necessary that economic relationships consciously aim towards the common welfare."[10]

Meanwhile, the question of the conscious direction of action clearly cannot be solved by scientific thought (or reductionist philosophy) alone. Our actions must be formed, undertaken, and judged by nothing less than the full range of our experience—by impressions and reflections on our own diverse individual and social requirements, interests, and goals. The elucidation of their general meaning is an attempt to explain the living intentionalities of human existences. Isn't this properly the entire purpose of philosophical inquiry and understanding?

Pragmatism, of course, has paid attention to all the complexities of this problem. George H. Mead systematically dealt with the mutual relationships between humans and environment, self and society, and culture and the world. His point of view—a point of view centered on process, emergence and the emergent system, principles of the dynamics, evolution and perspectives, behavior and society—deserves a favorable reevaluation and application today.

Mead, like Dewey and other pragmatists, raises to a higher level our understanding of experience as a natural process. Directed and shared actions (in which the natural activity of humans is fulfilled) call forth and are pervaded by cognition from the perspective of these actions themselves. This recognition of the irreducibly perspectival character of cognition signifies that the goal of cognition is the organization and advancement of the activities, already underway, which called it forth and influence it. In the event that this goal has been adequately interpreted by cognition in this situation, the different and various factors in cognition attain a factual unity, and this resulting unity in cogniton promotes the fulfillment of the activities underway.

This account of cognition in the concrete circumstances of particular problematic situations permits Mead to avoid speaking of cognition "in general" and to avoid striving toward any universal scheme of knowledge or reason. Mead, like Dewey, placed cognition, its nature, goals, and means in intrinsic connection to and dependence on its cosmological, biological, and social contexts. This contextualist account points to the possibility in theory and the need in practice for the elimination of the influences on thought of both authoritarianism and dogmatism: cognition of facts depends entirely on activities and practices, and thus these activities can and must be informed by inquiry rather than fiat, superstition, or speculation. This activity of inquiry is a necesssary condition for the authenticity of knowledge. To the extent that a philosopher insists on this, that philosopher comes forward as a proponent of principles of justification and warrant of assertions, or of their sufficiency for attaining goals. Such a position opens significantly a far wider possibility for changes or corrections of existing knowledge in those cases where living situations undergo change, than in the case where the primary truth of past principles attempts to become fixed "despite everything."

In the context of contemporary problems, this focus on human activity is equivalent to the recogntion that men and women, before everything else, are moral actors—moral actors searching for meaning and capable of something other and more than blind obedience to propaganda. This pragmatic faith (that lies at the heart of Dewey's philosophy) may incline one to optimism—or optimistic meliorism—even in the face of the complexities of the current day development of humanity. Through the development of cognition and inquiry in activity, men and women can cease to be passionless observers and victims of their situations. They can exert influence and direction on the course of their lives and societies. Each may stop being an alien in his or her own land. The pragmatists, especially Dewey and Mead, help this to be understood: "Mead's understanding of human nature as social at its most fundamental level suggests that we have been too quick to accept the dire claims of those who portray the human state as one of alienation and who maintain that humans are by their nature cut off from one another, isolated and alone."[11] The significance of this is that it clearly undermines the bases of both traditional idealistic metaphysics and more recent totalitarian politics that accept, legitimize, and sanctify the factual estrangement and actual divisibility of people, most often by means of the secret influence of world ontology. The course of contemporary development of civilization sufficiently and convincingly shows that, instead of political conformism and belief in the unconditional value of the recent past, the creative and research abilities of the people should be encouraged and cultivated. This would allow people to focus and concentrate energy on the inquiry into, and practical decisions about, life's important problems—especially those of primary importance for present times, including problems of the very survival of human life and nature.

In such fashion, pragmatism's naturalistic and practical account of rationality in action may acquire a higher capacity for creative activity (as opposed to mere creative theory). Of main theoretical importance now is that this principle be cleansed of distortions connected with its one-sided technocratic, scientistic, economist interpretation and application. In this vein, a contemporary Russian researcher writes: "an unexpected consequence of scientific-technical progress has turned out to be that the anxiety about the creation of 'formal' intellect became much sharper than the anxiety about the development of the spiritual potential of society, which alone can triumph over soulless intellectualism. Scientific-technical progress led to a deformation of education, since for its success it required a subject of action."[12] In other words, the realization of expedient action in and of itself does not ensure any increase of human spirituality.

As for pragmatism: By having developed a powerful naturalistic and practical account of human activity, including cognition, it now puts forward the question of the possibility of the unity of particular, concrete actions and general, shared spiritual meanings. This means that the current pragmatic task of development for pragmatism itself is nothing short of a transition from past pragmatism as a philosophy of action to future pragmatism as a philosophy of the soul.

Notes

This essay was translated from Russian to English by Douglas J. Hile, with assistance by Igor N. Sidorov and John J. Stuhr.

1. John E. Smith, *The Spirit of American Philosophy* (Albany: State University of New York Press, 1983), p. 188.

2. Marcus G. Singer, "The Context of American Philosophy," in *American Philosophy*, ed. M. G. Singer (Cambridge: Cambridge University Press, 1985), pp. 19–20.

3. Y. F. Tarasov, *Tendencies of the Development of Psycholinguistics* (Moscow, 1987), pp. 115–116, emphasis added.

4. Ibid., p. 102.

5. V. S. Rotenberg, "Two Sides of One Mind and Creativity," in *Intuition, Logic, Creativity*, ed. M. I. Panova (Moscow, 1987), p. 40.

6. Y. V. Ponamarev, "The Fundamental Links of the Psychological Mechanism of Creativity," in *Intuition, Logic, Creativity*, p. 13.

7. G. W. F. Hegel, *Encyclopedia of Philosophical Science* (Moscow: 1974), sec. 231, pp. 415–16.

8. Ibid., p. 416.

9. G. A. Davydova, "On the World-Outlook Nature of Philosophical Knowledge," *Questions of Philosophy* 2 (1988), p. 49.

10. V. I. Solovyov, *Collected Works*, vol. 1 (Moscow: 1988), p. 418.

11. James Campbell, "George Herbert Mead: Philosophy and the Pragmatic Self," in *American Philosophy*, p. 111.

12. V. P. Zinchenko, "Science—An Integral Part of Culture?," *Questions of Philosophy* 1 (1990), p. 45.

Objects of Knowledge

H. S. THAYER

The question "What is Knowledge?" is thought to be a typically philosophical question—so typical, indeed, that to ask it is to *be* philosophical while the mood persists. It has been asked and answered often enough to have succeeded in making a history for itself and to become a branch of philosophical study, namely, epistemology. Since a question about the nature of knowledge is unlikely to arise in the absence of some existing knowledge to ask about, this is not the skeptical quandry as to whether anything can be known at all. One grants that human beings possess knowledge, and science is usually cited as a commanding example. The question is rather about what qualifies something to be something known; what does "knowledge" mean? There has never been complete agreement about the answer.

The currently favored characterization of knowledge is "true justified belief," which is not altogether different from Dewey's definition of knowledge as warranted belief or warranted assertibility. But a precise specification of justification has proved difficult, and the notions of truth and belief continue to provoke controversies. Perhaps it is the fate of typically philosophical questions to remain unsettled. It is a fate not typical of most of science.

Dewey took the question about the meaning of knowledge seriously. In various ways and to some degree it is present in all of his writings and is the explicit subject of several of his major philosophical works.[1]

The question is of intrinsic interest and also an inducement to a clearer awareness of a vital part of one's self and of being one's self. In the wider sphere of social life beliefs about the nature and scope of human knowledge shape the way that education, social and political institutions, and moral deliberation and practices are understood. Dewey argued that influential philosophical theories of knowledge reflect and often serve to perpetuate certain dominant features of the cultures in which they find expression (MW 9:342–55). Social and economic divisions between labor and leisure classes, ruled and rulers, may be traceable in philosophic theories to prejudicial dualisms that separate body and mind, sense and reason, practice and theory, the material and spiritual. Dewey envisioned his own philosophical efforts in a similar way as implicated in the culture of which he was part. His theory of knowledge and education, he said, was an attempt to connect "the growth of democracy with the development of the experimental method in sciences" (MW 9:3).

We can thus appreciate why the question about knowledge was important to Dewey. For how the question is received and judged is profoundly revealing of the beliefs of people about themselves, their world and their prospects. Since knowledge is a significant cause of changes in human experience and society, the more it is understood the better the chance of administering it as a force for human good.

It is for the above reasons that Dewey was moved to frequent and occasionally severe criticism of philosophical expositions and explanations of the meaning of knowledge. The intellectual travail and endless controversies of "the epistemological industry" (as Dewey characterized it) are the inevitable result of uncritical reliance on dualistic assumptions guiding the analyses of the mental and physical, of knowing and objects known. The assumption that minds and material objects are inherently different kinds of existence yet somehow connected so that through internal mental processes the external objects are known defeats at the start any attempt to provide an adequate explanation of knowledge. While the assumed dualism was frequently propagated as authorized by modern scientific knowledge, it ensured that a "problem of knowledge" was insoluble.

It is not denied that there are genuine problems in epistemology; problems about what knowledge is and how it is attained. But these are problems of logic as Dewey understood them—that is, logic as the theory of inquiry.

The theory of inquiry is Dewey's theory of knowledge or its theoretical core: "Knowledge is related to inquiry as a product to the operations by which it is produced" (LW 12:122). In renouncing various dualistic interpretations of thinking and knowing and in focusing on how behavior is modified by thinking—and how thinking is a way of behaving—Dewey elaborated a comprehensive and novel theory of deliberative thinking. It is a theory that many philosophers have found of little or no relevance to logic or epistemology as ordinarily conceived.

In many respects Dewey's work is a radical departure from traditional and established beliefs about the nature of knowledge. Because of the tenacity and sweep of its criticism of accepted doctrines and because of its own innovations of orientation and argument, Dewey's thought has made for difficulties of understanding and assessment. It is not just that new ideas usually meet with resistance and opposition—although that is a predicament. Dewey's sustained critique of historically entrenched and recurrently accepted assumptions about mind and knowing leads to a reconceptualization of the subject matter and a reconstruction of the language of philosophic inquiry and analysis. He proceded to articulate and advance the main lines of the revisionary perspective. In going against habitual persuasions and conventional terminology, his work appears at first unfamiliar and in some ways incongruous and awkward; it thus strains our powers of recognition and judicious representation. The history of Dewey's thought has been marked to an unusual degree by controversy over issues of interpretation and meaning.

A fundamental doctrine that has proved especially troublesome in discussions of Dewey's theory of knowledge forms his conception of an object of knowledge. He writes:

> The object of knowledge is eventual; that is, it is the outcome of directed experimental operations, instead of something in sufficient existence before the act of knowing. (LW 4:136)

He also says that the act of inquiry initiates a "new empirical situation" such that "the *consequences* of directed operations form the objects that have the property of being known" (LW 4:70).

Dewey seems to be saying that an object of knowledge does not exist before it is known. And in a very special sense he is saying that. But he was not espousing a version of subjective idealism according to which thinking brings its objects into existence. He was often asked to explain what an object is before inquiry or before it is known. His answer, that he could not consistently presume to know anything about objects before they are inquired into, seemed evasive.

Part of the problem is verbal. Dewey's theory of inquiry required limiting the notion of "object of knowledge" to the warranted conclusions of inquiry. This narrowing of the use of the term was not a willful flouting of accepted idiom. Dewey had his reasons as we shall see. But the revised usage was apt to pass unnoticed and so to engender misunderstanding. The other and more serious part of the problem was rooted in deep philosophical differences between Dewey and his critics.

We are accustomed to think of objects of knowledge as on par with objects generally, known or unknown, They are labeled objects of knowledge when *we* come to know them. But the label has nothing to do with the object in its own right. Whether we succeed in knowing them or not, as objects they are—so Bishop Butler advised—just what they are and nothing else. Dewey appeared to be controverting this venerable common sense. He was asserting that objects of knowledge are not so much *discovered* as *produced* by inquiry. As Ernest Nagel remarked in his introduction to Dewey's *Logic: The Theory of Inquiry,* "this claim is not compatible with what is usually believed to be the status of objects of knowledge" (LW 12:xxii).

A minute but effective agent in this controversy is the pronoun 'it.' Speaking of an object and pondering how *it* comes to be known, the pronoun encourages an uncritical assumption that *it*—the object—has a fixed nature or character prior to and independent of any thinking about it. Else, what could be the referent of 'it'? Furthermore, the object, *it*, is the decisive factor on which the truth or falsity of what we think and say about it depends. Use of the pronoun in these senses easily extends into the more recondite notions of the externality and identity of subsances and the notion of a thing-in-itself.[2] So a metaphysical realism invests the use of language. We are predisposcd to adopt a conviction about independently existing objects with enduring essential natures.

It is in the light of this inveterate way of thinking about object of knowledge that Dewey's views seemed so odd and mistaken. To argue that objects of knowledge are produced by knowing them, or that they do not exist before they are known, appeared paradoxical. We seem to be unable to account for the objects before and in the course of our coming to know them. To catch them, as it were, in their unguarded moments before pinning them down by knowing them, is evidently like trying to jump on one's own shadow.

The sense of paradox is reinforced if one presumes that thinking and knowing are essentially internal activities and accomplishments of minds. Thus something becomes an object of knowledge not because of what may pertain to *it* (note the pronoun at work), but by virtue of an intellectual exercise carried on in the mind. The change effected by knowledge, then, is a change in someone's mind—a clarification or illumination—not a change among objects.

A central feature of Dewey's theory is that inquiry does not begin with "objects" already demarcated and determined; it begins with a situation that is problematic or doubtful. Even sheer "awareness" or "consciousness" is *of* something and is felt to occur in relation and with reference to something. The "something" *and* the active reference are discriminations and selective acts of thought. But a selection presupposes the existence of a plurality of factors affecting both the way a selection is made and what is selected. This complex of existing factors is a situation. And since a situation provides the existing conditions for the distinctions and selective activities of thinking, it is temporally and causally prior to thought and inquiry. We can see here how Dewey might have answered the question mentioned earlier about the status of objects before inquiry. What is or comes before inquiry is not objects but a situation. Furthermore, the selective modes of thinking and discourse are preceded by some immediately felt quality of a situation. For every situation has its distinctive "dominant qualitativeness," says Dewey, an inhering pervasive mood or coloring or tone.[3]

There are, of course, all kinds of qualitative situations that can elicit many kinds of response. But it is those situations that are markedly and qualitatively doubtful or questionable that form the subject matter and origin of inquiry. Attention to what is felt and experienced as problematic is the first stage in the transformation of that quality into something that is identifiable as a problem. Distinctions and terms are required in order that the problem can be stated. It should be noted that with the accession of language the originally felt situation and problem is changed in its constituents and quality; the qualitative subject matter begins to be "represented" and "abstracted" in definitions and propositions, its texture rendered in coherent terms as objects of thought. "Objects" in this stage of thinking, are not things-in-themselves, but selected qualitative elements abstracted from the whole situation in their bearing on the problem. They form objective conditions for inference in promoting inquiry. Objects—or objective conditions—thus acquire an instrumental function in the development of inquiry. It is only when inquiry is brought to a close and a doubtful situation is reconstructed into one that is coherent and resolved that an object of knowledge is established. The object of knowledge is the object known—an object of a judgment warranted by inquiry. Objects *in* inquiry are, so to speak, objects in transit, and in the making of inquiry. Objects of knowledge are the products as outcomes of inquiry.

In passing it should be mentioned that not all thinking is confined to inquiry. There are many occasions in which the achievement of knowledge is not a paramount concern. Entering my room I immediately recognize my chair. I do not need to conduct an inquiry before I can "know" what it is or can safely be seated. If all thinking had to take the form of inquiry we could never get started out of bed when we awake in the morning. Failure to make the obvious distinctions here or to insist that there is no other sense in which we can be said to "know" an object unless we have been inquiring about it would leave us with a theory not of intelligent action but of intellectual paralysis. Dewey was well aware that we often speak of "knowing" an object immediately and directly on sight. He calls this "apprehension" and distinguishes it from knowledge that is mediated by and results from inquiry. But he was concerned to argue that cases of direct apprehension of objects do not justify philosophic doctrines of a special kind or source of knowledge. To "know" something by immediately apprehending it is an application of learning and a product of past experience and inquiry. It is a curious fact that Dewey has been repeatedly faulted for not making these distinctions. As we have seen, that is mistaken, although it continues to inspire more or less bizarre criticisms of the sort just aired above.

Since inquiry terminates or eventuates in knowledge, it is not so surprising that Dewey should say that "the object of knowledge is eventual." Nor is it astonishing to declare that "the object of knowledge" is not "in sufficient existence before the act of knowing." All kinds of things including the objective conditions of a problem and the changes brought about by inquiry are in existence prior to the act of knowing. Dewey is very careful in stating these matters. He does not say that objects do not exist before the act of knowing them. He says an object of *knowledge* is not in "sufficient" existence. That is, with respect to *knowledge*, it is incomplete, and so is the act of knowing. Because of the process of inquiry new properties and relationships emerge to qualify a new and changed situation in which an object known and knowledge of it are complements conjointly and integrally.

Nonetheless, the idea that objects are altered by being known has perplexed many of Dewey's readers. Russell, among others, asked how knowledge of a star could in any sense be said to alter the star.[4] Dewey's reply aptly illustrates the theme we have been considering. Knowledge of a star does not begin with the star. It will have its origin in direct experience of a sparkling light observed in the heavens. It may have been the subject of myth and philosophical speculation. In time, the immediately apprehended light formed the subject matter of expert inquiry; a new kind of object was eventually established: the star as an object of knowledge and scientific astronomy. The star is an ancient part of the universe. But as an object of knowledge and something known, it is a relatively recent occurrence in the history of the universe. The occurrence of knowledge of the star has effected existential changes in relations among some parts of the universe. One such change is in the character of our direct experience of the sparkle of light. For knowledge of the star and its causal relation to the experience of seeing the sparkle of light enlarges and deepens the meaning of that experience.

The general thesis, then, that the object and situation in which inquiry is completed consists of existentially changed constituents and relations from that with which inquiry begins, is neither absurd nor unreasonable. But it will continue to baffle those who regard knowing as an internal activity in minds. Finally, it should be mentioned that a peculiar absurdity was often attributed to Dewey in ascribing to him the view that the object of knowledge is modified by knowledge of it. Dewey does hold that knowledge is a change in existences and a modification also of experience. Hence knowledge is a factor in changing and affecting all sorts of other things. But knowledge is not a modification of objects of knowledge. Knowledge does not convolute into modifying itself or *its* objects. Knowledge is not an alteration of knowledge.[5]

So much for some problems of interpretation. It may be of interest to try to see how the foregoing themes bear on some currently discussed issues in the theory of knowledge.

I will start with a typical and simple case. Someone (call him Smith) seeing an apple on the table says "there is an apple on the table."

Aside from the unaccountable brilliance of the bon mot, the facts appear to be simple. There are no simple facts, however, and the example is already shaped by selective interests. But let us take as facts the compound object of apple on table, Smith's presence, and his declarative utterance. A psychologist will be interested in what it is about Smith that has equipped him to perform this action. The focus will be on dispositions and training that go to form a rational response. (We suppose that the explanation will be some joint contribution of physiology and social and linguistic psychology.) The epistemologist will be primarily interested in what it is that makes Smith's statement true and knowledge of its truth. Some general definition of 'truth' is needed here, of course; but the interest leads into matters of belief and, perhaps, of intentionality and propositional attitudes to be ascribed to Smith in this case.

These days psychological and epistemological research into the explanation of rational behavior have become interrelated in complex ways. And the interrelations are augmented by the more recent work on artificial intelligence and cognitive psychology.

Here, then, is a subject matter of active investigation and also of considerable controversy. A very large and diverse literature will substantiate this impression. It is not my intention to venture into any of the issues of the controversy. At best, I hope to indicate how some of the features of Dewey's approach to the analysis of thinking and rational action may provide insights enabling us to reconsider certain limitations on how the problems have frequently been conceived and formulated.

To go back to Smith. We have what the engineers call "input"—the apple and table as stimulus conditions—and shortly thereafter Smith's "output" as a stated sentence. Between input and output is the region over which speculation turns with some intensity. It is where the physical input is transformed into a rationally motivated and accomplished end product. It is, of course, where notions of mind, mental events, beliefs, and dispositions are centered. It is an area of some mystery.

Most philosophers and psychologists argue that some kind of representation—be it mental or a brain event—plays a role in the transformation.

And it is tempting to envision a nice fit between Smith's thinking and belief about the apple and the sentence he utters. Smith thinks or believes *that*..., and says *that*.... The gap is filled by a proposition, a direct object of the verbs *thinks* or *believes*. Thus the now familiar notion of a propositional attitude. The notion was first developed by Russell. Originally (in 1914) he called it a "propositional verb." In any case, the main idea is that the proposition is "the content of belief," which is a guarded way of saying that it is, or expresses, the meaning of a belief.

In the subsequent critical literature grave doubts have emerged over the nature of 'proposition' and 'meaning.' These terms are just as elusive as the concepts of thinking and believing which they were enlisted to explain. Russell had acknowledged some discomfort at the start since, as he saw it, thought and belief were psychological data while propositions are logical constructions. He sensed that propositional attitudes were hybrid products of dubious origin. I think Russell's reservations were prophetic of a source of variance in later philosophical analyses of mental phenomena.

In the early period Russell was interested in the logical form and symbolism of belief and other attitudes.[7] Much later he continued to point out that analysis of propositional attitudes involved a mixture of syntactical and empirical questions.[8] But propositions, as distinct from sentences, were later taken to be empirical "psychological and physiological occurrences."[9]

I remark on Russell's views here because I think that even when not explicitly acknowledged in later literature his influence has been and remains very great. And this brief glance at so limited an aspect of Russell's work helps bring out a general question about logical representations (or "symbolism") and analytical procedures in contemporary theorizing about knowledge and about minds. It is a question that occurred to Dewey and prompted his mistrust of Russell's program of logical atomism.

To confine our attention first to Russell: the question is how propositions as logical structures become identified as psychological and physiological occurrences. Was this a case of projecting the properties of symbols into the subject matter being symbolized? The more general question is not confined to Russell only but to more recent trends in the theory of knowledge. It is to ask whether and to what extent current philosophical investigations of thinking and knowing exhibit a similar questionable tendency to convert the method of analysis and representation into ontological traits of the subject matter.

Dewey argued that analyses of propositional forms as logical and semantical structures remain incomplete because of an exclusive preoccupation with formal properties of truth and reference or denotation. For in addition to reportorial uses of terms and sentences there are vital regulative roles of propositions in the organization and promotion of behavior. In this latter capacity linguistic forms are biological and social adaptations whose functions are inseparable from organic and environing interactions in the maintenance of human life.

If we follow Dewey's lead in attempting to understand the example of Smith—or any number of more complex cases—we must start by recognizing the primary context in which and by reference to which an analysis of the subject matter is to proceed.[10]

The case of Smith seeing and speaking is a simplified instance of an inquiry. For it is also a case of knowing. It is then, in Dewey's terms, the occurrence of a certain kind of change in existential and organic materials and relations in a situation with Smith and an apple as the primary constituents (for us). There is also the temporally subsequent occurrence of Smith's speaking.

A very simple rendering of this scene would go as follows: Given the stimulus conditions—the presence of an apple on a table—and Smith's mastery of language, Smith is induced to respond with the utterance: "there is an apple on the table." If the utterance is true we have evidence of Smith's understanding of how to rightly apply the terms 'apple' and 'table' and thus also some evidence that he has knowledge about apples and tables.

We noticed earlier that for Dewey an object of knowledge is not a preliminary part of a situation in which knowledge is attained. *Something* exists and is immediately present, of course. Dewey is a realist in this respect. There is a subject matter and there is also the presence of some objects already known as the result of prior inquiries. *Something*, we may say, demands inquiry and "wants knowing." What it is, is the "object" of a problem. Thus, this present *something* is an apple and object of knowledge only proleptically. In its status before inquiry is exacted and completed it is an "objective" of inquiry but not an "object of knowledge."[11] The argument is not merely that an object may become an object of knowledge as a consequence of inquiry. That is a commonplace. The significant point here, as we have observed previously, is that inquiry brings about certain existential changes of some of the properties of an object and its relations to other objects (including persons engaged in inquiry). The occurrence of knowledge is a specific transmutation in the order of existences; one of inumerable ways the world is made to change.

The simple account would have it that Smith's sentential comment is the response to the apple as stimulus. But this response would then be a report of something already known: that an apple is there. The report may be in answer to a question, perhaps, or as directing someone's attention to the apple. The report is not a case of knowing. As we have seen, it would be a form of noticing or "apprehension" for Dewey.

In order for the apple to be a stimulus other conditions are necessary. The stimulus must come to be present; it must be noticed. But noticing is itself contingent on other factors. There will be prior activities and noticings, and sometimes speech, all of which precede the stimulus and into which the stimulus enters as an interruption or arresting of attention. A beam of light strikes the apple, say; or the apple falls onto the table. In any case, the stimulus events must be received into some ongoing course of behavior if a stimulus is to be formed. Something *becomes* a stimulus, then, by virtue of activities that are receptive and responsive to it.

In our example, the stimulus object is not the apple—that is, the apple that is eventuaily known. The stimulus is the disturbing flash of light in some place against some background. Or, it is the noise of something striking something else. Sight and hearing are directed to a place. The spatial coordinates involve reference to the position and movements of the body and head. The activities of responding are performed in order to determine what the stimulus is, and *what* it is has become the problem of locating and defining of a problem. All this will depend largely on Smith's capacity and training for integrating and interpreting immediate qualities of light or sound into stimuli for response. The sense qualities of light or sound then become functional as signs of something else. The development of Smith's responses to these immediate sense qualities issues in a mutually qualified product. The result is a new kind of qualities as having become *significant* as conditions for inference and as means to further action.

There is more. Seeing and hearing are connected with various bodily movements which in turn activate other sensory coordinations—such as reaching with the hand for touching. No doubt a network of coordinations is alive in Smith as he begins to respond to what will shortly later be distinguished and denoted as the apple.[12] Due to some of the associations and inclinations related to seeing and touching, he may even begin to salivate. Thus a response, or process of responding, is not some simple reflex but an extensive network of coordinated dispositions and activities in play and affecting the formation of any one response.

At some stage, in the example we are imagining, there is the remarkable advent of language. Smith says, "There is an apple on the table." How that transition from organic and physical interactions with light or sound evolves into the use of language—how light and sound stimuli are transmuted in value into verbal forms—is far too intricate to be traced out here. It is indeed a wonder.

There is a prevailing inclination of philosophers in treating of the theory of knowledge to regard the linguistic act—notably the statement—as the end product or completed fact for analysis of knowledge. But the trouble is that this approach overlooks certain important functional roles that statements may possess in different stages in the acquisition of knowledge. The differences of function (thus, in some sense, of meaning) are not reflected in the syntactical structure or in any one semantical interpretation of a statement.

Dewey offers interesting suggestions concerning the functional roles of statements in the process of inquiry. I will briefly illustrate some of these in reference to the example we have been studying.

Smith's statement about the apple is not the conclusion or summing up of an act of knowing. It has an intermediate place; it serves at first as a means to a conclusion. We must think of the statement as one further segment of and development in the network of coordinations mentioned above. There are several unifying functions the statement performs that deserve to be mentioned.

Smith's statement about the apple on the table might serve to reinforce some and inhibit other parts of an established coordination between seeing and touching. The link to touching might ordinarily function to confirm a response to what is seen. As Hume showed, one's seeing something is often regularly associated with expectations of touch and taste. But in the present case, the act of stating that there is an apple on the table can work effectively to minimize the elaboration of other inferences and tests. (Purely on the linguistic level, to state that an apple is there is to negate a host of other possible predications.) Hence the statement serves at least three closely related purposes.

1. The statement operates as a principle of economy of effort. In stating that an apple is there, Smith counsels himself (and perhaps others) that touching and tasting are not required. A shortcut over possible confirming practices is thus effected in the route to knowledge. Of course, one can go wrong—even perilously so; but ordinarily the saving in labor is worth the risk and the gaming instinct will contravene logical scruples. In a different but related way, the statement may serve to postpone any felt need of direct action. For, if the pagmatists are right, the statement is a formulation of hypothetical conditions and possible consequences that would occur if it is tested or acted upon. And knowing what would happen if one acts is often a good reason for not acting at all.

2. The statement is central to organizing and directing subsequent action on the basis of what is—and is declared to be—significant in the prior acts of seeing or hearing. For language articulates and completes those natural operations in their function of signaling or signifying as they occur in the immediate activities of seeing or hearing. The statement translates the unspoken "information" of the senses. It plays an intermediate role, then, in ordering and focusing previous sensory activity in preparation for subsequent behavior.

3. Finally, Smith's statement is spoken to be heard. He communicates with other persons usually, or he could be speaking to himself. In either case, he would normally hear himself speak. The others who are addressed by Smith—including that part of himself in the role of listener—are responsive (we suppose) to what he says. The original situation which had Smith and the apple at it center is now enlarged to include other persons. The network of coordinations which had Smith at its center is now expanded into a system of social relations. The responses of others to what Smith says come in to affect Smith's own responses to how he had responded to earlier stimuli. We have Smith and other persons responding to one another; in effect critically modifying responses formed earlier in serial interchanges by reinforcing or weakening some of them, as the case may be, under the pressure of a socially instituted preference for uniformity and agreement in settling observation and knowledge claims.

For Dewey, this social situation of mutual reinforcing and coadapting of responsive behavior among persons (and within Smith himself) is literally a *co-respondence*. The persons who hear Smith speak (including Smith) eventually arrive at a uniform and coherent response to what has been stated. An object of knowledge is then established.

In this last stage of the natural history of Smith and his utterence there is a change in "meaning" or function of the statement made. It is the "same" statement in wording only; for it has become a "warranted" assertion. It thus stands to the initial stimulus conditions that led to its formulation as an answer to what had originally been questionable and uncertain. The problem situation which provoked attention and inquiry has become clarified and resolved. And a particularly effective instrument in that resolution is the use of language—in this case, Smith's speech response and its functional role in establishing that, indeed, there is an apple on the table.[13]

To sum up. I started out with some reflections on Dewey's conception of an object of knowledge as a product of antecedent changes brought about by inquiry. The excursus on the example of Smith and the apple which then followed was illustrative of the thesis. But it was also intended to suggest some of the complexities of the subject matter of an empirical theory of knowledge—at least according to how Dewey conceived the prerequisites of the theory of knowledge as inquiry.

Inquiry is a transformation of immediately experienced qualities and events into objects of knowledge. Objects of knowledge, in turn, render immediate experience coherent and significant. For objects are how experience becomes ordered and how connections with future experience can be regulated and anticipated.

If inquiry is a distinct kind of change in existing things it also embodies changes in its own consecutive phases and relations to a changing subject matter. It is implicated in the transformation of situations which it serves to effect and promote. The primary instrument of control in inquiries is language. One of the difficult and subtle problems of a theory of knowledge is that of recognizing and distinguishing the interrelations of linguistic forms with their specific yet variable functional uses within the process of inquiry. We noticed one such instance just previously: Smith's statement as initially a hypothesis or proposition in the organization of inquiry and its later role as a warranted assertion in the completion of inquiry. Clearly, important differences of function and evidential value invest the "same" linguistic structure.

In this transition of roles Smith's statement becomes one of the factors contributing to its own confirmation or warrant in the closing of inquiry.[14] This kind of transformation of the functional roles of propositions is an important feature of Dewey's conception of the operation of language in inquiry. Thus Smith's statement exhibits a change from a stage in which it served as a *representation* of stimuli to one in which it is established as *representative* of an object. The change is parallel with and the logical counterpart of the existential change by which a subject matter under inquiry becomes an object of knowledge as a result of inquiry.

Finally, I have said nothing about one of the more familiar kinds of object that is present in and affected by the outcome of an inquiry. I have in mind the mind, or, as Dewey preferred to call it, the *person*:

A *person* is an object, not a "mind" nor consciousness, even though because of his capicity for inquiry he may be said to have a mind. (LW 12:518)

The style and subject matter of Dewey's *Logic* is highly impersonal. And that is as it should be according to how he viewed the aim of logical theory and his concern to keep questions of logic free of subjective doctrines of the "mental." There is nothing personal or "mental" about the logical forms and operations of inquiry, although it is persons who make inquiries happen.

Persons can also be objects of inquiry, of course. Dewey maintained that the way we are able to know about persons—including our own person or "mind" or "mental states"—is not in principle or method different in kind from the method of observation and controlled inference comprising inquiry into any natural subject matter (LW 15:27–33). That we are able to have and directly apprehend our own thoughts and feelings is not denied. But that fact does not force us to conclude that there is a special kind of immediate introspective knowledge. One's "awareness" of some immediate qualitative event as *had*—a sudden pain, say—is one thing; *knowledge* about it involving its connections with other events, causal and consequential, is another matter. The having of a thought or feeling or experience is not another kind of knowing it.

This argument continues to be controversial, however, and cannot be pursued here. I have raised it only to prepare the way for a concluding reflection.

Let us think of an inquiry having as its subject matter the person who is inquiring. This is a case of inquiry into one's own self or "mind." Some capacity or trait is felt to be perplexing and needing understanding. The inquiry might be a solo performance or carried on with the aid of other persons. The doctrine that has occupied us in these pages is that inquiry is a transformation of a subject matter and is productive of a newly qualified object: an object of knowledge. Accordingly, one's inquiry into one's own person, if reliably administered, will issue in a changed object, a qualitatively new person.

It is in this line that one might proceed to translate into Dewey's terms the famous Socratic injunction to self-examination. If it has merit, the idea suggests one of the many possible extensions and applications of Dewey's theory—one that for reasons unknown to me, Dewey never developed beyond some valuable hints. The idea might be worth investigation as a way of clarifying procedures and contributing to what is meant by knowing and knowledge of one's self.

Notes

1.   This paper enlarges and revises my "Dewey and the Theory of Knowledge," *Transactions of the Charles S. Peirce Society,: A Quarterly Journal in American Philosophy* 26, 4 (Fall 1990), pp. 443–58. It appears here by permission of the *Transactions of the Charles S. Peirce Society: A Quarterly Journal in American Philosophy* and its editor, Peter H. Hare.

2.   Dewey presents an important argument for his own approach to some of the philosophical issues here in his 1905 "The Postulate of Immediate Empiricism" (MW 3:158–67).

3.   In this and the next paragraph, I apply some of the suggestions in Dewey's remarkable essay, "Qualitative Thought" (LW 5:243–62). One of Dewey's objectives here is to develop a naturalistic interpretation of the background and starting point of all thinking as consisting of immediate pervasive qualities. The argument is a critical alternative to the theories of immediate experience held by Bradley and James. It is worth noting that parts of Dewey's discussion in this paper reappear in his *Logic: The Theory of Inquiry* almost word for word, and that the paper is twice referred to and footnoted in *Art as Experience*. For a valuable recent discussion of

the central ideas in this important essay, see Thomas M. Alexander, *John Dewey's Theory of Art, Experience, and Nature: The Horizon of Feeling* (Albany: State University of New York Press, 1987).

4.   Bertrand Russell, "Dewey New *Logic*" in *The Philosophy of John Dewey*, ed. P. A. Schillp (LaSalle, Ill.: Open Court, 1939), pp. 137–56. See also the critical discussions of the problem by A. E. Murphy and the more sympathetic treatment by Donald Piatt in the same volume. For more recent discussions, see George Dicker, *Dewey's Theory of Knowledge* (Philadephia: Philosophical Monographs, 1976) and Ralph W. Sleeper, *The Necessity of Pragmatism* (New Haven: Yale University Press, 1986), pp. 113–116, 120–127.

5.   Dewey had explained as much in his 1911 "Epistemological Realism: The Alleged Ubiquity of the Knowledge Relation" (MW 6:121; on the example of knowledge of the star, see MW 6:105–107). The point is restated in reply to Russell in *The Philosophy of John Dewey*, p. 547.

6.   Bertrand Russell, The Philosophy of Logical Atomism" in *Logic and Knowledge*, ed. R. C. Marsh (New York: The Macmillan Co., 1956), p. 127.

7.   Ibid., p. 216, 224.

8.   Bertrand Russell, *An Inquiry into Meaning and Truth* (New York: Norton and Co., 1940), p. 250.

9.   Ibid., p. 237.

10.   In some of the discussion that follows, I rely on Dewey's 1922 essay, "Knowledge and Speech Reaction" (MW 13:29–39), in which Dewey acknowledges indebtedness to Mead.

11.   See note 3 above.

12.   It is at least of passing interest that this part of the process is often said to be determining the "value" of the stimulus.

13.   This is a relatively simple conclusion to an admittedly simple example. A more impressive inquiry might proceed from the question of why the apple is nourishing or what an apple is. Or, it might be the inquiry of an artist where the problem is how the apple might be made the subject of a work of art.

14.   Dewey remarks in his 1915 essay, "The Logic of Judgments of Practice," that the "proposition is itself a factor in the completion of the situation, carrying it forward to its conclusion" (MW 8:16).

12

The Human Eros

THOMAS M. ALEXANDER

This chapter explores the relation between our desire to exist meaningfully through action and the question which this poses for philosophy. My thesis is simple: we are erotic beings. Our Eros, however, is neither divine nor animal. It is distinctively human: we are beings who seek meaning imaginatively through each other, and the locus of this transformative encounter is the community. This pragmatic model stands in opposition to traditional views of human beings as rational individuals or "epistemic subjects" whose primary function is to generate propositional claims about the world. It also stands in opposition to more recent neopragmatist accounts of human existence in which meaning is simply a function of relations of power.

Five Basic Claims

The Delphic injunction, "Know Thyself," forces us to confront some basic, simple realities. I believe five important claims about us can be made: a) We exist *temporally*, and the shape of our temporality is dramatically structured through the nature of *action*; b) we exist in a *human world of culture* and not merely in a physical environment; c) our understanding of ourselves and the world emerges as a *dynamic process of learning and growth*, and not as a static range of well-justified beliefs; d) our experience is fundamentally *aesthetic* rather than cognitive; and e) at the root of our existence is a *drive to live with a funded sense of meaning and value*, a "Human Eros."

If we accept these claims, after exploring them in more detail, serious consequences must follow for the practice of philosophy and its self-understanding. Let us begin with the first claim.

We do not exist merely as temporal objects, persisting from one moment to the next, nor even as biological beings continuously proceeding from birth through maturity to death. We exist in the *experience* of time configured by action into a *dramatic* process whose coherence is captured through *narrative* understanding. Our consciousness emerges from a prereflective world of desire, experience, and action in which this temporality of our being is presupposed for anything to make sense. This is illustrated in the temporally complex modalities reflected in the tenses of the verb: the perfect of completed actions, the imperfect of actions done but not completed, the future which looms ahead as well as the present immediately at hand. The moods of language—subjunctive, conditional, imperative, and indicative—exhibit how ontologically intricate our human understanding is and how deeply it is rooted in our active bodily comportment to the world around us. This temporality gradually emerges to conscious reflection through action. From the simplest sensori-motor manipulations to extended projects and traditions of whole communities, the structure of action builds up a web of interconnected meaning, a "world." The infant begins by struggling to master simple affairs of physical coordination, out of which a world of primary objects emerges. Human cultures aim at articulating a complex web of interpretive structures which coordinate shared action and constitute the range of ideal objects embraced by the world of the culture.[1]

Action has a *teleological* and *narrative* structure: by aiming at an end to be realized through definte means, action takes on the configuration of having a beginning, middle, and end in which the aim is realized or fails to be. The baby reaches for a toy, and the toy is either grasped or it is not, whereupon satisfaction or frustration ensues. The world is thus *dramatically* encountered as a projected field of possible and actual actions developing in time; our dramatic embodiment provides the structures of our understanding, permeating and guiding conscious, reflective thought.[2] Any theory of human existence or meaning that disregards these features, focusing instead on an ideal of mere formal correspondence or which epitomizes us in terms of static "states" will only have mystified our most fundamental manner of understanding ourselves and the world.

Second, human beings are also born into *worlds*, not just environments. At birth we are as much new members of a community, with its languages, beliefs, traditions, and values, as we are biological beings. Left abandoned or uncared for at birth, we die: that is a *fact* about us as a species. The fragile organism of the newborn is vitally bound to its world by the love and care it receives. Thus a human birth is more than a biological act: it is a cultural event fraught with all the meaning, mystery, and celebration of a new arrival. A social context of care and cooperation is *presupposed* along with the physical environment in the very needs of the baby's flesh. The infant also transforms a couple into a family and initiates a long process of development on their part. Not only do birth and upbringing result in a new member participating in the world of the culture, but the lives of the care-givers are changed. They are called upon to grow and know themselves in demanding ways. Care is a discipline. As the child develops, new needs develop into an ever-expanding world of affection, attachment, and meaning. A complex emotional world colors the aesthetics of all human relationships and it is directly tied to our actions which sustain or damage the project of care. How we manage to secure and cultivate enriching relationships with others is a primary quest of human life. How we have been raised and treated colors our consciousness as a whole.

Third, *learning* and *teaching* are also required for our entrance into the symbols and values of the culture so as to become communicants in its reality. By nature, then, we are not only social beings, lovers, helpers, and protectors, but also teachers and learners. In addition to the dramatically temporal, care-oriented social structure of our experience, we must recognize the fundamental nature of our existence as beings living together in a community bound by meaning-giving traditions which must be taught to be acquired, and without which love, cooperation, communication, and culture would be impossible. The way whereby we come to inhabit this cultural world is one of constant learning and adaptation. Growth is a process of transformation. Even if a culture believes its dogmas possess changeless, absolute authority, each individual spends the first formative years endeavoring to *learn* the world. Our experience is cast and recast constantly in a developmental process of growth which not only shapes our adult consciousness but which, as a *process*, has a narrative structure. Our self-understanding is deeply rooted in this experience. Our lives are punctuated by conflicts or problems demanding resolution. These may be temporary, minor shifts in our attitudes or major crises which strike to the core of our innermost being, determining our subsequent attitude toward the world and each other. The "self" is not a timeless, ahistorical ground for propositions, a spectator of the world or itself. The process of life belies such a characterization. We understand ourselves as having a history whereby we gradually develop the broad experience and trained habits to function effectively in our physical and cultural worlds. We have struggled to achieve a fluency and continuity in our experience. The "self" is a dramatic process of development.[3]

Fourth, our encounter with the world, moreover, is primarily *aesthetic*. Our experience is pervaded with a *sensed* texture of order, possibility, meaning, and anticipation. The world offers itself to us through our capacity to be lured into its aesthetic orders which in turn become the flesh of meaning. Our immediate experience of even the simplest, most mundane objects resonates with memory and expectation which are directly embodied *in* the world. If we encounter the day with boredom, arriving at the office and seeing "the same old desk" oppressively heaped with papers, with "*Work!*", with the cold cup of yesterday's brackish coffee and the dying plant in the windowsill, this suffusion of experience in its complexity and totality must be called aesthetic as much as those moments in which the thrill and beauty of life meets us in a cascade of vibrancy and joy. The pervasive, qualitative horizon of the aesthetic dimension of experience is always present with us. We seek the possibility of fulfillment; action is a pursuit in response to the lure of the world. The fine arts, Dewey argues, merely raise this dimension of experience to full consciousness. Through the medium of the living human body, we engage in the active and responsive experience of meaning. Human experience engages world and self primarily in the complexity of a pervasive aesthetic awareness: at each moment we are attuned to the world.[4]

Finally, I wish to make perhaps the most radical of all my claims: At the root of our lives we manifest a deep-seated drive *to exist with a sense of meaning and value*. Unfortunately, the terms "meaning and value" cannot be given precise definition here, for they are understood to denote the richest and profoundest ways in which we exist. Quite simply, we seek fulfillment on a number of levels and flourish when we find it and wither when we do not. A human life which has been denied or stripped of love, friendship, happiness, creative work, curiosity, awareness of mystery and beauty, and, above all, hope has been destroyed. This drive for meaning and value will allow us to endure suffering and even death for the sake of love for another person or for an ideal. Most literature and many religions take this as their theme, and rightly so. Our lives are projects guided by this most profound human need which truly holds the bonds of community together and constitutes the energy for creative activity of civilization. Our cultural worlds are shared creations whereby human beings seek to fulfill this common drive. Culture is not then simply the web of practices which the anthropologist may categorize. The web itself is a delicate structure opening up a world which enables the human project to continue its quest for meaning. When our meaning-constituting practices and ends are shattered, a crisis ensues, for individuals singly or for entire cultures. The loss of all meaning for the individual may generate a hopeless depression ending in suicide or self-destructive behavior; it may direct itself outwardly in acts of anger or in the obsessive pursuit of an ideal. A disintegrating culture is riddled with anxiety, despair, and confusion. Like individuals, such cultures also may embark upon frantic quests to reassert the values of the past, adopting fanatic ideologies, or may continue to fragment, succumbing to alien values without retaining any coherence of their own. The spread of the Industrial Revolution throughout the world, an event of unprecedented extent and power in its ability to dislocate the values, beliefs, and institutions of cultures, has led to a crisis in meaning and self-understanding for human beings as such.

Culture, then, is the expression of a drive for enountering the world and oneself with a sense of fulfilling meaning and value realized through action. Such a radical impulse I call the "Human Eros." When this drive is frustrated or negated, resulting in the sense of the loss of any meaning or value to our existence, it readily becomes transformed into a highly destructive power which may be directed outwardly or inwardly. One of the primary aims of civilization is to secure conditions whereby this Eros can develop, and it is the function of reflective intelligence in particular to address the crises which threaten it in order to avert its transformation into a drive for annihilation.[5]

I begin by noting these five conditions, our dramatic temporality, our social existence, our developmental self, our aesthetic experience, and the Human Eros, because I think that if we hold onto them, serious consequences must follow for philosophy. Much, if not all, of contemporary philosophy is remarkable for the willingness with which it has allowed itself to forget these great, simple facts of who and what we are. Our human temporality is hardly acknowledged in Anglo-American philosophy (described at best as a mere passage of brain states), while the development of our human consciousness in a process of social care and narrative understanding is ignored in the quest to analogize the brain to a digital computer. Though the theme of temporality once dominated continental philosophy, most poststructural thought has dissolved historical or narrative time into the fictions of social empowerment which, when deconstructed, expose only the ruptures and reconfigurations of the so-called arbitrary patterns of language and desire. Although Freudian psychoanalysis does concern itself with the complexities of the growth and emergence of the human personality, it adopts a model as reductionistic as that promoted by behaviorism or artificial intelligence theory. Finally, most theories of meaning simply ignore the rich complexity of human life. For example, one must turn, with a few exceptions, not to philosophers but to literary writers, psychologists, and theologians to explore the meaning of love. The versions of materialism in Anglo-American philpsophy have nothing to say except to dismiss the cultural world of our "manifest image" as "folk psychology." Poststructuralism also opts for dissolving the self as a construct of sublimated desire, which constantly exceeds and undermines its masks.[6]

If we accept these five features of human existence as constitutive of that existence, then we must fashion a new path for philosophical inquiry. In reinterpreting ourselves, we must reinterpret philosophy.

Beyond the Community of Contingency and the Community of Power

Before expanding on the emergence of the community through the dialogue of the social imagination, it is necessary to indicate that the themes discussed have been seriously neglected or misrepresented in current neopragmatism. Two instances may be briefly indicated, Richard Rorty and Stanley Fish. Both these thinkers seem to argue, on the one hand, for the importance of imagination and, on the other, for the role of the community in guiding the process of meaning and interpretation. But both have such attenuated views of the nature of the imagination, the community, the process of growth, the aesthetic nature of experience, and the human drive for shared fulfillment, which I think are so central, that their "pragmatism" easily turns either into an irrationalist philosophy of contingency and flux, as in the case of Rorty, or into a theory of community and meaning masking the brute force of power, as in the case of Fish.

In *Contingency, Irony and Solidarity*, Richard Rorty sets forth his most forceful vision of the human condition. True to his antifoundationalism, Rorty seeks to expose the vanity of any appeals to some essence of human nature. But here he begins to raise the disturbing political question: What justification can there be, on such conditions, for one social structure, like liberal democracy, over others? His conclusion takes a form of libertarianism reminiscent of J. S. Mill. A free society is one which recognizes its nonfoundational character and therefore allows its citizens to be "as privatistic, 'irrationalist,' and aestheticist as they please as long as they do it on their own time—causing no harm to others and using no resources needed by those less advantaged."[7] Such a view Rorty calls "ironism" because it is committed to certain values, such as the removal of as much pain and humiliation as possible, without having any absolute rational grounds for doing so. What Rorty offers in place of appealing to rational principles is the ideal of developing imaginative sympathy, "the imaginative ability to see people as fellow sufferers."[8]

Rorty sees the development of our imaginative and aesthetic abilities as crucial for the prospects of a free society, but his analysis of imagination and aesthetic awareness is deeply indebted to the Enlightenment position he repudiates. In his discussion of the role of creativity in language, for instance, Rorty wishes to stress the importance of the role of imagination and creativity in shifting the webs of meaning. But because he is so locked into a quasi-positivist theory of meaning, he can make no sense of such transformations and so must come to regard any imaginative, creative moment as an irrational intrusion into the rule-governed habits of conventional meaning. This is brought out especially in his treatment of metaphor, which closely follows Davidson's analysis. Metaphoric expression, when it is genuinely novel, is a *nonsemantic* event; it is like interrupting a conversion to make a face or kiss someone or point to something—anything which succeeds in "producing effects on your interlocutor."[9] The even flow of linguistic meaning has been suspended by a physical event. Thus when Dylan Thomas said, "The force that through the green fuse drives the flower/That blasts the roots of trees/Is my destroyer," Rorty believes that *at first* he had said something quite meaningless, though he had *done* something. Once, however, this became a conventional expression, memorized and repeated so that it evokes an habitual response, it gains meaning—but of course has ceased to be an imaginative or creative expression. For Rorty, to say something "without a *fixed place* in the language game is, as the positivists *rightly* have said, to utter something which is neither true nor false. . . ."[10]

Note that Rorty cannot explain how such an event *ever* makes sense. Sheer repetition does not establish a convention which makes sense. If one person's hopping on one leg while reciting the Gettysburg Address adds nothing to the content of the speech, neither will it be affected if everyone does it. How then does such an expression *become* accessible? This is the question Rorty cannot answer because his view of language and meaning is, at the root, one which seeks meaning in the traditional terms of true or false propositions justified by a system of practices, rather than one which takes imagination and process as central. In the compact nature of his style, Dylan Thomas has said "I am driven by a force of life, the same which drives all living things, and which destroys them." The transformational relations that are set up are between his "green youth" and life of plants, and so of all living nature. This is a force that also destroys: the word "fuse" connects the implicit image of the stem with a bomb. The movement of the verse goes from flower to root, from youth to destruction, suggesting a temporal process, a development. The powerful totality of the expression is reinforced by the "root-flower" relation: the *whole* being, then, is in the grip of a force of life which brings blossoming and destruction: while the plant may flower at the top, at the root lies the power of its being destroyed. The expression at first may not be accessible (and there certainly are instances in Thomas' poetry that must remain so), but we can begin to work with the *evocation* of meaning which the mysterious phrase imparts, and we do so by a series of transformations and connections which essentially employ imaginative and metaphoric reasoning. Through this we come into a relation with the poet who is indicating something about our common human condition.

Rorty not only cannot make sense of the nature of metaphoric expression, but the entire realm of symbol, mythology, historical interpretation, and the articulation of ideals must be equally opaque to him. Yet this is where most human life is meaningfully lived. He is left with a view of the self which is as radically contingent as Hume's (though he strangely lays upon it the Nietzschean injunction of "self-creation") and a view of the community simply as a contingent web of practices shifting randomly throughout time. Needless to say, this does not give him much to go on for his defense of liberalism, other than an appeal to our contingent, ironic desire not to see others hurt.

This failure to come to grips with the interrelation of imagination and community appears also in the work of a "neopragmatist" literary figure, Stanley Fish.[11] The fundamental problem facing interpretation theory of course is whether there ever is something which is "the" true meaning of a text or whether interpretation is a purely relative response. Fish, seeking a moderate position, hit upon the idea that what limits individual interpretations are the accepted practices of the "community of interpreters." In *Is There a Text in This Class?* Fish appeals to this device because, though the accepted practices of interpretation shift over time (and thus not only affect what the meaning of accepted literary works may be, but what "literature" itself is and what texts are classified as literary and what are not), there is not an "anything goes" relativism in which anyone's interpretation is as good as anyone else's. Though one might be tempted to see such a move as covertly justifying why there must be designated individuals who are empowered by society to read its texts authoritatively (i.e., professors of English), Fish has made the question of community central to the problem of interpretation.

Fish's problem in one sense is the opposite of Rorty's: How to stablize meaning instead of acknowledging the pervasiveness of contingency. Hence Fish sees the appeal to the community as a crucial step in securing meaning: "Indeed, it is interpretive communities, rather than the text or the reader, that produce meanings and are responsible for the emergence of formal features. Interpretive communities are made up of those who share interpretive strategies not for reading, but for writing texts, for constituting their properties."[12] But what ultimately constitutes a community of meaning for Fish? Nothing but agreeing on a set of interpretive practices, and this itself cannot be further resolved *methodologically*: "there is no single way of reading that is correct or natural, only 'ways of reading' that are extensions of community perspectives.... The business of criticism ... was not to decide between interpretations by subjecting them to the test of disinterested evidence but to establish by political and persuasive means (they are the same thing) the set of interpretive assumptions from the vantage point of which the evidence will hereafter be specifiable.[13] There can only be persuasion and social coercion at the basis of any set of interpretive strategies accepted by a community. Rhetoric, langauge in the service of irrational power, constitutes the community because it is the maker and unmaker of the rules of the game.

Rorty's and Fish's views indicate how deeply we need to consider both the nature of imagination and community to arrive at an intelligible and humane theory of meaning. But their versions of "pragmatism," instead of drawing upon the insights of the classical pragmatists, like John Dewey, are really more the products of theories of meaning stemming from analytic and ordinary langauge philosophy of the past few decades.[14] The question of the pragmatic result of their position must also be raised. Not only do their views offer a remarkably attenuated view of meaning, imagination, art, and the community, but they recommend dubious practices. Rorty's view of the incommesurability of private self-creation with any public concern abandons seeing how public affairs are really implicated in our private worlds or how our private actions may have broad public consequences. He thus encourages the retreat into a private world of aesthetic description with the hope that it eventuates in a "sentimental education" which somehow bolsters the project of liberal demcoracy. Fish's approach would result in a cynical endorsement of present interpretive methods which must regard any innovation as a challenge to an established locus of authority and power. If a community is forged through a rhetoric of power which fixes shared strategies, one rejects the idea of meaningful change or criticism. It also ignores the idea of a community founded on the ideas of self-experimentation and a pluralistic imagination. Neither really can make sense of the idea of a community as constituted through an imaginative exploration of the possibilities of meaning resulting in a continuous process of transformation and growth. Nor is there a place for the creation of ideals to be used as critical standards of present practices.

The Community of Social Imagination

I will now explore an alternative approach, developed from Dewey's concept of aesthetic experience and his and Royce's analysis of the community. The idea of the community that emerges is one which through its imaginative, dynamic intelligence actively seeks for conditions that fulfill the deep aesthetic needs of human beings to experience the world with meaning and value in an expressive, reflective, and self-critical way. Our quest for community is also a quest to encounter others; we experience the meaning of the world *through* each other, and art is a preeminent perfection of this practice. Contrary to postmodern theories, the work of art (alias, "the text") becomes a medium through which we imaginatively embrace new habits of understanding that give meaning to our old habits by allowing them to develop and grow. Through others we expose the genuine *possibilities of the present* which give us intelligent ways of evaluating and developiing its tendencies toward fulfilling rather than destructive ends, achieving a continuity of meaningful experience. It is this dramatic, imaginative, embodied, communal engagement of the present in its possibilties as well as histories which allows us to experience meaning, and this is "art."

Culture is a web of highly flexible practices that allow us to enter imaginatively and actively into each's others lives. After acquiring a basic mastery of our infant bodies, we commence the arduous process of social understanding. Gradually we begin to engage the immediate others in our world, those who give us care, and through them we encounter the emerging self we will be. Dewey and Mead have emphasized how we dramatically learn to take the role of the other to develop our sense of self. I wish to stress that this is an *imaginative* need. We must constantly project ourselves into the stances of many other people to gain an organized perspective of ourselves and become self-reflective. This is more than mere sympathetic substitution of the other for ourselves. The other enters into the creative process of *interpretation* and *understanding* which we have of ourselves and the situation. This projection seeks a continuously integrative attitude through the possibility of a coordinating end of action. We only experience the meaning of the world through this process of social interaction structured along the lines of narrative temporality in which there is ongoing continuity, not mechanical routine interrupted by random change. When human life takes on the pattern epitomized in the theories of Rorty and Fish, it is life on the edge of becoming meaningless, a point at which the destructive force of the frustrated Human Eros will emerge, either outwardly or inwardly.

Others enter into the interpretation of my activities. Imagine a simple game of catch. I must throw the ball to you: but this is not just aiming and throwing at a target. I must anticipate in my throw the way you will respond, knowing also that you are anticipating my action of throwing. You have dramatically projected yourself into my activity as thrower and I have projected myself into your activity as catcher. This *mutual effort to anticipate together* creates a dramatic fusion of our fields of action and interpretation through which we can both coordinate our individual activities toward the shared end of playing a game. I do not lose my self-identity through this process; my self-identity becomes more definite because of my ability to take "the social standpoint," as Mead called it. A range of possibilities opens up which would not exist if I could not do this, thus creating new projective lines of action which extend from my present circumstances into the future. We both grasp this common end, though we each may perform distinctive but complimentary activities (such as the difference between the role of pitcher and catcher in baseball). But without this guiding end functioning as an integrative ideal, we would not be able to coordinate our actions in this manner. If anything, the actions of the other would be regarded as impediments to the realization of our actions.[15]

Most human activity lacks the clearly presented ends of games (perhaps this explains why the artificial constraints of games are so popular—games offer clear instances where such simple ends are set forth and can be rather easily embraced and followed, allowing individuals to experience in an aesthetically vivid manner the dynamic but meaningful projections of participatory interpretive activity). Communities are bound together by hazier ideals and we need to find more definite ends to achieve cooperative activity providing a context for the realization of value and a sense of meaning in our lives. The possibility of community, then, lies as much in the ability to *search out* and *discover* integrative ends as it does in the conservative practices of its traditions. Indeed, traditions are highly valued largely because they provide such a stable network for guiding and interpreting *future* activity.

The aesthetic immediacy of experience is pervaded by these social features. Our actions aim at ends which fulfill us; we need to be able to make evaluative, intelligent decisions which can be understood as ways of organizing our present actions toward sustaining and enriching ends. Acting in light of those ends, our activities become imbued with the heightened experience of meaning. Our experience is illumined not only by recognizing it as the outcome of a history but by seeing the present possibilties of conduct which *develop* that history: we can act so as to find fulfillment and we find this process an unfolding event of meaning which we inhabit. This theme is forcibly articulated by Dewey in his concept of *"an* experience." The aesthetic possibilities of experience are not limited to a uniqne class of purely "aesthetic" objects, such as those found in the fine arts. Any activity which succeeds in realizing the possibilities of a present situation so that it becomes pervaded by a sense of completeness, closure, and expressive signficance exhibits the features of *an* experience. Dewey stresses the temporal development of any such experience. It is not just that any experience takes time, but *an* experience constitutes a genuine temporal process having a "narrative structure" of beginning, middle, and end where the parts are organically related to the whole and are the means through which the whole experience is realized. A bar of music, for example, does not merely take time and make noise; when heard *as* music it occupies a dramatic moment in a dynamic process, having a relation to the part of the piece which has preceded and anticipating the part yet to come. (LW 10:218ff.).

The way *an* experience fills out time is quite significant. Human time is not a mere succession of moments, but is governed by the complex interweaving of developmental, narrative patterns of interpretation built out of the teleological structure of actions. Our activities aim at completion. In some cases, the end lies in a specific goal, such as finding food, reaching for a ball, or removing the hand quickly from a hot dish. In others, we aim at more persistent conditions of equilibrium, such as the maintenance of oxygen in the blood or securing a constant food supply. We organize our world from our earliest days by achieving simple, basic acts of coordination which aim at controlling the body to anticipate the world for the achievement of ends. These acts have a teleological, intentional structure and as they become connected with each other, new and more complex acts and ends become available as ways of organizing our experience and giving it new meaning. Mastery of simple sensori-motor coordinations links a number of previously discrete acts, such as grasping and arm movement, into new and more complex actions, such as the act of picking up and throwing an object. Gradually these acts form an elaborate and expanding network which constitutes a structural horizon against which consciousness itself emerges. When it does, it characteristically apprehends "the world" not as a static object but as a field within which one must act, as a *dramatic* context in which one lives *forward*, but also has a past, a *history*. Through the early years of childhood eventually one comes to understand oneself as living a life in which one's actions greatly determine the meaning and shape of one's existence.[16]

These two points, the imaginative projection into the stance of others and the teleological structure of human experience, may now be combined. Our meaningful experience of the world arises less from purely individual acts than from our *social* mode of existence. Our social environment acts upon us and calls out a social response. *We inhabit the world through our imaginative embodiment of others which we learn from their imaginative embodiment in us.* The field of intentionality arises from this shared dramatic space in which we struggle to anticipate together. This allows us to communicate and thereby to interpret and understand ourselves so that we can assess, evaluate, and coordinate our particular activities toward a shared world of meaning which is not static or final but in constant developmental play. The teleological structure of these actions gradually engages the complex web of culture, which might be described as the symbolic storehouse of the social imagination. The shape of one's individuality emerges through the appropriation of the culture, which is not merely an environment of coexistent others, but a *world*, a nexus of meanings and values embodied in a range of symbolically interpreted practices through which human beings can be meaningfully present to each other. A "world" is thus the interpretive horizon within which we encounter and realize our humanity in acts of expressive communication. It extends beyond any group of individuals, embracing traditions, history (sacred or mythic as well as secular and historical), practices, institutions, and the narrative possibilities which are available for individuals to use in the process of participation in the society. A world allows a culture to have a narrative past and to act in light of a range of ends which define a meaningful, valuable future. It allows for a genuine community to exist through creating the possibility of a *process of social interpretation.*

Josiah Royce's profound exploration of the interrelation of time and interpretation to the community can illuminate the previous remarks, standing as an important challenge to the idea of interpretive communities offered by Rorty and Fish. Royce acknowledges that a community "is essentially a product of a time process," having a past and a future.[17] Like an individual, a community exists temporally. The interpretive meaning of an individual's present experience is set within a context of memory and anticipation; so too a community is constituted insofar as its members share a *"community of memory"* and a *"community of hope."*[18] The members identify themselves in terms of accepting a certain history as their own, a history which helps explain who they are and which articulates a range of values, meanings, and practices. Part of the shared human project of self-understanding requires that we have a shared past as well as an individual past. This is the interpretive act of discerning the "community of memory." But communities, like individuals, live forward: the shared range of hopes and expectations constitutes the "community of hope." These are interpretive horizons without which the community of the present could not exist, and they function as the means whereby a continuous process of action is possible. The nature of the cultural world extends through the social imagination so as to frame a background of a past and the foreground of a future; the community is thus a process with the distinctive temporal structure of *narrativity.*[19] Cooperation alone does not define a community, according to Royce, unless there is an "ideal extension" of the meaning of each member's activity to the community of memory and community of hope which allows for mutual interpretation in the present to be possible and for them all to share a commitment to a common life which generates loyalty and even love. "The time-process and the ideal extension of the self in this time-process," states Royce, "lie at the basis of the whole theory of the community."[20]

Royce connects this to the nature of interpretation: "A community. . . depends for its very constitution upon the way in which each of its members interprets himself and his life."[21]

Behind the diversity of specific human purposes, there is the need for each individual to make sense of his or her life through the life of others. Adopting Peirce's triadic semeiotic theory, Royce argues that interpretation is a constant *process* with three terms involved, the object interpreted, the sign or interpreter, and the one to whom the interpretation is addressed, the interpretant. This applies as much to my interpretation of my past self to my future self, such as when I recall a promise which thus mediates between my past and future selves and determines the meaning of who I am and will be, as to my interpretation of a text or event.[22] For Royce, the community as such exists as a process of interpretation, mediating past and future through the symbolic configurations of the present. *Human temporality is socially appropriated through the process of interpretation.* Time itself is understood as an order of possible interpretation. Temporality is seen to be one of the essential features of human understanding; it is made available through our social imagination.

Furthermore, since each sign calls for a *new* sign to interpret it, the life of the community calls "in ideal, for an infinite sequence of interpretations."[23] A community exists through a *continuous process* of generating *new* meanings which do not rupture with the past so much as render the whole temporal configuration of human existence intelligible. In other words, if meaning originates with our experience of community, we anticipate a future in which new lives and new standpoints are *required.* Temporal development and novelty are implicated in the idea of process itself. These new meanings cannot be successfully imagined to be mere products of a rhetoric of persuasion masking a will to power; they are anticipated as continuations of *our* community. Of course, communities may be destroyed, their cultural ideals annihilated. But the community as a project anticipates its continuity through an extension into a future which sustains and develops its meaning.

"Man," says Royce, "is the animal that interprets; and therefore man lives in communities and depends upon them for insight and salvation."[24] The "Will to Interpret" is this striving to overcome the radical separation and individuality of each person, thereby constituting a community whereby the meaning of each can be present to the others and to himself as well. The desire to interpret aims at a "community of interpretation," an ideal which gives structure and guidance to the "community of memory" and the "community of hope." Human beings approach each other through the possibility of sharing an integrative world of meaning which allows them to be members of a community, truly present to each other. Interpretation occupies a special function in the community, articulating those symbols whereby there can be shared insight and understanding. As Royce observes, this has tremendous ethical and religious value, for it is "interpretation which is the great humanizing factor in our cognitive processes and makes the purest forms of love for communities possible."[25] By enriching our understanding of our past and articulating possible ideals for the future, we have constituted and extended the community of the present and the meaning it holds for those living within it.

Royce's analysis up to this point poses a serious challenge to the attenuated views of the "community of interpretation" discussed earlier. First, we now can acknowledge the way in which human beings come to inhabit a shared cultural world through the narrative structure of action and traditions which render that world articulate, allowing us to participate as members in the meaning of that world. A cultural world is a narrative web which grasps a horizon of shared meaning. Every culture has a set of stories which serve to organize the "community of memory." These stories are marked out as sacred in archaic and religious cultures. In nontribal cultures there are also fundamental "myths" which serve the same purpose—essentially any *story* which functions to define and articulate the basic meanings, values, and history of the community. The stories of the discovery of the New World, the flight of the Puritans, the Revolutionary War, and so on, historical facts though they be, serve to define the range of values and meanings out of which a "community of memory" for American citizens is generated, even for those whose American genealogy does not extend that far back. The fight to alter these stories, so as to include the stories of native Americans, blacks, Hispanics, and women, is a fight to modify the ideal used to constitute the values and social identities of our culture so that those which have been "faceless" may also be meaningfully present. Many conflicts throughout history are conflicts of stories commanding our ideals because they constitute the meaning of who we are and the world in which we live. Behind these conflicting ideals is the desire for living a shared life of meaning, what I have called "the Human Eros."

Here a more Deweyan conception of community is needed to supplement Royce's idealistic emphasis on integrative transcendence. Communities need a pluralistic orientation to maintain their imaginative creativity and self-interpretation. Instead of the "private project of self-perfection," we need to make the distinctive activities of individuals truly expressive and so shared by others to enhance the intelligence and imaginative horizon of the community. As Dewey stressed, art is a prime example of the way in which highly distinctive visions have not only been shared, but have *generated* new modes of understanding by showing how seemingly dead-end practices could be radically altered and redirected. The conception of painting as realistic representation was changed by nineteenth-century painters from Monet on by exploring new styles. They did not "rupture vision," but taught us to see with their styles in new ways. They educated vision. The same is true of political reformers who, unlike revolutionaries or a hostile enemy who seek to destroy a culture, have managed to reinterpret a culture's meaning through exposing new possibilities in its practices. The progressive inclusion of blacks and women into the full rights enjoyed by all citizens is an enlargement, not a rupture, of the ideal, the meaning, of freedom and equality. Reformers like Martin Luther King or Susan B. Anthony have also educated vision. A community is sustained through the continuous process of self-interpretation, that is, self-education.

A community exists, Dewey argues, by developing the art of expression and communication. This is what allows human beings to organize themselves in a variety of ways that expand the horizon of meaning. A rich background of symbolic understanding is needed as well as the trained imagination that explores new modes of response and enters flexibly into the possibilities presented in the encounter with others. A society that trains its citizens to understand and appreciate the diversity of our worlds of meaning is more likely to be able to resolve conflicts in ideals as well as to articulate inclusive ideals that sustain a pluralistic culture. A democratic culture is not a Babel of pure difference held together by the loose, temporary end of the private pursuit of personal happiness; it is a culture that can actively understand a variety of worlds. Mutual indifference as to how each other live does not prepare one to communicate, much less to understand alternative worldviews. Instead of the narrow ideal of cultural dogmatism, which excludes the meaning of the other, Dewey stresses that democracy flourishes when the aesthetically educated imagination, disciplined through the self-regulation of the experimental method, aims at securing the conditions whereby a community can adapt, develop, and grow.[26]

We can now see the need for theory as imaginative extension of the interpretive ideals that make the community possible, opening up intelligent courses for action and self-understanding. Theory, as Dewey said, liberates practice. It can do this through articulating ideals to be explored rather than by making dogmatic claims for having achieved a fixed, closed system. Insofar as we are constantly caught up in the *process* of trying to make sense and understand each other, we are rarely faced with pure instances of self-evident intentionality. All who regard intentionality as the perfect lucidity of meaning have simply idealized the product of the fixed, reflex habit. If we focus instead upon the moment of discovery and learning, a different view offers itself. Intentionality for Dewey is what points us toward the shared encounter of the future, in its ambiguities as well as its anticipated stabilities. It is our quest for the community where meaning is aesthetically encountered, where life is lived as narrative development and not as a bare succession of tomorrow after tomorrow after tomorrow: time can be a tale told by others than idiots. Our shared strategies of understanding do not have to be masks for the rhetoric of power; they can be instrumentalities toward creative action, lured by the ideal of the aesthetics of meaning, forging a community through hope and memory.

Such a community Dewey called "democracy" because it would engage itself in the realization of the distinctive potentialities of each individual toward participatory action and shared benefit. Only through the social can the individual come to be. The result would not be a life entirely subjected to collective ends, as Rorty supposes, but one that can intelligently distinguish between genuinely shared public concerns in need of social direction, and those innumerable private transactions that are not.[27]

This indicates a unique function of the humanities in general and philosophy in particular in developing a democratic society. The humanities are the practices which seek to grasp the symbolic life of human existence. They explore the horizons of cultural meaning and so educate the democratic imagination. Through this they enhance the possibility of communication, the understanding of others, and articulate the possibilities for intelligent development and action. Those who are the interpreters of the humanities must be energetically engaged in the task of constituting the community of memory and the community of hope. This also involves the creation of inclusive ideals whereby the present communities may achieve new visions of self-interpretation and greater enhancement of meaningful action. The theory of the humanities posed by Rorty or Fish presents a serious challenge for the role of the humanities in the modern world. It is doubly tragic that they have adapted the name "pragmatism" when it is pragmatism which offers a view of the humanities as central to the cultivation of imagination and the growth of a self-critical community. We need a theory that does not make a neglected riddle of the imagination or community and sees the creation of those worlds of cultural meaning as the expression of a primary human drive to live a life that can embody a value-rich, intelligible existence with others. Our ideals are the sources of our deep commitments and may have the most tragic as well as beneficial consequences. We must foster those which sustain the Human Eros rather than those which evoke its darker nemesis.

The result for philosophy is important: Philosophy, as the preeminent humanistic practice, can serve the Human Eros by articulating those meanings that can secure a community which actively pursues the ideal that human beings can live meaningful lives. But we must appropriate the aesthetic and imaginative aspects of human understanding in order to put philosophy back in constructive dialogue with humanity's quest for meaning, and we must understand the social nature of imagination and the communicative nature of aesthetic expression. The Human Eros possessing philosophy recovers humanism.

Notes

1. I articulate this position as it is developed by the classical pragmatists, especially John Dewey. It also is found, of course, in descriptions of human existence in Martin Heidegger's *Being and Time*, Maurice Merleau-Ponty's *Phenomenology of Perception*, and Paul Ricoeur's *Time and Narrative*. My development of this view also owes much to the personal influence of Mark Johnson.

2. For discussion of the employment of the "schemata" of our embodied action, see Mark Johnson, *The Body in the Mind* (Chicago: University of Chicago Press, 1987) and George Lakoff, *Women, Fire, and Dangerous Things* (Chicago: University of Chicago Press, 1987).

3. See William James' "The Sentiment of Rationality," *The Will to Believe, The Works of William James* (Cambridge: Harvard University Press, 1979), pp. 57–89. Also see the extension of this theme in Dewey's "The Reflex Arc Concept in Psychology" (EW 5:96–110), *Interest and Effort in Education* (MW 7:151–97), and *Human Nature and Conduct* (MW 14).

4. For a more extensive discussion of the "qualitative horizon" found in Dewey's *Art as Experience* (LW 10), see my *John Dewey's Theory of Art, Experience and Nature: The Horizons of Feeling* (Albany: State University of New York Press, 1987).

5. This alludes to but differs from Sigmund Freud's reductionistic materialism. Though the pragmatic theory of the unconscious is not much developed, it recognizes the capacity of unconscious experience to be "civilized" through intelligent habits. Dewey illustrates this in the operation of such prereflective intelligence pervading and structuring the meaning of experience in works of art (cf. LW 1:228).

6. Much contemporary philosophy is remarkable for its willingness to forget these great, simple facts of who and what we are. Anglo-American philosophy, for instance, hardly acknowledges our temporality. Most poststructural thought has dissolved historical or narrative time into fictions of social empowerement that await deconstruction and exposure of so-called arbitrary patterns of language and desire. Much could be made, I think, of the consequences for contemporary Continental semiotics flowing from Saussure's dualistic, dyadic semiotic which made the relation of signs to world entirely arbitrary. This opened the path for Nietzschean and Freudian views that there is nothing behind language except some sort of irrational will or unconscious desire. Rorty and Fish, discussed below in section II, seem to accept this. By contrast, Peirce's triadic semiotic

grounds the process of meaning in the world through the community of interpreters, discussed below in section III.

7. Richard Rorty, *Contingency, Irony and Solidarity* (Cambridge: Cambridge University Press, 1989), p. xiv.

8. Ibid., p. xvi.

9. Ibid., p. 18.

10. Ibid., emphasis added.

11. Fish now describes himself as a "Marxist," though the reasons for this are not terribly clear.

12. Stanley Fish, *Is There a Text in This Class?* (Cambridge, Mass.: Harvard University Press, 1980), p. 14.

13. Ibid., p. 16.

14. Rorty's own long commitment to analytic philosophy is well known. See his confession, in reply to critics, that he is not widely read in pragmatism, "Comments on Sleeper and Edel," *Transactions of the Charles S. Peirce Society* 21, 1 (Winter 1985), p. 39. In *Is There a Text in This Class?* Fish indicates that he has been most influenced by analytic theories of language, especially those of Austin and the later Wittgenstein.

15. This theory of meaning is discussed by Dewey in chapter 5 of *Experience and Nature* (LW 1), by George Herbert Mead in *Mind, Self, and Society* (Chicago: University of Chicago Press, 1934), and by myself in chapter 4 of *John Dewey's Theory of Art, Experience and Nature.*

16. See William James' discussion of teleology of intelligence in chapters 1 and 4 of *The Principles of Psychology* (Cambridge, Mass.: Harvard University Press, 1981). See Dewey's discussions of this topic in "The Reflex Arc Concept in Psychology" (EW 5:96–110) and *Human Nature and Conduct* (MW 14).

17. Josiah Royce, *The Problem of Christianity* (Chicago: University of Chicago Press, 1968), p. 243.

18. Ibid., p. 248.

19. See Ibid., p. 290. Royce's social hermeneutic emphasizes the constant need for new ideas to interpret the past to the future. By contrast, Alasdair MacIntyre's recent discussions of community and tradition mostly look backward, except to ensure that future conflicts are resolved so as not to threaten the integrity of the existing tradition.

20. Ibid., p. 268.

21. Ibid., p. 274.

22. Royce offers a lucid interpretation of Peirce's doctrines in Lectures XI, XIII, and XIV in *The Problem of Christianity.*

23. Ibid., p. 290.

24. Ibid., p. 298.

25. Ibid., p. 318.

222   THOMAS M. ALEXANDER

26.   Dewey's idea of the "experimental method" is a continuation of the social hermeneutics of the democratic community. For Dewey, science is an extension of the social, imaginative nature of experience as it seeks to educate itself through inquiry into nature. Experimental methodology is a discipline for constant learning and thus provides an important self-limitation in the fallibilistic quest for meaning.

27.   See Dewey's discussion of community in *The Public and Its Problems* (LW 2). Dewey's rejection of the individual-social dichotomy undercuts Rorty's efforts to separate projects of private self-creation from those of public policy. Despite his professed admiration of Dewey, Rorty seems unaware of this central feature of Dewey's social philosophy.

13

Liberal Irony and Social Reform

LARRY A. HICKMAN

It is not necessary to subscribe to any of the various formerly or currently popular cyclical views of history to recognize extraordinary similarities between our own time and an earlier one, some 100 years ago, that was coterminous with the formative years of John Dewey's public career.

Both are periods marred by racial strife, by a deterioration of the living standards of working men and women, and by the neglect and exploitation of children. Both are periods characterized by unchecked personal and corporate greed, by a capitulation on the part of federal and state governments to social Darwinist economic principles, by the activities of powerful groups of religious fundamentalists[1] which seek to impose their supernaturalist agenda on a wider public, and by extensive (and controversial) waves of immigration. Perhaps even more significant, both are periods that exhibit widespread and unpenalized corruption within government and a steadfast flight from reality on the part of the voting-age public.

John Dewey's response to the deplorable social conditions of the last decades of the nineteenth century was to call for social reform—a cultural reconstruction in which philosophy would play several important roles. First, philosophy would serve as a reminder to the other disciplines (as would the other disciplines to it) of the importance of an ongoing reconsideration and reconstruction of its own ontological commitments. In this regard Dewey argued that philosophers must abandon their usual and too-intimate attachment to doctrines and prescriptions worn threadbare by habitual and uncritical use. He thought it essential, for example, that philosophers recognize the futility of attempting to describe reality in a general sense; that they abandon their hoary quest for certainty; and that they abjure supernaturalist and extranaturalist metaphysics in favor of a radical, experimental empiricism.

Should philosophers persist in clothing themselves in these comfortable but worn-out garments, he suggested, they would no longer be welcome in the company of those conscientious men and women in business, in the sciences, and in the technological fields who take it as their task to identify, to resolve, and to reconstruct genuinely problematic situations. Their conversations would consequently lack the solid ring of relevance and would degenerate into jargon tossed to and fro among themselves.

A second role prescribed by Dewey for philosophy went beyond these admonitions. Philosophers, he argued, have at their disposal both a unique subject matter and a distinctive set of tools. Their unique subject matter is the method of inquiry by means of which distinctions are drawn and adjudications made between values that are immediate and those that are ulterior, that is, between what is apparent and what is eventual. This method works in ethics, in aesthetics, and even in logic itself, that is, in the very theory of such inquiry. It also works in all the other arts and sciences that consider particular cases of the relation of already-possessed tools and goals to their better, but not-yet-attained, alternatives.

The philosopher's distinctive set of tools includes both those instruments that are appropriate for use in philosophical inquiry in general, and the specific instruments that are unique to the various areas of his or her concern, such as aesthetics, ethics, or logic. An example of a general philosophical instrument is the recognition and avoidance of what Dewey called "the philosopher's fallacy." This mistake is committed when an inquirer analyzes a complex situation into its constituent parts for the sake of resolving some perceived difficulty, but then insists that the parts secured by means of inquiry were present all the while—*prior* to inquiry and in some absolute sense, in a way that is unrelated to the goals or ends-in-view that initially prompted their isolation from the total situation. Dewey's work offers an extensive account of general methods, such as the avoidance of the philosopher's fallacy, by means of which inquiry itself is illuminated, tested, refined, and suggested for use in the other arts and sciences.

An example of the more specific instruments available to the philosopher are those tools developed specifically for use in aesthetics, in ethics, and in logic. These include theories of representation and expression in aesthetics, various deontological and consequentialist theories in ethics, and notions of class inclusion and of warranted assertibility in logic.

It is, Dewey argued, of great functional importance to differentiate these three things: the unique subject matter of philosophy, the set of general tools that it brings to bear on philosophical questions *qua* philosophical, and the specific tools that have been found to be of use in each of the specific areas of philosophical inquiry. And it is also important to recall that for Dewey what functions as the unique subject matter of philosophy—the general method of intelligence that he thinks is present wherever and whenever genuine problem solving occurs—also functions as a general tool for the other arts and sciences. The difference is one of reflection: philosophy undertakes a self-conscious and systematic study of the general method of intelligence that is merely used, albeit often improved upon in use, by the other disciplines.

Were one to confuse the general method of intelligence *qua* subject matter of philosophy with the general method of intelligence *qua* tool of the other arts and sciences, one might be tempted to think that philosophy has no unique subject matter, or that philosophers have no particular role—beyond their roles as good citizens—in the pursuit of social reform.

These are conclusions that have in fact been drawn by a sizeable contingent of contemporary philosophers. Richard Rorty, for example, has written approvingly of what he takes (mistakenly, I will argue) to be Dewey's desire to "rub out" the distinctions among art, science, and philosophy, and to substitute for those distinct methods a "vague and uncontroversial notion of intelligence."[2] I believe that Rorty's confusion in this matter has led to terminal problems for his "liberal ironist." I shall return to Rorty's interpretation of Dewey presently.

That Dewey thought the general method of intelligence to be the subject matter of philosophy is apparent from his remarks in the final pages of his 1925 *Experience and Nature*. Philosophers, in Dewey's view, are capable of occupying a unique niche in the broad and ongoing enterprise called social reform, or the reconstruction of culture, because one of the functions of their discipline involves a "criticism of criticisms." "Philosophy," he wrote, "is inherently criticism, having its distinctive position among various modes of criticism in its generality; [it is] a criticism of criticisms. . ." (LW 1:298).

On at least one occasion, Dewey put this point in terms that exhibit overt reference to the threefold distinction among categories that had earlier been elaborated by C. S. Peirce. First, the philosopher, as well as the practitioner of the other arts and sciences, has the task of going beyond the immediacy of "conscience in morals, taste in fine arts and conviction in belief" (LW 1:300) that characterizes inherited, habitual, naive, and other stances that are utilized daily and in an uncritical fashion.

In our own time such uncritical immediacy of response has included the emotional fever pitch generated by the use of patriotic symbols, such as the flag, during political campaigns. In the arts it has taken the form of preference for kitsch and sentimentality over thoughtful and engaging studies of complex human situations. In the realm of religious taste it has meant literalist reinterpretations of what were formerly regarded as allegorical supernaturalist myths and consequent attempts to censor well crafted and insightful literary and performance works on the grounds that they are immoral or even "satanic." In the area of mass media it has taken the form of an insidious sensationalism that conflates information with entertainment.

It may be objected that this list contains only negative instances, and that "conscience in morals, taste in fine arts and conviction on belief" may also include instances that have led to positive results. Dewey's answer to this point was the same as that of Peirce. Where unrefined experience leads to a good consequence, no more than luck can be claimed. It is, on the other hand, the function of intelligence to go beyond luck and to make sure that what is found to be valuable is secured.

The philosopher, then, shares with the political scientist, the historian or critic of art, the sociologist, and the media theorist the task of criticizing and refining uninformed impulses such as those just mentioned. Because it utilizes the general method of intelligence, however, in addition to the specific tools of each of the disciplines, this work can hardly be said to be uniquely philosophical.

But it is also the task of the philosopher (and Dewey thought it uniquely so) to operate in a venue that lies beyond those critical judgments of fact—Peirce's seconds—that are a part of the task of the individual arts and sciences, from anthropology to nuclear physics and from mathematics to video art. One of the crucial functions of philosophy, in short, is to ensure that criticism operates at a level of generality not unlike Peirce's thirdness, a level at which it is "aware of itself and its implications, pursued deliberately and systematically" (LW 1:302). It is at this level that both general philosophical tools, such as the philosopher's fallacy, and tools that are unique to the more specific areas of philosophical concern, such as theories of "truth" as warranted assertibility, come into play. Taken together, these are the tools that have arisen from the activity Dewey called "criticism of criticisms."

Dewey detailed some of the consequences of undertaking such a criticism of criticisms: they include the regulation of "the further appreciation of goods and bads," the engendering of "greater freedom and security in those acts of direct selection, appropriation, [and] identification," and the "rejection, elimination, destruction which enstate and which exclude objects of belief, conduct and contemplation" (LW 1:302). If Dewey's language regarding this matter fails to be elegant, it at least has the clarity and directness required to dispel any doubt concerning what, in his view, needs to be done.

Above all, the work of the philosopher is for Dewey situated in a cultural matrix from which it takes its problems and to which it must return for the checks and cues that afford its results a power that is both solvent and constructive. This is tantamount to saying that the role of philosophy in social reform has two moments. The first is an *excursus* from experience that is immediate and unrefined, as well as from the data and working hypotheses of the individual arts and sciences. The second, once such material has been secured, worked over, and designated for use in the philosophical task of reformulation and transformation, is a *recursus* to the contents and the methods of the arts and sciences and to quotidian experience in ways that insure that "freer, richer, and more secure objects of belief are instituted as goods of immediate acceptance" (LW 1:320).

These two moments, one solvent and the other reconstructive, constitute the drumbeats to which Deweyan social reform marches: the first is the resolution of problematic situations into meaningful parts and pieces by means of the application of instruments invented or chosen for that specific task; the second is the eventual and eventful *re*construction of such situations on the basis of the new meanings and the new possibilities that follow upon the intelligent application of appropriate tools to problematic situations.

A pivotal word in the Deweyan lexicon of cultural reconstruction is "refinement." Dewey's arguments in *Art as Experience* reveal that he had few illusions regarding the tendency of most human individuals to take any available pleasure impulsively and without admixture. But he also understood that calls for censorship or for suppression of what is common, crude, or (short of violent) even patently disgusting to a majority is most often counterproductive. This is so because expression that is naive, intuitive, and unreflective often carries with it an energy that is fueled by cultural disturbance—distress that simmers outside of officially sanctioned channels of expression.

Dewey resolutely opposed those who would counter such expressions with instruments of suppression. His tactic of choice was instead the transformation of the raw materials of cultural disharmony by working to refine them, by focusing their energies, and by turning them toward ends that were better and more appropriate.

Dewey's views on the subject of the role of philosophy in cultural reconstruction are by no means uncontroversial, even among some "neopragmatists" who claim to be his ardent adherents in general terms.

As I have already indicated, Richard Rorty, whose variety of neopragmatism currently enjoys considerable popularity,[3] has written approvingly of what he takes to be Dewey's desire to "rub out" the distinctions between art, science, and philosophy, and to substitute a "vague and uncontroversial notion of intelligence."[4] It is therefore surprising that even as he fuzzes these boundaries, putatively on Dewey's authority, Rorty establishes an implicit hierarchical privilege for the literary arts. As did Foucault and Heidegger before him, Rorty holds that science is now quietly receding into the background, and that it is being replaced by poetizing. A poet, in his broad definition of the term, is "one who makes things new."[5] But when he comes to specifics, it is usually spoken or written language that is the poet's subject material.

The effect of Rorty's hierarchizing is that science is not merely deemphasized, but eclipsed as a tool of social reform. Rorty thinks this an important part of his task of laying bare the faults and failures of the Enlightenment project, which had in his view instituted a kind of cultural hegemony for science. His "liberal ironist" responds to this alleged eclipse of science with a shrug of her shoulders; she thinks that liberalism centers around novels, plays, and poems, and not around science. She recognizes no particular vocabulary as more important than any other, just so long as there is enough overlap to allow one speaker to enter into another's "fantasies." In her view, the setting of science and the dawning of irony is just a case of one form of conversation being replaced by another. Her deconstructivist redescription may, Rorty suggests, serve quite as well to expand "our chances of being kind" as did the old scientific liberalism. It may even do better; it does not hold out the ungrounded hope of being "progressive" and "dynamic."

What, then, is Rorty's own view of the social function of philosophy? Unlike Dewey, he thinks that it has none. It would be better, he suggests, "to avoid thinking of philosophy as a 'discipline' with 'core problems' or with a social function."[6] To be sure, Rorty holds and presents certain ideas concerning what a good society would be like. It would be one in which free discussion was the norm rather than the exception, in which everyone had equal access to the means for self-creation, and in which, given that level playing field, people were then left alone to "work out their private salvations."[7]

Rorty singles out for special criticism what he takes to be Habermas' view, that cooperative political action requires a common vision of what is universally human. Such a position, he argues, is unsatisfactory because it fails to come to terms with the failure of the Enlightenment idea of a foundational human nature on the basis of which its programs of absolute rationality and perfectibility were constructed. He recommends instead a view that what binds political groups are shared vocabularies and common hopes.

It would be redundant to present here an extended case that Rorty's work exhibits nothing that could be called a coherent social program. Richard Bernstein, Cornel West, and John R. Wallach have expended considerable ink in the process of establishing precisely this point.[8] My point is rather to illuminate the ways in which Dewey's notion of cultural *reconstruction* works by contrasting it to the liberal ironist's program of *deconstruction*.

What is remarkable in Rorty's neopragmatist-deconstructivist account of what philosophy does is that some of the most important philosophical underpinnings of Dewey's program for social reform drop out. It is as if Rorty has taken one half of Dewey's prescription for cultural reconstruction—its analytical or solvent moment—but ignored the other half—the moment in which it undertakes active reconstruction. Perhaps that is why the social dimension in Rorty's work, unlike that of Dewey's, turns out to be a liberalism without social action.

Dewey strenuously and consistently argued that the sciences and the arts constitute different types of inquiries in that they have different subject matters and different sets of tools. From a Deweyan perspective, Rorty's liberal ironist is correct on one important matter: there is no ultimate *ontological* distinction between the arts and the sciences. The liberal ironist is also correct that the arts, the sciences, and philosophy utilize the same general method of intelligence. But from Dewey's perspective she is mistaken in her conclusion that neither is there a *functional* distinction on which the differences between the arts, the sciences, and philosophy rest.

It is precisely against this plank in the liberal ironist platform that Dewey's argument is so effective: "different types of problems demand different modes of inquiry for their solution..." (LW 12:82). He maintained that it is the function of the arts to comment upon the life and institutions of a particular culture and to express and intensify the meanings they find there—to render situations more perspicuous than they would otherwise be, to free experienced values from contexts that tend to militate against their use and development, and to enlarge the response of the imagination to perceived impasses: in short, to "perpetuate, enhance and vivify in imagination the natural goods" (LW 1:305).

Implicit in this characterization of the arts as a tool of cultural reconstruction is an argument against governmental interference in the arts, or of the restriction of government support to one type of art on the grounds that it is "safer" or less controversial than another sort. Dewey's position with respect to this matter is as relevant in our own time as it was when he first advanced it. As I write, the news contains regular accounts of attempts to politicize the National Endowment for the Arts, that is, to create a political test for funding and to restrict support to those works of art that are considered "safe."

But what makes art art is not whether or not it is "transgressive," that is, characterized by some as containing subject matter that is obscene because it examines themes that are sexual or violent. What makes art art is its success in the performance of the functions just enumerated—freeing, enhancing, and expressing meanings. In the most general of terms, art must be expressive in ways that are not so much uplifting as clarifying, and not so much inspirational as insightful.

On this view, the difference between pornography and art, when art contains sexual material that some or even many find offensive, is that pornography only serves to excite and exploit erotic fantasy, whereas art expresses such fantasy in ways that lead to its examination and refinement. On this definition, most of the images of women on MTV are pornographic, even though they are deemed socially acceptable and are viewed in millions of American homes. And the performances of Karen Finley, which have been judged pornographic by the director of the National Endowment for the Arts under admitted pressure from Senator Jesse Helms and others, are legitimate artistic expression.

The function of the sciences, in Dewey's book, differs markedly from that of the arts. The distinctions he draws between these disciplines is not prescriptive, however, but descriptive. They take into account what artists and scientists *do*, not some fixed ideal by means of which their activities are measured. The sciences disclose relationships in ways that can be generalized to ever broader instrumental use, taking the term "instrumental" in the general sense of quantifiable and productive of new methods of quantification. In the arts, relationships are expressed. In the sciences, relationships are stated and then stabilized by means of quantification, that is, by developing ever more complex languages which allow for ever greater precision and sophistication with respect to the substitution of variables. Science develops noetic—or at least cognitive—instruments which allow the comparison and contrast of things that were not theretofore understood as or taken to be relative, except perhaps by luck (LW 4:101).

Dewey provided an excellent example of this point in 1925, in the last chapter of *Experience and Nature*. Writing of the contributions of Jeremy Bentham and John Stuart Mill to the reform of the social ills of their time, Dewey suggested that their work had lacked the precision available when scientific instrumentation is utilized. Their work, he argued, was more like that of the literary artist, Charles Dickens, whose expressed insights into the malaise of his time stirred individuals of good will to undertake meaningful reform. Their work operated, as he put it, as "literary rather than as scientific apparatus" (LW 1:323), though it would certainly be wrong, he was quick to add, to demean the work of any of these men. It is, after all, a function of art to refine and express brute experiences and to inspire action.

Mill's essay on *The Subjection of Women* provides an excellent example of Dewey's point. As a polemical tract, one which involves a narrative account of perceived injustices and whose reasoning is predominantly analogical, Mill's story can not have failed to touch and to sensitize a careful reader. Even today it functions as does good art. But it lacks a dimension which can now be furnished by careful empirical studies that go beyond the anecdotal in order to assert and defend detailed quantitative analyses of pay scale differentials, the increasing feminization of poverty, and the consequences of legislation that restricts access to means of reproductive control, to mention only three of many areas of current scientific focus in this broadly problematic area.

This difference between the respective roles of the sciences and the arts in social reform can perhaps be made more clearly by eliciting some contemporary examples. The first involves successful works undertaken by artist and scientist which function in different but complementary ways to express, analyze, and reconstruct a particular social difficulty. Dewey's view regarding the unique function of philosophy is also manifest in this case. Because philosophy involves the study of the general method of intelligence, it is uniquely positioned to criticize the methods of the distinct disciplines that employ it. And because it functions as a criticism of criticisms, philosophy is also uniquely capable of arbitrating the differences and highlighting the similarities involved in alternative approaches to the same material.

Photographer Stephen Shames has done for the public of the 1990s what Jacob Riis[9] did for his own public a century ago. Shames' *Outside the Dream*[10] expresses the meanings of the poverty and homelessness of many of America's children in ways that are unique to the work of the skilled artist. As an artist, Shames' task has been to refine and detail those meanings; he has sensitized his public in a manner that constitutes a call to action, but does not define the means and methods involved in such action.

Shames' work, and its consequences, are thus of a radically different sort than the quantitative efforts of the behavioral scientists who have interpreted and published the data associated with the growing gap between rich and poor. Their charts, graphs, and tables do not so much "express" meanings as they serve to "state" them in ways that serve to render them stable and manageable.

If Shames, as heir to Jacob Riis, has raised our consciousness and *expressed* the meanings of poverty and homelessness, then the more quantitative treatments advanced by Kevin Phillips' *The Politics of Rich and Poor*[11] and the editors of *Scientific American*,[12] to take only two of many possible emamples, have *stated* those meanings in ways that constitute a call for specific action and set out the means by which it is to be undertaken. The difference between the function of the arts and the sciences in this case is clear in terms both of method and result. It is a difference that Dewey emphasized throughout his written work as one that must be understood in order for deliberate social action to be successful.

But this is also a difference that Rorty's liberal ironist tends to fuzz. The very different efforts of Shames and Phillips go well beyond the Rortyan palliative of "entering into one another's fantasies." Their example involves distinct methods and tools that function in ways that are complementary. There is no vague and "undifferentiated" method of intelligence at work here. Instead, the works of scientist and artist are successful only as their different methods contribute to defining and sharpening an overarching method of intelligence, and then finding ways for that continually reconstructed method to feed back into their disciplines.

Productive liberalism, a liberalism that involves social action, thus involves a variety of methods and techniques that go beyond a simple attempt "work out our own salvation." Further, although both the arts and the sciences utilize the general method of intelligence, neither discipline has that method as its subject matter. The analysis of that method, and of the ways in which it operates in a feedback relation with respect to the various disciplines, is one of the most important functions left to philosophy. Philosophy, as Dewey puts it, is a kind of "liaison officer" between and among various disciplines.

At times the arts and the sciences come into direct conflict. It is in such cases that philosophy can fulfill an important social function, engaging the "criticism of criticisms" which Dewey characterized as one of its unique functions. News reportage on television offers an excellent case for such analysis.

Some media critics have argued with great cogency that the very format of television militates against careful and detailed analysis of public issues. Because it is a mass medium and because it also constitutes a covert form of advertising (NBC, for example, is owned by General Electric), television news tends to reduce complex matters to their superficial aesthetic-affective dimensions and to reinforce common prejudices. In its quest to mimic the short bursts of simplistic, high-energy information developed and utilized so effectively by advertisers to condition their audiences, television news coverage has largely abandoned the critical debates that are an essential ingredient in the objectivity and fallibilism of the sciences. It has settled instead for highly stylized and aestheticized renderings of information, all the while claiming for itself a special ability to represent the facts of a case in a rigorous, definitive, fashion (as "eyewitness" news, for example). To its critics, however, it functions at best as a defective art form—defective in the important sense that unlike the successful arts it consistently fails to treat its materials with honesty.

Nowhere has this criticism been more warranted than in the televised coverage of the war in the Persian Gulf. The story Americans saw was one dominated by visual material furnished by the Department of Defense and its contractors, and by analysis and commentary furnished by the same sources.

Detailed, quantitative, scientific studies of the reportage of the Gulf War have begun to emerge, however, and they highlight the inadequacies of the medium and its practitioners. Janet Steele[13] and others, for example, have examined the backgrounds of the many consultants who were invited to appear on network news programs, including "Nightline," during coverage of the war.

Steele found that representatives of think tanks with Pentagon funding were rarely identified as such, and in some cases were actually misidentified in ways that contributed to the impression that they were objective analysts. One guest, for example, who appeared 56 times during the period from August 1990 to March 1991, and who was identified as a "University Professor" and "National Security Analyst," was actually employed on the staff of a conservative Republican senator.[14] For its part, the editors of the journal *Extra!* surveyed the sources on NBC, CBS, and ABC nightly news during roughly the same period and found that "of 878 on-air sources, only one was a representative of a national peace organization. . . . By contrast, seven players from the Super Bowl were brought on to comment on the war."[15]

It is little wonder, then, that one public opinion poll found that only 13 percent of those sampled knew "that the U.S. responded to Iraq's threat to use force against Kuwait [in July of 1990] by saying it would take no action. . . [whereas] 81 percent of the [same] sample could identify the missile used to shoot down the Iraqi Scuds as the Patriot."[16] The televised news coverage of the Gulf War may have functioned well enough as an art form designed to create and maintain public support for American involvement in the hostilities, but it was precisely to that extent that it failed to deal adequately with its putative materials. In Dewey's view, the methods of the arts and the sciences at their best are also the methods of democracy. Where an art form works in an antidemocratic fashion, it compromises its own methods and loses its claim to artistic integrity. Under such conditions, "news" becomes little more than propaganda.

The matter of the distinctive functions of the arts and the sciences was the subject of Dewey's attention in 1934, in chapter 4 of *Art as Experience*. Once again, Dewey clearly articulated his view that it is the function of the sciences to *state* meanings, whereas it is the function of the arts to *express* them. Dewey thought that science functions as does a map or a directory: it sets out some of the conditions that must obtain if a particular experience is to be undergone and appropriated. But it is not that experience itself. An important difference between faulty science and good science corresponds to the degree of adequacy with which the supplied directions serve to lead to the desired experience. A formula for the combination of two chemical elements to form a third is adequate insofar as what has been predicted actually occurs under the specified conditions.

There is, however, a major difficulty in the way that some have interpreted the role of the sciences. Philosophers and scientists of the seventeenth century—and they were in many cases the same individuals— clearly attempted to assimilate science to art: they expected science to be an expression of the inner meanings of things. But when science is thus asked to perform the function of art, when something is expected of it that it has not promised and that it cannot deliver, the resulting confusion is inevitable.

It was Dewey's view that this confusion of scientists and philosophers of the seventeenth century, their attempt to assimilate novel instrumental techniques to an outdated art form—a contemplative metaphysics of fixed and finished categories—was a great impediment to what might have been even greater progress during their time. What they in fact accomplished was highly productive: their *de facto* treatment of science was as a matrix of indicators and as a directory of expectations. But what they *thought* they were doing, and the way they described their activities, turns out in retrospect to have functioned as a brake on their actual accomplishments: they persisted in their description of science as expressive of the final and inner nature of things.

There was thus a great gap between what seventeenth-century scientists thought they were doing and what they actually accomplished. They thought that they were getting ever closer to a final picture of reality, but, as Rorty's liberal ironist correctly points out, this turned out to be a dead end. Their original accomplishment lay in what they did in fact, that is, their opening up of new horizons by means of the development and the refinement of new tools and artifacts.

The move of the liberal ironist, then, is to reject that unfortunate assimilation by seventeenth-century science and philosophy of the experimental method to an art form that claimed to be expressive of "reality." And she is certainly correct to do so. Where she goes wrong, if we accept Dewey's account of the matter, is that she fails to grasp the full extent of the error of seventeenth-century science. She has consequently repeated it in another form. Whereas the seventeenth century assimilated science to an old and now for the most part disused art form, namely the attempt to express the nature of ultimate reality, she assimilates science to a newer and currently popular art form, namely the expression of experience through literary forms. Viewed from this perspective, her argument ultimately begs the question: since science can no longer be assimilated to the old art form, it must therefore be assimilable to some new one. Her unspoken premise, as well as her conclusion, is the hierarchical privilege of the arts over the sciences.

The fact that the liberal ironist ignores is that science had its own voice during the seventeenth century, and that its *de facto* voice spoke loudly and clearly above the *de jure* claims that were being made for it. Moreover, science continues to have its own voice even today. The accomplishments of scientific technology in medicine, in the exploration of space, in the manufacture and delivery of consumer goods, and in innumerable other areas constitute more than simply "another vocabulary." They constitute real indications of how real problems may be articulated, resolved, and reconstructed.

As I have indicated, an important consequence of the liberal ironist's assimilation of science to the literary arts is that science becomes only one "vocabulary" among others with no particular privilege. The point that she misses is precisely the point of Dewey's social reformer, namely that both the arts and the sciences continue to be privileged, but not hierarchically so. Each is privileged within its own peculiar domain, and each utilizes the other in its own investigations. A sculptor, for example, may use data generated by the sciences regarding the strength and stress loads of various materials; and a scientist may utilize instrumentation whose design expresses the aesthetic qualities of glass, metal, plastics, wood, and other materials. In the contemporary examples just enumerated, the artist may utilize scientific data on poverty to target areas for aesthetic investigation, and the scientist may utilize the work of the artist to motivate his own interests and to engage his reader in the human dimension of abstracted data. In the same vein, the work of social scientists could be of great service to the artists who construct televised news, were they to avail themselves of it. Televised news might then open itself up to a wider spectrum of opinion, and work more diligently to construct balanced and defensible presentations of events that inform as well as entertain. What is important in each of these cases is that neither the scientist nor the artist, *qua* scientist or artist, performs the unique function of the other, and that the philosopher has a unique social role as critic.

In the view of the social reformer, if it is the function of the sciences to lead to an experience, it is the function of the arts to constitute one. The scientific or prosaic is set forth in propositions which indicate what is required for an experience. The artistic or poetic is "super-propositional": it involves what Dewey calls "an immediate realization of intent" (LW 10:91).

A significant point of difference between Dewey's social reformer and Rorty's liberal ironist, then, is that whereas the social reformer argues that the sciences and the arts constitute different types of inquiry, each with its peculiar subject matter and set of tools, the liberal ironist wants to blur that distinction. Further, the social reformer not only differentiates between the arts and the sciences, but is ready to indicate some of the ways in which they are related.

Dewey's social reformer, for example, reconstructs the popular notion, prevalent since the seventeenth century, that technology is "applied science." He thinks that the fault of this popular definition is that it is too "scientistic": it tends to make science the measure of all other dimensions of human experience. So the social reformer views science as functionally embedded within technology; he treats it as a special type of technological activity. But the social reformer does not stop there. For him, science could not operate in the absence of the "consummatory" moments of aesthetic experience. As Dewey wrote in 1948, in a reply to Benedetto Croce, "[N]ot only is scientific inquiry as it is conducted a highly skilled technology, but the consummatory fulfillments that are characteristic of the esthetic phase of life experience play a highly important part in attaining the conclusions reached in science" (LW 15:98).

The social reformer thus easily avoids the charge of scientism that is a central feature of the liberal ironist's frontal attack on the Enlightenment project and its manifestation in seventeenth-century science, as well as a feature of her attack on the progressive social reformer himself. Science is privileged, according to the social reformer, but only in its own domain. Far from being a paradigm for human experience, science is at most instrumental to "the enrichment of immediate experience though the control over action that it exercises" (LW 10:294).

According to the social reformer, progress is not only possible, but a frequent feature of our actual experience. It occurs whenever the possibility for amelioration is recognized, when scientific and other types of instruments are utilized to actualize and fructify what was theretofore only desired or hoped for as an "end-in-view," and when the resultant super-added value is enjoyed both for its own sake and as a platform for further progress, that is, as a means to enlarging meanings and securing further benefits. For Dewey, an important part of human life is a process of tech-nological or artifactual production, among whose tools is scientific inquiry.

The social reformer's view of progress is therefore not bound up with practice, as some Marxists have suggested, or with contemplation, as Hannah Arendt has argued, or even with enjoyment, as some aesthetes have thought. Progress is rather a cycle of production: this includes the production of new significances, the production of new feelings, the production of new means of enjoying, and the production of new techniques of production. For the social reformer, to be human is to be involved in production, to generate an increase over what nature has given, to reconstruct ourselves on a continuing basis. This is one of the most important meanings of technology.

In the second volume of their admirable *A History of Philosophy in America*, Elizabeth Flower and Murray G. Murphey call to our attention a distinction that sheds considerable light on these matters. Characterizing the views of the mid-nineteenth-century German-American Hegelian Peter Kaufmann, they describe his socialism as one that "shares the Hegelian view of history as a process in which good emerges from evil through alterations and reform of the social institutions which transmit and mold values." They contrast this view with "the prevalent New England view that social reform depends upon the individual's change of heart."[17]

This distinction may in fact be an important factor in understanding the difference between Dewey's social reformer and Rorty's liberal ironist. One finds Dewey's social reformer active in education, politics, the arts, the sciences, and every area where there are problems to be solved. Institutions are viewed as there to be improved. Social movements are viewed as opportunities for amelioration. Sleeves are rolled up, instruments are invented and applied, and matters are altered for the better. The project of amelioration undertaken by the social reformer includes a continuing analysis and reconstruction of *both* the manifestations of our selves and the social institutions in which those selves are embedded.

But Rorty's liberal ironist is timid by comparison. The focus of her attention lies not in social institutions but in a change of heart—a conversion experience on the part of each individual. As Rorty put it, her hope is that individuals will be able "to work out their private salvations, create their private images, reweave their webs of belief and desire in the light of whatever new people and books they happen to encounter."[18]

What Flower and Murphy have called to our attention is that the position of the liberal ironist is a kind of secular Calvinism. Calvin had argued that there is a kind of pride associated with the use of natural and acquired tools, and that philosophy is of little use in the larger program of finding our place in the world. His emphasis, like that of the liberal ironist, was upon conscience and upon individual regeneration. As with Rorty's liberal ironist, so with the Calvinist; liberalism is possible, but it is a liberalism without social action. And a liberalism without social action, to use Rorty's infelicitous but revealing phrase, offers only "ungrounded" social hope.

Ralph Sleeper has articulated this distinction between Dewey's social reformer and Rorty's liberal ironist with great precision:

> The trouble comes, not with Rorty's recognition of Dewey's pervasive "antifoundationalism," but with his construal of its consequences. We are left, he tells us, with "ungrounded social hope" and a philosophy that can provide us with nothing more than occasional illumination to dispel the gathering gloom.

Philosophy, according to Rorty, is to give "edification," and there doesn't seem to be anything very edifying in Rorty's attenuation of philosophy's function to the point where it becomes indistinguishable from that of literary criticism. What rankles is Rorty's insouciant reductionism. Pragmatism—at least Dewey's sort—had seemed to offer us more than that. It had seemed to be teaching us how to transform the culture that is decaying around us, rather than just how to "cope" with its collapse."[19]

Following William James, Dewey thought that the question was not so much whether social hope was "grounded" in some final way as whether ways could be found to bring into existence what was hoped for. That novels, plays, and drama can and do set social agenda, motivate enthusiasm for social action, and promote common vocabularies is both undeniable and a source of great good. But to assert, as does the liberal ironist, that amelioration depends solely, or even principally, upon the "awareness of the power of [literary] redescription,"[20] that the methods that have been so effective in the natural and social sciences have no special place in social inquiry, is to amputate one half of the method which has been tested and urged upon us by the social reformer. In giving up the reconstructive moment for the sake of the solvent or analytical one, the deconstructivist liberal ironist abandons all hope for social actions.[21]

Notes

1.   Fundamentalism, of course, refers to a religious view based on the 1910 tracts, *The Fundamentals*. Nevertheless, each of the five items of the fundamentalist agenda had been around for some time before 1910. These included: "the literal truth of the Bible, the authenticity of all its miracles, the Virgin Birth of Christ, His Resurrection, His substitutionary atonement for the sins of man." Ray Ginger, *The Age of Excess* (New York: The Macmillan Company, 1965) p. 283.

2.   Richard Rorty, *The Consequences of Pragmatism* (Minneapolis: University of Minnesota Press, 1982), p. 51.

3.   See Konstantin Kolenda, *Rorty's Pragmatic Humanism* (Tampa: University of South Florida Press, 1990).

4.   Richard Rorty, *The Consequences of Pragmatism*, p. 51.

5.   Richard Rorty, *Contingency, Irony and Solidarity* (Cambridge: Cambridge University Press, 1989), p. 13.

6.   Ibid., p. 83.

7.   Ibid., p. 85.

8.   John Wallach, "Liberals, Communitarians, and the Tasks of Politcal Theory," *Political Theory* 15, 4 (November 1987) pp. 581–611. Richard

J. Bernstein, "One Step Forward, Two Steps Backward," *Political Theory* 15, 4 (November 1987) pp. 538–63. Cornel West, *The American Evasion of Philosophy* (Madison: University of Wisconsin Press, 1969) esp. pp. 192–209.

9. Jacob A. Riis, *How the Other Half Lives: Studies among the Tenements of New York* (New York: Dover Publications, Inc., 1971).

10. Stephen Shames, *Outside the Dream* (Washington, D.C.: The Children's Defense Fund and Aperture Foundation, 1991).

11. Kevin Phillips, *The Politics of Rich and Poor* (New York: Random House, 1990).

12. Paul Wallich and Elizabeth Corcoran, "The Discreet Disappearance of the Bourgeoisie," *Scientific American* 266, 2 (February 1992) p. 111.

13. Janet Steele, *Enlisting Experts: Objectivity and the Operational Bias in Television News Analysis of the Persian Gulf War* (Washington, D.C.: Woodrow Wilson Center Media Studies Project, 1992).

14. See "Press Clips," in *The Village Voice*, December 24, 1991, p. 8. The individual identified as a "university professor" was in fact an adjunct professor at Georgetown University. There is crucial difference between a faculty member who teachers on a part-time basis and whose primary employment is as a member of a congressional staff, on the one hand, and a full time faculty member who pursues research in a scientific and objective fashion. This is precisely the distinction that was obscured.

15. See *Extra!* 4, 3 (May 1991) p. 5.

16. See *Extra!* 4, 3 (May 1991) p. 11.

17. Elizabeth Flower and Murray G. Murphey, *A History of Philosophy in America*, vol. 2 (New York: G.P. Putnam's Sons, 1977) p. 469.

18. Rorty, *Contingency, Irony and Solidarity*, p. 85.

19. Ralph Sleeper, *The Necessity of Pragmatism* (New Haven: Yale University Press, 1986), p. 1.

20. Rorty, *Contingency, Irony and Solidarity*, p. 89.

21. I am indebted to Ralph Sleeper and Michael Eldridge for numerous suggestions regarding the material in this chapter.

14

The Pragmatics of Deconstruction and the End of Metaphysics

R. W. SLEEPER

Frozen at the threshold, metaphysics stands like the wanderer in Trakl's famous poem commented on by Heidegger, paralyzed: no table is set for it with bread and wine, however.

Set you that down.

—Ruben Berezdivin, ''In Stalling Metaphysics At the Threshold''[1]

The encoded messages that we are getting from philosophers who practice deconstruction are often puzzling. It is not that breaking the code is so difficult. Deconstructionists delight in providing us, if not with translation manuals, at least with "code-breakers," openings through which we can peer at the game going on inside. It is just that after the decoding is done and the game is over, we have the sinking feeling that we are not much better off than before.[2]

Thus Berezdivin, in the essay from which the epigraph installed above is taken, traces the deconstructionist hostility to metaphysics to its source in Plato's dualistic distinction between philosophy and poetry. It is "fiction versus fiction" from then on, Berezdivin tells us; hope for anything closer to the truth than that is forever "stalled," foreclosed. Metaphysics is *over* even before it begins. But where does *that* leave us?

According to Richard Rorty the irony of the situation that Berezdivin reports is just what deconstructionist criticism intends. Deconstructionists are *trying* to leave us in the condition of aporia they often ascribe to the failed philosophies they scorn. It is easy to think of this as the "foundationless" condition that Thomas Kuhn wants us to think of as "The Essential Tension," or that Rorty himself thinks of as the "ungrounded" contingency of his "social hope."

But *that* condition, surely, is just the condition that John Dewey taught us to think of as "problematic." Since it is not a condition we happily rest with, he urged upon us a range of options under the general rubric of "inquiry." Inquiry, Dewey held, is "melioristic" across the board. The logic of experience that inquiries exhibit sustains this holding and shows how the range of inquiry's varied practice hangs together. There is a "continuity" that links these intelligent behaviors, Dewey believed, connecting and involving them with the natural world of all sorts and conditions of existence.

In the end Dewey found himself compelled to admit that the practice of inquiry had enabled him to create something like a philosophical "system" of connections and involvements, of events and their outcomes. It was a provisional background theory of the world of existences and our experience of them that might aid in resolving the tensions that crop up in that world. It worked like a contingent map of the pathways that had led to a surprising, if incomplete, record of successes; to what he sometimes referred to as "consummatory" experiences. The achievement of these successes, he reminded us, is the purpose of inquiry and the end of metaphysics.

Dewey made no apology for his antifoundational use of the term 'metaphysics' as an antidote to dualism in *Experience and Nature*:

> ... the text of my book makes it clear that I was proposing a use of the terms so different from the traditional one as to be incompatible with it... what it names and stands for is here emphasized because in my treatment philosophy is *love of wisdom*; wisdom not being knowledge but knowledge-plus; knowledge turned to account in the instruction and guidance of life.... (LW 16:389)

It is in this Deweyan sense that my essay is a metaphysical inquiry into the practice of deconstruction in philosophy. I shall be trying to escape the aporetic atmosphere, the almost "Cabalstic" air, that sometimes surrounds it. I want to get clear on why deconstructionists are so hostile to metaphysics. But I also want to keep up the Deweyan sense of the "meliorism" of inquiry, the sense that the practice of inquiry is not just intended as criticism, but as a practical necessity. I mean the criticism of practice that is necessary if we expect to go on with the practice of criticism.

It is intended to be *helpful*, not just in respect of the "problems of philosophers," as Dewey himself put it, but in respect of the "problems of men." Another way of putting this is in terms of the sense that philosophical investigations can be "therapeutic"; the conception of philosophy that John Dewey shared with Ludwig Wittgenstein despite the divergent routes they took in exploring their common territory of language and the culture that discourse makes possible. As Wittgenstein's investigations show, there are different ways of releasing the fly from the fly bottle. So why should we think that different maps of a single landscape *must* be mutually exclusive? In the practice of explorations like this they may reenforce each other: be mutually edifying.

Richard Rorty wants us to see how Dewey and Wittgenstein are joined in this task of philosophical and cultural amelioration by Martin Heidegger. He wants us to see how Dewey's criticism of the "Tradition" converges, not just with Wittgenstein's, but with Heidegger's account of the perverse role of metaphysics in that "Tradition." He wants us to see that deconstructionists, philosophers like Derrida, Foucault, and Berezdivin, are just trying to write another chapter of the "original story" that Heidegger tells. They are trying to overcome the metaphysics of "foundationalism" as Heidegger did, Rorty tells us, and to scotch the traditional belief that "epistemology" may be helpful to culture.

But it is not that easy to bring Heidegger's "forgetfulness of Being" into line with Dewey's aim of "meliorism"—to suggest that Heidegger's "original story" is just another version of Dewey's effort to "intellectualize" our cultural practices. Or that Heidegger was just trying, as Wittgenstein was, to diagnose and dispel our fixations with "certainty" and "truth" as amelioritive aids to the improvement of culture. It is not that easy to see that Heidegger was taking the "naturalistic" turn in metaphysics and epistemology that Dewey and Wittgenstein were. Indeed, the reading of Heidegger that deconstructionists favor seems to belie the very role that Rorty wants to ascribe to him.

The deconstructionists want us to think that Heidegger's "story" is not just about the "collapse of Western metaphysics" but entails the impossibility of its reconstruction. They want us to see Heidegger's acknowledgment of the failure of his "early" project of disclosing the "meaning of Being" as an acknowledgment of the failure of metaphysics altogether, rather than as the beginning of some new thinking about metaphysics. They want us to see the "late" Heidegger as rejecting epistemology rather than as trying to recover something like its original (Greek) sense in *techne*. The deconstructionists think that we ought to dispense with metaphysics and epistemology altogether, that culture will be better off *without* foundations of the sort that sustained it from antiquity through modernity. And, because he is largely in agreement with this contention of the deconstructionists, Rorty defends them.[3]

The practice of deconstruction is, according to those who practice it, indefinable *except* in practice; lexical definition of deconstruction is less than useless. Its meaning, they tell us, can only be grasped by the showing of its consequences; it is only in use that its meaning can be shown. Pragmatists (and Wittgensteinians) have often made similar points about *their* practices as well. And they have pointed, as deconstructionists do, to ways in which traditional philosophical problems can be dismissed, as well as at different ways of dealing with those that can't because they are not *just* philosophical problems but are human problems, problems of culture, as well.

But pragmatists don't think that getting rid of some ancient (or modern) philosophical quandary is one sort of task and helping men and women cope with the perennial problems of existence, of living *with* one another, as problems of a different sort altogether. They see both as parts of a continuous task, as aiming at much the same thing and as making use of much the same resources. Deconstructionists seem to think of these as quite different matters altogether, for they are much better at pointing out practices that we ought to drop than at limning or outlining those that we ought to accept.

Pragmatism has always leaned towards "consequentialism" and "verificationism" in matters of belief: there is always something like a fact of the matter, or eventual outcome, at stake in making a judgment or launching a criticism. Heidegger's thinking followed a similar path, both early and late.[4] But the deconstructionists tell us that our judgments are not involved with matters of fact, or anything even remotely like them, at all. Questions which *seem* to call for "objectivity" are simply not answerable by reference to what is anything even close to the objects themselves, or the outcomes of our ways of treating them. And Richard Rorty takes the deconstructionist side in this by pressing the point that it is very likely that there *isn't* a "fact of the matter" about such matters as we ordinarily think that there *must* be a "fact of the matter" about.

Deconstructionists want us to see that even such questions as what Rorty calls the content of our "final vocabulary" (by which he apparently means our most basic beliefs) are texts that can only be discussed *in* texts and in relation to *other* texts. We sometimes get the impression that most deconstructionists think that there is nothing outside the texts, or that *everything* is a text. But they are not making *that* ontological judgment, or any other. They are just *not doing* ontology. Ontological reference is as impossible as metaphysics; as Derrida points out, the problem of the *reference* of such texts is intractable. Rodolphe Gasché tells us that the serious point that Derrida makes in *Grammatology* is just that the *meaning* of such texts is "undecidable" by syntactical analysis, which leaves the questions of semantics to the texts themselves. Yet the deconstructionists are neither pantextualist nor nihilists; it is just that there is nothing outside the texts against which we can measure our judgments for better or worse. They want us to see that all we philosophers can do is offer descriptions and redescriptions of such events as the texts themselves describe and redescribe.

Deconstructionists want us to give up the idea that we might hit on a description that states the *truth* about what's happening when the Berlin Wall is dismantled, when Solidarity seems divided against itself in Poland, or what the "life in truth" claimed by Czech dissenters like Václav Havel and Václav Malý *really* means.[5] They want us to drop the idea that some fact of the matter or collection of them could be capable of disclosing the truth about what's going on. It is not that they want us to think of the removal of the Berlin Wall, the fragmentation of Solidarity, or Czech dissent as meaningless. *Of course* these events are meaningful; it is just that they are meaningful only in terms of the language of the texts in which they *become* meaningful.

The deconstructionists, moreover, *do* want us to think that deconstruction is *both* destructive and reconstructive. They want us to see it as destructive of what is no longer useful in understanding the meaning of events, what is no longer, like metaphysics itself, *philosophically* useful. Like both Dewey and Heidegger, Richard Rorty seems to be engaged in reconstructing the history of philosophy as if, somehow, the reconstructed product would help us cope with our *own* problems better than the unreconstructed version did those who constructed it. But, *unlike* both Dewey and Heidegger, Rorty and the deconstructionists want us to see that any attempt at the reconstruction of *metaphysics* won't work, that even the history of philosophy may be *over*. Philosophy itself may no longer be useful—or even interesting.

Like pragmatists, deconstructionists want us to agree that, as Hilary Putnam puts it from the pragmatist side, there just isn't any convenient "God's-Eye View" we can take in order to sort things out. But Putnam adds: "Of *course* philosophical problems are unsolvable; but as Stanley Cavell once remarked, 'There are better and worse ways of thinking about them.' "[6] This is a point that deconstructionists *have* to agree on, or relinquish the only defense that they have of their own ways of thinking and writing. Like the phenomenologists they want us to give up the notion that there are independently real things-in-themselves that we can know, any noumenal criteria or a priori categories, or any ideal foundations upon which to ground our value systems. They *don't* want us to give up the Husserlian idea that there are better and worse ways of thinking and writing about the "things themselves." It is just that they want us to give up thinking of them in terms of *true* and *false* ideas of the ways of being.

So they *do* want us to give up Husserl's idea that we can reach "objectivity" by means of "transcendental subjectivity." They want us to give up the idea of objectivity altogether, the way that Heidegger gave up on the question of the "meaning of Being."

But the deconstructionists *still* think of themselves as successors to Husserl and Heidegger, and sometimes as inheritors of the mantle of Wittgenstein and Dewey as well. They think of themselves as the inhabitants of the linguistic world that is the bequest of these thinkers. But if the "limits of my language are the limits of my world," as Wittgenstein suggested in the *Tractatus*, it is because "my language" and "my world" are already *"inside"* a world that contains them, as he pointed out in the *Investigations*. And if communication is a "miracle beside which transubstantiation pales," as Dewey once suggested, it's because it's involved in our transactions with the natural world of which it's a part and in which it participates.

The deconstructionists' practices belie these claims and the "naturalized" view of the epistemology and ontology of language they share. Critics like Stanley Fish think that deconstructionists have arrived at a naturalized view of their *own*, a view of language that is so good that it no longer *needs* any epistemology. He thinks that we should stop pretending that language has anything to *do* with ontology; we are better off without these standard aids to criticism, doing what comes "naturally." By treating language as the "house of Being" (in Heidegger's terms) and themselves as its occupants, as if there is *nothing* outside with which language is decisively linked, it is hard to see deconstructionists as either Wittgensteinians or pragmatists. Perhaps their claim to be heirs of Husserl and Heidegger is equally suspect.

Deconstructionists want us to relinquish such staples of pragmatism as the ontology of the transactional involvement of the knower with the known, the objectivity claimed for warranted assertions, and the possibility of an empirical metaphysics. They want us to reject all Kant-style transcendental arguments, Husserlian transcendental subjectivity, and all talk of essences, even phenomenological ones. But, as I've said, they protest that deconstruction is *not* just nihilism. They want us to see that if "anything goes," in Feyerabend's pregnant redescription of inquiry, that everything remains the same. Except that *we* are supposed to be better off. Unlike nihilists, deconstructionists want us to see their practices as breaking through the bonds of metaphysics and as opening new vistas of meaning, new horizons of hermeneutical freedom.

They want us to see that deconstruction is *not* just an evasion of philosophical responsibility, an aimless practice, wanton, a waste of time. The deconstructionists are not just kidding around despite their air of insouciance, *not* just showing off their brilliance in the art of verbal manipulation, or the copious erudition they bring to their dissections of the history of philosophy.

They want us to see the practice of deconstruction as criticism, after all, *serious* criticism that—in Rorty's apt expression—is part of the "conversation of the West," an attempt to "keep the conversation going." They want us to see that their use of descriptions and rediscriptions are not just cavalier exercises, or lessons designed to improve our vocabularies. They want us to see that in performing such exercises we are likely to hit on what Rorty called (in a gloss on James that comes close to the sense of Putnam's reference to Cavell) what it is "better for us to believe." But they want us to stick to the *texts* of these descriptions and redescriptions rather than the events described and redescribed; the very syntax of our descriptions are treated as doubtful "infrastructures" so that the "real" or "true" meanings are, as a matter of principle, "undecidable."

Deconstructionists want us to see, as Rorty once put it, that "*language* is a more suitable notion than *experience* for saying the holistic and anti-foundationalist things which James and Dewey had wanted to say."[7] But deconstructionists, as I've pointed out, think that these "holistic" and "antifoundational" things can't always be said—or, better, "inscribed"—in decidable syntax.[8]

How, then, *are* we to decide what *any* text means? It looks as if the answer to *that* question is itself undecidable if we take the suggestion of Stephen Watson. He begins his essay on "Regulations: Kant and Derrida at the End of Metaphysics" with some memorable lines from Beckett:

> Vladimir: . . . We could start all over again perhaps.
> Estragon: That should be easy.
> Vladimir: It's the start that's difficult.
> Estragon: You can start from anything.
> Vladimir: Yes, but you have to decide.
> Estragon: True.
> > *Silence*
> >
> > *Godot*[9]

But even Watson concedes that silence itself is an aporia; that Vladimir and Estragon will soon resume their chatter, if only about how difficult it *is* to decide. For silence itself becomes unendurable if that's all that there is. As Wittgenstein pointed out, solipsism offers little repose.

Rorty thinks that the best alternative to silence in filling the void left by the absence of metaphysics and epistemology is to resort to the vocabulary of irony. Perhaps I can give some idea of how this is meant to work by citing the irony of the jokes that people who are involved in such situations as the removal of the Berlin Wall, the fragmentation of Solidarity, or Czech dissent, tell on themselves.

Miroslav Holub, the distinguished Czech poet and immunologist, commences his "Prague Diary" with a text describing a cartoon that helps clarify the meaning of dissent in the context of his own country's situation:

> One of the latest cartoons by Vladimir Rencin—who belongs to that strong group of poets of the political drawing which flourished in this country during the Seventies and Eighties— shows two middle-class gentlemen with glum crestfallen faces. The gents are saying: "The good old times—wine, women and the Communist Party. . . ."

And he follows up with a joke from the past:

> The situation (in Prague) can be defined by a joke from the distant Thirties: socialism is a system in which the people, by their heroic efforts, overcome obstacles that would never have otherwise arisen.[10]

Holub wants us to see how ill prepared his countrymen are to face the demands of reconstructing democracy by their years of underground resistance to a totalitarian regime for which they had no responsibility. There is irony here, as there would be in a possible definition of deconstruction that runs like this: "Deconstruction is the practice of criticism in which philosophers, by their heroic efforts, overcome obstacles that would not otherwise have arisen."

There is, I take it, something in definitions like these that works, despite the fact that we are not likely to find them in any future dictionary. They work because they tell us something; something that's so. We get the message, as we say; like the message of the fifties (and sixties) from Pogo, the possum who addressed us from the text of the cartoon strip of life in the Okefenokee Swamp: "We have met the enemy and they are us." To get such jokes is to see how the situations about which they *are* jokes tend to self-destruct and, perhaps, to disclose a facet of deconstruction's practice. To get such jokes is, somehow, to grasp the disclosure of their meaning and, by that means, the meaning of the situation joked about. It is, *perhaps*, a way of stumbling into the sort of experience that Dewey inscribed as "consummatory," of edging up on Heidegger's "*aletheia*."

What these joke texts share, and why I resort to them in an effort to see what's happening in deconstruction, is just that they help to show why deconstructive criticism so often ends in aporia, the situation that I compared to Dewey's "problematic" situation above. It is not so different from what Yossarian, the American bombardier in Joseph Heller's memorable text, taught us to think of as a "Catch 22" situation. Noticing that one's situation is like that of Yossarian's is not exactly a "solution" of the problem, but it helps us to grasp the *meaning* of the situation, of something that's so. Even if it *is* just one dimension of the problem.

The irony is in the discovery that deconstruction works only on what we—here I use the 'we' in its broadest possible sense—have ourselves first constructed, and is doubled by the discovery that "overcoming the tradition" inevitably lands us, already, *in* a "tradition." A *new* one, perhaps, but nevertheless a "tradition." As when Sartre discovers the irony that, for those who have been "condemned" to freedom, there is, in the end, "No Exit." Or when Heidegger discovers the irony that the collapse of classical metaphysics has landed us in an ontological situation where, as he put it in a famous interview, "Only a god can save us."

In his own "Diary" piece—the text of which resonates with Holub's "Prague Diary"—Richard Rorty essays a gloss on the irony of Heidegger's situation and the possibility that Heidegger might all along have been "Thinking Like a Nazi," even in philosophical texts *outside* the texts of his political lectures. Rorty deconstructs both such texts—that is, the philosophical ones *and* such texts as the famous inaugural lecture and the remarks in the interview—by means of the text of a "possible world" in which Heidegger avoids complicity in the Nazi world, divorces his viciously anti-Semitic wife Elfrida, marries a beautiful and adoring Jewish student who produces a son named Abraham, escapes to America, and rejoins his countrymen only after the war, whereupon he resumes his role as—to quote Rorty's text—the author of "an original story about the history of Western philosophical thought." The irony of all this, Rorty tells us, is just that: "In our actual world Heidegger was a Nazi, a cowardly hypocrite, and the greatest European thinker of our time."[11]

It is helpful to remember that Rorty is not, in this passage, eliciting a fact of the matter, but is trying to get at what he thinks it is better for us to believe. Lest the irony of his vocabulary escape us we have to remember that he is not *just* telling an amusing story, even though we are encouraged to *find* it amusing. (The notion that Heidegger *might* have married a student of his named 'Hannah Arendt,' is particularly encouraging!) The story that he tells about Heidegger's "possible world" *is* a joke, after all, just as "funny" as the jokes that Holub tells about the situation in Prague, and that Pogo tells on *us*. It is just that we must remember that telling such jokes is among the most serious things that we do. For Rorty's joke, his deconstruction of the texts, is seriously meant to deter us from an impulse, as he puts it, to "brush aside the books of people influenced by Heidegger—Derrida, de Man, Foucault—as just more of the same discredited claptrap."[12]

Thinkers like Derrida, de Man, and Foucault have taught us to find the seeds of deconstructionist thinking in Heidegger's account of the "forgetfulness of Being," that is, in what Rorty refers to in his "Diary" as "an original story about the history of Western philosophical thought." It is, they tell us, a story of the distance that we have traveled from life in the "truth of Being" down the centuries since metaphysics was first constructed as truth's foundation by the likes of Anaximander and Parmenides, and meddled with by Plato and Aristotle. The historical deconstruction of *their* construction—its *destruction* is not yet complete, according to the deconstructionist reading of Heidegger, though the "End of Metaphysics" is at hand in the "Technological Age"—ends, as Eliot put it, "not with a bang, but a whimper."[13]

Eliot's "trope" is not just evidence that he shares Heidegger's "distaste for democracy," in the sense inscribed in Rorty's "Diary," but evinces Heidegger's romantic vision of a lost world as well. (Or another to come.) It evokes the scent of the "Blue Flower" of German romanticism which blooms so ubiquitously in Heidegger's texts, both early and late. It has the sense of aporia that so often appears in the inscriptions of the deconstructionists, or the poignancy of Rorty's "ungrounded social hope" and his nostalgic vision of a future of human "solidarity." It is, in a sense, a nostalgia for a world that never was and never will be, for a world in which we might have truly *achieved* the end of metaphysics, life in the "truth of Being," rather than suffering its collapse.

On this deconstructionist reading of Heidegger's story, it is not so much that God has forsaken us or that we have forsaken God (although, both are possible). It is just that *metaphysics* is over. It is no longer a possible way of grounding our value systems, no longer a possible foundation on which to build our criticism. It all ends in the displacement of the vocabulary of classical metaphysics by the vocabulary of the natural sciences and the technological praxis of "Modernity" in a culture fallen under domination by the necessities of the "technological age."

All that is left to lighten the gathering gloom are the occasional glimpses of the "truth of Being" unconcealed—and yet concealed—in the disclosures of *aletheia*.

The "original story" that Heidegger tells of how all this could have happened is not at all unlike the story that John Dewey tells in his Gifford Lectures, *The Quest for Certainty*. They converge, Michael Zimmerman tells us, in accounting for the "collapse of traditional Western metaphysics" by the futility of the search for the absolute, of the quest for the "meaning of Being." But they diverge in their respective assessments of where this "collapse" leaves us. Zimmerman thinks that Dewey relies on "science" to fill the void left by the absence of "transcendent, absolute values," while

Heidegger believes that *nothing* can fill that void. While Dewey waxes optimistic about technology as an engine of progress, Heidegger sees nothing but the ruin of culture in the "technological age."

Like Rorty, Zimmerman concedes that Dewey *tried* to reconstruct a naturalistic metaphysics of existence, and thinks that this attempt was a failure. He departs from Rorty's reading of Dewey only when he claims that Dewey was caught up in a strain of Hegelian historical determinism, asking:

> Is not Dewey's notion of man as Nature becoming more rational merely another form of "subjectivism" in which man remains the measure of all things *not* because of his ties to the transcendent but because man himself wills to be that measure?[14]

Zimmerman thinks that this lands Dewey in the same aporia at the end of metaphysics as Heidegger. Rorty, by contrast, just wants us to forget about Dewey's metaphysics altogether on the grounds that it was a bad idea in the first place. We are to concentrate, instead, on how Dewey's story of the quest for certainty parallels Heidegger's story of the forgetfulness of Being. While Zimmerman wants us to see Dewey's metaphysical effort as a failed attempt at the *continuation* of "traditional Western metaphysics," an attempt that lands him in the same aporia of "subjectivism" as Heidegger, who (on Zimmerman's reading) thinks that this "enslaved" state is the destiny of Dasein. But it is more or less obvious that, in deconstructionist terms, the hermeneutical difference between Rorty's Dewey and Zimmerman's is no 'differance' at all (in Derrida's sense). Nothing is changed by the alternatives and everything remains the same.[15] For both Zimmerman and Rorty philosophy had better accept the irony that no metaphysics is going to help us escape the inevitable consequences of the "subjectivism"—*however* defined—that follows the "collapse of traditional Western metaphysics."

Zimmerman sounds like a deconstructionist because he thinks that the late Heidegger's "*Kehre*," his "new thinking" that followed the collapse of the project of *Sein und Zeit*, was a failed attempt to reconstruct the metaphysics of Dasein as a metaphysics of existence. But Rorty and the deconstructionists don't think of the late Heidegger as even *attempting* a metaphysics. They think of the late Heidegger's antifoundational writings as *blocking* such attempts, and justify their own hostility to metaphysics by appealing to Heidegger's "original story" of the damage that metaphysics has done in bringing on the "technological age."

By contrast Mark Okrent thinks that Heidegger's "new" approach to Dasein was continuous with his early reliance on pragmatic "argument structures" (that reflect what Okrent calls a "pragmatic metaphysics"). He thinks that Heidegger gave up on the metaphysics of Being because of his failure to discover the transcendental arguments that were both premised by and promised in *Sein und Zeit*.[16] The "new" metaphysics is designed to replace the metaphysics conceived of in *Sein und Zeit* and which was, as early as 1935, criticized by Heidegger himself.

I think that Okrent is right in thinking that Heidegger's project takes a decisive turn away from the metaphysics of Being toward the metaphysics of existence early on, owing at first to what he saw as the difficulty, then as the failure, of the transcendental arguments required to disclose the "meaning of Being." In *Sein und Zeit* the understanding of Dasein is stymied (*in die Quere*) by the fact that Heidegger thinks that the question of Dasein's meaning cannot be resolved unless and until the question of the "meaning of *Being*" is resolved. There's the rub, or at least *die Quere*! Absent the "meaning of Being" there is no hope of a solution to the predicament of Dasein's contingent existence. The classical and phenomenological transcendental arguments that were supposed to disclose the "meaning of Being" don't work.

In a recent text Michael Zimmerman introduces a new and surprising analysis of Heidegger's treatment of technology with a famous quotation from the text of "What Is Called Thinking?" that translates like this:

> Our age is not a technological age because it is the age of the machine; it is an age of the machine because it is the technological age.[17]

The surprise (and the irony) is that in this new text, Zimmerman finds that Heidegger's account of the "collapse of traditional Western metaphysics" into the "subjectivism" of the "technological age" suffers from the same flaw that he had earlier *thought* that he detected in Dewey's account. Heidegger, it now seems, was just as stuck on Hegel's deterministic conception of history, as Zimmerman had earlier suggested that Dewey was.

Moreover, in this new text, Zimmerman takes pains to scotch the notion that Heidegger abandoned the task of metaphysical inquiry simply because the "productionist metaphysics" (as it is now described) of the classical tradition is over. It seems that Heidegger, repelled by what he saw as the disastrous consequences of *that* tradition in the "technological age," turned to the task of a reanalysis of Dasein. Zimmerman argues that this reanalysis of what is *actually* involved in production— or work—was, for Heidegger, a genuinely "new beginning" of metaphysics.

It thus seems clear that Zimmerman has come to reject the deconstructionist's claim that the "late" Heidegger abandoned all hope for metaphysics. It is just that Heidegger failed to develop the new metaphysics that he was trying to work out as the alternative to the "metaphysics of

Being" which he had been compelled to abandon. He failed, according to Zimmerman, to get that new metaphysics off the ground owing to his predeliction for thinking of the destiny of Dasein in terms of *Blut und Boden* and the *Geist* that haunts German romanticism thereby masking the duality of essence and existence behind the vocabulary of "Being as self-emergence" and "Being as appearing." He failed, in short, because he was *still* trying to find a way to disclose the *meaning of Being*.

But what is most striking about Zimmerman's reading of the late Heidegger is not just that he sees the failure of Heidegger's new metaphysics to get off the ground (of Being); it is that he sees that Heidegger came to the realization that the only way to break the grip of the old metaphysics is by replacing it with a *new* metaphysics. In this insight, of course, he comes close to agreement with Okrent's view that Heidegger was *all along* practicing a kind of "pragmatist" metaphysics. A metaphysics that Heidegger was, at first, prepared to suppress, but that in the end was all that he was left with.

But Zimmerman still fails to recognize that Heidegger's new metaphysics was an attempt to shift its focus away from Being to existence, to Dasein itself rather than "Being itself." Zimmerman had already failed to see that Dewey was doing just that in *The Quest for Certainty* and *Experience and Nature*. Zimmerman discounts, as Rorty does, Heidegger's criticisms of the argument structures featured by classical logics from Leibniz to Kant in his *Leibnizbuch* and the *Kantbuch*. He fails to see that Heidegger, like Dewey, had a lifelong concern with the connections and interconnections between logic and ontology. Like Heidegger, Dewey set out early on to "de-stabilize" the foundations of classical metaphysics and the theories of logic which, he thought, were grounded in those foundations. He "deconstructed" them, in a sense; a sense that Richard Rorty makes use of in his own criticism while ignoring the contingent *reconstructions* which Dewey offered in their place. Unlike Heidegger however, Dewey recognized early in his career the very "duality" that Zimmerman finds to be a "puzzling" element in Heidegger's thinking. Moreover, Dewey not only recognized it but blamed it for just about everything that had gone wrong with both metaphysics and logic right from the start. Like Wittgenstein's moves, Dewey's "naturalizing" strategies in logic and epistemology, his "reconstructions" in metaphysics and the theory of valuation, were designed to overcome *"die Quere"* that crosses the pathways of Heidegger's thinking and cancels them out.

The consequences for Dewey's thinking about inquiry, accordingly, could not be much further from Heidegger's than they are. Here is how Larry Hickman sums up the way that Dewey "naturalizes" epistemology and ontology:

Drawing on the metaphors that accompanied Darwinian evolutionary theory, Dewey argued that human beings are organisms
within nature and that their tool use is one of the developmental
edges of natural activity. Tools and artifacts are no more neutral
than are plants, non-human animals, or human beings themselves: they are interactive within situations that teem with value.[18]

This results, Hickman tells us, in a conception of inquiry that views
technology as a possible means of resolving the "problems of men" rather
than as reducing them to subjects of its sovereignty. In consequence,
Dewey regards irresponsible technology, the bane of Heiddegger's
conception of "productionsist metaphysics," as due to the failure of inquiry
into existences of all kinds, and not to the "forgetfulness of Being."
Heidegger's "new thinking" about the predicament of Dasein, and Dewey's
about the "problems of men," converge on techne, the art of "knowing"
in Dewey's jargon, the art of "disclosure of meaning" in Heidegger's.

Dewey thought that a metaphysics that describes the "generic traits" of
all kinds of existences could be of assistance to techne. Heidegger did too.
But because he was still caught up in the belief that *Dasein* must, somehow,
have an *essence* within, an essence that "productionist metaphysics" distorts
and that must both disclose itself and *be* disclosed by techne his "new
thinking" could barely get started.

Like the deconstructionists Dewey thought that we should give up
on the whole idea of fixed essences and eternal forms that are "out there"
in a transcendent reality. Destabilizing such notions is the stock in trade
of both. But Dewey didn't think that meant that we should give up the
idea that inquiry deals with existences, that we had to limit our
investigations just to the "language games" that people play, any more
than Wittgenstein did. I don't think that Heidegger did either. But
Berezdivin is right, in a (perverse) sense. The *new* metaphysics that
Heidegger spent such a large part of his life in trying to produce never
did make it (out) across the "threshold" of language. It is just that
Heidegger could never bring himself to relinquish the vocabulary of
classical dualism that haunts his descriptions and redescriptions of Dasein.
Sometimes it is phrased in the language of "objectivity" versus "subjectivity." But the dualism of "essence" versus "existence" is what it comes
down to in the end.

The collapse of *that* dualism is what John Dewey's philosophy, his
conception of metaphysics and of inquiry, is all about. It is *not* just about
the "collapse of Western metaphysics" in the sense that Rorty thinks it
is, or about the hostility to metaphysics that deconstructionists ascribe to
Heidegger either. It is about the "life in truth" that Dewey calls "wisdom."

Not just knowledge, but "knowledge turned to account in the instruction and guidance of life." Wittgenstein and Heidegger thought that was what philosophy was all about too, even if they sometimes found themselves blocked by the Weltanschauung of classical metaphysics.

When he came face to face with the same aporia, the same old Weltanschauung that confronted Heidegger in the "forgetfulness of being," Wittgenstein put the problem more presciently than Heidegger was ever able to do and concisely enough to serve the end of epigraphy in bringing this chapter to its inconclusive close:

> *Ich will also etwas sagen, was wie Pragmatismus klingt. Mir kommt hier eine Art Weltanschauung in die Quere.*
> —Ludwig Wittgenstein, *On Certainty*[19]

Notes

1. Reuben Berezdivin, "In Stalling Metaphysics: At the Threshold," in *Deconstruction and Philosophy: The Texts of Jacques Derrida*, ed. John Sallis (Chicago: University of Chicago Press, 1987), p. 59.

2. John Sallis's "Introduction" to the volume of essays mentioned in note 1, above, provides a brief introduction to the deconstructionist vocabulary. Rodolphe Gasché's *The Tain of the Mirror: Derrida and the Philosophy of Reflection* (Cambridge: Harvard University Press, 1986), provides a more complete account, as well as a rationale of the movement.

3. It should be clear from what follows that I do not think of Rorty as a "deconstructionist"; it is just that it is hard to think of him as a "pragmatist" either.

4. Mark Okrent, *Heidegger's Pragmatism: Understanding, Being, and the Critique of Metaphysics* (Ithaca: Cornell University Press, 1988).

5. For the Czech leaders' use of "life in truth" see Erazim Kohák, "What's Central to Central Europe," *Dissent* (Spring 1990), as cited in *Harpers* (June 1990), p. 18.

6. Hilary Putnam, "Realism with a Human Face," in *Realism with a Human Face*, ed. J. Conant (Cambridge, Mass.: Harvard University Press, 1990), p. 19.

7. Richard Rorty, "Comments on Sleeper and Edel," *Transactions of the Charles S. Peirce Society* 21, 1 (Winter 1985), p. 40.

8. Rodolphe Gasché, "Infrastructures and Systematicity," in *Deconstruction and Philosophy: The Texts of Jacques Derrida*, pp. 12–13.

9. Stephen Watson, "Regulations: Kant and Derrida at the End of Metaphysics," in *Deconstruction and Philosophy: The Texts of Jacques Derrida*, p. 71.

10. Miroslav Holub, "Prague Diary," *London Review of Books* (June 14, 1990), p. 25.

11. Richard Rorty, "Diary," *London Review of Books* (February 8, 1990), p. 21. I owe to discussion with my colleague, Alan Rosenberg, much of my appreciation and understanding of the importance of this essay in the context of Rorty's work.

12. Ibid.

13. As far as I know Heidegger never wrote of metaphysics as something that is "over" in the sense that deconstructionists use that term. He did think that *classical* metaphysics achieved its fulfillment (*Vollendung*) in the "Technological Age" in which the "forgetfulness of Being" is manifest. But to speak of this "Age" simply as marking the "End of Metaphysics," or of philosophy, is notoriously ambiguous. Rorty has avoided the ambiguity of the latter, but not the former, in *Mirror*, by distinguishing between "Philosophy" and "philosophy."

14. Michael Zimmerman, "Dewey, Heidegger, and the Quest for Certainty," *Southwestern Journal of Philosophy* (May 1978), p. 92.

15. Jacques Derrida, *Speech and Phenomena and Other Essays on Husserl's Theory of Signs* (Evanston: Northwestern University Press, 1973), p. 141. See also, "Differance," in *Margins of Philosophy* (Chicago: University of Chicago Press, 1982). I am indebted to Edith Wyschogrod for unpacking the important difference that "differance" makes for Derrida.

16. Mark Okrent, *Heidegger's Pragmatism*, pp. 221–22.

17. Michael E. Zimmerman, *Heidegger's Confrontation with Modernity: Technology, Politics, Art* (Bloomington and Indianapolis: Indiana University Press, 1989), p. xiii. The points that follow are to be found mainly in chap. 14, pp. 222–47, but see also p. 248. This thoroughly non-deconstructionist reading of Heidegger is the best available account of Heidegger's "Thinking Like a Nazi."

18. Larry Hickman, *John Dewey's Pragmatic Technology.* (Bloomington and Indianapolis: Indiana University Press, 1990), p. 202.

19. Ludwig Wittgenstein, *On Certainty* (San Francisco: Harper and Row, 1972), p. 54 (#422). The published English translation is: "So I am trying to say something that sounds like pragmatism. Here I am being thwarted by a kind of *Weltanschauung*." But this is controversial and permits a reading that would contest Wittgenstein's intention as stated in the first sentence. Rather than being "thwarted," it is, I think, that Wittegstein was "diverted" by traces of the old Weltanschauung that remained present in Moore's "certainty."

15

Body-Mind and Subconsciousness: Tragedy in Dewey's Life and Work

BRUCE WILSHIRE

It is not easy to think of John Dewey as a tragic figure. There are too many pictures of his kind grandfatherly face, or of him dandling school children on his knee, or of him meeting notables. He achieved fame and influence fairly early in his lifetime as a thinker and educator, far beyond what any American philosopher had gained before. Moreover, he lived to a very old age, active and honored practically to the end.

But there is another side to the picture. Before World War I two of Dewey's children died quite young, and the advent of the war itself was profoundly shocking. Its gruesome absurdities shook Dewey's optimism badly, and its occurrence coincided precisely with his sizeable mid-life crisis. At fifty-seven he had pretty well summed up his views in the magisterial, tightly organized *Democracy and Education* (1916). He had no idea, of course, that he would live for thirty-five more years, and he entered a period of distraction and depression (his views on the war prompted harsh criticisms, which did not help). He became romantically involved with a woman not his wife (although the relationship was probably not consummated physically), and he hied himself to the psychobiotherapist, F. M. Alexander.

Dewey had been criticizing Cartesian psycho/physical dualism for decades. But when his personal problems were confronted in the startling light that Alexander's body work threw upon the limitations of consciousness, Dewey produced a much deeper critique. Two years later, in 1918, he accepted an offer from Stanford University to give a series of lectures on morals (published in expanded form in 1922 as *Human Nature and Conduct*). Dewey acknowledged Alexander's influence, but it would be clear to an attentive reader even if he had not. Vivid allusions occur both to psychoanalysis and to the war. What could drive supposedly reasonable people to such insane carnage, Dewey wonders? He notes William James' seminal "The Moral Equivalent of War," and observes that the traditional motives—glory, heroism, fame, booty—have been complicated and attenuated by the nation-state organized technologically. Anticipating to some extent Hannah Arendt's idea of "the banality of evil," Dewey writes,

> The activities that evoke...a war are of...a collective, prosaic political and economic nature...Universal conscription, the general mobilization of all agricultural and industrial forces of the folk not engaged in the trenches, the application of every conceivable scientific and mechanical device, the mass movements of soldiery regulated from a common center by a depersonalized general staff: these factors relegate the traditional psychological apparatus of war to a now remote antiquity.... The more horrible a depersonalized scientific mass war becomes, the more necessary it is to find universal ideal motives to justify it.... The more prosaic the actual causes, the more necessary is it to find glowingly sublime motives. (MW 14:81)

On the eve of his sixtieth year Dewey reconsidered the very meaning of individual identity and individual behavior for us humans—essentially socialized, group members that we are. And he wonders what we are to make of groups when they are organized according to scientific and technological principles. Moreover, he reconsiders the meaning of science itself. And it is not surprising that he would examine the powers of psychoanalysis to peer behind our cheap talk about motives and to disclose what really makes us tick. But at best, he can give psychoanalysis only a mixed review:

> It exhibits a sense for reality in its insistence upon the profound importance of unconscious forces....Every movement of reaction and protest, however, usually accepts some of the basic ideas of the position against which it rebels. So...psychoanalysis... retain(s) the notion of a separate psychic realm or force. They add a...statement of the existence and operation of the "unconscious," of complexes due to contacts and conflicts with others, of the social censor. But they still cling to the idea of a separate psychic realm and so in effect talk about unconscious consciousness. They get their truths mixed up in theory with the false psychology of original individual consciousness. (MW 14:61–62)

Despite Jung's and Freud's creative work, they are stuck, Dewey thinks, with unsuspected and unattacked Cartesian assumptions. In effect, Dewey launches himself on a new career that will see him expose "the false psychology of original individual consciousness" with a severity and thoroughness never before seen in his work, or perhaps in anyone's. But if the psychological conception of the subconscious that he puts in its place is correct, any indepth knowledge of human beings will be extraordinarily difficult to achieve, as will be any effective educational program and any sane reconstruction of culture. At age seventy, long a famous and extraordinarily influential educator, Dewey writes,

> We have at present little or next to no controlled art of securing that redirection of behavior which constitutes adequate perception or consciousness. That is, we have little or no art of education in the fundamentals, namely in the management of the organic attitudes which color the qualities of our conscious objects and acts. As long as our chief psycho-physical coordinations are formed blindly and in the dark during infancy and early childhood, they are accidental adjustments to the pressure of other persons and of circumstances which act upon us. They do not then take into account the consequence of these activities upon formation of habits....Hence the connection between consciousness and action is precarious, and its possession a doubtful boon as compared with the efficacy of instinct—or structure—in lower animals. (LW 1:239)

In 1938, nearly eighty, Dewey published *Experience and Education*, an attempt to explain to his many "followers" in "progressive education" what he was up to. But most of them, despite their good intentions and hard work, had not a clue as to what this very difficult philosopher was doing. Nor did most professional philosophers, for they too, despite their intelligence and logical rigor, had left Cartesian psycho/physical assumptions in place, and had succumbed to simplistic views of human identity, science, learning, and knowledge! There is something distinctly tragic about Dewey's career, and the tragedy centers on his profound, but never rounded out, views on subconscious mind. It is not just that his views were not really understood for lack of definitive clarity, or for lack of sympathetic and intelligent readers, but also that he exposed mountainous difficulties for gaining self-knowledge, difficulties that stagger the confidence of any intelligent educator or statesman.

Let us back up and explore what Dewey discovered in his work with F. M. Alexander, for this more than anything else drove him into his deepest critique of psycho/physical dualism. As I said, at age fifty-seven, already famous, he entered a period of personal as well as intellectual crisis. Like Dante's "Midway upon the journey of our life I found myself in a dark wood, where the right way was lost," life for Dewey was stale, flat, pointless—something was missing. All his efforts to achieve a theory that integrated body, self, and experience were blocked by the painful experience of his own life. He detected a rude discontinuity between his powers of inquiry and perception, and the very conditions of these powers in his functioning organism. His own consciousness seemed to split off from its conditions in his organism. It was a kind of waking nightmare in which Descartes' psycho/physical dualism could be expelled from Dewey's critical consciousness, but only to have it reappear in Dewey's own everyday behavior and carnal reality. This embarrassing turn imperiled Dewey's vision of goodness as vitality, as integrated, dynamically interactive living. Indeed, it is not too much to say that it imperiled his life. Dewey began to suppose that there are factors at work in our bodily selves that condition and limit consciousness to such an extent that it cannot grasp these factors. He suspected that consciousness is a closet lined with mirrors. So in 1916 Dewey consulted the pioneering psychobiotherapist.

Alexander had discovered means for altering consciousness by altering bodily movements and postures. He had made advances in the conscious use by the body-self of its own organism to achieve ends of fuller vitality, integration, and above all, consciousness of itself. Judging from the way Dewey talked and held his head and neck, Alexander said "he was drugged with thought." It was indeed as if his mind were dissociated from his body.[1]

Does seventeeth-century psycho/physical dualism return? No, Dewey thought, but he knew he faced immense personal and theoretical difficulties. He discovered something fundamental about the limits and conditions of his own consciousness. It was only *after* Alexander manipulated Dewey's body into unaccustomed positions and postures that Dewey could imagine even the *possibility* of them!

So *the body must take the lead* if consciousness is to become aware of its closet; body must be jolted by itself. But how can the body do this without being conscious, and how can it imagine new ways of living if it must do so with the old consciousness? In fact, a leap of faith by consciousness seems to be required, one in which the body is allowed to take the lead. Also intervention by *another* conscious body, another person, may have to be allowed. Only then, perhaps, can sensations be generated that both *form* revealing hypotheses about one's body-self and test these.

It is self-deceivingly abstract to limit truth to propositions writable on a blackboard. Nor can self-knowledge be limited to a set of facts that a consciousness spies in the "outer world." The truth of self-knowledge demands that a body-self intimately and courageously interact with itself to lead to consummations revealing of itself. Alexander concentrated on altering the way in which Dewey's head rested on his neck. His habitual positioning was so integral to his self's identity that Dewey could not imagine the new positionings until Alexander effected them manually. Caught up by the tacit belief that its consciousness floats free from its body, the body-self is not open to its own deepest impulses to integrate itself— either with its own past or with the surrounding environment.

When the head—the heavy head—is not balanced atop the backbone, a dynamically integral part of the body, the most intimate continuity of self is knotted or blocked. This continuity is experiential time lived viscerally. One's senses are constrained and warped by fixed ideas, unable to grasp new possibilities of growth. Instead of acknowledging one's origins, and building upon them, one is captured by some of them. Head tilted up perhaps, cramped, gritting teeth, holding back breath, holding back tears, the little child's tensions and fears still held in the muscles and joints of the middle-aged man's jaw. Lacking a strong body and a secure position in the world, the child as head has tried to go it alone. To reconnect and readjust the head and neck properly may be sufficient to release this archaic fixation and to free the self for mature behavior. To straighten out the body is to begin to straighten out lived time, to undo fixations! The past is not always present beneficially—to put it mildly. Such therapy may be sufficient to liberate consciousness by opening it to some of its own conditions and potentialities *here and now* in the body. One has to grope and intuit trustingly if one is to open one's consciousness and know one's own bodily being.

"Know thyself!"—words inscribed on the temple of Apollo at Delphi. These words that haunted Socrates haunted Dewey and, along with many lessons from Alexander, enabled him to deepen his thought during the next three decades of his life. Science that does not lie upon us oppressively stifling our freedom and our dreams—that does not lie upon us "like an incubus"—science that becomes intelligence, cannot be divorced from patience and courage, or from that aesthetical-ethical satisfaction that is "rectitude of organic action." Science that becomes intelligence cannot be divorced from greatness of person. These virtues are not merely "values" inside some subjective consciousness, but structures of the body-in-the-world, and they must emerge if we are to live sanely and vitally. To achieve this "rectitude of organic action," Dewey writes, we must get in touch with

> our immediate organic selections, rejections, welcomings, expulsions. . . of the most minute, vibratingly delicate nature. We are

not aware of the qualities of most of these acts. . . .Yet they exist
as feeling qualities and have an enormous directive effect on our
behavior. (LW 1:227)

Dewey here puts his finger on the nub of the subconscious mind, the point
at which we can begin to understand human beings' irrational exclusions
and aggressions, their ecstatic inclusions and engulfments in groups, and
even the ways in which they can be numbed or hypnotized, inured in
routines, dulled into mindlessly obeying orders, and cast into the banality
of evil. We can begin to understand this without fabricating or reifying
"consciousness" as some strange entity or nonphysical substance, and then
imagine that there is an even stranger incarnation of it that is somehow
not conscious, "unconscious consciousness," as Dewey derisively labels
such a sport (thereby anticipating by decades Sartre's critique).

Now let us follow the main contours of Dewey's inquiry into mind—or
rather, body-mind—and those of its workings that do not involve
consciousness. We will see that he completely reverses Descartes' procedure. Instead of beginning with consciousness as the most certain reality
and tying knowledge of everything else some way to it, Dewey articulates
a view of the world in which consciousness is understood as momentary,
fleeting, and highly derivative. His is a developmental view in which
consciousness emerges from mind—some of which is not conscious. And
mind emerges from the psychophysical, and the psychophysical emerges
from the physical. The question becomes reversed: Instead of, How is
anything but consciousness possible? the question becomes, How is
consciousness possible?

Dewey describes *the* philosophical fallacy as the tendency to think that
something achieved eventually through a process existed prior to the
process and caused it. It is true that at some stage, under certain
circumstances, there can be some consciousness of consciousness. But it
does not follow that an essentially self-reflexive consciousness exists on
its own prior to what is achieved under certain circumstances, and that
it lies behind this process, simply unveiling itself through it. To think that
consciousness is a self-sealing, self-illuminating "substance" of some kind
is a remnant of substantialist metaphysics and its tendency to reify the
reference of nouns. Since we can quantify and speak of "one consciousness" we tend to infer mistakenly that consciousness is some kind of
individual thing referred to.

There is an echo of Aristotelianism in Dewey's view. *What* something
is (its "form" or "formal cause") is best understood as a realization of some
of the potentialities of the organism. Mind itself comes into being, is
formed, and "can be understood in the concrete only as a system of

[habitual] beliefs, desires, and purposes which are formed in the interaction of biological aptitudes with a social environment" (MW 14:3). But Dewey's idea of what something is (its "form") is radically different from Aristotle's. For Dewey "form" evolves, *gets formed*, through habits of interaction building up between organism and a total environment. There is no showcase of eternal, finished forms. Mind itself is an evolving pattern of habits of interaction. It is a realization of the potentialities of stages of habits prior to mind-habit, and it itself *may or may not* become "material" for realization as consciousness. Characteristically Dewey writes,

> Habits may be profitably compared to physiological functions, like breathing, digesting. The latter are, to be sure, involuntary, while habits are acquired. . . . Walking implicates the ground as well as the legs; speech demands physical air and human companionship. . . natural operations. . . and acquired ones like speech and honesty, are functions of the surroundings as truly as of a person. They are things done *by* the environment by means of organic structures or acquired dispositions. . . .They involve skill of sensory and motor organs, cunning or craft, and objective materials. They assimilate objective energies, and eventuate in command of environment. . . .They have a beginning, middle and end. (MW 14:15)

Mind is not a substance, it is minding, it is the habitual ways an organism and environment assimilate, interact, and coordinate so that needs of the organism (and probably also the environment) are satisfied. At what point in complexity of interaction does minding emerge? Is an earthworm adjusting to its environment minding it? It is essential to Dewey's approach—and no mere defect of learning on his part—that he cannot tell us precisely what this point of emergence is. There are untold numbers of borderline cases. Continuity—or continuum—is the key concept in Dewey's worldview, and definitive of a continuum is that it not be constructible out of discrete units or stages. Dewey's practice is to take leaps along the continuum until he locates positions that clearly exhibit different properties. Not that this consistently relieves us of difficulties. For example, he says that minding emerges when an organism interacts with the social environment, or when it engages in a language. But don't dogs, for instance, have their own society and their own language? Dewey is not quite sure how to handle that. "Language" remains ambiguous in Dewey's writings, at least as far as I can see.

But he is still telling us something very important about human beings. Even if we say somewhat arbitrarily that minding "in the full sense" emerges with human beings engaged in human language, we must also say that minding emerges within a background of human and prehuman organic habits that is never simply discarded and left behind. Minding, he says, involves *meanings*, and meanings are always tied up in some way with *means*—the means whereby an organism interacts in some more or less effective way with the environment. Dewey profoundly undercuts psycho/physical dualism. Minding is the activity of body-mind organizing itself and the world around and within it so that dominant needs are satisfied. The *means whereby* this is accomplished includes the responses of others—present and actual, or remembered or anticipated—which the organism incorporates within itself to deal with the world around it and to make sense of it. "Objects" are events with meaning, that is, individuations or "cut outs" emerge within the processing, interfusing world as the cocreation of organism and environment: the means whereby adjustment is achieved show up on "the other side" as the meanings of *things*. "Objects are habits turned inside out," he writes (MW 14:127). But a habit of interaction and adaptation may cease to be fruitful, and may be superseded, in whole or part, by another habit pattern, and so a new inventory of "the items of the world" must be toted up, an inventory that can never be final or complete.

Dewey writes, " 'This,' whatever *this* may be, always implies a system of meanings focused at a point of stress, uncertainty, and need of regulation" (LW 1:264). There must always be an element of uncertainty, because there is no assurance that ongoing, habituated means and meanings will achieve accustomed satisfactions. Due to changes in organism or environment, old habits may be disrupted. If so, conscious-ness may arise, says Dewey, for consciousness emerges only when there is some hesitation or some failure in habitual adjustments. However, there is no point in saying, Consciousness can stretch its imagination and imagine sorts of things that haven't happened yet. For if consciousness does emerge, Dewey says, it can do so only within bodily and other material conditions and limitations that determine the scope of its imagination, *and that typically lie beyond that scope.* There is no reason to think that consciousness can predict which meanings will arise, so of course there is no reason to think that consciousness can predict which of these meanings will become conscious.

That is what Dewey learned so surprisingly and sometimes so painfully from Alexander, and what he is trying to theoretically reconstruct in his treatises. There is no primacy of "immediate givens of conscious-ness"— "images," "sense-data," whatever—for if these figure in conscious-ness it is because they are factored out of the processing continuum and come to be as "individuals" when the occasion for focusing analysis arises. But that occasion arises as a result of circumambient stimuli and organic adjustments that cannot at that moment be precisely or exhaustively known by anyone. Consciousness cannot reliably predict even its own course. There must always be some not yet adjusted to stimuli as well as some organic adjustments, means, and meanings that are not conscious. "The present moment is the darkest in the whole series," as William James put it. Consciousness is conditioned within a matrix that is not itself conscious.

We begin to see what Dewey means by subconscious mind, and it is a veritable enormity. He cannot conceive it as being some backwater or far corner of consciousness which a sedulous reflexive or introspective use of consciousness could detect just by "looking." All mind, so all subconscious mind, is body-mind, and all of body-mind's means-by-which-adjustments that have become habitual will comprise subconscious mind—no matter when these adjustments were induced and no matter under what straitened, oppressive, or disintegrative circumstances. *If these responses are habitual and "work" in some minimal sense, they will not generate consciousness.* Not only that. Since they are a part of the subconscious matrix that conditions and limits consciousness, they will typically fall beyond the scope of consciousness when and if it arises. Consciousness does not even know what to look for. All it can do is stand open to the possibility that body-mind will reveal something if body-mind is allowed to spontaneously display itself. To be sure, consciousness may prepare the ground for discovery by allowing the body to be manipulated by another body-mind who knows the sort of things to look for—another body-mind in the very unusual language community of therapist and patient. Consciousness might prepare itself to be startled. By incorporating the other's attitudes and manipulations, the other's means-by-which, one's own behaviors may be given conscious meaning, stand out, finally be noticed. But one's own consciousness "by itself" cannot change one's person at will. I put "by itself" in scare quotes, because there is *no such thing* as *a* consciousness. Such a meaning is a trick of language, not a precipitate of an effective means of adaptive behavior that leaves an effective meaning, a legitimate individual, cut out and individuated in the world.

Dewey grapples with the concept of the subconscious in two key chapters of *Experience and Nature,* "Nature, Life, and Body-Mind," and "Existence, Ideas and Consciousness." Note well this key quote from the opening pages of the latter chapter:

> There is thus an obvious difference between mind and consciousness; meaning and an idea. Mind denotes the whole system of meanings as they are embodied in the workings of organic life; consciousness in a being with language denotes awareness or perception of meaning. . . . The greater part of mind is only implicit in any conscious act or state; the field of mind—of operative

meanings—is enormously wider than that of consciousness. Mind
is contextual and persistent; consciousness is focal and transitive.
(LW 1:229–30)

Several points must be emphasized. Although Dewey speaks of "a system
of meanings," this misleads if it suggests a coherent system. As we will
soon see, he himself means anything but that! Notice next the crucially
vague phrase "consciousness... denotes awareness or perception of
meanings." He does not tell us if he means awareness of meanings *as*
meanings—reflexive, semireflexive, or thematic awareness—or whether
it is awareness merely in the sense that means are used voluntarily (in
some sense), and meanings are conscious in some *implicit, prereflexive* way.
He allows for the latter when he writes of "sense:"

> Sense is... different from signification. The latter involves the use
> of a quality as a sign or index of something else, as when the red
> of a light signifies danger, and the need of bringing a moving
> locomotive to a stop. The sense of a thing, on the other hand,
> is an immediate and immanent meaning; it is meaning which is
> itself felt or directly had. (LW 1:200)

I believe it is only when we keep the latter meaning of "meaning" firmly
in mind—"sense of a thing," "immediate and immanent meaning"—that
we can appreciate fully what Dewey has to say about prereflective or
nonthematic consciousness. It is a via media between reflective consciousness and subconscious minding. It leads us in the direction of the latter.

Finally, with respect to that vagueness that is brought on in part by
the very nature of Dewey's approach through evolution and continua,
notice his words quoted above, "consciousness is focal and transitive." But
by his own admission he follows James in believing that the largest part
of consciousness is marginal, not focal; it is "on the fringe;" it is
nonthematic meaning brought to consciousness by some disturbance in
habitual adjustments. This interpretation coheres with his own overriding
belief in continuity; and the fact that sometimes a semiconscious or
preconscious process connects in some way with truly subconscious
processes does not soften the punch of what he can tell us about
completely subconscious minding.

A whole monograph could be written about the maddening semantic
problems in these two key chapters of *Experience and Nature.* Many of them
could have been avoided by adopting the phenomenological distinction
between thematic and nonthematic meanings. Without further ado, I will
construe his terms in ways I believe best exhibit what he is trying to say
about subconsciousness. I am particularly intent upon rescuing a sense
of "organic means" and correlated "meanings" that need not be thematic,

and need not even be—though they might be—marginally conscious. Whether subconscious or preconscious, they lie beyond the focal abilities of refexive consciousness to identify, calculate, and control.

Let us return to the point that subconscious means and meanings do not form a coherent system. Dewey's exhibition of this devastates any optimistic view of the human condition. He thinks the "soul of modern man" is a hellish mess. I will quote at some length from pages that should forever dispell the illusion of the kindly, grandfatherly, benign and optimistic Dewey. That these pages are seldom quoted by commentators reveals the typical squeamishness of intellectuals brought face-to-face with the facts of life, facts of body-mind and subconsciousness. In this material are some key lines already quoted:

> Apart from language, from imputed and inferred meaning, we continually engage in an immense multitude of immediate organic selections, rejections, welcomings, expulsions, appropriations, withdrawals, shrinkings, expansions, elations and dejections, attacks, wardings off, of the most minute, vibratingly delicate nature. We are not aware of the qualities of many or most of these acts; we do not objectively distinguish and identify them. Yet they exist as feeling qualities, and have an enormous directive effect on our behavior. If for example, certain sensory qualities of which we are not cognitively aware cease to exist, we cannot stand or control our posture and movements. . . . Meanings acquired in connection with the use of tools and of language exercise a profound influence upon organic feelings. In the reckoning of this account are included the changes effected by all the consequences of attitude and habit due to *all* the consequences of tools and language—in short, civilization. Evil communications corrupt (native) good manners of action, and hence pervert feeling and subconsciousness. The deification of the subconscious is legitmate only for those who never indulge in it—animals and throughly healthy naive children—if there be any such. The subconscious of a civilized adult reflects all the habits he has acquired. . . all the organic modifications he has undergone. And in so far as these involve malcoordinations, fixations and segregations (as they assuredly come to do in a very short time for those living in complex "artificial" conditions), sensory appreciation is confused, perverted and falsified. . . . Activities which develop, appropriate and enjoy meanings bear the same actualizing relation to psycho-physical affairs that the latter bear to physical character. . . . The actualization of meanings furnishes psycho-physical qualities with their ulterior significance and worth. But it also confuses and

> perverts them.... the casual growth and incorporation of
> meanings cause the native need, adjustment and satisfaction to
> lose their immediate certainty and efficiency, and become subject
> to all kinds of aberrations. There then occur systematized with-
> drawals from intercourse and interaction...: carefully cultivated
> and artificially protected fantasies of consolation and compensa-
> tion; rigidly stereotyped beliefs not submitted to objective tests;
> habits of learned ignorance or systematized ignorings of concrete
> relationships; organized fanaticisms; dogmatic traditions which
> socially are harshly intolerant and which intellectually are institu-
> tionalized paranoic systems; idealizations which instead of being
> immediate enjoyments of meanings, cut man off from nature and
> his fellows. (LW 1:227-29)

Dewey has put himself in position to understand—although perhaps not
to change—much of the irrational behavior of human beings. As a chief
instance, he stands on the verge of uncovering pollution phobia, the
phenomenon of untouchable others, other human beings. He sees how
we "individuals" must incorporate the views of others if we would make
sense of things, and how this catches us up in the corporate body, the
group as its own sort of individual. Identities are formed through tacit
or manifest purification rituals which broadcast, in effect, "I and my group
are what we are because we are purely ourselves, wholly other from you
others." And in his suggestion that the psycho-physical has its own level
of sense and meaning, he opens up the possibility of grasping the body-
mind's immediate if subconscious sense of its own inner fluids, movements, processes, postural stances, and attitudes, as these respond nearly
automatically to the stimulating environment. We need arts of various
kinds—fine arts, social arts, healing arts—if we would express and grasp
these responses instead of being engulfed in them. We need expression
that is intelligent, but is not mere rational prediction and calculation.
Typically our expressions erupt from fanatical group allegiances that
brutally exclude outsiders. Or some insider may threaten our bodily
envelope and posture, our precariously defended adjustments, and incur
our fear and rage. Or some expression of ours gets locked into a fixated
constellation that pulls away from our other needs, and a spastic,
disintegrated, vitiated personality results.

Now, what is an educator—or anybody else—to make of all this? How
much rectification of this mess can we reasonably expect in any public
institutions, even if they were operating under the very best conditions,
and with the best and the brightest personnel? Is it "sylabub and flattery
and spongecake" (James's phrase) to even speak of "The Reconstruction

of Culture"? Brilliant and courageous man that he was, even Dewey himself seems to have been appalled by what met his eye under the tutelage of F. M. Alexander. Working into his seventies and eighties he turned out brilliant works, for example, *Art as Experience* and *Logic: The Theory of Inquiry*. They contribute suggestive additions to his view of the subconscious, but they do not directly face the mess that I quoted above. As far as the late *Experience and Education* goes, Dewey was so far ahead of his "disciples" (or is it far beneath, *de profundis*?) that he seems to suspect that he cannot confuse or discourage them further with any significant talk of subconscious mind. His is a titanic attempt to write an educational primer, but it is also poignant and pathetic. As far as professional philosophers were concerned, he thought it was nearly hopeless. Writing to his sometime collaborator, Arthur Bentley, Dewey corresponds on the eve of his ninetieth year in rejoinder to two analytic philosophers who had criticized his logic:

> Church and Smullyan don't realize, in the first place, that logical form, instead of being set over against subject-matter, is itself a distinction in subjects matter, and in the second place, in consequence, they translate what we say into what it would be *if they* held it—its as if we're part of their system—a kind of criticism I've received most of my life from my professional colleagues.[2]

Dewey is saying that these professional intellectuals will not listen, cannot listen—will not, cannot, stand open to another person's life and thought. Their sharply focused consciousness is conditioned and limited by factors and forces that fall beyond their consciousness. These factors and forces are typically fear of, and aversion toward, anything *other* that might disturb the categories in which they try to neatly catalog the world and to keep it at arm's length. The other *as* other is sensed just enough—sensed consciously and unconsciously—to be the target upon which are plastered one's own projections. Insofar as the brilliant focus of an intellect eclipses the surrounding world of bodies—and one's own body—it alienates consciousness from subconscious life, alienates self from others, and self from self.

The obstacles to reconstruction of culture that Dewey discovers are enormous. It is left to us to try to work out a program of action and education. In introductions to some of Alexander's books, Dewey supplies clues, particularly autoconditioning of responses by body-self. A crucial example of this appears in his critique of Pavlov's program of animal conditioning. In the introduction to Alexander's *The Use of the Self*, Dewey writes that since there are central organic habits that condition every act we perform, we can hope to locate these, bring them under conscious direction, and convert "the fact of conditioned reflexes from a principle of external enslavement into a means of vital freedom."

But can such therapeutic work be incorporated in public education in the way in which the "three R's" are? In legislating such a program to enhance human freedom wouldn't we be violating the very principles of pluralism and privacy essential to a democratic society? How *is* this therapeutic work to be coordinated with formal education and social reform? Most of our social institutions daily become more professionalized, depersonalized, alienating. But there must be a sphere of inviolable privacy and personal initiative. Daily the social and the personal pull farther apart (except for scandal sheets that exploit the private lives of the rich and famous and TV talk shows that seize on ordinary folk if their personal lives are sufficiently bizarre, obscene, or anguished to hold attention for a moment). What is needed is thoughtful coordination of the personal and social spheres.

A vision must be achieved that coordinates existential resolve and insight with the most penetrating critiques of society, politics, economics, and technology. I think that this is what some thinkers are trying to accomplish. A threshold of consciousness may be reached, I think, a threshold that will allow consciousness to discern some of its own conditions and limits. But there is no assurance that we can stand upon it and take appropriate action in time to avert disaster to our species— and perhaps to the rest of living Nature.

I have just seen a movie—"Total Recall"—and have watched Arnold Schwartzenegger's character tear people's bodies to pieces as if they were excrement. Some children were in the audience. Just "protecting and enjoying first amendment rights"? Is that a convincing justification for such a spectacle? Do we have any idea of what we are doing with our technologies of communication, for example? Are we simply releasing dangerous impulses through "fictions" in a more or less safe environment? Or are we prompting acting out behavior in the "real world"? And aren't these alternatives simplistically framed? In their generalizing don't they gloss over the ineluctable particularity of particular people at particular moments in particular situations trying to cope with their particular subconscious or preconscious devils? In an ever shrinking and inter-dependent world how many technologically outfitted and pecariously balanced madmen can the planet tolerate? I am as appalled as was Dewey when the lid is pulled off subconscious mind. Its too frequent "corruption" and "perversity"—brought on in large part by civilization itself—are clearly evident. Only with this in mind can we truly appreciate the adage, We have met the enemy and it is ourselves.

I detect in myself conflicting tendencies, one of which is to simply give up (Do others detect this sort of thing in themselves?). I think that on some subconscious or preconscious level my body-self recoils in the face of difficulties and complexities that seem insurmountable. Then, before I know it, this deep fear and weakness is rationalized in consciousness in endless ways—for example, by finding scapegoats, such as, "the scum of the earth who make Hollywood movies." I don't mean that criticism of Hollywood films need be untrue or unhelpful. But the very truth of a criticism aimed at a blatant ill can augment the force of rationalization (in the psychoanalytic sense). That is, the truth can provide a "justification" for throwing up one's hands in despair, and for relieving oneself of the task of making a sustained critique of oneself and of the culture.

It is no accident that Kant included in the most basic questions we can ask ourselves, For what can we hope? The great pragmatists concur: Survival depends upon the difficult feat of combining intelligence and hope. At times, we must hope against hope. For if we do not, if we do not try to ameliorate our situation, we are *surely* lost.

So, very briefly now, how does our study of Dewey point to possible amelioration in two problem areas: education and ecology. The first point to be made with respect to both is obvious: only when we recognize the size and complexity of the problems—without frightened recoil before them—will we mobilize sufficient thought and force to make any real difference. The second point to be made with respect to both problem areas is fairly clear: as long as we persist in thinking of ourselves as individual consciousnesses connected somehow with individual bodies, we will produce artificial analyses of educational and ecological problems and get nowhere in resolving them.

Take education: If Dewey is right, our conscious attitudes arise within a matrix of unconscious organic adjustments conditioned from our earliest days on earth. It follows that our highest national priority should be the earliest education that a child receives. We need a Marshall Plan for our own reconstruction, and a Peace Corps comprised of the best and the brightest of our college graduates who will devote themselves to teaching on the "lowest" levels. We must also, somehow, enlist the cooperation of parents, and we can do so, of course, only by not invading their privacy. Strategies must be worked out.

As for "higher" education, the Cartesian fiction of nonbodily individual consciousness has resulted in separate "faculties of the mind" (a kind of phrenology of pure consciousness), a hyperspecialized, bureaucratized, departmentalized, research-obsessed university that typically fails to address the education of persons, *integral* beings. We need professors who actually *are* what their social role implies they are: educators, integral beings, good persons, who can teach by example, not just by lecture or scientific demonstration, and who are rewarded in a career-sustaining way for their efforts. This doesn't mean that all professional "distance" must be eliminated, or that universities need be turned into vast sanitoria or Esalen Institutes.

Now—just for a moment—the problem area of ecology: The Cartesian fiction inclines us to divide ourselves from our bodies. But this leads to alienation from all matter. It becomes just stuff to be exploited for immediately understandable and enjoyable gain. We become impious with respect to our natural environment and pollute, deface, or destroy the matrix without which we cannot live—Nature, our "home," as Dewey put it (geography should be the central discipline in schools, he thought).

We face *basic* difficulties, I mean difficulties that cannot be solved by science alone. As Dewey knew, philosophy must be reconstructed so that it relates to the problems of men and women. And people must *see* that this is so, which means that professional philosophers—or at least some of them—must return to Plato's and Dewey's idea that philosophy is the general theory of education.

Of course, given the momentum of the military-industrial–comfort-society complex, all this may turn out to be "pie in the sky." Still, the only intelligent thing is to hope against hope.

Notes

1.   Frank P. Jones, *Body Awareness in Action: A Study of The Alexander Technique* (New York: Schockcn, 1976), pp. 94–105.

2.   *John Dewey and Athur F. Bentley: A Philosophical Correspondence. 1932–1951*, eds. S. Ratner, J. Altman, and J. Wheeler (New Brunswick, N.J.: Rutgers University Press, 1964), p. 590.

16

Why Bother: Is Life Worth Living? Experience as Pedagogical

JOHN J. MCDERMOTT

We must beware of our penchant to dismiss the cliché phrase, especially posed as a seemingly trite rhetorical question.[1] At first glance, the query as to whether life is worth living strikes us as somewhat routinely jocular, a sort of throw-away question to which one would not expect a reply, let alone an answer. Nonetheless, if we take the question at dead reckoning (pun intended, for the inquiry, after all, is about death, that is, my death) then its seriousness leaps to the fore.

The Question

So, let us ask ourselves, each in turn, is *my* life worth living? Surely, we must avoid a present-minded response for at some time, the *yin* and *yang* in most of our lives, the only appropriate refrain would have been to wit: I wish I could die.

Yet, even if we extricate ourselves from an immediate personal crisis, an identical plea, justifiably, could be entered. The arrangement of my own death, despite its chilling finality, does bring with it two salient advantages. First, it is a free act and, for that matter, perhaps my only free act, ever. Second, its very finality is also liberating as in the sadly bravado comment, "Well, I shall not have to put up with that (or anything) anymore."

If the reader-listener finds this too lachrymose or riddled with the allegedly nasty vice of systemic despair, I counter by offering a brief diagnosis of what it is to 'do' living.

The Setting

The first, foremost, and permanent ontological fact of our human situation is that we were born to live but sure to die. The awareness of this central, irreducible, incontrovertible fact comes to each of us at different times in our lives. For me, being full-blooded Irish-American, the awareness came very early, at age four or five. The setting was traditional, no less than participation in that glorious linguistic piece of self-deception, the 'wake'. And just why, I would boldly ask, is Aunt Peggy asleep, here in the parlor? I was told that this sleep was necessary if she were to 'wake' again, as in the powerful and oft-healing biblical motif, paraphrased as "if the seed does not die, ye shall not have eternal life."

I came to accept that explanation, albeit with the canny dubiety often found in the not so virginal mind of a child. And, the click of tall glasses filled with rye and ginger created a domestic celebratory atmosphere that could only bode well for the future of Aunt Peggy. It was much later in my life that I became sadly aware that the alcohol was far less a celebratory liquid amulet than an attempt to deaden intractable pain. The searing truth of this reached a crescendo when I drank my way through my father's wake, a pain still throbbing.

Some among us believe that in time we shall be redeemed. I do not so believe. Some among us believe that death is *au naturel*, or as Marcus Aurelius contends, a sort of spiritual nitrogen cycle, knit by an inexorable and holy bond. I do not so believe. Still others refer to us in our future state of finality, as "the grateful dead." I do not so believe.

Neither you nor I were asked if we were willing to start on this journey. Our conception resulted from the acts of others. Is it not plausible, then, that we may come to resent being told that we must finish a journey begun tychastically by us, willy-nilly as it were. Our opponents charge us with *hubris*, an important Greek word which means pride, nay stubborn, self-destructive pride as testated by Achilles sulking in his tent.

My version of *hubris* is that it means the acting out of a perpetual adolescent protest. Yet, is *hubris* an accurate description of those of us who have serious doubt about whether life is worth living and who refuse to accept a supine gentility as the appropriate response to mortality? I think not. To the contrary, and paradoxically, I offer that only a response of refusal to accept the righteous character of the inevitability of death can make it possible for life to be worth living.

The Problematic

So much for a general philosophical landscaping. Let us now come closer to hand by means of a phenomenological diagnosis of our "text," namely, indeed, is life worth living? The term 'life' can be only used retrospectively as in my life, or, if you knew of my life, or, what a life I have had, or, I have no life, or, plaintively, this is a life? The term 'living,' on the other hand, is a process word, a present participle, a happening and a witness to the "specious present." Following John Dewey, we live only at this time and at no other time and so life is an abstraction, perched above our living as a desperate effort to identify ourselves, to become existentially instantiated. Yet, the only part of our past which exists is the past that is present to us. And the future is but a "gossamer wing," vapid, elusive, and most always, by far, doomed to be different from the futured intentions of our present.

Our living is not out of something or in something. Nor is it about something, or on behalf of something. Rather, our living is constitutive of our person. Who we are at any moment is precisely our living. Obviously, spatial metaphors fail us here. Analogous to our physiological activity, which goes on always until it stops, forever, so too does our personal living proceed inexorably, without respite, without any extrapolation for purpose of an objective view; for that, too, is our living. Our language, especially in its fidelity to a subtle yet pervasive Aristotelean bequest, leads us to believe that stasis, substance, place, thing are where we are, what we hold as if we moved from box to box, external to the flow which courses through us. My version emulates the female body, that is, I see us as uterine, a permeable membrane, eating, breathing, "livering" all the while. For me living is a journey, the origin of which is not of our making. The goals are *en passant* and the end is ontologically tragic, although for many of us, alas, it may be salutary, even unfortunately welcome.

The Journey

If it is so that the meaning of the last, ultimate end is unknowable, then at best our human journey involves risk. More, the ultimate end, should there be such, seemingly has no significance for me, personally, at all. The philosophical question as to the "beginning" and the "end," if there be either, and the still deeper question, "Why is there something rather than nothing?" are precisely that, questions; fascinating, intriguing, nagging, perplexing in the sense of Maimonides, yet irresolute. Their obduracy is not due to our failure, thus far, to unlock the argument, but rather to being cast in such a way that however we turn we face an experiential surd. Whatever else one wishes to say about Parmenides, he is right when he cautions us about the attempt to discuss *nothing*. In roughhouse terms, with regard to the ultimate meaning of existence we do not and can not have a clue. Does it not follow that a homely question emerges, namely, why bother?

Yes, why bother? Why *should* we live it through to our end? This is a revealingly different question than why *do* we live it through. The answers to the latter question are as old as human consciousness. They appear as brilliant constructs, anthropologically, liturgically articulated and often accompanied by repressive totems, warnings, advice and claims, none of which have any ultimate certitude.

If I do not know the ultimate meaning of when, of how, of why, and I am deeply skeptical of the integrity of those efforts to explicate those questions so that I shall behave as cajoled, demanded or in response to a promise, the most fake of all the attempted resolutions, then again our question comes to the fore, why bother?

It may justly be asked that if one does not bother, what else does one do? The answer is very singular and clear. One should commit suicide. Granted that this decision has to be a careful one for it is the final insulating cut, the permanent withdrawal from the process, from the fray and the end of hope for a way back in and out. We have no way of knowing whether those among us who have committed suicide have actually made a liberating decision, for the famous and infamous suicide note is always anticipatory. There can be no reportage on the aftermath from the doer of the deed. The assumption here is that the person committing suicide is fully aware of what he or she is doing. It is not true that suicides are 'crazy' people, for the latter rarely kill themselves. It is also not true that suicide is necessarily a selfish act in that it leaves behind gaping wounds in the lives of others. Obviously, that can be and often is the scenario. Just as often, however, suicide is an act of moral courage and altruism, putting an end to the mayhem and hurt caused by the person who no longer believes that life is worth living. *Straight out then, living should be a personal choice made over against the existential, viable, often plausible and certainly liberating option of suicide.* Certainly, to choose to go on living should be more than a response to those quietest phrases: "life goes on" and "so it goes," "round and round we have it," as "the world turns."

As of this moment, I am living. At one point in the recent past, I chose not to go on living. Before my decision was consummated, I was personally seized and forced to reconsider. Alike with Dax Cowart, the Galveston burn victim, I have mixed feelings about that reprieve. Still, having it granted, I now undertake to ground the decision to go on living, hoping to answer the question, "Is life worth living?" affirmatively.

The sentence for which I reach to assist me does not come from the *Bible* or from the *Tao te Ching* or any other spiritual literature. It is from *The Myth of Sisyphus* by Albert Camus and reads, "I want to know if I can live with what I know and only with that." An understanding of the life and thought of Camus, especially as found in his early North African essays, makes it obvious that, for him, "to know," is not to be construed in a narrow, traditionally epistemological way. Knowing for Camus is ringed with ambience and is inclusive of the tacit, the inchoate. In my version, personal knowing is best found in our affective experiences, which no matter how dangerous, how trivial, never lie. As we feel so do we know. Concepts, set in the brilliant schemata of the philosophers, trail our percepts, wooing them into coherence, correspondence or with Ockham, *flatus voci*. As with William James, when faced with the problem of living I lean to "knowledge by acquaintance" rather than "knowledge about," unless one means to be up and about or hanging about.

The Journey: Suffering as Texture

Now as I decide to bother, both by acquaintance and by about, I ask myself the question, just what is it that is coming at me as I am living in the world? Is there a message, an *utter*ance, a voice from the *logoi* of persons, nature, things, and artifacts? As I listen, I hear, for the most part, the voice of unrequited suffering. If one does not believe, as I do not, that in the long run, *sub specie aeternitatis*, that all will be well, be one, be redeemed, or in the die-cast metaphysics of Las Vegas, even out, then the voice of the unrequited takes on a shrill, chilling, razor-sharp quality. The voice threatens to unseat any and all efforts at equanimity, let alone serenity.

Those among us who are reflectively knowledgeable are all too aware of the grisly fact that since the beginning of human history, most persons did the living in a grinding, precarious, and repressed setting. In this century alone, yet to close, despite (or because of) its exquisite technical and scientific accomplishments, more than fifty million people have met death prematurely, violently, vulgarly, even obscenely at the hands and minds of other human beings, chasing one absolute or another due to religion, region, ethnicity, language, skin color or race. Has life been worth living for those who for decades have suffered under periodic eruptions of attempted genocide, local internecine strife, or as featured by the twentieth century, worldwide narcissistic bathing in rampant destruction?

These disasters have not befallen me, thus far. And so, is this jeremiad on behalf of collective, long-standing, seemingly intractable suffering, any skin off my nose? Question! To what extent should I allow the suffering of others affect my version of life's being worth living? The responses to this question are very revelatory as to how we understand ourselves, have ourselves as it were, as a human living creature, a person. (The ongoing destruction of our ecosystem and our treatment of all living creatures is surely germane to our question but is not of reach in the present context.)

One response, callous, but widespread, is that the suffering of others is neither our problem nor our concern. A second response, delusive, self-deceptive for me, is that there but for the grace of whatever, whomever, go I. This is a sort of talismanic approach in which the Greek notion of *moira* is transformed into the American notion of luck. Of this, I offer that Descartes was closer to the truth when he flirted with the possible existence of a *mal genie*. The Manicheans were closer still when they posited good and evil in an eternal, irresolute embrace. But did not the Calvinists, terrifying though they be, have it right when they held that some are saved and some are not and the reason is arbitrary?

A more affectionate position, despite its character of self-preservation, holds that we cannot afford (the pun is foreboding) to allow others' suffering to enter into our personal ken because its enormity will paralyze us or render us hopeless. There is again a strand of self-deception here but this version at least acknowledges that not all is well. The upshot, however, of each of these responses is that we should do nothing or we can do nothing to resolve either the existence or the meaning of collective unrequited suffering.

One further and treacherous rationalization abides in the mind of our own self-styled mandarin class, planet-wide. I refer here to a legitimation of human history by virtue of our collective monuments, historical moments of dazzling heroism, reflective accomplishment, and human creations greater than the sun, the moon, and the earth as John Keats once wrote. Just how does one reconcile the magnificence of the Pyramids, Angkor Wat, and the Great Wall with how they were built, by whom and at what human price. Can we afford, spiritually, psychologically, to reflect on the plight of our Irish and Chinese forbears as we Amtrak our way from Chicago to Los Angeles? Do we not then invoke the Spartacus syndrome forgetting the history of Thrace while thrilling to the courageous if abortive rage of one who carries for us just a glimmer of liberating possibility? I have no way out of this masking of the terror of our past. It would seem that Hegel was accurate when he described human history as a slaughter bench, riven with victims, rescued only in meaning by those "heroes" who epochally embody the *Phenomenologie des Geistes*. And just what do we think, only recently, of the contrast between our being appalled at the potential destruction of the archaeological treasures of ancient Mesopotamia and the also present destruction of the lives of thousands of children, as innocent in that debacle as they have been in all of the pockmarked millenia preceding? Is it not true that deep within us, the cultural remains take precedence, for, after all, they are immortal, whereas the children, like we, are mortal? And so it goes.

The Journey: Amelioration as Nectar

Some decades ago, an unusual refrain was heard over and over as part of a political campaign. After a litany of problems and afflictions, Robert Kennedy would say that "we can do better." This is hardly the stuff of rhetorical flourish, and, yet, the use of the word "better" is a very important choice, for it replaces all of those halcyon words; cure, resolution, and those metaphors of comfort, as in to straighten out things, make everything whole, all on the way to a great society and a new world order. Unfortunately, these are the seeds of cynicism, for as I look over the wreckage of the human historical past, I see no hope for any resolution of anything humanly important.

This baleful perspective does not, however, obviate other responses such as healing, fixing *en passant*, rescuing, and yes, making, doing, having things better. These approaches are actions on behalf of metaphysical amelioration, which holds that finite creatures will *always* be up against it and the best that we can do is to do better.

Yes, I acknowledge that the strategy of amelioration is vacant of the ferocious energizing that comes with commitment to an absolute cause, ever justifiable for some, somewhere, in spite of the nefarious results that most often accompany such political, religious, and social self-righteousness. A moral version of the maxim of Camus, cited above, would read, can I believe in helping when, *sub specie aeternitatis*, I hold that there is no ultimate resolution. Put differently, the original meaning of the ancient medical maxim, *primum non nocere*, was to do no harm. How and why did the maxim come to mean, keep the patient alive, at all cost, including the cost of dignity? What is it about us that cannot abide the sacrament of the moment as we reach for a solution, an end game, an explanation, a cure, nay, immortality?

I try as hard as I can to believe that the nectar is in the journey and not in its final destination. I stand with T. S. Eliot, who warns that "For us, there is only the trying. The rest is not our business." Perhaps I can describe my philosophical position as a Stoicism without foundation. Walt Whitman says it for me better than I can say it for myself. "The press of my foot to the earth springs a hundred affections, they scorn the best I do to relate them."

For what it is worth, and that, too, is a perilous question, I now believe, shakily, insecurely and barely, that life is worth living!

A Deweyan Pedagogical Appendix

Now if I choose to 'bother,' it becomes incumbent upon me to build out from the aforegoing diagnosis. In so doing, I try to leave no stone or thinker unturned in my search for a way to continue the journey, while not becoming unfaithful to my rejection of those traditional moorings which have now lost both their viability and their integrity for me.

One version of the human condition that I find wise and energizing is the aesthetic pedagogy of John Dewey. In his *Art as Experience*, Dewey issues a profound and yet stern warning with regard to the way in which we have our experiences.

> The time of consummation is also one of beginning anew. Any attempt to perpetuate beyond its term the enjoyment attending the time of fulfillment and harmony constitutes withdrawal from the world. (LW 10:23)

Before we break open this text of Dewey, which comes to us as an alternation between a source of liberation and a dirge, a *dies irae*, it will be necessary to understand Dewey's quadruple phases of "having an experience," namely the inchoate, the anaesthetic, the aesthetic, and the consummatory. These appellations of our experience as undergone are not to be taken as hierarchical, nor are they mutually exclusive, one of the other. Actually, the inchoate is always with us and its significance depends on our ability to flush out the hidden ambience that lurks in the everyday, the ordinary, the scene, the sounds, the smell, the feel, the dreams, the rich symbolic hinting as present in our time passing. To the contrary an experience as consummatory is rare, whereas the aesthetic and anaesthetic versions of our experience are pervasive, a sort of systolic-diastolic rhythm in our personal living.

Taking these phases now in turn, what can we say of the inchoate as characteristic of our aesthetic sensibility. We each carry with us, subcutaneously, as Dewey would say, all of our experiences ever undergone. To retrieve them we have obvious activities, such as memory, and more determined attempts such as retrospection. We are also subject to flashbacks, startling intrusions from our past into our present consciousness. At times, we can trace the relational netting that gave rise to these eruptions but at other times their origins are vague, unknown, as if they were self-propelled from our past into our present presence.

What is startling and pedagogically crucial about our experience of the inchoate is that when it makes an appearance in our consciousness we realize the originating power and the surprising novelty of experiences we once 'had' and yet of which we were unaware in our daily consciousness. I offer as an instance, that if we were to recollect a place in which we had spent long and intensive personal time, a home, a neighborhood, a city, a work-site, and then asked ourselves just what do we miss, the response is often jolting. Deep beneath and ambient to the layers of our everyday consciousness there resides and abides the inchoate fabric that subtly penetrated all that we did, thought and underwent in that previous time and place.

Some years after moving from the sensorially rich environs of New York City to the profoundly sparse, comparatively, location of south central Texas, I asked myself what do I miss. Immediately, a flood of obvious, no longer present, events and stimuli came to mind. Yet, in truth, I did not seem to miss them in a deeply sad and lachrymose way. Pressing further, the real loss came to the fore of my awareness, namely, the omnipresence of *water*. For forty-five years, I had lived and worked on the island of Manhattan and on Long Island, surrounded by rivers, a sound, and most of all the great Atlantic Ocean. When in New York City, this water presence, remarkably, was taken for granted and its deepest significance was inchoate. When in Texas, the absence of the water forced its earlier presence to 'surface' and, paradoxically, yet helpfully, I nostalgically brought its healing character to bear on my new life and situation.

Each of us, in our own way, can have access to the inchoacy of our past. I now find that by retrieving these heretofore vague experiences,[2] I am able to thicken the frame of my person such that the possibility of spiritual nutrition is enhanced.

Striating everything we do, think, and in all of our experiencing are the crossover rhythms of aesthetic and the anaesthetic. The former, for Dewey, is quite straightforward, a living on the edge, on the *qui vive*. He compares it to the ever-alert nostrils of a fine animal, whose quivers anticipate and attend the slightest perturbation. To be aesthetically alive is to be touched when we touch, and to allow each of our experiences to bathe us, penetrating our affective response and transforming all that we have experienced, no matter how distant from our present consciousness.

Yet, as Martin Buber wisely warned us, we have a melancholy fate in our inability to sustain a relationship that is sacred, with the world of "Thou". Often, very often, we find ourselves insensate and drifting in the world of "it". For Dewey, the abiding and notorious enemy is the humdrum, the routine, which lulls us into patterns of autonomic response such that experiencing becomes numb. The anaesthetic will cause the self-fulfilling nadir of inanition. Long before the spate of medical literature on the pathology of clinical depression, Dewey accurately diagnosed the perils which await us when we sever ourselves from the messagings of the everyday, the ordinary, and the aesthetic rhythm indigenous to allowing our experiences to speak directly to us. A person knows that a negative answer awaits the question, Why Bother?, when even one's things, precious, personal things, no longer speak, no longer resonate, no longer matter. To the contrary, when a person is open to the multiple voices of experiences, inclusive of the apparently inert presence of things, the inchoate and the riot of sounds and colors, nutrition is at work such that one, indeed, might decide to, bother.

Now as we pay increasing attention to the aesthetic rhythm of how we have our experiences, the possibility of profound enrichment emerges, called by Dewey consummatory experiences. They are not of the run of experience, even aesthetically undergone. Rather they are constituted as special, as *an* experience set off in verve, in implication, in sheer delight, in ambience, and in exquisite intensity.

For some consummatory experiences we may prepare, while knowing full well the risk of failure and the collapse of our anticipation, our expectation, our thick promissory dream. A second, ludic origin of consummatory experiences may be simply one of surprise. The only preparation here, although it is indispensable, is that we live our lives as always aware of the symbolic nuance that accompanies all of our experiences and we remain ever on watch for even the slightest novelty in the message. Further, to the extent that we allow ourselves to hope for that moment, which sings uniquely and to us, immediately, then significantly such moments will occur with frequency.

Consummatory experiences may be large, even gigantic in input as our presence at the winning, overtime goal in the Stanley Cup or singularly personal as the surprise announcement that our underachieving child has been admitted to medical school. Or, these consummations may be of a cameo nature, a chance meeting with an old, never-forgotten but long-lost friend. Again, serendipitously coming upon a once-treasured love letter or the return of our favorite bird from its winter habitat.

Still, as Dewey has warned us in the text above, these consummations have their appropriate duration and then they, as we, in time, cease to be. We cannot and should not attempt to string out a consummatory experience beyond its own distinctive presence and rhythm in our life. To do so will be an act of spiritual necrophilia as we try to suck life from the frayed, the dessicated husk of once glorious experiences. To know when to stop is as demanding a need as to know when to start. Consequently, it is the journey which yields the nectar. To ask of our journey that it yield surety as to its meaning other than its meaning *en passant* is to court spiritual arrogance. In time, the arrogance is sure to self-destruct and then sets in for us the ultimate spiritual disease, cynicism. When cynicism arrives, the question as to Why Bother? is not only unaddressed, it is not asked. We close down and become helpless, hapless and mean-spirited.

The thought of John Dewey does not answer the question, Why Bother? in any peremptory or stentorian way. The question, however, pervades his life and his work. Of one thing we can be sure, for Dewey, cynicism is not a creative option but a deadening one.

Pedagogically, it is salutary to teach ourselves, others, and especially the children that it is not necessary to have certitude in order for a person to live a meaningful life. It is a hallmark of the thought of C. S. Peirce, William James, and John Dewey that the risk of failure is attendant upon forays into the future. Our lives are riddled with the presence of the tychastic and no probability theory, however sophisticated, will obviate the persistence of that strand in all we do. And Dewey is especially helpful in his denotation of the ever pervasive rhythm existent between the stable and precarious generic traits of existence.

Possibility cuts both ways, for it can be foreboding or enriching. Yet, we have no guarantee of which direction our possibilities shall take. In short, we move slowly hand over hand, reading the consequences of our actions and our thoughts as they emerge in the crucible of existential experience. I tell myself to savor the nectar and bury the dross. And even when I founder in so doing, I do not fail to tell that to my children, to my grandchildren, and to my students.

If the nectar is not in the journey, where else could it possibly be?

Notes

1.   This paper enlarges and revises my "Why Bother: Is Life Worth Living," *Journal of Philosophy* LXXXVIII, 11 (November 1991), pp. 677–683. It appears here by permission of *Journal of Philosophy* and its managing editor, Michael Kelly.

2.   William James alerts us to the importance of the vague. He writes, "It is, in short, the re-instatement of the vague to its proper place in our mental life which I am so anxious to press on the attention." *Principles of Psychology*, vol. 1, *The Works of William James* (Cambridge: Harvard University Press, 1981), p. 246.

Thomas M. Alexander is Associate Professor of Philosophy at Southern Illinois University at Carbondale. The son and grandson of philosophers, he was born and raised in Albuquerque and received his B.A. from the University of New Mexico, and his M.A. and Ph.D. from Emory University. He has published several articles on American philosophy and is the author of a book on Dewey, *John Dewey's Theory of Art, Experience, and Nature: The Horizon of Feeling*. He also has written essays on Classical philosophy, social and political theory, and aesthetics. He currently is working on a study of the moral imagination and the theory of democratic culture.

Raymond D. Boisvert is a Professor in the Department of Philosophy at Siena College in New York. He received his B.A. from Providence College, his M.A. from the University of Toronto, and his Ph.D. from Emory University. He is the author of a book on John Dewey, *Dewey's Metaphysics*, and several essays on American philosophy and the thought of Dewey. In addition, he has written many articles and reviews on literature, painting, film, and aesthetics, and recently has received a Fulbright Fellowship in American Studies at the University of Lyon in France.

James Campbell is Associate Professor of Philosophy at the University of Toledo. Following undergraduate study at Temple University, he earned his Ph.D. from the State University of New York at Stony Brook. In addition to many articles and essays on John Dewey, George Herbert Mead, and themes in American culture, he is the author of *The Community Reconstructs: The Meaning of Pragmatic Social Thought* and editor of *Selected Writings of James Hayden Tufts*. He is a member of the editorial board of the *Transactions of the C. S. Peirce Society* and has recently completed a Fulbright Fellowship in American Studies at the University of Innsbruck in Austria.

James Gouinlock is Professor of Philosophy at Emory University. He earned his B.A. from Cornell University and his Ph.D. from Columbia

University. A former president of the Society for the Advancement of American Philosophy, he has published many articles, essays, and reviews on classical American philosophy, philosophy of education, and moral philosophy. He is the author of *John Dewey's Philosophy of Value* and *Excellence in Public Discourse: John Stuart Mill, John Dewey, and Social Intelligence*. In addition, he has edited a book on the moral writings of Dewey and coedited another on ethics in the history of Western philosophy.

Larry A. Hickman is Professor of Philosophy at Texas A&M University where he has received an award for distinguished teaching. He earned his Ph.D. from the University of Texas at Austin. He is the author of *John Dewey's Pragmatic Technology* and *Modern Theories of Higher Level Predicates*. A former editor of the *Southwest Philosophy Review*, he has edited three anthologies on the philosophy of technology, including *Philosophy, Technology, and Human Affairs*. In addition, he has published many essays and articles on a broad range of subjects, including American philosophy, the philosophy of technology, film studies, photography, and the culture of the American Southwest.

John Lachs is Professor of Philosophy at Vanderbilt University. He received his B.A. and M.A. from McGill University and his Ph.D. from Yale University, and has received several awards for excellence in teaching. A past president of the Society for the Advancement of American Philosophy and the C. S. Peirce Society, he has written many articles on American philosophy, philosophy of mind, metaphysics, social philosophy, and ethics. He is author of *Intermediate Man*, *Marxist Philosophy*, *Mind and Philosophers*, and *George Santayana*; editor or coeditor of *Animal Faith and Spiritual Life*, *Physical Order and Moral Liberty*, and *The Human Search*; and co-translator of Fichte's *Science of Knowledge*. His latest book is *Human Natures*.

Thelma Z. Lavine, Clarence J. Robinson Professor of Philosophy and American Culture at George Mason University, received her Ph.D. from Harvard University and holds teaching awards from Brooklyn College, the University of Maryland, and George Washington University. She is the author of a nationally televised PBS course in philosophy, the author of *From Socrates to Sartre: The Philosophic Quest*, and coauthor and coeditor of *History and Anti-History in Philosophy*. In addition, she has written many essays on continental philosophy, sociology of knowledge, psychoanalysis, interpretation theory, and American philosophy and culture—including an introduction to a volume of *John Dewey: The Later Works*.

Peter T. Manicas currently directs the Liberal Studies Program at the University of Hawaii where he also teaches in the Sociology Department. He received his B.A. from Syracuse University and his M.A. and Ph.D. from the State University of New York at Buffalo. He is the author of many articles in journals in philosophy, political science, history, sociology, education, rhetoric, accounting, and psychology. He has written books in logic, the history and philosophy of the social sciences, and political and social philosophy, and, most recently on the historical relations of democracy and war. These books include *A History and Philosophy of the Social Sciences* and *War and Democracy*.

John J. McDermott is Distinguished Professor of Philosophy and Humanities at Texas A&M University. He earned his Ph.D. from Fordham University, and has received teaching awards at: Queens College; City University of New York; State University of New York at Stony Brook; and, Texas A&M. He is the author of: *The Culture of Experience: Essays in the American Grain; Streams of Experience: Reflections on the History and Philosophy of American Culture;* and many essays on philosophical and cultural issues. In addition, he is editor of a cultural introduction to philosophy; *The Philosophy of John Dewey; The Basic Writings of Josiah Royce; The Writings of William James;* and is a founding advisory editor of *The Works of William James.*

Sandra B. Rosenthal is Professor of Philosophy at Loyola University, New Orleans. She received her Ph.D. from Tulane University, and has served as president of the Society for the Advancement of American Philosophy, the C. S. Peirce Society, the Southern Society for Philosophy and Psychology, and the Southwest Philosophical Society. She has written extensively on pragmatism and the relations between pragmatism and continental philosophy. In addition to scores of articles on these subjects, she is the author or coauthor of: *Speculative Pragmatism; Mead and Merleau-Ponty: Toward a Common Vision; The Pragmatic A Priori; Pragmatism and Phenomenoloy: A Philosophic Encounter;* and, *Thematic Studies in Phenomenology and Pragmatism.*

Charlene Haddock Seigfried is Professor of Philosophy and member of the American Studies and Women's Studies Committees at Purdue University. She received her Ph.D. from Loyola University, Chicago. She is the author of many articles and two books on William James: *Chaos and Context* and *William James's Radical Reconstruction of Philosophy.* In addition, she has written on methodology in the continental and American traditions of philosophy, feminist theory, aesthetics, and philosophical psychology. She currently is editing a special issue of *Hypatia* on feminism and pragmatism and writing a book on the same topic.

Igor N. Sidorov is a professor of philosophy at St. Petersburg State University in Russia. His major teaching and research interests are classical and contemporary American philosophy, philosophy and culture, and recent Russian thought. He is the author of a book on American philosophy and America culture, *Filosofia diestviya v SShA: ot Emersona do D'yui* (*Philosophy of action in the USA: From Emerson to Dewey*). A former Fulbright professor at the University of Oregon, he has lectured extensively throughout the United States.

R. W. Sleeper is Professor of Philosophy Emeritus at Queens College and Graduate Center, City University of New York, and teaches courses in American philosophy, ethics, and philosophy of law at the University of New Hampshire and Plymouth State College. He earned his Ph.D. at Columbia University, and has written extensively on pragmatism, the thought of John Dewey, and contemporary philosophy. In addition to many articles, he is the author of *The Necessity of Pragmatism: John Dewey's Conception of Philosophy*, and coeditor of Robert Sylvester's *The Moral Philosophy of G. E. Moore*.

John. J. Stuhr is Professor of Philosophy and Director of the Humanities Center at the University of Oregon. He earned his B.A. at Carleton College, M.A. and Ph.D. at Vanderbilt University, and has held fellowships in Germany, Australia, and Russia. He has received awards for excellence in teaching, and has written on pragmatism, continental philosophy, ethics, education, and politics. He is author of *John Dewey*, editor of *Classical American Philosophy*, coeditor of three books on professional ethics, and an editor of the *Personalist Forum*. He is completing a book on Dewey's theory of experience and a collection of essays on philosophy, experience, and community, and is coediting a volume on Michel Foucault.

H. S. Thayer is Professor of Philosophy Emeritus at the City College of New York. He received his M.A. and Ph.D. from Columbia University, and taught at Columbia, the New York School of Psychiatry, and the Graduate Center, City University of New York. A recipient of many scholarly awards including both Guggenheim and National Endowment for the Humanities Fellowships, he has published extensively in American philosophy, Peirce, James, and Dewey, and ancient Greek philosophy and the history of philosophy and science. He is the author of *Meaning and Action: A Critical History of Pragmatism*, and editor of *Pragmatism: The Classic Writings* and *Newton's Philosophy of Nature*.

Bruce Wilshire, Professor of Philosophy at Rutgers University, earned his B.A. at the University of Southern California and his M.A. and Ph.D. at

New York University. He is the author of *William James and Phenomenology: A Study of the Principles of Psychology* and editor of *The Essential Writings of William James*. He also has written on a wide range of issues, including: *Metaphysics: An Introduction to Philosophy*; *Role Playing and Identity: The Limits of Theatre as Metaphor*; *The Moral Collapse of the University: Professionalism, Purity, and Alienation*; and, just completed, *Wild Hunger: From Nature's Ecstasy to Addiction*. He has received a distinguished teaching award from Rutgers, served as co-director of the Society for Phenomenology and Existential Philosophy, and is the vice-chair of the Society of Philosophers in America.

Index